Systems Science and Collaborative Information Systems:

Theories, Practices and New Research

Emilia Currás
Autonomous University Madrid, Spain

Nuria Lloret Romero
Universitat Politècnica de València, Spain

Information Science
REFERENCE

Managing Director:	Lindsay Johnston
Senior Editorial Director:	Heather Probst
Book Production Manager:	Sean Woznicki
Development Manager:	Joel Gamon
Development Editor:	Myla Harty
Acquisitions Editor:	Erika Gallagher
Typesetters:	Adrienne Freeland
Print Coordinator:	Jamie Snavely
Cover Design:	Nick Newcomer, Greg Snader

Published in the United States of America by
Information Science Reference (an imprint of IGI Global)
701 E. Chocolate Avenue
Hershey PA 17033
Tel: 717-533-8845
Fax: 717-533-8661
E-mail: cust@igi-global.com
Web site: http://www.igi-global.com

Library of Congress Cataloging-in-Publication Data

Systems science and collaborative information systems: theories, practices and new research / Emilia Curras and Nuria Lloret, editors.
p. cm.
Includes bibliographical references and index.
Summary: "This book examines the impact of new information services on day-to-day activities from a range of contemporary technical and socio-cultural perspectives"--Provided by publisher.
ISBN 978-1-61350-201-3 (hardcover) -- ISBN 978-1-61350-202-0 (ebook) -- ISBN 978-1-61350-203-7 (print & perpetual access) 1. Information science. 2. Information organization. 3. Information retrieval. I. Curras, Emilia. II. Lloret, Nuria, 1966-
Z665.S895 2012
020--dc23

2011038480

British Cataloguing in Publication Data
A Cataloguing in Publication record for this book is available from the British Library.

All work contributed to this book is new, previously-unpublished material. The views expressed in this book are those of the authors, but not necessarily of the publisher.

Table of Contents

Subsection
Information, in Collaborative Information Systems, as a Science in Itself

Subsection
Vertical Integration of Collaborative Information Systems

Section 2
Technology in Collaborative Information Systems

Subsection
Metasearching / New Search Interfaces

Subsection
Automatic References

Subsection
Open Source Software to Collaborative Information Services

Detailed Table of Contents

In this chapter, there is an attempt to consider an organization of knowledge regarding a vertical integration of science, which is focused as a systems unity of greater complexity then what has been considered before. An ascending or descending vertical integration of science might be to interpret questions posed by human in general and information scientist in particular. It could provide answers that they are looking for. All aspects of the global information could have a widest sense, appear to be treated, and the problems need to be freshly addend as required solutions. This vertical integration of science is considered here from the vision of the systems science theories. A study of this integration, with all its complexity could provide important solutions for an adequate organization of knowledge.

This chapter uses the concept of system to enquire into the concept of information, trying to separate the different senses in which this core concept is used in Information Science and other sciences, that is, physical or "raw" information, messages, knowledge, news, documentation and meta-information.

The concept of information is studied as a system of layers or levels, in which each new sense emerges from the previous one. Once each of these senses is clearly established, it is possible to provide more specific insights about the real scientific domain of Information Science: a science related to the design and maintenance of external social memories and the process of referring their contents to relevant personal and social activities. Its focus is, therefore, the optimization of the processes of social memory. So, in conclusion, Information Science is, first, a science of social memory and its use, and, even more specifically, of the methodologies and technologies (social or technical) that exist to optimize its functioning by means of external memories, references (metadata) and systems of metadata (ontologies).

Making an incursion in the forest of problems and theories of information, beyond observing a lack of mutual understanding among information theorists, we find out that information can be understood as a multifaceted reality. The variety of theories is in itself a reflection of the complex nature of information. A systematic approach to these theories, looking for common and divergent understandings render– so to speak – a cubist picture of what information really is, showing for instance its multi-dimensionality. In other words, when we say there is information in cables and organisms, in antennas and societies, in robots and mental states, we do not have to be mistaken: information is considered in each case in different aspects. Delving into the nature of observation, we will find a solid ground to pose information as a bridge between objects and subjects, therefore providing the possibility to overcome the inveterate segregation of the objectivist and subjectivist understandings. As we will see, such vision also provides the possibility to articulate an understanding of information in its multifaceted reality.

In this chapter an epistemology, based in the information, as the paradigm, that rules our lives, is stated - Informationism -. Information, or perhaps the message, reaches the brain as tiny impulses - quanta or useful information -, hitting and activating the neurones; as a consequence becoming quanta of useful information which produce knowledge, science and wisdom. Some definitions of information are quoted, as well as its connotations and peculiarities. The physical, psychic and pragmatic, etc. connotations of information are studied, including its energetic aspect; within a Cosmovision of it. Some neuronal theories are also studied.

This chapter reflects objective and subjective principles to organize and disseminate information. It presents the human condition in the dynamic of searching and using information by making explicit the informational need of the user with learning theories, information organization, and user studies as subsidies. This is done in order to increase the development of cognitive trajectories to search, select, and use information, bearing in mind the permanent process of modifiability to face new environments. Finally, the text focuses on the social and economic development promoted by the science and technology advances, pointing out the social gap that has emerged from this reality.

People develop attitudes toward things in many ways. While direct experience can be the foundation of permanent attitude formation, both indirect experience and referential input from others are strong influences on both attitude development and changes in personal attitude. The psychological factors that govern attitude are varied. They are documented in the scholarly literature of many fields, and frequently reference the study of people and technology. Research in the use of information systems (IS), however, does not typically aggregate the psychological factors influencing user attitude. The purpose of this chapter is to bring together the divergent empirical evidence of IS user attitude formation. A grounded theory approach is used to formally identify and analyze this evidence. Such analysis can provide a more cohesive understanding of what is known about user attitudes toward information systems, and can offer an ontological framework for more formalized study of the relationship between people and information systems.

E-collaboration and collaborative systems bring geographically dispersed teams together, supporting communication, coordination and cooperation. From the scientific perspective, the development of theories and mechanisms to enable building collaborative systems presents exciting research challenges across information subfields. From the applications perspective, the capability to collaborate with users and other systems is essential if large-scale information systems of the future are to assist users in finding the information they need and solving the problems they have. This chapter presents a review of research in the area of creating collaborative applications and taxonomies. The author analyzes previous literature, and examines some practice cases and research prototypes in the domain of collaborative computing. Finally the chapter provides a list of basic collaboration services, and tools are presented relating to the services they provide. All surveyed tools are then classified under categories of functional services. In conclusion, the chapter highlights a number of areas for consideration and improvement that arise when studying collaborative applications.

Subsection
Metasearching / New Search Interfaces

This chapter discusses using context in Information Retrieval systems and Intelligent Assistant Agents in order to improve the performance of these systems. The notion of context is introduced and the state of the art in Contextual Information Retrieval is presented which illustrates various categories of contexts that can be taken into account when solving user queries. In this framework, the authors focus on the issue of task-based context which takes into account the current activity the user is involved in when he puts a query. Finally they introduce promising research directions that promote the use of Intelligent Assistant Agents capable of symbolic reasoning about users' tasks for supporting the query process.

The traditional system for searching for documents in archives is based on correct preparation of the description instruments: guides, inventories, catalogues and index cards. The emergence of three factors in the last few decades has made the system, used by archive institutions for centuries, no longer the most appropriate for information retrieval. These three factors are information and communication technologies, and electronic indexing, preferably using appropriate thesauri. This chapter is an attempt to analyse which technological elements and which description and indexing elements directly impact information retrieval of documents. As a result of the analysis, some requirements are proposed that must be observed in archival information systems installed in organisations with the aim of optimising effective information retrieval.

Subsection
Automatic References

Taking into account the fundamental role of online public access catalogs in the dissemination of scientific and technical information, it was considered relevant to look into the situation of user interfaces of OPACs Web of university, special, public and national libraries in Latin America. A quantitative methodology has been adopted and a checklist of system functions (Hildreth, 1982) updated was used as data collection tool. A sample of 846 OPACs was obtained from predefined search queries and classified according to type of software, type of library and country. A subset of 374 units was selected of those whose system presented a frequency of appearance ≥ 10. The percentage of presence of functionalities in each area was calculated and functionalities were compared according to type of software by test of independence. It was then possible to typify the interfaces of the analyzed OPACs according to the selected types of software and in relation to their category.

Subsection
Open Source Software to Collaborative Information Services

The purpose of this chapter is to describe how the concepts and principles from the Systems Approach may be helpful in understanding and modeling the collaborative group cognitive processes in information handling in an academic library. In order to address complexity and dynamics, this chapter analyzes several theoretical positions, which together may help us to shape the academic library from a comprehensive and systemic point of view (such as Systems Approach, Communities of Practice, Activity Theory and the Viable System Model). This chapter suggests focalizing on the activity (performed by a community) as the basic unit of analysis in studying the complexity of academic libraries. This activity is what allows the transmission of tacit and explicit knowledge and the skills from an expert to a novice. Other elements in the activity are objectives, rules and regulations, and importantly the learning processes that occur dialectically between subjects and community. A model such as Beer´s in the way the authors presented it in this chapter fits well to decompose reality and synthesize it to analyze the proposed complexity. This may allow facing organizational problems by focusing in the way people act to transform the inputs into products and add value to them by teaching and learning.

The Internet has become the essential media for daily work of cultural management professionals. Its richness of contents and the fast evolution of technologies do even exceed the capacity of adaptation and decision of the professionals due to the wide range of possibilities that the Internet offers. It is in this new context where technologies and cultures get mixed up as cultural institutions cannot play the same roles as they did in the analogic world. Not only the classical functions of conservation, research, commission or exhibition have to be valued, but also in the role of broadcasting, doors to communication 2.0 should be opened, getting into the social networks, not only sharing but also listening what the users have to say. This new step has to be managed by institutions that are able to understand and add the new philosophy 2.0 in their corporative and communication culture. It is not longer one-way communication as the role of the users is essential. The author will analyse the strategies and models of some institutions that have incorporated digital practices and culture in their organizations and communication and therefore, the way they connect with their different audiences (Creators/artists, users and other organizations.) have changed.

The author describes Coagmento, a system that provides integrated tools and workflow for doing collaborative information seeking in online environment. Coagmento's inception followed a need to provide essential tools to collaborators without them having to learn an entirely new system or work in an unfamiliar environment. Here they describe how the author designed, developed, and deployed Coagmento. The design of this system was facilitated using several pilot runs and cognitive walkthroughs. A fully functional version of Coagmento was then developed and evaluated using laboratory study, and its design optimized using participatory design sessions. Finally, the author describes how they made the enhanced version of Coagmento available to wider group of users, along with issues and challenges faced. They summarize lessons learned and provide a guideline for designing and developing such collaborative information seeking systems.

Foreword

The shifting sand of our global information systems is extraordinary, with the content and search driven systems of the past playing only a small part of the information landscape. As we move from systems that provide documents to those that connect us to key experts, as we move from the desk to mobile computing, as we move from local networks to the cloud, information system value is driven by an elementary but critical factor – good design. When they're good, information systems are simple and easy to use, but as the editors and authors of this important work fully understand and explain remarkably well – simple and easy designs are rooted in a deep understanding of user needs and information seeking behavior.

Systems Science and Collaborative Information Systems: Theories, Practices and New Research provides a rich discussion of the need for this deep understanding of users, their needs, and the context that they bring to an information system, as well as their backgrounds and behaviors. The work is as innovative in its approach as it is comprehensive in its scope. There is a clear international focus to this work, with authors from Spain, Mexico, Brazil, France, and the United States. This is no surprise, as the editors, Professor Emilia Currás and Dr. Nuria Lloret Romero, have international research and system design experience and have assembled a premier group of scholars to explore these issues and how information systems are changing as a result.

This awareness of information shifts and the challenges of users navigating available information systems form the core of the research and theoretical discussions in this book. While most of the general public takes information for granted, the researchers featured in these pages understand and describe the myriad factors that go into high-quality systems. The variations in information availability around the world, systems for managing information sources, cultural framing in information-rich settings, adapting to search requirements, and user attitudes toward data systems, are all explored in the book's chapters. The study of information seeking behavior is important, as it builds on our understanding and interaction with the world around us. Increasingly, our physical and cognitive approaches to dealing with our social and professional environments are framed by the information we have consumed. Examining how that information came into our lives, how we go about getting more information efficiently and our reactions as humans in a world of complex information systems sheds light on our potential future as information consumers and the present-day challenges of systemizing information feeds.

Toward that end, this book opens by considering which information systems are available to key emerging populations around the world. Jointly written by Elsa Barber, Silvia Pisano, Sandra Romagnoli, Verónica Parsiale, Gabriela de Pedro, Carolina Gregui, and Nancy Blanco, the inaugural chapter, "Management Systems of User Interfaces functionalities in Latin-American Web OPACs," examines the online public access catalogs (OPACS) changes facing university, special, and public and national libraries throughout the region. These researchers have developed a quantitative method for evaluating such systems, which removes ambiguity about information availability in critical, functional categories.

Moving from what's available to the challenges of navigation and search, the book explores inherent system complexities, impacts of dominant culture management systems, and "informationism" – the new paradigm replacing industrialism in the modern world. Aida Varela and Marilene Lobo Abreu Barbosa take the lead with "The Complexity of Finding Information in Collaborative Information Systems: Cognitive Needs," followed by Margarita Cabrera Méndez's "Cultural Management 2.0" and "Informationism, Information, and its Neuronal Theories," and "Vertical Integration of Science. An Approach to Including Information, Knowledge, and Its Organization" by Emilia Currás.

The systemic approaches to information gathering and analysis discussed by these researchers build on the body of knowledge that is needed for an acceptable organization of data points. This body of knowledge is then challenged by José María Díaz Nafría, who argues in his chapter, "Information: A Multidimensional Reality," that the field lacks consensus, and, as such, has constructed information as a multifaceted reality for consumers with decidedly geometric traits.

Delivering usable services and information is in the eye of the consumer, and this issue is addressed squarely in the chapter: "Adaptive Information Retrieval Based on Task Context" by Bich-Liên Doan and Jean-Paul Sansonnet, which describes the role of artificial agents in information searches. Francisco-Javier García-Marco's discussion in "What is Information? An Enquiry Beyond Information Science From a Systemic Point of View," examines from a unique perspective the nature of content and how it is related to end-user (human) experiences and perception.

Turning back to a key tension in the book, "Metadata for Information Retrieval in Archives" by Vicent Giménez Chornet, discusses the issue of the diminished stature of traditional information management systems. The ability to search electronically has revolutionized the industry since the 1990s, but according to Chornet, the heralded metadata and discovery systems have not yet caught up. Proposals and action plans to marry the two forms is covered, with the aim of achieving optimal information retrieval methods.

Of course, even the most efficient systems are worthless if no one finds them useful or easy to use. "Understanding User Attitudes Toward Information Systems: A Grounded Theory Approach" by David A. Jank examines how people form their mindsets around information systems and how those mindsets or attitudes can actually shift system use. Where user attitudes and the context they bring to information systems are better understood, better system tools and functionalities result without question in Jank's view.

User needs give way to administrator and community concerns in the final chapter. "Academic Libraries as Complex Systems" by Álvaro Quijano-Solís and Guadalupe Vega-Díaz looks at several theoretical positions for library management, both on the back end with staff and on the front end where community members are interacting with the systems. In this way, the authors suggest that only by taking into account both viewpoints can such complex systems grow over time and become optimal.

Each of these researchers offers a different and innovative view of the new collaborative information systems rapidly emerging in the market. By perusing each section carefully, it is possible to come away with a new understanding of the current leading edge thoughts around the nature of information, as well as how systems no longer inform and transform our lives with mere content or more search, but rather through a rigorous understanding of users, their information needs, the diverse information contexts they bring to problems, and their complex information-seeking behaviors.

The Information Age has dawned, and the sun has steadily moved its journey through the sky. In a world overflowing with information systems, increasing our knowledge of users beyond the noise and the methodologies of information technology may allow us to make better sense of our world before the sun once more meets the horizon.

John J. Regazzi
Long Island University and Partner, Focused Connections

***John Regazzi** is currently Professor, Dean Emeritus and Director of the College of Information and Computer Science at Long Island University. In 2005 John was appointed Dean of the College of Information and Computer Science and Dean of Palmer School of Library and Information Science. In September 2001, he was appointed to the position of Managing Director, Market Development of Elsevier. This appointment was in addition to his duties as President and CEO of Elsevier Inc. and a member of the Elsevier Board of Directors. Previously he was also Managing Director of Elsevier Electronic Publishing, globally. As Managing Director, Market Development, John was responsible for Elsevier's research, advanced technology, and new strategic market initiatives. Prior to joining Elsevier, John was President and CEO of Engineering Information, Inc. (Ei), from 1988-1998, and he oversaw the company's incorporation into Elsevier Inc. John received his doctorate in Information Science from Rutgers University in 1982. He is a graduate of Columbia University, where he earned an M.S. in Library and Information Science. He also holds an M.A. in Religious Studies from the University of Iowa and a B.A. in Psychology from St. John's University. John has been active in the information profession through publications and presentations, and he maintains a number of professional affiliations, including among others: American Association of Publishers, Division of Professional and Scholarly Publishing; Board of Directors (1999 - 2002); CABI, Board of Directors (1998 - current); Ei Foundation Board of Directors (1998 - current).*

Preface

This book can be considered unique in its kind, in that it broadly explores collaborative systems from the viewpoint of information systems. Also considered are the theoretical and practical aspects of these systems from a collaborative standpoint. In this regard, it is assumed that there is a relationship of dependency between information and collaborative systems.

Nowadays, the structure of society, culture, research, industry, in short all human activity, is dependent on information systems from differing backgrounds and whose areas of specialty varies. Any human activity bases its daily work on information, whatever it may be.

As part of the theoretical and practical studies relating to the so-called "electronic techniques" and given the progress reached in the last 50 years or so, the interaction between man and machines has been seriously explored. There have been studies of so-called HCI = Human Computer Interaction, and in some cases Interaction" has been replaced with "Interface", or also by "Interconnection".

The influence of computer use on humans, both in terms of construction and users, is truly worrisome. People are increasingly more dependent on computers, and. everything is seen, studied, or disseminated using such machines. Human beings, as users, end up changing physically. For example, their vision may be affected. In a recent op-ed I authored, which was published in the journal *Mi Biblioteca*, I dared to say that "Internet is the devil's punishment".

The reason I point this out is that "collaborative systems" are included in the study of HCI and can be considered as a branch, or as an application of such systems.

This book focuses on collaborative systems and their applications, which have rapidly evolved in very recent years. The peculiarity of this kind of systems is that the users are both actors and managers of their layout, as well as their use. Therefore, there is a shared relationship of knowledge and experiences, or in other words, of information, a relationship which is rich in informational power.

Collaborative systems must fulfill some conditions for their effect to be positive. The phases of coordination, cooperation and dissemination must all be completed and must be fully supported by "digital technology."

As collaborative systems have evolved, a complete nomenclature has been developed, a terminology which properly defines the constituent parts and practical aspects, etc. In this respect, practical and adaptive collaborative systems are referred to, as well as functional interfaces, collaborative services and collaborative organization. In other respects, there is talk of taxonomies and of collaborative classifications.

As for their use, they have resulted, for example, in the famous social networks, which are diverse and varied. Likewise, Web 2.0 is an application of these systems, which requires understanding the relationships between users and participants in a process of "information sharing".

This book is structured into sections, which in turn, are divided into the following subsections:

1. Theoretical and Scientific Aspects in Collaborative Information Systems
   a. Theoretical and Philosophical Principles: Informationism
   b. Information Systems from the Systems Science Theories
   c. Information, in Collaborative Information Systems, as a Science in Itself
   d. Vertical Integration of Collaborative Information Systems
2. Technology in Collaborative Information Systems
   e. Historical Review
   f. Metasearching / New Search Interfaces
   g. Automatic References
   h. Open Source Software to Collaborative Information Services

The first chapters are in some way related to theoretical aspects. These chapters discuss information, which, after all, is the basis of the entire contents of the book.

Information is everything and nothing at the same time. In Roman times, Titus Lucretius Caro (99 - 55 BC) defined information as "not being, but allowing to be".

It cannot be seen or touched, and is timeless and recyclable.

It activates our brain and gives us the ability to understand the world around us and to acquire knowledge. As the Spanish neurologist, José Manuel Rodríguez Delgado said, "knowing takes up space", it takes up space when putting our brain into action. The German professor Helmut Arntz said that people changed from hominids to humans when they began to acquire information from their environment. So how do we refer to information relating to news reporting, for example? This is the question. Information needs support of some type. In our case this support is configured by certain systems called software or programs and by certain machines known as hardware. These are handled and powered by humans.

We often forget that behind all these devices and programs there is a human being, whose mental faculties our now so developed that he is able to build programs for everything that computers do today. This is amazing and even more so when it comes to mobile phones. In this regard, the Spanish physicist Felix Vidondo speaks of "Thinkware" as a human element, along with software and hardware.

CHAPTERS

Let us now briefly discuss the contents of the chapters in this book, following the order shown in the Table of Contents.

The first chapter is entitled "*Vertical Integration of Science: An Approach to Including Information, Knowledge and Its Organization*", Emilia Currás, Universidad Autónoma de Madrid.

As the author of this Preface and of this first chapter, I find it very difficult to objectively criticise it. However, I will try.

First science and the way it can be defined are studied, two possible definitions being highlighted: a summary of everything known to date and a way to access knowledge which arises.

The way in which science as a unit can be vertically integrated is then studied.

Since ancient times human knowledge has been integrated horizontally. However, if we attempted to vertically integrate this knowledge, perhaps we could understand and solve certain problems posed by humankind today. This idea is not entirely new, and other authors having outlined this type of integration, but without specifically mentioning or focusing on it. The novelty and may I dare say, originality, lies in the vertical integration of all of science.

Obviously for reasons of space, only certain knowledge, such as knowledge of sociology, computers, information, etc., is used to outline what the vertical integration of a unit of science might be.

In the full chapter, vertical integration is graphically presented and the explanation provided can be summarized as follows.

Let's look at how this integration can be accomplished. Each piece of human knowledge forms a column, where the other pieces of knowledge involved in gaining this knowledge are placed. Each piece of knowledge added to a column constitutes a block, or holon (term used in Systems Science).

Also, for reasons of space, we will use "computer science" as just an example of a piece of knowledge with which a column will be built. Now, some knowledge and tools necessary for its development are taken into account, such as, electronics, communications, computers, biology, culture, history and information. These pieces of knowledge are placed in the column so that each forms a block or holon.

Let us now take another example: "Information" which will require the following pieces of knowledge to evolve and be used: inter alia, psychology, sociology, communications, computer science, and history, etc. The related column is built and the aforementioned holons are placed within it.

The same is then done with each successive piece of human knowledge. The whole forms a polyhedron, a polyhedron of a unit of science. It can be observed that some pieces of knowledge form a complete column while others are holons in another column. To study which relationships between one and another are both logical and practical, and consequently, to understand their vertical integration, it will be necessary to resort to the principles of Systems Science.

The next chapter is entitled: "*What is Information? An Enquiry beyond Information Science from a Systemic Point of View*", by Francisco-Javier García-Marco, Universidad de Zaragoza, (Spain).

In reality there are few researchers who address the issue of information and of information science from a theoretical and practical standpoint using Systems Science. This author is one of them and to support his arguments, he devotes part of his chapter to the study of these issues. (*Note: he uses the word "systemic". In my opinion, he should use the term "systems" as a possessive. This term is most commonly used internationally by all researchers in Systems Science.*)

The author divides the chapter in different sections and subsections, where he sets out his ideas, assumptions, assertions and conclusions. He begins by differentiating between Information Society, Information Science and Science of Information. He says that information has become a fundamental part of society and its varied cultures.

This information is the result of automatic data processing and dissemination. Additionally, information is fundamental in the study of cognitive science, communication sciences and computer science. Its importance in Library and Information Science (LIS), which is his field of study, cannot be overlooked either. There are enough studies and research to be able to define what information can be. This chapter only concentrates on its meaning and concept in the fields where information appears in the form of raw information, and as knowledge, messages, news, documentation and meta-information. All these come under the tenets of Systems Science or General Theory of Systems.

Additionally, it treats information as a target of human reality and in terms of its role in modern science, using a metaphor relating to water being where the fish of science swim, which emphasizes waters' key role in fish' development.

It also emphasizes the importance of information which is useful in scientific philosophy so as to place it alongside time, space, matter, energy and information.

Additionally, it stresses physical information contained in many of the studies of LIS (Library and Information Science), where such information is required to be reported. There is no communication without information, nor does the former exist without the latter. According to this author, they are the two sides of the same coin.

Additionally, he highlights the cognitive information forming part of processes of knowledge acquisition and learning. Information is not knowledge, but it is the vehicle enabling such knowledge to be reached.

In relation to Information Science, after conducting a complex and systematic study, he concludes by identifying the following issues: invariant (taken from the outside), where knowledge comes from (due to the influence of information), this is where the language to express it originates, which results in a message prior to documentation. By handling this information (through processes of classification, indexing, etc.) meta-documents are created. He explains that a Matryoskka can be organised, like in the case of Russian dolls, where information is subsumed under other information.

Information science is essential for human beings, their social life and their evolution. It helps to preserve, conserve and circulate (disseminate) knowledge, contributing to scientific development and the preservation of historical memories.

The third chapter was written by José María Díaz Nafría, Universidad de León, (Spain), and is entitled "*Information: A Multidimensional Reality*."

This very extensive chapter describes the BITrum project born in 2008 and dedicated to studying the nature of information. BITrum stems from BIT, like information and *vitrum* is taken from Latín, and was defined as a glass window, made up of many parts of multiple colours. Here it is used to refer to multi-variety information.

60 university researchers from different countries take part in the BITrum project. It is funded by the National Institute of Communication Technology and is headed by the University of Leon under the European Union.

The chapter focuses on discerning and reasoning on the nature of information in a detailed and thorough manner. The theories of other authors are cited for the purpose of making them known and to use them as a basis for the author's own theories.

His main interest is to emphasize *the nature of information,* considering and distinguishing between objective and subjective information.

Factual information is related to objects of very diverse nature and features. Here the focus is on machines and their varied applications and uses, as well as computer science and its tools. These are objects whose general usage is varied. Some believe and others process and use information in one way or another.

For this author, subjective information refers to mental processes as varied as the mind can achieve. These include the sciences, like physics, chemistry, biology, ethics, psychology, etc.. The ultimate aim is to achieve an understanding between the two types of information so as to define what the nature of information may be. Information forms a bridge between objectivists and subjectivists.

To develop his arguments, he refers to information as such. He begins by focusing on the variety of information theories that exist and the lack of a mental understanding between theoretical researchers. He says the information is presented as a multifaceted reality, with a very complex structure, which could be studied under the principles of Systems Theories. This would highlight its multidimensionality, evidencing its differing features.

He also sets out the concepts that have emerged from the Greek and Roman times until very recent years. The reality of subjective information is backed by studies on modern science, and for the purpose of structuring his ideas, he devotes a great deal of this chapter to their study and discernment.

In this same connection, the author also discusses the diversity of cultures and explains that information is produced when these cultures come into contact. Communication is established between them. In this way, he also refers to their social aspects, which are highly complex.

In other paragraphs, he refers to information as being key to creating uncertainty, and the aspect of intentionality is not left out. When disseminating information, intentionality must always be taken into account.

Another section of this chapter focuses on the objectivity and subjectivity of information. In this regard, he points out that Wiener does not agree that information is a type of energy or matter like other authors such as the Italian Paolo Manzelli and myself, who see information as a very subtle form of energy which could lead to matter.

He claims that information can be studied from the standpoint of epistemology, which may also encompass its anthropological aspect. So considered language then appears. However, he emphasizes that the language is shown as a manifestation of information. He believes that language establishes relationships between objective and subjective language, and that it does not necessarily have to be human language. There are many different kinds of languages.

Another significant section of this chapter refers to the dimensions and levels of information. It sets the levels from an interpretive, syntax, systematic and pragmatic perspective, emphasizing the multidimensionality of information. He again emphasizes that the nature of the information is based on the interface between object and subject, and insists that an understanding should arise between objectivists and subjectivists to discern the long-awaited definition of the nature of information.

He also undertakes a detailed study on what it means to develop feeling, perception and intelligent perception in order to reach a coherent union of the nature of information.

In terms of future research plans, he believes it is appropriate to follow the path already started by focusing on the fields of cybernetics, infocomputación, etc. In another vein, studies should be extended to dynamic logic, measurement theory, etc. His aim is to achieve a common understanding as to what the nature of information may be in the information age. He places emphasis on the use of information in the connection of cultures, and identifies a common understanding between objectivists and subjectivists. (*Note: this is something, which as stated in this chapter, must be very difficult.*)

The next chapter discussed, which I myself wrote, is entitled "*Informationism, Information and Its Neuronal Theories*".

This chapter begins by highlighting the phase of transmutation through which mankind is passing, which affects all walks of life, and consequently, information. As a result, the various definitions of information are explored. It is considered as an attribute, an object's quality, and an added value. Additionally, it states that information is assumed to be a typical and normal process undergone by living beings, by which they try to adapt to the environment in which they live. In this sense, information is an ontological process, which includes intelligence and which produces knowledge, science and wisdom. It explains how knowledge is produced, asserting that the brain receives impulses from outside, and upon impact with neurons, activity starts. (*Note: In our previous chapter, we mentioned that "Learning takes up space."*)

The impacts of forms of energy are converted into useful information. These are called *"quanta of useful information"*.

It is said that the information transmitted, received and understood, is essential for setting up human societies, and possibly other types of societies. And perhaps most importantly, it makes reference to their utility. Information should be used for society to evolve, both in the theoretical (e.g. science), and practical (e.g. industry) fields.

In another vein, information is considered, firstly, as a "phenomenon" and secondly, as a "process". Information as a "phenomenon" is one that reaches our brain naturally, consciously or unconsciously, and which produces knowledge.

Information as a "process" is one that is handled and treated for the purpose of being used and which would be the basis of information science, discussed in detail in subsequent pages.

Of great interest are the successive pages, which offer a historical review of trends followed during the past years, both in former and in very recent times. Its influence on the development of humanity and its life forms is highlighted, giving rise to the "Information Society" where it acquires a transcendent value.

Subsequently, a question is posed. "Information, what is it?", which is followed by a detailed discussion of new aspects and definitions of information. It is very instructive to read, as are the paragraphs entitled: "Information in its definitions" or its "Important characteristics" and its "Ontological aspects". It is noted that human beings find themselves on Earth, but also within the whole cosmos, and consequently they receive information from the Cosmos, which could be considered as Cosmic Information.

The subject of "quanta of useful information" is again explored in detail, followed by a description of certain theories of neural information, where information is situated in different ways and times. Cited are the neural theories of C.E. Shannon, John McHale, Fred, I. Dretske, Thomas Y. Feulich, R. M. Bergstrom, S. Brier,, Alexander King, Norbert Henrichs, Peter Ingwersen y A. N. Leontiev, as being the most outstanding and original.

In this chapter, which is also very long, "Informationism" is left for the end, after citing some neural theories of information and emphasizing the definitions, connotations, characteristics and uses of information. All the above is meant to emphasize the importance of informationism, which has led it to become a science in itself, similar in some ways to the other branches of human knowledge, within the whole of science as a unit.

Although Informationism is the concept of most significance in this chapter, being that it is a *new unprecedented and original theory of knowledge*, a large amount of space is not devoted to this topic in the commentary to this chapter.

In short, it is explained that if information is so important in all walks of life and has anthropological, psychological, social and socioeconomic connotations, etc., a new *epistemological theory* called "Informationism" can be sketched where the *central paradigm* turns out to be *information.*

Informationism will be comparable to other epistemological and gnoseological theories, such as Positivism, Realism, Existentialism, Chemicism, etc.

The true significance of this chapter lies in disseminating this *new theory of epistemological knowledge,* called Informationism and the fact that *"the Informationism period has arrived"*, also ensuring that *"nothing without information, and everything because of"*.

In the future Informationism will continue to be researched. (*Note: In a note at the end of the chapter by Garcia-Marco, it is stated that a reference to informationism was found in Wikipedia, suggesting that the name informationalism be used. I have not been able to find this reference, but I do not see any reason for this change. This is a new epistemological theory, and it should follow the same nomenclature.*)

Having discussed the theoretical chapters, which are critical to laying the groundwork for how information may be defined and taking into consideration the consequences and effect of its dissemination and use, following is a discussion of the subsequent chapters focusing on "Collaborative Systems."

The first chapter on this topic is by Aída Velera and Marilene Lobo Abreú Barbosa (both Brazilian), entitled "*The Complexity of Finding Information in Collaborative Systems: Cognitive Needs*".

It is said that in these times where the collaborative system known as Web 2.0 has emerged, the processing and dissemination of information has completely changed, and "everything is for everyone" and "many to many" is the standard that is currently being followed at many libraries and documentation centers. These changes suggest that the cognitive processes also suffer a change, a change which is dealt with in this chapter.

In this sense, it is important to consider the cognitive processes required to obtain a collection of information, its storage and the search therefore, providing a use which is efficient and effective to users, who are the actors, i.e., both the providers of information and their users.

The authors study quantitative processes from a psychological standpoint and also from the standpoint of cognitive psychology, analyzing the impacts that the brain receives from outside. Also considered are inter alia, certain processes of capacity, necessity and orientation required to achieve full brain capacity. The authors discuss the types of human interfaces produced in back and forth relationships, so as to form a mode of knowledge, whose orientation depends on the information received and needed.

The theories of other researchers are analysed, and Feuerstein, Chov, Kuhlthatt and Kuhlthan Teixeira are cited in relation to processes that take place in collaborative systems to find and research information to make it available for dissemination.

Theories of learning which lead to the creation of knowledge are also discussed. For this purpose, the theories of Piaget, Lucien Goldmam, Vrgostsky, Paulo Freire, Morin and Feuerstein, (more thoroughly) are also studied.

The next step is assumed to be the study of the behavior of users searching for information, which is the other side of collaborative systems. Ethnographic methods which differ depending on the type of ethnic groups have recently been used for this purpose, and provide answers to many questions. The theories of several scientists who are specialists in these areas are then studied. The authors Bertram Brookes, Wilson, K Caral Kuhltham (again, more extensively), Peter Ingwersen, Hjorlan, Devin and Ellis, are cited as being most representative.

So far, the foundations for collaborative systems have been analysed and laid down. Both the cognitive processes used to create information and the learning process used to achieve its assimilation and, hence, its dissemination and usage, are studied.

Through ethnographic studies it is shown that not all people behave the same way, and the differences occurring in Brazil are used as an example. The authors believe that these discrepancies are caused by a lack of finances and suggest that entities and countries establish means and opportunities which can remedy these situations.

Studies on users are then discussed. The next chapter entitled "*Understanding User Attitudes Toward Information Systems: A Grounded Theory Approach*", was written by David A. Jank, from the University of Long Island, (USA), who states that the purpose of this chapter is to fill in any gap and converge any difference as empirical evidence of the behavior of information system users. This author is interested in studying the attitudes that users of information systems acquire, and attempting to change them if the system so requires. Today, as everything evolves, a change in attitude might be necessary.

Actually, this is a study on users, which takes into account psychological research. Discourse analysis and bibliometrics were also used. The number of features to be taken into account when studying the attitudes of users was determined and epistemological aspects were also considered.

A qualitative analysis of published literature was used. Support was sought from research and theories of a large number of authors. All research was performed after 2000, i.e. In other words all of the studies are very recent. Collaborative systems were introduced as a result of the changes in information systems. It was concluded that a change in attitudes is necessary, taking into account the environment, the place, including different countries, and the type of companies, etc.

This author's reasoning is shown in the tables under Figure 1 which provide an overall view of the epistemologic values of the attitudes of information system users. (*Note, this author frequently repeats certain terms*). These attitudes are studied from the standpoint of the taxonomy used and the meaning of the term terms relating to these possible attitudes. Topics such as psychological health, ontological bases, social attitudes, etc. are introduced. In Figure 2, called "dendrogram", the terms used are related by means of lines which are interleaved according to the degree of similarity of the terms. The type of terms is always the same. The author attempts to show that the user attitudes are not so different and offer few variations. Up to this point, reference is made to users as groups. However, he also studies them individually, placing emphasis on their behaviour within their environment. In response to information science, individual users behave the same way individually as they do in a group. The same reasoning is applied to them.

In the future, research on this topic should be continued, especially in reference to multidisciplinary studies.

The next chapter was written by Nuria Lloret Romero, Universitat Politècnica de València (Spain), the other co-editor of this book.

It is entitled: "*Review and Brief History of Collaborative Systems: Taxonomy, Services and Classification.*"

This chapter is very interesting in that it presents a historical review of what has been done in relation to the creation and applications of collaborative systems. She also analyses the literature on the subject and examines certain case studies and research projects, all within the field of computer supported collaborative systems.

These systems have evolved over the years and the year 1968 is mentioned as the possible starting date. This was the year in which the CSCW (Computer Support Cooperative Work) which is essential for new research, was presented.

In 1975 a program appeared which allowed for the use of shared screens, telepointing and videoconferencing. According to the data found, in 1981 the term "groupware" began to be used. Looking to the future, these systems have evolved so quickly that there is hardly any specific data. Everything appears to have happened at the same time.

Taxonomically, the author goes on to define some terms related to these topics, such as Groupware, CSCW, Role, User, Shared/Objects, Wokspace, Session, Tool, Setting, Collaborative Associations, Shared/Repository, Telepointer, Protocol, View, Meta-protocol, Awareness and Avatar, among others.

The evolution of collaborative systems is then described more extensively. HCI (Human Computer Interaction) systems are first explored. Due to the influence of successive inventions and software, these systems have changed very significantly to reach the so-called Web 2.0 approach. (*Note: Nowadays there is talk of Web 3.0.*)

With the advent of personal computers and more recently, mobile phones, a new technological development in collaborative systems has again arisen. The consideration of the space-time parameter has recently contributed to these developments.

The author offers a description of the most popular collaborative systems, starting with videoconferencing, chat, electronic meetings, electronic voting, shared whiteboards, co-authoring, multiuser hypermedia, collaborative virtual environments, planning groups, audio conferencing, online social networking, document management, etc. A large section is devoted to describing SNSs (Social Network Sites), which are services based on Web technologies enabling you to build a public profile, have a list of users, and browse by connection lists. The examples cited are Myspace, Facebook, Twitter, LinkedIn, Friendster, Myspace, etc. In conclusion, she effectively shows us a wide range of collaborative networks and their evolution over time.

The next chapter is entitled "*Adaptative Information Retrieval Based on Task Context*", by Bich-Liên Doan and Jean Paul Sansonnet (France).

In this chapter, the authors study the importance of introducing the appropriate repository, whether already programmed or new, in information search and artificial intelligence domains. These fields, which are so different, can be complementary. They can also influence each other, if the need to establish connections with the creators of information systems and their users is taken into account.

A detailed study has been carried out on what may perhaps be a science, i.e. information search science, based on contexts, which, for example, are from an information center, where the previous processes of collecting, indexing and repository filing have been carried out.

With the current increase in the mobility and ubiquity of the users, and taking into account the diversity of existing repositories, tools and interfaces, you can easily access information, but some conditions should be required. The repositories should be constructed in accordance with their aspects, such as nature, structure, behavior and peculiarities. The psychological factors of the creators and users will also have to be taken into account. Studies of philosophy, psychology, linguistics and computer sciences should be performed. Human aspects should also be considered, such as perception, representation, interpretation, and the use of reference systems.

The author then explores topics relating to the search for already structured information using the system under study, taking into account interactive, adaptive or personalized searches. It highlights the importance of user-computer relationships, advocating for systems which are the easiest and most commonly used such as Yahoo and Google.

Adding certain system devices to make the search easier is also discussed. In this regard, the way in which users make questions is discussed. It is curious to observe how users who are searching for the same answer ask the related question in different ways. Computers (programs and software built by humans) have to interpret the question and offer the appropriate response. For this purpose there are certain programs allowing for interaction, dialogue, questions and answers, which make the question to be answered by the computer more exact. The issue of natural language is very important. The computer should understand the language in which .you are working

With the advent of digital systems, software becomes more complicated. This is where large changes have occurred in the "question-answer" mode. Not only has the computer changed its structure and programs, users have also changed their attitudes. This is something which is very difficult.

As a result, language (human) and the appropriateness of the questions formulated have become a topic of debate once again. Some graphics and explanations are provided to illustrate this topic.

In the future, the influence of virtual systems should continue to be studied in order to build a unified platform which combines both symbolic and formal models so as to give positive responses to users.

In all the chapters of this book in which users are studied, the same reasoning, problems and performance techniques are repeated. The databases or repositories have to be organised using the rules in force. There must be classification, indexing, and storage systems which are appropriate in each case, and finally, specialists in the subjects covered.

The chapter entitled "*Metadata for Information Retrieval in Archives*" by Vicente Giménez Chornet, Universitat Politècnica de València, (Spain), deals with a special case relating to archives.

The above conditions are repeated, and emphasis is placed on the fact that the archivists must be specialists in the subject and care must also be taken to assure there are enough archivists to carry out the required mission. Many times, the lack of personnel leads the organisation of the archives to be neglected, causing confusion among users.

A number of paragraphs are devoted to the study of the application of the rules in force. Not all rules are appropriate for every kind of archive.

Another issue the author considers to be important is the addition of a new document to an archive which has already been created. When the archive is historical, the problem is even more serious because it is necessary to know the dates of the document. It is advisable to follow the rules, and in any case, not to create a parallel archive. However, it may be advisable to include an additional note. This is true in both the case of manual archives which do still exist and in mechanized archives.

This author proposes continuing the same line of research.

The next chapter entitled "*Management Systems of User Interfaces Functionalities in Latin: American Web OPACs*", was written by Elsa Barber, Silvia Pisano, Sandra Romagnoli, Verónica Parsiale, Gabriela de Pedro, Carolina Grogui y Nancy Blanco, all from the Universidad de Buenos Aires, (Argentina).

We are told that the process of mechanizing libraries began in the 1880s in Latin American countries, at times when these countries were experiencing poor political and economic conditions. This negatively affected the development of such mechanisation, and these effects are still noted today. The studies focus on the university libraries in Latin American countries.

It was concluded that of most importance was to have well organised libraries where OPAC systems were installed.

Subsequently, the authors present a detailed study of research by a number of specialists from many different countries. These studies evidence the gaps found over the years in this region of the planet. It was highlighted that by percentage, the most advanced countries are Mexico, Brazil, Argentina and Colombia.

These authors once again discuss collaborative systems and state that the most suitable to meet the needs of the user are the OPACs in Web 2.0, which are the systems most commonly used, given their functionalities.

They emphasize the need to disseminate knowledge using ICI (Information Computer Interaction) systems, through units of information in all of Latin America in order to take part in collaborative systems and create network knowledge.

The conclusion is that the situation in certain countries is quite acceptable and that university libraries are on the right track. These topics will continue to be researched.

The next chapter by Álvaro Quijano-Solís and Guadalupe Vega, (both from Colegio de México), is entitled "*Academia Libraries as Complex Systems.*"

These authors once again focus on the topic of university libraries, but this time from the standpoint of Systems Theory. They begin by defining academia (university) libraries as systems pertaining to a higher education institution of a broad spectrum. They supply information resources and other similar services to professors, researchers and students.

Academia libraries have undergone major changes in recent years, both in terms of organization, structure and distribution, and in terms of political, economic and social conditioning factors. The authors extensively describe their functions, tasks and obligations. They emphasize that these are collaborative systems, which implies that they are also social systems.

It is very important to take into account both educational and social aspects, all within an environment which is now based on Internet. The introduction of electronic working methods has led to the change being experienced in these times. This type of library must focus on a learning environment rather than a teaching environment. Users, whether teachers or students, look for materials and information, in order to solve problems they face in their research or studies, all based on so-called Information Technology. In order to provide users with appropriate information, intelligent and cognitive processes must be followed which satisfy users acting both individually and as a group in a balanced way.

In fact, Systems Theories in which the library is considered as a highly complex system, have been relied on in order to be able to organise a good and efficient university library.

The authors then describe how a system can be defined and what it should consist of: structures, the "objects", their composition and the environment where they are located. The objects in this case are the library collection. On the other hand, there should be cooperation between the collection and users to make the system work. They refer to communities of practice and learning communities.

Communities of Practice are studied in depth. Definitions are provided and numerous variants are cited. For the purpose of studying such communities, the principles of the Activity Theory are applied. As a result, a new definition of library is outlined. The Activity Theory continues to be applied, and human activity is referred to highlight that in the operation of a university library, of most importance is the human factor.

Now, an academia library is described as a "complex system" where contextual activity is considered as a whole consisting of the following subsystems: data collection, coordination, organization, strategy, planning, development, background, learning module and innovation module.

They the authors propose a model from a systemic standpoint, which takes into account the properties of communities of practice and Activity Theory in order to address organizational problems, so that people (users) can transform inputs into products and add value through teaching and learning models.

In the future, this topic will continue to be researched.

The next chapter of this book is by Margarita Cabrera, currently from the, Universitat Politècnica de València, (Spain) and is entitled "*Cultural Management 2.0*".

In this chapter 2.0 systems are explored from the standpoint of organization and dissemination of culture. The 2.0 program is situated within the field of electronic techniques, and specifically digital website systems, which is why they are referred to as Web 2.0 systems. When they appeared it was assumed that an end point had been reached. However, there is already talk of Web 3.0.

The main objective is to describe the state of the art (looking at the past to some extent) of organizational culture, from the standpoint of Web 2.0. The author analyzes where we have come from and where we are going, as far as culture is concerned. We come from an analog world and are headed towards a more complex digital world. The latest cultural institutions are cited and discussed, being considered as social communication systems. Their evolution over recent years is also explored. In fact, Web 2.0 is an advanced version of protocols and communication and dissemination programs within the organizations of culture.

They base their studies on communities of users, in a special field of services of a varied nature. Despite everything, their importance is not technological in nature, but rather is related to attitudes towards Web 2.0 and to society as a whole.

In these systems, of most relevance are the users. This converts them into an existential phenomenon of research and applications among participants (real users). The author also explains that the user is a figure generating organizational models that can help improve the services provided in social institutions, taking into account social participation and media.

The author then lists the conditions the user or team must fulfill in order to make use of Web 2.0 in social networks. From a long list, highlighted are those that seem most relevant, such as: immediacy, freedom, transparency, being close and accessible, being constant, and so on. It is equally important to consider the issue of natural languages used

With digital tools specific to Web 2.0 environments, you can create intelligent cultures which act by themselves as automatons or robots. The greatest difficulty posed by these practices is dissemination. It is pointed out that the content agents, actors and organizations must be good professionals, and they should be very knowledgeable about the issues with which they work.

In the future, research on the creation of more independent and intelligent cultural and social Web 2.0 systems will be continued.

The final chapter of the book is entitled, "*Coagmento: A Case Study in Designing a User-Centric Collaborative Information Seeking System*", by Chirag Shah.

In this chapter, the author describes Coagmento, a system that provides integrated tools and workflow for doing collaborative information seeking in online environment. Coagmento's inception followed a need to provide essential tools to collaborators without them having to learn an entirely new system or work in an unfamiliar environment.

Here they describe how the author designed, developed, and deployed Coagmento. The design of this system was facilitated using several pilot runs and cognitive walkthroughs. A fully functional version of Coagmento was then developed and evaluated using laboratory study, and its design optimized using participatory design sessions.

Finally, the author describes how they made the enhanced version of Coagmento available to wider group of users, along with issues and challenges faced. They summarize lessons learned and provide a guideline for designing and developing such collaborative information seeking systems.

COMMENTS

It may be wrong for me to say so but this is indeed an original book with important developments. There is a point of originality in all the topics discussed. The authors may deal with issues which are already known, but they do so from fresher points of view.

Information is studied in great depth, giving rise to new ideas and reasonings not seen before, useful reasons which may enable us to discern what the characteristics, use and nature of information may be.

The studies of vertical integration of sciences and informationism are pioneering in that we have heard little about these subjects to date.

The chapter devoted to the evolution of collaborative systems based on reliable data is very illuminating.

The different chapters devoted to studying users in one manner or another present new and unknown characteristics, attitudes and practices which had not been explored to date. The chapter on the status of collaborative systems in Latin America, shows us unfamiliar situations and perspectives. The chapter on university libraries presents a serious study of their status and current activities, both now and in the near future.

This book is enjoyable to read and you need not be a specialist in these subjects to understand them. I would even dare to say that these pages contribute to increasing general culture. However, they are also essential for specialists, scholars, teachers at any level of education and students.

Here you are provided a basis from which to draw on for your own teaching and to discuss these topics in classes, or when you have to give a lecture, or prepare a presentation for a conference. This information is also useful for students who wish to expand on the notes they have taken in class.

This book should not be missing from any university or general library or from the office of any scholar, professor and user of all the systems dealt with in this book.

I predict it will be quite successful.

Emilia Currás
Autonomous University Madrid, Spain

Nuria Lloret Romero
Universitat Politècnica de València, Spain

Section 1
Theoretical and Scientific Aspects in Collaborative Information Systems

Subsection

Theoretical and Philosophical Principles:

Informationism

Chapter 1
Vertical Integration of Science:
An Approach to Including Information, Knowledge and Its Organization

Emilia Currás
Autonomous University Madrid, Spain

ABSTRACT

In this chapter, there is an attempt to consider an organization of knowledge regarding a vertical integration of science, which is focused as a systems unity of greater complexity then what has been considered before. An ascending or descending vertical integration of science might be to interpret questions posed by human in general and information scientist in particular. It could provide answers that they are looking for. All aspects of the global information could have a widest sense, appear to be treated, and the problems need to be freshly addend as required solutions. This vertical integration of science is considered here from the vision of the systems science theories. A study of this integration, with all its complexity could provide important solutions for an adequate organization of knowledge.

Take up your torch and walk, walk...

Mankind, both now and the future.

need you to pave a way

E.C.

DOI: 10.4018/978-1-61350-201-3.ch001

1. PRELIMINARY CONSIDERATIONS

Mankind is clearly at a transcendentally important point in history, in that there is a transmutation of all forms of life: intellectually, socially and also politically and economically. This crisis situation has been noted by many authors and the author of this chapter has mentioned it in other papers. It is also something that requires no proof; its indicators and consequences are well known.

When, about 30 years ago, people began to speak about society begin in crisis, and the effects of this were first felt in daily life, it seemed daring and even pessimistic to think that this was the beginning of a period of transformation or transmutation. To relate crisis to transmutation was considered as audacity of avant garde and eccentric thinkers. So much has been written and the symptoms are so obvious that there is now no alternative but to accept these ideas and realities. Proposed solutions have been few and those applied or adopted even fewer.

Given the situation, why are we incapable of finding solutions and putting them into practice? The reason is that we have to change our mentality. "A new man" should be born, with new ways of thinking and of acting in response. For a good numbers of years -it is difficult to define how many-, thinkers from all disciplines and of all ideologies have talked about the change in mentality which is necessary in order to focus on solutions for the problems of today. Of these, the best known to the author of this paper will be mentioned. M. Jackson, I. Progogine, W. Gasparski, E. Andreewsky, R. Rodríguez Delgado, Fernando de Elzaburu, E. Laszlo, Alwin Diemer, Heidegger, John McHale, Fichte and Hegel, amongst others.

If emphasis has been given to the present situation of mankind and the need to undergo a change in mentality, it has been with the idea of upholding the following reasons which will be explain along this paper. (Figures 1 and 2).

2. CONSIDERING THE SYSTEMS SCIENCE

One of the changes in mentality, now becoming evident, is from consideration of the superiority of the whole over each of its parts. This is the first and principal postulate of systems science. For example, the Club of Rome maintains that questions should be treated globally, albeit applying local solutions. R. Rodríguez Delgado speaks of the need to create a theoretical framework containing a global vision of knowledge and human activities. Bogdanov, in his *Tektology*, advocates a holistic way of thinking as a source of development which he considers as a systemic philosophical principle. Fichte and Hegel refer to the passing of the philosophy of facts to that of the environment. Fritjof Capra offers a new vision of the universe as a dynamic weaving of interrelated events, in which no property of the parts is fundamental and it is the union of all the peculiarities and mutual relations that determines the structure of the whole. All these ideas and postulates are likewise based on the principles of systems science.

In fact, from the point of view of the author of this paper, systems theory with its vision of a whole, where mankind can be considered as a complex evolving and fuzzy system; in which the participating subsystems are in dialectic interaction among themselves and simultaneously with their environment, can provide solutions for our present situation and provide the mental impulse that we need to implement this much required change in mentality.

3. INFLUENCES OF SCIENCE

Science is one of the pillars in the evolution of mankind. Science can be considered as a unity of the branches of knowledge, as well as a way to acquiring these branches. These ideas are precisely one of the first indications of the advocated change in mentality.

Not long ago, and even today, science was considered to refer only to a knowledge of nature, and what was objectively real and existing. The study of matters related to the manifestations of the spirit, such as philosophy and art, history...,etc, belonged to the world of the humanities, opposed to, and at odds with science. L. van Bertalanffy made efforts to demonstrate that both manifesta-

Figure 1. "Mankind" flowchart 1

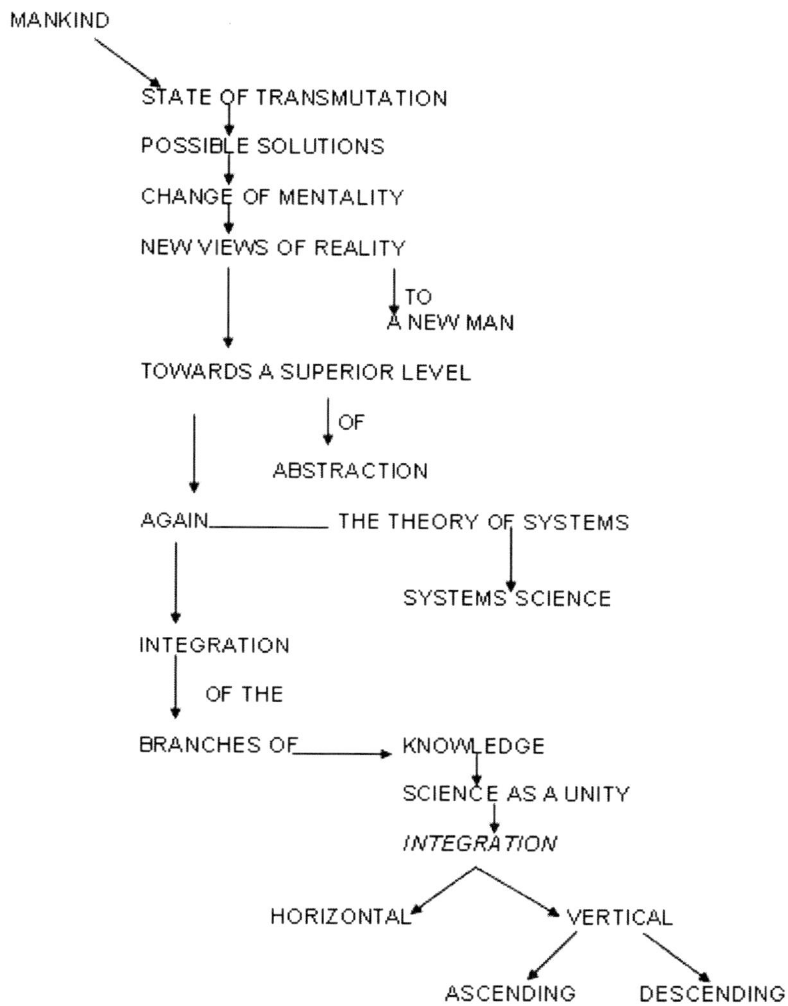

tions of the human intellect are intimately related. Teilhard de Chardin said that science is the sister of the humanities. Perhaps those who carry out highly specialized and technical activities might still propose differences. However, the idea of a fraternal union was growing and gradually spreading, along the times, so that today is almost generally accepted.

The idea of science as a unity of the branches of knowledge is not new. The postulates of Tao refer to this. However, we know that ideas (which are rarely new and original) recur in cycles of varying length, tracing a curve of maxima and minima along a central line which represent the evolution of mankind. We find them, from 2500 BC to present times, the same ideas reflected at varying intervals by the thinkers of the times, for instance, Hermes Trimegisto, Albertus Magnus, Karl Marx and more recently Schrödinger and Morcillo Crovetto. From recent times we can mention: Heisenberg, who quantified development in the search for the unity of science; Weizsäcker, who tells us that our spirit is looking for the unity of science: and Elzaburu, who refers to science as

Figure 2. "Mankind" flowchart 2

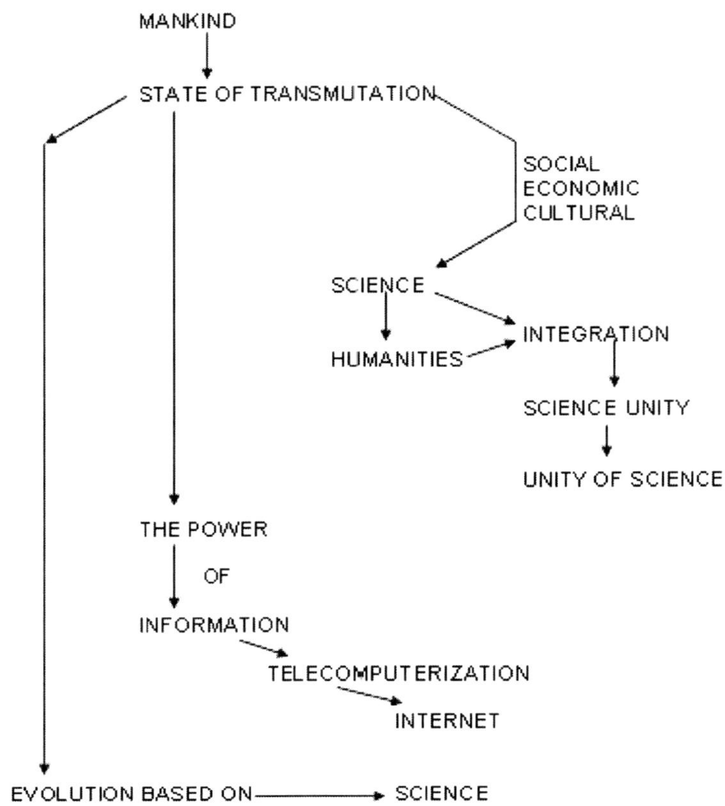

a knowledge that directs the sense of behaviour, Alexander King generalizes even more by combining knowledge with the close relationship between phenomena, events and states of understanding.

Science embraces all learning accumulated to date, the ways to achieve such learning and the ways of acquiring new knowledge. When expressed in such a general way, it becomes ambiguous and inconsistent. However, if one delves into these postulates, one find the inclusion from mere definitions to theories and applications, scientific methods, research procedures, manufacturing processes, the influence of various factors such as information, prospection techniques, in fact everything that contains science and makes science.

Science is both unique and plural. As a system, it is made up of subsystems, basic elements which Koestler and Smyties called "holons". These holons are not simple but are composed of other subsystems, similarly complex. All this is influenced by vectors, fluxes and refluxes in dialectic interaction, as the author of this paper postulate in the article "Dialectic interaction in science".

When reading studies about science and other subjects we can find, without perhaps realizing it, references to these ideas on the vertical integration of sciences. In the 6th Book of the Tao, for example, it is mentioned that when it is considered that things integrate, it is possible to understand the nature of Heaven, Earth and all things. The integration here is downwards, from the supernatural (perhaps only universal), to the nature of knowledge, to the social, economic and political (composing "all things"). Eric Schwartz refers to the man-cosmos integration. Here it is understood that the relationship of the aforementioned parts of the science is made by means of an upwards integration, the opposite of the previous case. Paolo Manzelli postulates that classical physics does not help in understanding the energy-matter-information relationship. For this it is necessary to introduce intermediate processes where the chemical processes play an important role. Likewise, F. de Elzaburu assures us that biology derives from physics, which means a vertical leap from the latter, considered as a basis, to the former, as a final climax. Mario Bunge, on the other hand, proposes that all systems contain five interdependent aspects: cultural, political, economic, biological and environmental. In other words, five manifestations of a further five branches of science in ascending degrees of complexity. Bohm and Chew coincide in that the "conscience" or moral sciences should be included in the future theory of physical phenomena or physical sciences, if we widh to understand the essential aspects of the universe. In their fundamental ideologies, these authors coincide with the theories of Fritjof Capra, and are not far removed from the principles of the Tao of Physics. From another point of view, Karl Popper considers psychology becomes part of physics. Likewise, taking psychology as a primary part of science as a unit, medicine can be included in psychology. (Table 1)

These examples are enough to show that the vertical integration of sciences is an underlying idea in the minds of contemporary thinkers.

4. VERTICAL INTEGRATION OF SCIENCES

Science is thus composed of the different sciences (branches of whole knowledge or wisdom systems) in a highly complex integration of systems in state of interrelations. This complexity increases with advances in the evolution of mankind and of all vital phenomena on our Planet, and the future of the Cosmos itself. The process of integration has traditionally been studied from a horizontal viewpoint. If it is held that all manifestation and successes of the human intellect have a place in a given aspect of science, i.e. in one of the sciences of which it is formed, such as historical, legal, chemical or biological, there is understood to be a concordance between them, relating them on planes at the same level. This line of thought involves significant difficulties when the real aim is to look for solutions to the crisis which we are facing.

It is true that there are no superior or inferior sciences. All hold equal importance in the union of the branches of learning, and all should be studies individually as a complete whole with its own characteristic and peculiarities. However, when one wants to study the interrelations between some sciences and others, in processes of integration that provide global views of where to extract practical and local solutions for the evils in any aspect of our life, be it political, social or economic, we have to change our way of thinking,

Table 1. Some authors who postulate the idea of the unity of science

Tao La Tse	*2500 BC*
Palto	*427-337 BC*
Alberto Magno	*13th century*
Pedro Calderón de la Barca	*1677*
Bogdanov	*1923*
Henri Pointcaré	*1964*
Ludwig von Bertalanffy	*1968*
Alexander King	*1976*
Aurelio Peccei	*1984*
Ilia Progogine	*1988*
Fernando de Elzaburu	*1988*
Mario Bunge	*1988*
Emilia Currás	*1988*
J.J. Scala Estatella	*1991*

our mentality. We have to enter a new level already postulated by David Walsh, Bela H. Banathy, I. Prigogine, M. Jackson and F. de Elzaburu, among others (Figure 3).

Let us try then by considering the integration of sciences in a vertical sense. Each of the different sciences (branches of human knowledge) constitutes a block within science as a unity. This block is influenced by different blocks, or sciences, to an extent that is determined by the knowledge´s environment to each in relation to the rest, or to a specific one under study. In order to achieve complete knowledge of each branch of the science, it is necessary to start with the one which serves as a basis and then move up or down, introducing other more complex sciences or complementary means, within the environment of learning to which the science under study refers.

It might then appear that we are considering some sciences as principals and others as being complementary. This could be within each of the sciences (branches of human knowledge). In one instance a particular science might play a principal role, and a complementary role in another. Likewise, certain sciences affect all the rest, while others relate only to a few, within their degree of affinity.

Figure 3. Different branches of learning

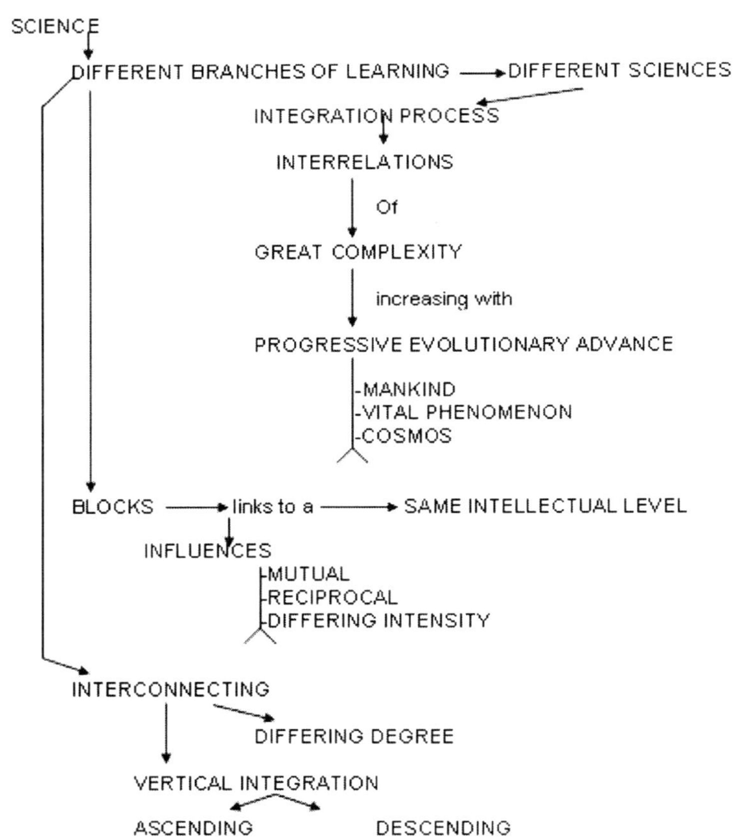

5. STRUCTURE OF SCIENCE AS A SYSTEM IN ITS VERTICAL INTEGRATION AND ITS INTERACTION WITH THE OUTSIDE

5.-I.

It has to be agreed that the difference branches of human knowledge which make up the unity of science exert varying degrees and levels of influence on each other. Such an example is chemistry, which is influenced by physics, biology, meteorology, zoology, etc. In psychology one has to take into account the influence of sociology, morals, biology, etc.

In information, as a branch of human knowledge, information theory, electronics and philosophy intervene among other. We likewise should agree that certain sciences appear to be the basis for acquiring full knowledge of another science.

Figure 4. Polyhedron example

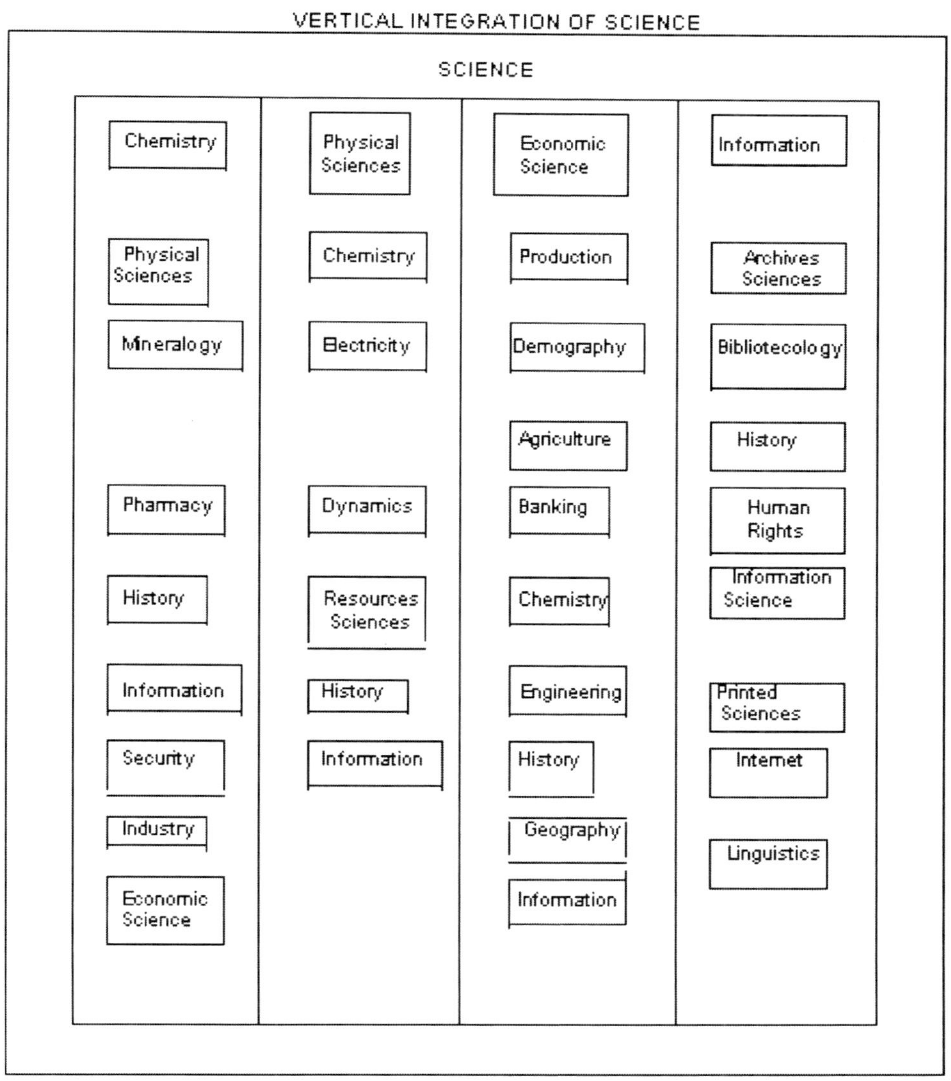

Physical science is the basis for the study of chemistry, medicine for studying psychology, and botany is the basis for agriculture. It is also true that certain sciences intervene in the development of other branches of knowledge. It is evident that history, mathematics (particularly in its practical and statistical applications), geography, ethics and information in its information science form, are all sciences that should be included in the study of any science. The degree of dependence and influence of a science on others would vary according to each case, so that the network of relationships appears as complex with concordant and discordant interrelationships all evolving in space and in time.

Let us imagine a polyhedron with rectangular faces. Internally, this polyhedron is made up of a series of columns, formed of *blocks* or bricks of differing height and weight (Figure 4). If we were to build a real model we could use colours for the different blocks and thus illustrates their interactions.

Each column represents a branch of the unity of science. Hence, we would have physics, chemistry, ecology, economics, law, philosophy, history, science, and information, etc., each forming a basic unit, or holon, of the system. This holon in turn is not simple, it is complex and forms a subsystem of a complexity similar to that of the global unitary system.

The holons are made up of *blocks* that vertically, either upwards or downwards, form and complete the column. The blocks, in turn, form branches of science. In other words, at times a certain science appears as a principal holon and at others as one of the blocks forming another holon. This can be illustrated by certain practical cases. In order to study medicine, it is necessary to start with biology, and perhaps even with embryology, and then to add blocks such as sociology, psychology, physics, chemistry, history, information and finally ecology.

When wanting to study ecology, mineralogy should be taken into account as well as adding botany, zoology, agriculture, meteorology, sociology, economics, history, statistics, information, etc. In the case of philosophy, one would have to being with neurophysiology, which embraces research on brain processes when creating a line of reasoning, and continue with epistemology, ethics, etc. When considering Information, it should be the basis, which will be added with, Archives sciences, Bibliotecology, Information science, knowledge organization, classification theories, linguistics, History, Internet technique, etc. (Figure 5).

It is necessary to understand here "information" as a branch of human knowledge, as was stated before. As such, no other branches, or sciences, can be developed without using information. A difference is made also here between "information" –a branch of human knowledge – and "information science" as a component together with library and archives sciences (examples in Figure 4).

The contribution of each science to the development of another cannot be the same in each case. In the development of the historical sciences, for example, agriculture, mineralogy or ecology do not play the same role as ethics or art because their influence in the development of agriculture is not so important. Therefore, the blocks within the columns are not always of the same size.

It should be understood that there are mutual and reciprocal influences of varying intensity between the blocks themselves and their columns. This is a complicated network or flux and reflux vectors, where an input loop can become an output flow in another column. Dialectic relationships are established which affect the evolution of the principal system, science as a unity, and each of its component parts. This is a development led by the time –space parameters which then mark a dialectical evolution to get a transformation of the whole system in a continuous process of varying intensity.

Figure 5. Vertical integration of science

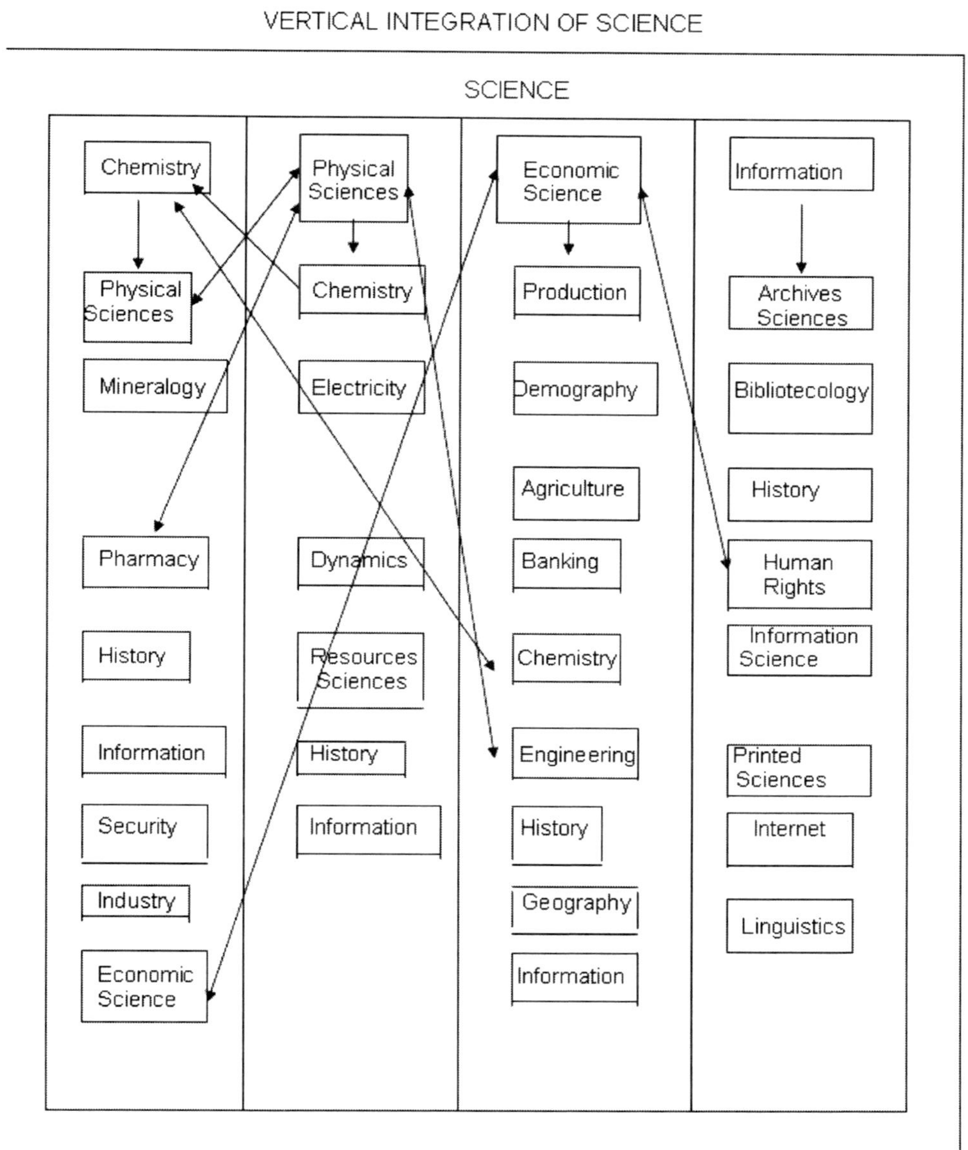

5.-II.

The system of science as a unity is also immersed in the environment that it has created, within the Planet Earth and within the Cosmos, which is mainly unknown. Inputs flowing into our system are generally in the form of continuous and intermittent, but not uniform, items of information. It has been shown how a saturation of information causes a transmutation in the system. This saturation occurs in increasingly shorter periods of time, when considered from the standpoint of our human terrestrial dimension. Events show that at present science is saturated with information, hence its transmutation process, affecting all thoughts of mankind in the present state of crisis. All this points to a change in mentality, a jump in level.

6. THE SPACE-TIME PARAMETERS

It is necessary here to dedicate a few paragraphs to the subject of the space-time parameters in which all human, and therefore science unity, activities are carried out. I am not really sure if we clearly understand what these are, both space and time, in our concept of unique and unrepeatable human beings as individuals, who are also negligible parts and particles within the Universe or Cosmos as a whole. As each of us consider ourselves important, we approach all questions affecting us from our own human point of view, as living beings on the Planet Earth. Space is that in which we move, slightly increased with space flights and large telescopes. Regarding time, we know that it passes and creates differences in our actions and behaviour, and we measure it in terms of physical phenomena, likewise related to our Planet.

Philosophical and mathematical studies have in fact been carried out to examine in depth both time and space, always from man´s subjective point of view and his existential meditations. Now, a change of mentality is also needed. Both space and time are arbitrary dimensions created by man himself to provide an explanation for a series of questions relating to mankind.

What has to be taken into account is that time is conditioned by space. Whatever the latter, so will be the former. As an example, for humankind a terrestrial "minute" has not the same measure as a minute on Saturn, which means that time is conditioned by space. Everyone agrees up to this point. However, when focussing on certain other questions we cling to our terrestrial idea and won't leave it. If we tried to put ourselves on higher levels with "our feet still on the ground", with new concepts of space and time, we could explain many questions which still remain a mystery.

7. MORE CONSIDERATIONS

From this paper, the vertical integration of science, we have to think of the discontinuity in the development of the different branches of science, both in time and in space. If a certain branch evolves faster than another, in which it is an intermediate block, a swelling can arise which disorder and unbalance. The whole column, or branch of science, will undergo a change due to this input. Equilibrium is regained by studying the phenomenon, taking into account a higher degree of complexity that provides solutions. In other words, one would have to pass to a new conceptual level, which is wider and more generalized, according to each specific case. If electronics evolves faster than acoustics, within the physical sciences column, harmony no longer exist between the two, nor within the holon itself. An imbalance has been created. If chemistry, or rather the chemical industry, evolves faster than mineralogy, within the column formed by economics, everything changes. If Bibliotecology evolves faster than classification theories, or cataloguing, a disorder is taken place and if knowledge organization evolves faster than thesauri theory happens the same. Various examples could also be given with similar phenomena resulting, as it is in information, as well if retrieval process goes faster than the classification systems (knowledge organization) an unbalance is created.

Likewise, it should be remembered that different branches of science do not develop in the same way, neither with the same intensity in different countries not in different periods in history. These variable, discontinuous and, at times, negative vectors of flux have to be considered when studying the system of science as a unity, as well as their influence on mankind' s future and of all life on Earth. This all shows that questions have to be approached in a different manner, from a higher level that is at once more global, but at the same time more specific and precise.

Another factor to consider is the development of mankind in its evolution towards an understanding of the world in which it lives. There is still plenty to be discovered and invented. Our brain is capable of highly superior development. Human life on Earth has only just begun.

8. SYSTEMS INTERACTION

Science as a unity is vertically formed by columns representing the different branches of human knowledge, and by blocks located within each column representing the unique contribution of each branch to whole of the column, which are interrelated by applying systems theory (or systems science).

These interactions are made by means of vectors and parameters established within the overall system, In other words, in the polyhedron drawn above (Figure 4), the system is considered to be highly complex, situated in the living realm of human beings. This system is composed by a number of subsystems (columns), which in turn are composed of subsystems. A complex structure is thereby formed in which there are ebb and flow relationships of varying intensity and length of time. A polyhedron is formed which includes the aforementioned vectors (Figure 5). The true values

Figure 6. Integrating sciences

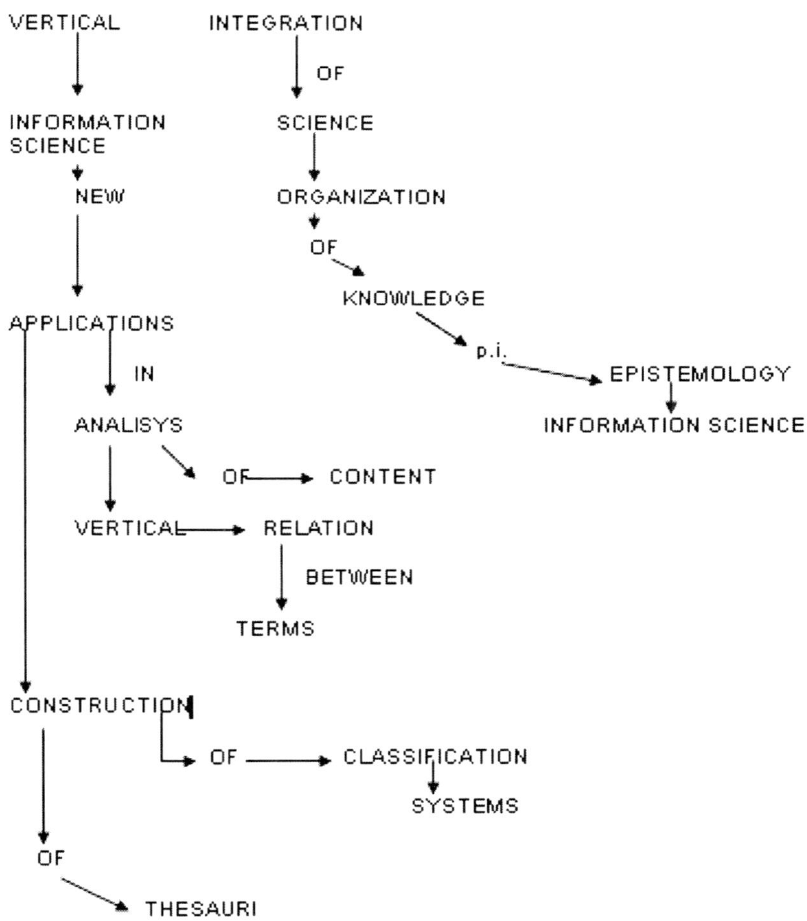

of these data are calculated using mathematical formulas in accordance with the rules of systems science.

9. HUMAN KNOWLEDGE ORGANIZATION IN ITS NEW CONCEPT

This approach to the vertical integration of different branches of human knowledge, sciences, within the unity of science, involves a new order in the same philosophical theories for organization of knowledge or epistemology. It would be a new trend in the manner of understanding or realizing part of epistemology. The concept is not new, as was indicated above when mention was made of some authors who have argued for this vertical way of ordering human knowledge. Here it is organized in a different way, placing the different sciences in vertical columns, one for each specific science, where other sciences which contribute to its information and development form blocks with different sizes and influence.

10. ROLL OF INFORMATION SCIENCE

Since this idea of integrating sciences in a vertical way within the unity of science involves a new method for the organization of knowledge, it could also be applied to information science. As a matter of fact it can be applied; for instance in content analysis, as when a vertical relation is established of terms in a classification system or in a thesaurus. It is precisely in the thesauri where relations between generic and specific terms involve a vertical relation form greater to smaller conceptual content (Figure 6).

Figure 7. Vertical system

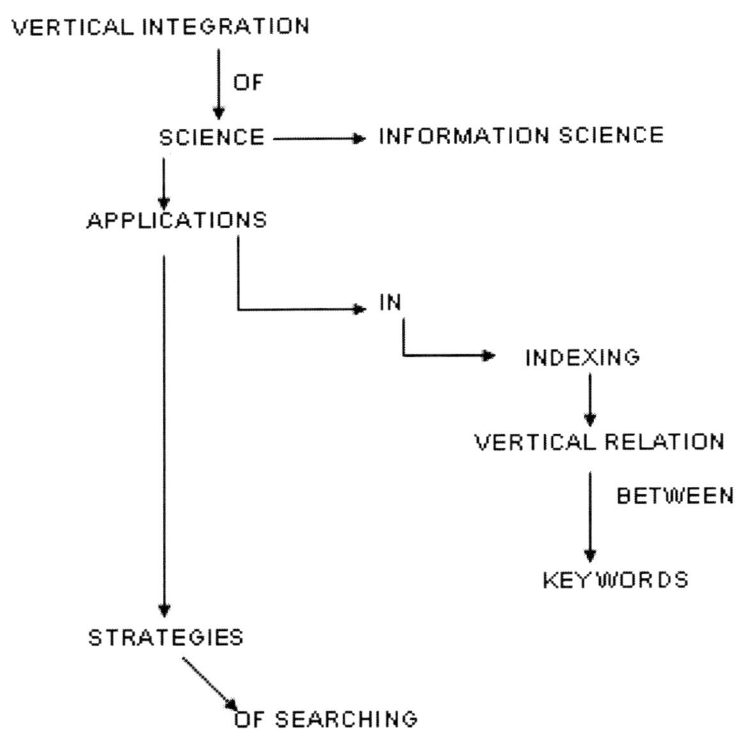

In like manner an arrangement of terms, or concepts, can be observed in information retrieval and in the formulation of searching strategies. If we proceed from greater to smaller, or vice versa, the keywords can be more easily arranged and information retrieval will be more efficiently achieved. (Figure 7)

Once more, the usefulness of the vertical integration of sciences in the sciences unity is confirmed, and this is also valid in the case of information science.

This vertical system of arranging and integrating sciences can be defined as a different approach to classification of sciences including the classic and traditional ones, from the mediaeval trivium to the more modern classifications, where data processing is now included as well as computer science, sociology and environmental sciences.

In the author's view, one cause or reason for this transmutation, is the development of progress, whether scientific, technological or cultural, etc. Should progress be stopped (…!!!); but who would dare? Since such a possibility does not exist, other solutions must be sought.

CONCLUSION

In this chapter an attempt is made to find solutions to our world today, where major transformations have arisen in all ways of life and activities. One of the main, if not the only reason, which has led to and continues to encourage such transformations, is information in all of its diverse definitions, characteristics and connotations. Of course information itself acts as a driving factor in science. Science evolves in response to the boost in human intelligence. An attempt is made to study, or perhaps, foresee the most importance causes of the transformation, or mutation of society currently being experienced.

This chapter aims to make some changes in human thought, which to date have not been considered conceivable: as may be in the organisation of science, knowledge and wisdom.

To date, science, i.e. unity science, as a set of all branches of knowledge, has been organized horizontally into layers overlapping each other. An attempt is made to organize science vertically, considering it to be a unit composed by the various specific sciences (branches of knowledge) forming a whole. These different sciences encompass, for example, chemistry, information, medicine, etc., organized together vertically. This would lead to relationships which are harmonically positioned and in dialectical opposition. The interpretation and resolution of such relationships could be solved using the principles and practices of systems theory.

Vertical integration of sciences in unity sciences, leads to the building of a polyhedron, composed by blocks (branches of knowledge or specific sciences) which establish a harmonious, and at the same time, dialectic relationship. Everything is related to everything else and to the environment in which it is situated.

In order to better understand this vertical integration, reference is made to several sciences, including inter alia, chemistry and information. Naturally, reference is made to information, as a science in itself, and to knowledge and its organisation both in the human realm, and with respect to the very specific information science, which is the overall theme of the book in which this chapter could be included.

ADDITIONAL READING

Bertalanffy, L. (1968). *General System Theory. Foundations, Development, Applications*. New York: George Brazilier.

Bonsack, F. (1990). Ouverture verticale et ouverture horizontale. *Bulletin de l'AFG*, *55*, 5.

Bunge, M. (1989). El enfoque sistémico de los Recursos Humanos. *Rev. Int. Sist.*, *1*(3), 247–356.

Capra, F. (1984). *El giro decisivo: una nueva visión de la realidad. Ecofilosofías. Diseñando nuevas formas de vida*. Barcelona: Integral Ediciones.

Checkland, P., & Howell, S. (1998). *Information, Systems and Information Systems*. London: Wiley.

Currás, E. (1987). Science as a system of cyclic process of generation, processing, accumulation and transfer of scientific information. In *Theoretical Problems of Information. Place of Information in the Global Problems of the World, FID, 659* (pp. 11–26). Moscow: VINITI.

Currás, E. (1990). Dialectic interaction in science. In *Actes du Congrès Européen de Systemique. Association Française pour la Cybernetique Économique et Technique.* (pp. 5-17). Lausanne: AFSCET.

Currás, E. (1990). Un nuevo concepto de información científica. (A new concept of information in scientific integration). In *Proceedings of 44th FID Conference and Congess.* La Habana: FID.

Currás, E. (1995). Information science-information as a dialectic interactive system. In *Second International ISKO Conference, Madras, 26-28 August (Sarada Ranganathan Endowment for Library Science, Bangalore, 1992).* Also in IFID 20, 1, (pp. 31- 42).

Currás, E. (1996). *Tratado sobre Ciencia de la Información (Treatise on Information Science)*. Rosario: Universidad Nacional de Rosario.

Currás, E. (2005). *Ontologías, Taxonomía y Tesauros: Manual de construcción y uso*. Gijón: Trea.

Currás, E. (2008) *Ciencia de la información bajo postulados sistémicos y sistemáticos*. Madrid: edición personal.

de Elzaburu, F., & Martitegui, J. (1988). *La crisis mundial. De la incertidumbre a la esperanza (The world crisis. From incertitude to hope)*. Madrid: Espasa Calpe.

Gilchrist, A. (2003). Thesauri, Taxonomies and Ontologies – an etymological note. *The Journal of Documentation*, *59*(1), 7–18. doi:10.1108/00220410310457984

Gutiérrez Ríos, E. (1975). *La ciencia en la vida del hombre (Science in man's life)*. Pamplona: Eunsa.

Hernández, A. J., & Gómez, M. J. (1983). *Hacia una concepción integrada de la naturaleza" (Towards an integrated concepttion of nature)*. Spain: Nancea.

Jackson, M. C., & Keys, P. (1984). Towards a system of systems methodologies. *The Journal of the Operational Research Society*, *35*, 473–486.

King, A. (1989). The great transition. *International Forum on Information and Documents*, *2*(14), 3–8.

Kloestler, A., & Smyties, J. R. (1969). *Beyond Reductionism*. London: Hutchinson.

Manzelli, P. (1989). Energia, materia e infromazione. (Energy, matter and information). *Civitá Cibernetica*, *1*(IX), 9–17.

Morcillo Crovetto, A. (1980). *Evolución y negantropía, el modelo matemático de la evolución en base a la teoría de sistemas" (Evolution and negantropy, the mathematical model of evolution taking as a basis the systems theory)*. Unpublished paper delivered at Seminar on General Systems Theory. Madrid: Politecnica University.

Parvu, I. (1996). La unidad del conocimiento científico en el marco de un enfoque tipológico de las teorías (The unity of scientific knowledge within the framework of a typological approach of theories). *Theoria*, *27*, 7–17.

Pointcaré, H. (1964). *El valor de la ciencia (The value of science)*. Madrid: Espasa Calpe.

Popper, K. R. (1967). *El desarrollo del conocimiento científico. Conjeturas y refutación. (Scientific Knowledge development)*. Buenos Aires: Paidos.

Prigogine, I., & Stengers, I. (1983). *La nueva alianza. Metamorfosis de la ciencia (The new alliance, Metamorphosis of science)*. Madrid: Alianza Universidad.

Rodríguez Delgado, R. (1987). Esquema del nuevo pensamiento. *Rev. Venezolana de Síntesis*, *1*, 55–57.

Simon, H. A. (1998). Economics as a historical science. *Theoria*, *13*(32), 241–260.

Snow, R. M. (1991). The integration of systemic and interpretative thought. *Rev. Int. Sist.*, *3*(1), 37–68.

Volkov, L. (1999). Information environment and some aspects of mankind's intellect. In *Proceedings of 4th Systems Science European Congress, Valencia-Ibiza (20-24 September 1999).*

Subsection

Information Systems from the Systems Science Theories

Chapter 2
What is Information?
An Enquiry beyond Information Science from a Systemic Point of View

Francisco-Javier García-Marco
Universidad de Zaragoza, Spain

ABSTRACT

This chapter uses the concept of system to enquire into the concept of information, trying to separate the different senses in which this core concept is used in Information Science and other sciences, that is, physical or "raw" information, messages, knowledge, news, documentation and meta-information. The concept of information is studied as a system of layers or levels, in which each new sense emerges from the previous one. Once each of these senses is clearly established, it is possible to provide more specific insights about the real scientific domain of Information Science: a science related to the design and maintenance of external social memories and the process of referring their contents to relevant personal and social activities. Its focus is, therefore, the optimization of the processes of social memory. So, in conclusion, Information Science is, first, a science of social memory and its use, and, even more specifically, of the methodologies and technologies (social or technical) that exist to optimize its functioning by means of external memories, references (metadata) and systems of metadata (ontologies).

INTRODUCTION

Information Society, Information Science and the Science of Information

Information has become a central concept in our societies and cultures. This is probably a result of automation of information processing and transfer. But, once information has achieved such a token status, its concept requires further elucidation and clarification.

This is even more important in Library and Information Science, which — as other sciences like Cognitive Science, Communication Studies and Computer Sciences — situates information in a central place of its conceptual system.

Establishing what information may be is by no means easy, and many people from different

DOI: 10.4018/978-1-61350-201-3.ch002

branches of philosophy and science are pursuing it[1]. In this chapter, we are going to concentrate only in separating some of the different senses of information — information, communication, knowledge, documents, metadata… — that are frequently used in Library and Information Science with the purpose of bringing them into a system of concepts with the aid of the theory of systems — or systemics.

Information and Systems

So, this chapter uses the concept of system to enquire into the concept of information, trying to separate the different senses in which it is used in Information Science and other sciences: physical or "raw" information, knowledge, messages, news, documentation, meta-information… The final aim is to gain more information to establish the distinctive field of Information Science and its relation with other fields of science that are also preoccupied and occupied with information.

As a result, a surprising conclusion comes out: Both concepts — those of information and system — complement each other, because information — as a form or as an interaction — is the most peculiar aspect of a system. You cannot explain what a system is without using the concept of information and its various modalities — interaction, organization… And, on the other hand, the concept of system results to be a great tool for illuminating the relation between information and its related concepts, because a system is born when the interaction between two or more elements is feed-backed, which is really the norm and not the exception.

The Problem of Information as an Objective or Human Reality

From the very beginning, a theoretical option of the author must be disclosed on behalf of the transparency of the discussion. The concept of information can be seen from two very different perspective. The first one is as a physical property or reality. The second perspective understand information as a function of the system that uses information, that is, of biological systems, human beings as a special category inside them, and also vicariously of information-processing artefacts.

Several authors have cleverly delved into both ways of approaching the concept of information, which have been summarized as the objective versus the subjective understanding of information (Fernández Molina, 1994; Martínez Comeche, 1995). As it is well-known, Michael Buckland (1991) enriched the distinction with a tripartite model —information as process (of informing), as knowledge or as thing—, with information-as-process mediating between both sides. The debate around the concept of information is also especially apparent in one of its main theoretical topics: the distinction among data, information, knowledge and wisdom currently referred as the DIKW hierarchy (Pérez-Montoro, 2003; García Marco, 2011 for extended references). These are concepts that are part of the basic vocabulary of any information professional or scientists (Moreiro, 2005).

Of course, there is a bridge between both sides, and with two directions. Information-processing systems are built upon physical reality, so information is part of them. They are informed in the same sense than the rest of the universe. But physical information is perceived and used only in the own — limited and emergent — terms of the cognitive system.

Anyway, in this chapter, and without forgetting that information must have an obvious correlation in the real world, information is treated as something very human. When we, humans, discuss the question of information, we are thinking together about the process of apprehension of our environment by us, human beings.

So, telling that "the world is informed" means that we detect invariants in the world that we can use for our purposes. And in our culture, information apprehension is mediated by information and communication technologies. So, in an even more contingent way, it could be said that the concept of information is nothing more and nothing less than the way in which IT-enhanced modern humans relate to reality.

In someway, objective or human perspectives of information are not irreconcilable positions. And this can be easily shown by a reduction to absurdity of both radical positions. If the concept of information had not a real substratum, the transfer of forms that happens in communication and creation would not be possible. On the other side, if information was directly and totally accessible per se, the pursuit of knowledge would not be necessary; on the contrary, our vision of what information may be is affected by our nature, our knowledge system and our perspective.

As a conclusion, our position on the ontology of information is that information exists as a reality, but that, when referring to human affairs, information is something quite specific, and must be studied in its own terms.

As ever, George Bateson (1972: 317-318) cleverly captured the dual nature of the concept of information when he gave his famous definition: "Information is a difference that makes a difference". The difference is objective, but the difference-making is the business of by a third party, the human agent.

THE MODERN CONCEPT OF INFORMATION

The Nascence of the Concept of Information

Though the word information is of Latin origin, the concept of information, as far as we know, was coined by the classic Greek philosophers (e. g., Sagredo & Izquierdo, 1983; García, 1998; Capurro, 2003, 2009).

It reaches its maturity in the Aristotle's theory of the four causes. From his point of view, information could be defined as the process by which an agent — efficient cause — gives its form — formal cause — to a matter — material cause — with a purpose — final cause.

It results still amazing that Aristotle — building on Plato's ideas and, of course, on the work of many preceding philosophers — had such a brilliant understanding of what information might be, as he puts the concept in the centre of his philosophy, by means of the theory of hylomorphism.

For him and in modern words, information could be defined as nothing more and nothing less than the effective transference of a form from one system to another.

The Age of Information

But, though information has a long history as a concept in Western philosophy, the modern emphasis on information has very practical and pragmatical roots.

It has become an axiom of both current popular, political and scientific sociology to state that we live in the age of information (Castells, 1996, 1997, 1998).

The basic idea is that we currently are in a new stage of the evolution of humanity, after the agricultural and industrial revolutions. The agricultural revolution (circa 9.000 b. C.) brought also urbanization. And the industrial revolution (c. 1800 a. C.), which was based in the generalized automation of physical work, which set the conditions for a global network of interconnected huge urban centers.

The new stage of the evolution of humanity (the information revolution) results from the combination of the telecommunications revolution — beginning at the end of the 19th century and the beginning of the 20th with the invention of the telephone and the radio — and the computer revolution, and means the automatic control of symbolic processing.

In fact, the information revolution can be considered the final stage of the industrial revolution in the sense that culminates the automation not only of physical work but also of symbolic work, and therefore of all the different processes that have information as its input — that is, logic, mathematics and communication. It can also be considered the culmination of modernity, the process by which western European societies gained the control of the world in the midst of great conflicts and a technological race.

The impact of automation on industrial civilizations has been enormous, and has changed radically the rules of economics, social life and politics. This has been also translated to international relations, provoking a rupture of previous equilibriums.

The same must be said of its for-the-moment final stage[2], information revolution. As a result, calculus and communications can be automated, and the whole sector of white-collar workers is being transformed into technology-based information managers or condemned to obsolesce. With the aggravation that each level of automation opens the door to new stages of complexity — e. g., databases and data control open the door to expert systems and computer-assisted management. The worldwide real-time transfer of information has accelerated the implosion of peoples and nations into a single global system, in the process that we call globalization.

But, information revolution is a new of stage of the industrial revolution not only in historical terms, but also in the sense that it is information that controls physical work; or, if you want, it is information that controls production. This fact has also an effect on the international division of work: the most advanced economies rely on superior control of all the aspects of the information flow — marketing, advertising, prospective research, management, education — and delegate industrial production in less advanced economies. Even financials have partially become a function of the real-time IT-based control of the economy, for example in the creation of money and debt.

In sum, the combination of increased physical and "informational" automation is changing the rules of playing in all the fields of social life, and information automation sits on top of the physical one. So, it is not strange that information had become the key cultural token, and that nowadays everything is seen throughout its prism.

Information as a Key Concept in Contemporary Science

This information-centric approach has also invaded the scientific debate, and now information is a pervasive concept in all the sciences. To express this new state of opinion, Emilia Curras (2008) has talked about "informationism"[3], that is, a scientific perspective by which everything is studied through the prism of information: physics, genetics and biology, neurosciences, cognitive psychology, society and mass media...[4]

But it is not only a question of the social impact of information and communication technologies, this new emphasis has also its own scientific roots.

The advance of mathematics and engineering, the explosion of mass media and its pervasive influence, and specifically the invention of communication devices and calculating machines made too obvious that information is something *per se*. Though very abstract, information — both its configurations and processes- became an object, something that could be studied in itself. Information — which for the most of the history of western philosophy and science had been considered to be a process — was objectified.

On the other hand, computer science has made possible a big leap forward in the computability and mathematical modelling of biological, economic and social problems, bridging the shores of hard science and humanities, separated to a great extent by the suitability of the scientific method for tackling their problems. It has allowed also the development of physics of complex systems, widening the number of problems that can be researched scientifically. These are all very information-rich fields, all of them supported by a heavy use of information technologies, in which information can be fully appreciated as a key concept of science.

In the past such complex problems were not computable, and the scientific method could only be applied to small or highly simplified domains. Such reductionisms made information transparent; it was not appreciated. Information is about difference, diversity, that is, about what makes each system different, and for many years science offered the biggest advances by studying simple problems of a very wide scope, like gravity. The information complexity of those fields was relatively low, compared with the realms of biology, social world and culture.

Using a common metaphor, it can be stated that, for the most part of the history of modern science, information has been the water in which the fish of science was swimming, so that remained unnoticed. Information processing made information visible, and this concept exploded across the whole system of sciences; and information has begun to be understood as a specific reality, a subject of study. Moreover, in the same way that occurred with matter and energy, the concept of information has proved a potential to provide a new construct to interconnect the different sciences and provide unity to science, forming a basic trilogy of primitives with the previous ones of matter and energy.

The Problem of a Definition of Information

But such a pervasive expansion of the concept of information has not occurred without consequences.

The practicalities of information have departed from the simplicity and elegance of the Aristotelian concept of information, and now this word is used in many contexts and from very different paradigms. It is not strange that, because of that, many definitions have been provided, and the concept of information has been the subject of a crescent amount of literature (Segal, 2003; Capurro and Hjørland, 2003).

As a result, a lot of confusion surrounds the concept of information. The problem overflows the field of semantics to invade also the ontological one: many intellectuals and scientists think that this is not only a problem of different contexts of use, but also that, being information a primitive concept like energy, matter, time or space, it cannot be properly defined.

This is quite challenging for a so-to-be Science of Information, which certainly has information as its scientific object and central concept. Undoubtedly, any ambiguity about its core concept will, almost certainly, result in its ontological and epistemological blurring, and, finally and more pragmatically, in a less competitive academic and professional body.

It is true that we should accept the argument that a primitive concept is quite difficult to be defined, but discussion on primitives is a characteristic of Western philosophy. Even more modestly, the mere semantic task of establishing the relation of the meanings of information with other related words remains an approachable one. We can certainly apply lexical analysis to the term and try to isolate its different senses.

In any case, an interdisciplinary approach to the concept of information has the potential to make library and information science more intelligible and better understood by a wider audience. Moreover, it should allow information scientists to establish in a clearer way their scientific domain, which is of the outmost importance in a moment when scientists from all the disciplines are making information a central concept in their research.

USING THE CONCEPT OF SYSTEM TO UNDERSTAND INFORMATION

Looking for a potential way to achieve the necessary level of generality that might lead to a proper interdisciplinary approach to the concept of information, the concept of system comes naturally to mind.

Systemics has been precisely a quest for a truly transdisciplinary approach to complex domains, and it could *a priori* provide a frame to grasp such a primitive, pervasive and complex reality as information.

The systemic approach provides many meta-tools that are useful for defining information. Some of the most important will be used in this chapter: the very concept of system, the articulation of systems (inclusion, imbrication and stratification), systems methodology (structural and dynamic analysis), and some discussed philosophical concepts like emergence and self-determination.

What Is a System?

As it was seen with information, there are also many definitions of system, also a methodological primitive, at the same level than the cause-effect pair. Most of them emphasize the idea of the relation among elements inside a totality and the interaction of systems with their environment.

One of the most popular definitions is that by Hall and Fagen (1956), who in a seminal publication stated that a system was "a set of interacting elements that form an integrated whole". This definition focuses on the key aspect of systems theory, that is to say, that it is an epistemological tool allowing at the same time synthesis (the whole) and analysis (elements) by studying the interactions among the parts that lead to the emergence of the whole.

A more precise definition is the one provided by Röel the Rosnay (1975). This author states that "a system is a set of elements in dynamic interaction, organized for a goal." Rosnay clarifies that the goal is the process that keeps the system together, e. g., survival and reproduction for living creatures, homeostasis for physiological systems, equilibrium and life sustenance for biosystems... Only when resulting from design, the goal must be considered intentional, like a computer programme or a tool. The interesting point about stating the aim of a system is that it immediately enlightens which is the functional property that brings a system to existence.

Systemics in Information Science

The systemic approach to information is not rare in our field and has been suggested by authors like Peter Checkland (e. g., 1981, 1998) and Emilia Currás (2008).

All the authors emphasize that the concept of system is overall a tool for studying complex questions that are destroyed by the usual analytic approach that makes science so powerful —simplifying and reducing the studied variables— and that fails with complex fields as human and social sciences. In particular, it is a methodology to consider *all* the relevant variables of a problem and their interactions, even if it does not result immediately in a quantitative model (soft systems methodology).

From our perspective, discussing the concept of information from a systemic point of view implies illuminating what information could mean inside such a definition of system. The subsequent subchapters will review information in the different layers of systems in which reality is organized: the physical realm (information as difference and relation), the biological world (information as messages and the phenomenon of reproduction), the psychological layer (information as knowledge), the social level (information as culture and reference) and, upon it, the human sphere (information, again, as creation).

PHYSICAL INFORMATION: DIFFERENCE PLUS RELATIONS

At the Beginning it was Difference...

There is a long way from Greek philosophy to modern science, but the concept of information has been there all the way, and now it has taken again the centre stage of Physics — etymologically, the science of the reality.

The simplest approach to information is to use the concept of difference. This is the approach for example that Shannon and Weaver (1949) take when separating signal from noise. As it cannot be otherwise, such an approach has been taken also in the study of more evolved systems, particularly in Psychology. For example, Gestalt Psychology is built around the concepts of form and background; and, as we have seen, another psychologist, Gregory Bateson (1973), defined information using the concept of difference.

In any case, the advances in mathematics and logic have converged into putting the concept of difference at the centre of the concept of information. From this point of view, information in a system can be defined as the specific configuration of a system among all the possible alternatives; and, therefore, it can be measured as the probability of this configuration among the set of such different possible states.

At the higher level of abstraction and from the very abstract realm of physics, information can be defined as the specific disposition of matter in space and time — or other potential dimensions, for the case. It results from the highest-level abstraction of all the possible differences that can be stated for all the systems that do exist or might exist in universe.

From this point of view, information is one of the five primitive concepts of science and material philosophy: time, space, matter, energy and information. Information is in this sense similar to configuration, structure, organization, system, etc.

... but there is No Difference without Relation

But, as it will be discussed in the next topic, the approach to information by Shannon and Weaver emphasises the static aspects of information, and leaves the relational ones for the concept of communication. It is not strange, as for Shannon and Weaver information was a thing to be transmitted, and their theory makes information a thing to achieve this practical aim. But, not only differences result in increased information, also relations do.

So, the two key aspects of 'physical information' are a) the identity-difference pair and b) relations.

The first one is static or structural. According to this point of view, information is the sum of all the differences — in position, in quality... — that exist in a system and its relations in this very moment in relation with all the alternative possibilities that have been detected or even those that might be imagined.

The second one is dynamic and relational. Information refers here to the relation between the different parts of the system along the line of time. From this point of view, information is the interaction existing among different subsystems or, if you want, 'events'.

If appropriately conciliated, combining both perspectives to create a unified approach to information would be very consistent with the systemic perspective. In fact, it is very common in systems methodology to take both approaches: the static description of a system, and the explanation of its dynamics (Rosnay, 1975).

The sum of differences and relations is precisely what brings an organization or system to existence. And, to gain an understanding of it, differences and relations in a moment (structure) are as equally important as differences and relations along the time (dynamics).

We should not finish this subchapter without reminding the reader of a topic of the major importance. The concept of difference is not completely objective. A judge must establish it always. Human scientists do not research all the differences but only those that they perceive and are interested in.

COMMUNICATION: FROM INTERACTION TO MESSAGES

Information and Communication: Two Sides of the Same Coin?

One of the key aspects of the concept of information is its indivisible relation to the concept of communication. After some analysis, this relation results so inseparable that communication and information appear to be the two sides of the same coin.

As it has been previously reviewed, in ancient Western philosophy information was understood mainly as a process. On the contrary, in our current cultural environment, information is generally comprehended as an abstract thing: a piece of news, or, more in general, the content of a document, a message or even a process.

This is also true of the most influential paradigm in the study of communication and information. As we have seen, in the theory of communication of Shannon and Weaver (1949) communication is the process and information the conveyed message.

This apparent aporia can be easily resolved from a systemic approach. From a systemic point of view, every reality inseparably has a spatial side and a dynamic or temporal one.

Sciences are full of examples of such a Janus nature of information. Light is at the same time a particle (photon) and a wave. Live results in forms (anatomy) and processes (physiology). When studying languages, we need to learn how a language is and how it evolves; and the same happens when studying societies. Even artefacts are designed considering its structure and its dynamics. And both sides of the coin are intimately joined.

It is difficult to know if this dual cognition is a characteristic of the universe or of our interaction with reality, that is, of our perceptual — and in general, cognitive — system. This a recurrent problem in all the sciences, beginning with Physics — quantum theory and the uncertainty principle — and ending with Psychology and Social Sciences —, and has been approached in different ways by contemporary philosophers, especially by constructivists.

But, in any case, we know something for true: when studying information and communication both sides of the same coin must be studied: the fixed photo of information structures and the moving motion of communication dynamics. This is the dual way in which we understand reality, which does not mean, on the contrary, that we are studying different domains.

In conclusion, from this point of view, communication is the process of forms functioning together in interaction with a subjacent principle; and information the abstraction of this relation in a fixed representation. Communication conveys information; information develops in communication. Both are the different sides of the same coin.

Second-Order Communication: Reproduction and Representation of Information

But there is a kind of communication that can be better defined as a second-order communication.

This happens when communication is not only the dynamical aspect of information — or, vice versa, information is the static side of communication —, but it results in the transference of a form from a system to another.

This process is the essence of life, or, in the systemic vocabulary, of biological systems. In information rich environments, some systems are able to replicate themselves. Systems reproduce themselves by imposing their form on a new matter along a period of time.[5]

In this case, it is not only that information implies communication, but that information — and therefore communication — can be actually communicated. Second-order communication[6] is usually understood as the transference of information — in the sense of the content of a message —, but it should primarily be seen as the imposition on another system of an information structure that exists in a previous system. In physics, this process is completely mechanical, in biology, mainly unintentional and unconscious; in Ethology, partly conscious and deliberate; and in human communication, more or less controlled by conscience and will.

The implications of second-order communication for the concept of information are philosophically very important, because if information can be extracted apart from the matter that has taken such a configuration, this is a point in favour of those who think that information must be some kind of distinctive and autonomous reality. In other words, if information can be transferred from one system to another, it must be something *per se*, not a kind of any other thing.

In the same direction, communication reinforces the idea that information is not attached to matter completely, but that constitutes a reality of its own and that can be studied in its own terms. From a systemic point of view, it could be stated that information is not the property of a system, but a reality that can be studied as a system in itself.

Finally, reproduction means something new — the re-presentation of information — in the sense that a form is presented again in another instance. Of course, representation is much more visible when a system reproduces using another vehicular system. This occurs in third order communication and it is going to be the matter of our immediate interest.

Third-Order Communication: Messages, Codes and Languages

In the more advanced forms of second-order communication, the transferred forms are stored in a vehicular system, which is called 'message'. Messages exist in the biochemical realm — NDA —, and also in the biological, sociological y cultural ones. They allow for the replication of systems — reproduction — and also of specific states of such systems, so that they can achieve harmony and result in a functioning macrosystem. Messages constitute information vehicles, travelling from an originating system to the target one, which will be thereafter transformed. These vehicles do not contain information in a fully developed form, like in primitive processes of reproduction, but only the necessary information to trigger the development of a new form in the receiving system. Of course, they need that the target systems are prepared for the message, in the sense that they have the necessary preconditions for its deployment.

Messages are formed with elements of the vehicular system. An abstraction of all the possibilities of such a system is what is called a code and, in its more evolved forms, a language.

Human beings are particularly good in developing codes, have a meta-linguistic capacity — they can study codes and recreate them —, and this is one of their main evolutionary advantages. But this, again, is the matter of the next topic.

KNOWLEDGE AND LEARNING SYSTEMS: CONTROLLING AND DEVELOPING INTERNAL REPRESENTATIONS

What is Knowledge?

Another qualitative leap happens when a system is capable of sending messages to itself, storing messages inside, and re-organizing them to integrate and produce more complicate representations, becoming therefore capable of controlling new actions on the external and internal medium of the system. This is the process that we call learning and its product is knowledge.

Learning is the capability of integrating information about the environment inside a system; elaborating these representations into new information; and retrieving them when necessary to act upon the medium[7]. Knowledge is *new* information acquired by a system and represented inside it.

Knowledge can be defined, from our perspective, as the process of incorporating information — the form or part of a form of an outside system — inside (by) a system that is able to use it in a due way. As a process, knowledge can be considered a synonym of learning.

Knowledge is also the result of this process: the re-present-ation of the form of a system inside another system, its connections with the rest of the available representations, and its potential for reconfiguration. We call 'memory' to the storage system, and 'memories' to the stored representations[8].

Human beings are — up to a certain point, but not only, as we will discuss later— information processing systems that thrive in rich-informed systems (media). Human beings, being part of such a network of interactions, are able to detect, use and even exploit them to pursue their purposes.

External information from the point of view of knowledge is any meaningful difference. And its meaning is given by the cognitive system itself, as a result of its context, purposes, structure... There is not something in "raw information" that makes it meaningful, but its relation with the learning system. We cannot easily understand the concept of meaning without referring to properties of advanced systems like self-logic, self-determination and emergence. Meaning is not in the message, but in the whole system of communication.

Which is the Purpose of Knowledge?

Why knowledge? Living organisms use knowledge to expand their immediate spatial and temporal frontiers; detaching their behaviour from the mechanical results of the immediate inputs they receive from their environments and the specific outputs that are programmed in their genetic code.

Knowledge means storing information, and such a process of storing provides the organisms that are able to develop it with the same kind of advantage that any kind of store — a central concept in the theory of systems — achieves for a system: enhanced autonomy from the environment.

Thanks to information transformed into knowledge, living organisms — and certainly intelligent organisms — can accomplish results that are unattainable without it. In particular, they extend the temporal and spatial frames in which and in which they operate, though only in a way that is directly proportional to the quality of the information they have. They create a virtual world that allows them to transcend the actual limits of space and time, though only in reference to their perceptual space, not their physical action[9].

Cognitive Information: Potential Information, Stored Information, New Information

From the point of view of a knowledge system, there exist three primitive basic forms of information: a) relevant information existing in the environment with a potential to be attended and integrated; b) information that has been stored in a system, which is what we usually call knowledge; and c) information that has been noticed but that it is not present into the system and is being attended to and in the process of being integrated, which is what is called news.

It is very frequent in many disciplines to identify information and news. In fact, news is, simply stated, new information for a subject or a whole audience. From this point of view, it is clear that equating news and information is taking the part for the whole, and, though this can be considered a clever rhetorical resource, from an ontological and epistemological point of view it should be considered a misstatement.

However, stressing the meaning of information simply as knowledge acquisition is very frequent in many disciplines, mainly in communication sciences and law.

CULTURE AND SOCIAL COMMUNICATION

Culture as Socially-Shared Knowledge

Humans are not isolated creatures. Like the majority of mammals, they are social animals, and their social life is extremely sophisticated, including division of roles, work and a complex life cycle.

This means that each individual acquires mainly the knowledge that is useful for the roles that he will have to play. And that the knowledge that a society needs to survive is scattered among its members, depending on the place they occupy in it.

As a result, such a complicate social system requires a strong social communication system to survive.

Societies — as systems of systems, of growing complexity — depend on information to reproduce themselves and also to organize their elements in compatible forms. Of course, they need it also to organize their environments to support their needs.

This body of social information is called 'culture' in social anthropology, usually including its material forms. Thus, culture can be defined as the knowledge that is shared by a society as a whole, and that is necessary for its reproduction and survival. In his theory of the three worlds, Popper (1972, 1978) defined it as the set of creations of the human mind in which we live, together with the worlds of nature and knowledge, and as a specific product of the world of knowledge.

Culture is both a form — an evolving form — and a set of mechanisms to control and improve all the information processes going on inside it. But in any case, culture is all about information, though a special kind of information.

Social Communication

To transfer knowledge, individuals download it to information, but this information is of a specific kind. This information is not "primitive" or "raw" information, but knowledge codified in another kind of information for communicational purposes.

Marking a clear difference with biological communication, social communication is intentional, at least in a substantial part, and can be governed by deliberate processes of emission and reception.

This sense of information is the typical one in Information Science, where physical and biochemical information are not at all the main problem and everything is about human[10] deliberate and intersubjective communication.

The Challenges of Social Knowledge and Communication

Culture brings new problems to the management of information — knowledge and news. Social knowledge, in the sense of knowledge that is known by a group or a society as a whole, can be centralized — at least in theory —, but is usually distributed. Knowledge must be continuously distributed inside a society and to each new generation. These processes require a considerable amount of resources.

This fact produces two contradictory problems: On one hand, knowledge can be lost if it is not transferred properly. In fact knowledge is being lost all the time. On the other hand, what it is new for a person can be nevertheless part of the culture. So oblivion and redundancy are the two extremes of a very complicate equilibrium.

The Problem of Oblivion

Oblivion is nothing bad per se. Everybody involved in the task of education — and in general anybody who has lived enough — knows that sometimes you have to forget and learn again, and that old knowledge can be a problem if interrupts the learning of more adequate models and habits. Another example comes from the field of Psychopathology, where it is very usual to stress the need to unlearn and re-learn.

But losing knowledge that is needed to take decisions is certainly dysfunctional, and forgetting completely past information reduces the possibilities of reflection — one of the most remarkable characteristics of human information —, the scope of the experience timeline and, also, of reusing past experience if old conditions return.

Putting knowledge in documents and these in archives is a technique to liberate the working memory without losing experience; and this is precisely the function of many diaries and in general of permanent archives.

The Problem of Redundancy

One of the big problems with information society has been that, as the cost of communicating has been sharply reduced, the messages are delivered throughout many channels and repeatedly, provoking a lot of redundancy and contributing to the phenomenon that has been called "infoxication" —incremented in the social web (Benito, 2009)—, mainly a question of saturation of the receiver's channel. Information Science can contribute and is contributing to mitigate this problem with selective dissemination and, notably, filtering. These are all solutions on the side of the demand.

It is true that redundancy is a great problem, but only in the storage and retrieval level, and especially if information overload, inconsistencies or silences result from it. In the level of social communication, redundancy is an intrinsic part of the process of socialising knowledge, and, thought it can be rationalized up to some point, it cannot be avoided without killing the informational process itself. Certainly, there is always something new in known 'news'. When news come once and again, this provides new information, specifically, about its importance for the people that are divulgating them. We could call it the 'news strength', and it has a great importance in the creation of social consensus and is widely used in social technologies. What is new here is not the content, but the number of messages.

Of course, as it happens in the most basic systems, redundancy is also a protection against errors in the process of communication, and some degree of redundancy is necessary, contingent to the probability that a message may be lost.

So, any approach to control redundancy in the side of the offer is due to provoke also many problems, if it does not take into due consideration the functions of social redundancy. An approach to solve the collateral problems of social redundancy without damaging its adaptive functions has been taken: inventing technologies to increase the force of a message without necessarily repeating it, like references (links in the web) or voting devices.

Information Fights and the Value of Information

A someway ingenuous and straight-minded approach to information is frequent in Information Science. Information and communication are considered positive processes by definition.

A distant perspective of physical and biological processes easily brings this approach into question. Information and communication can destroy a system. Infection by virus is a process of information and also a cancer. Biology and Ethology show us that competing species and individuals manipulate information processes to gain and advantage over their rivals. The same happens in human communication and in human societies.

Because of its very nature, messages imply the transference of a form inside another form, and this is a process of, so to say, invasion, which is to provoke changes in the receiving system.

From a wide point of view, human information and communication is also a part of life, and their goodness or wrongness is something that depends on each one's values and relative positions. When discussing human information, only from a high and realistic consideration of the receiver, can we judge the goodness or wrongness of a message.

SOLUTIONS AGAINST INADEQUATE OBLIVION AND REDUNDANCY: REFERENCE AND DOCUMENTATION

Two other kinds of information have evolved precisely to solve or at least minimize the problems that oblivion and redundancy pose: metainformation and documentation.

Metainformation: Information about Knowledge

One of the most interesting — and unique? — things about human knowledge is that includes some kind of second-level knowledge, that is, the ability to get knowledge about knowledge and its processes, and use such representations in the same way than knowledge to improve its cognitive and adaptive processes. This level is usually called metacognition.

In the field of culture — social knowledge — there exists also a kind of metacognition. In fact, the whole field of Information Science could be considered a science about a specific part of such a social metacognition: social memory (Garcia, 2010).

As the body of knowledge of an individual, a group or a society grows, managing this knowledge becomes increasingly important.

This knowledge about cultural knowledge is what we call references, which is properly a knowledge about a source of knowledge. The most primitive type of reference is pointing to an expert. But in our world, reference means also pointing from a document to other documents. As more and more references are available, the need to distinguish them adequately and to include information about the source and its utility increases, and the whole field of metadata explodes.

Complex referencing is impossible if a source is not available, and it only develops to its full potential if another social memory technology is available: documents.

Documentation: A Technology of Social Memory

Documentation is humanly-communicated knowledge that has been codified upon or inside an external stable holder. The purpose of this strategy is to surpass the limits of synchronous communication and avoid the problem of oblivion, which impose severe restrictions to the scope and duration of human communication.

Documentation is an external memory that can be shared. Knowledge — or better, as documents contain messages, seeds of it — is fixed outside the mind and can be recovered by any intelligent agent with enough motivation, background knowledge and cognitive capabilities.

In sum, documents are at the same time *communication and memory devices*, and this is common to the different generations of documents that have existed and continue evolving[11] (Figure 1).

It is true that no documentation technology is perfect, but it is always a way to move the spatial and temporal limits of communication a bit further away, and to externalize knowledge so it can be shared.

So, documentation is a very practical and brilliant solution, but, as other technologies, it inherently creates a new problem, at least as far as it is successful. As a tool of storage, it allows for the ever growth of records. And these records constitute a world of their own[12], which must be managed. The strategy is using meta-information, and of course, delegation in automata. This is exactly the scientific domain of Information Science.

Figure 1. Knowledge, communication, memory and documents

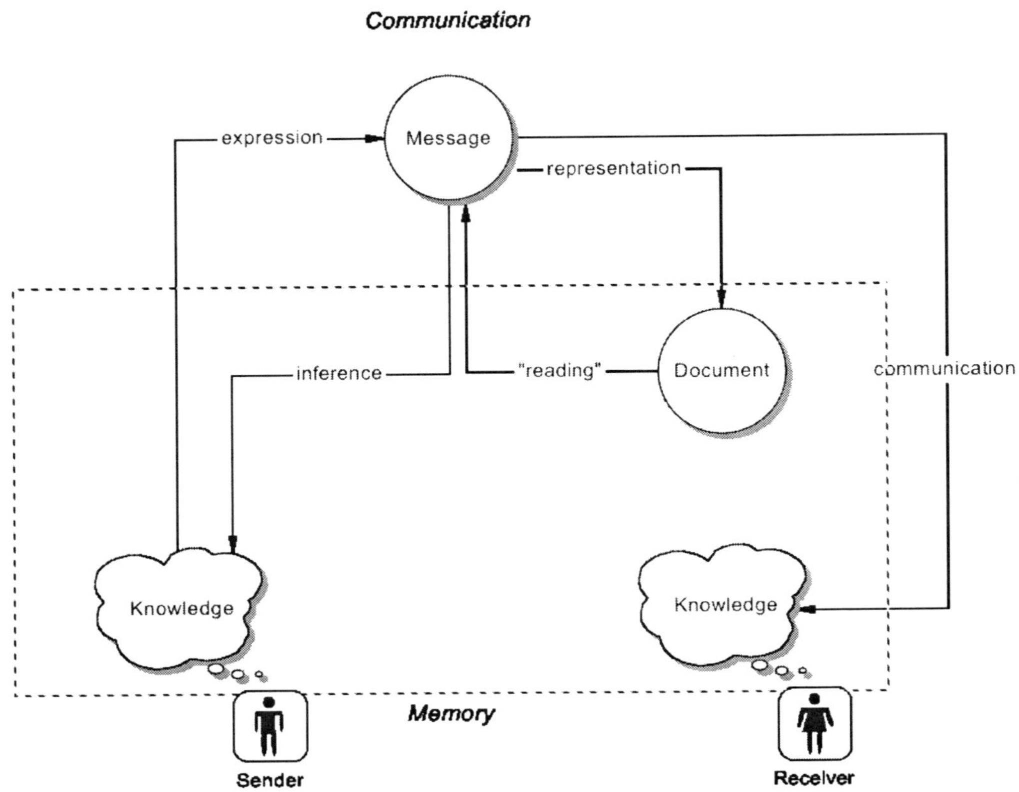

HUMAN INFORMATION: BEYOND REPRESENTATION

There is a final problem with information that should be addressed. Frequently, information in Information Science is seen only as an object, as a representation, and there is a tendency to overstate the function of knowledge and memory. This is logical up to a point: the emphasis of information science is on information preservation and circulation by means of the control of knowledge records, which are information objects.

But, in our reflection we have found two very different perspectives on information: one is centred on the outside world and is passive; and the other, on the learning subject and active. In the first one, information is objective, and must be grasped by the subject, creating a representation. In the other perspective, the subject that is trying to modify reality searches and creates information, and this representation — new information indeed — governs the agent's behaviour.

A key aspect of human information is that humans can walk both sides of the cognitive path. Information is not only gained from the environment, detecting invariants, representing them in the form of knowledge, communicating them among persons and machines with common codes, storing them in external memories that can be shared, and referring to such external memories with references.

No, human beings are capable of much more. They can create new information structures inside their cognitive systems — using also knowledge from other people and sharing with them if necessary or convenient —, and then impose this information on the external world. Moreover, human beings are even able to invent new goals, something that goes far beyond mere calculus.

This is the process of creation — of imposing form on matter — that was so cleverly identified by Aristotle as the centre of human nature, together with the possibility of using reason to gain a common shared perspective that can support conviviality among persons with different ideas[13].

In the systemic tradition, the relation between information and the emergence of new realities in systems is a classic. The use of information to generate new realities — as in technical invention or artistic creation — opens the door to further discussions about the nature of information, that, anyway, keep it at the centre of the anthropological, philosophical and scientific debate.

To sum up, and without taking a final position on these difficult and open questions, it must be observed that human information is not only about representation, but also about the creation of new forms. In other words, human information is not only about memory and reasoning, but also about imagination. Artistic creations, scientific models and methodologies and technical invention are inevitable evidence of this other side of human information.

CONCLUSION

The Different Senses of Information as a System of Emergent Layers

Along the previous pages, we have tried to show that the different senses in which information is used have a deep logic and form a system of emerging sub-types of information that have an ontological relation to the pyramid of reality and sciences that is common in the systemic approach and in the usual understanding of science.

We have departed from the Aristotelian concept of information, as giving form, that is — in systemic language —, as a system transferring forms to another system. From the most basic layer, information and communication seem the two sides of the same reality: the static and the dynamic Janus faces of a system. Difference and relation appear as the two basic logical primitives to define information.

In physical systems information is mainly about interactions. Biology introduces the complexity of messages and the reality of reproduction, which means that a form is replicated and even transferred through messages. In the next level, cognitive systems are capable of manipulating the messages that have stored inside into an ever more integrated and complex system of representations. In a new layer, the social nature of humans — cooperation and division of work — implies that they have to develop a common systematic world of representations, that we call culture. To manage the world of culture — and also the world of knowledge —, humans invented documents, a technology to store knowledge in external memories that can be also used for communicational purposes. Finally, to manage the increased world of documents, humans sophisticated a linguistic device — reference — transforming it into a complex tool to map documents among them and with knowledge needs, giving life to metadata.

Leaving aside the forms of information that are of the interest of physics, chemists and biologists, information science must deal at least with these five kinds of such an information

- *Invariants* — both recurrent events and structures or, for the moment, exceptional ones — of the real world (including the three worlds of Popper) that can be perceived by humans *and* are of their interest. As far as they are perceived, they have a strong relation with human purposes, at least as they emerge from the evolution of their perceptual system. We might have called such invariants "raw information".

- Representations of these invariants *inside* the human cognitive system, that we call *knowledge*.
- Representations of knowledge by means of a language to communicate it between persons, that we may call *messages*, and that constitute the backbone of the functioning of human groups, institutions and societies. Here it should be stressed that we are using a reduced meaning of the concept 'message', limiting it to acts of communicating human knowledge. As we have seen, messages are of a more general nature, and occur, notably and for example, in genetics, physiology and ethology.
- Representation of messages outside the human cognitive system, that function as external — and frequently interpersonal — memories. We can call them *documents*, records or, nowadays and quite imprecisely — to avoid the (for some outdated nature of the) concept of document — "information objects". I personally think we should keep the term *document* as the denomination for this class of "information objects", because it is very specific and etymologically has the potential to include all kind of information objects, whose purpose is, after all, showing — *docendum*, in Latin — other things that are not present.
- Finally, a special class of documents, in the sense of external stored messages, that refer to a document, which we may call *references*, which can be collected and have been called secondary or tertiary documents, bibliographical references or records, catalogues, etc. Nowadays references are commonly referred as *metadata*. Again, it must be remembered that reference is a second-order type of messages that is present in the layer bellow culture.

As it can be seen, each new kind of information can be understood as a specific class of the previous one: So, knowledge is invariants represented inside the cognitive system; messages are knowledge codified to be communicated; documents are messages stored on a medium; and references are documents about documents. From this point of view, they form progressive subclasses, or, more graphically a set of Matryoshkas, the famous Russian dolls (Figure 2).

But they are more that a set of subsets. They are also a structure of layers. Each level can be seen as preserving the properties of the previous level, paying respect to the law of inheritance. And it is also true that each new level, though preserving the properties of the previous one, adds something new; that is, it has an emergent nature and realizes a control over the one bellow, in a cybernetic sense[14]. So, knowledge allows people to control invariants; messages, to make possible knowledge transfer; documents, to control the preservation and reuse of messages; references, to deal with an unmanageable set of documents (Figure 3).

Implications for a Specification Scientific Domain of Information Science

Finally, establishing different levels in the concept of information has important implications for mapping the domain of Information Science.

In these pages we have proceeded from the concept of information in reality, to information in reproduction and communication, in knowledge and culture, and information has been revealed as a wide and interdisciplinary concept. Information scientists must be humble when confronting such a complex domain that crosscuts the whole domain of science.

Though Information Science is interested in information in general, it is clear that it cannot claim the whole phenomenon of information as its realm. Information is a multidisciplinary problem, which should be — and is — being treated in all the sciences — it is even central in information

Figure 2. The information Matryoshkas (no scale representation intended)

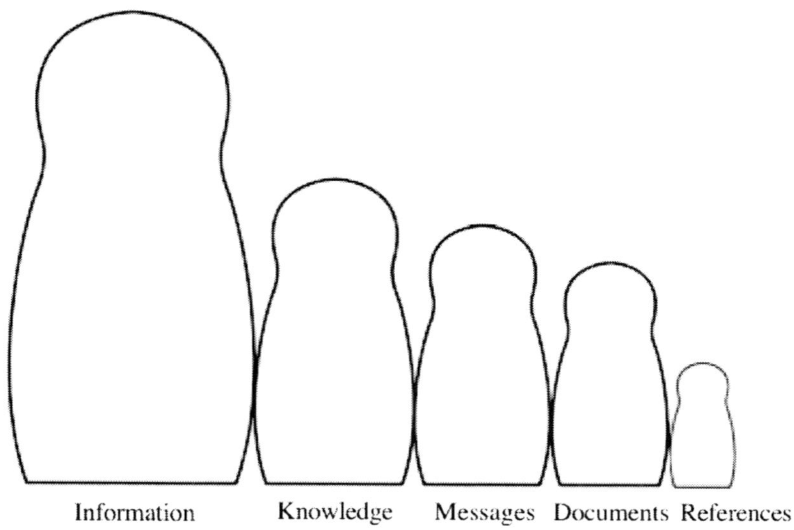

physics, biocomputing, cognitive sciences, computer science, etc. —, especially when information has been accepted as a primitive concept and automated information treatment is at the centre stage of modern science, and, we must say, as the infrastructure of social, economic, political and cultural activity in modern societies.

We suggest that information scientists should situate themselves in this complex and interdisciplinary environment, and try to establish their own specific field of study and their particular contribution.

So, has Information Science a specific scientific domain? It seems clear that this specific

Figure 3. The multiple-layer pyramid of information

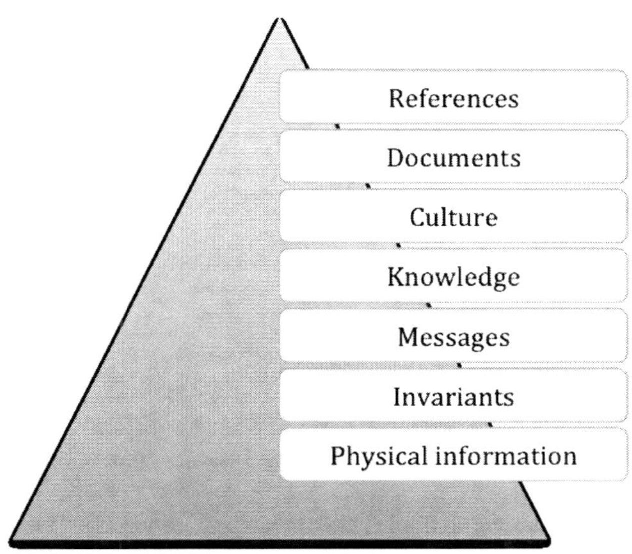

domain corresponds only to a specific sense of the concept of information: dealing with human messages that have been stored in an external memory for future conversion to knowledge. In this sense, information Science is worried with knowledge that has been codified in messages and stored. Probably, the only kind of information that is specific of information science in a special way is "reference".

So, in conclusion, Information Science is, first, a science of social memory and its use, and, but even more specifically, of the methodologies and technologies (social or technical) that exist to optimize its functioning by means of external memories, references (metadata) and systems of metadata (ontologies).

REFERENCES

Bateson, G. (1972). *Steps to an ecology of mind.* New York: Ballantine Books.

Benito Ruiz, E. (2009). Infoxication 2.0. In Thomas, M. (Ed.), *Handbook of Research on Web 2.0 and Second Language Learning*. London: Information Science Reference. doi:10.4018/978-1-60566-190-2.ch004

BITrum. (n.d.). Retrieved from http://sites.google.com/site/proyectobitrum/

Brillouin, L. (1962). *Science and information theory*. New York: Academic Press.

Buckland, M. (1991). Information as thing. *Journal of the American Society for Information Science American Society for Information Science*, *42*(5), 351–360. doi:10.1002/(SICI)1097-4571(199106)42:5<351::AID-ASI5>3.0.CO;2-3

Capurro, R. (2009). Past, present, and future of the concept of information. *TripleC: Cognition, Communication, Co-operation*, *17*(2).

Capurro, R., & Hjørland, B. (2003). The concept of information. *Annual Review of Information Science & Technology*, *37*, 313–411.

Castells, M. (1996). *The rise of the network society*. Malden, Mass.: Blackwell Publishers.

Castells, M. (1997). *The power of identity*. Malden, Mass.: Blackwell.

Castells, M. (1998). *End of millennium*. Malden, MA: Blackwell Publishers.

Checkland, P. (1981). *Systems thinking, systems practice*. Chichester: Wiley.

Checkland, P., & Holwell, S. (1998). *Information, systems and information systems: making sense of the field*. Chichester: John Wiley & Sons.

Covey, S. R. (1989). *The seven habits of highly effective people: restoring the character ethic*. New York: Simon and Schuster.

Currás Puente, E. (2008). Ciencia de la información bajo postulados sistémicos y sistemáticos. Caracas: Edición personal.

Díaz Nafria, J. M. (in press). What Is Information? An Enquiry Beyond Information Science From A Systemic Point Of View. In Currás, E., & Lloret, N. (Eds.), *Systems Science And Collaborative Information Systems: Theories, Practices And New Research*. Hershey: IGI Global.

Fernández Molina, J. C. (1994). Enfoque objetivo y subjetivo del concepto de información. *Revista Espanola la de Documentacion Cientifica*, *17*(3), 320–331.

Foundations of Information Science. (n.d.). Retrieved from http://fis.icts.sbg.ac.at/

García Marco, F. J. (1998). El concepto de información: una aproximación interdisciplinar: I: Hacia una definición objetiva. *Revista General de Información y Documentación*, *8*(1), 303–326.

García Marco, F. J. (2010). Las instituciones de la memoria ante el cambio digital: una propuesta sobre la articulación interdisciplinar de las ciencias de la documentación. *Pliegos de Yuste: revista de cultura y pensamiento europeos* (11).

García Marco, F. J. (2011). La pirámide de la información revisitada: enriqueciendo el modelo desde la ciencia cognitiva. *El profesional de la información, 20*(1).

Hall, A. D., & Fagen, R. E. (1956). Definition of a system. In Society for the Advancement of General Systems Theory, Society for General Systems Research & et al. (Eds.), *General systems: yearbook of the Society for the Advancement of General Systems Theory*, 1, 18. Ann Arbor, MI: The Society.

Martínez Comeche, J. A. (1995). *Teoría de la información documental y de las instituciones documentales*. Madrid, Spain: Sintesis.

Moreiro González, J. A. (2005). *Conceptos introductorios al estudio de la información documental*. Salvador, Bahía: EDUFBA.

Pérez-Montoro Guitiérrez, M. (2003). *The phenomenon of information*. Lanham, MD: Scarecrow Press.

Pinto Molina, M., García Marco, F. J., & Agustín Lacruz, M. C. (2002). *Indización y resumen de documentos digitales y multimedia: técnicas y procedimientos*. Gijón: Trea.

Popper, K. R. (1972). *Objective knowledge; an evolutionary approach*. Oxford: Clarendon Press.

Popper, K. R. (1978). Three worlds. *The Tanner Lectures on Human Values*, *80*, 141–167.

Rosnay, J. d. (1975). *Le macroscope: vers une vision globale*. Paris: Éditions du Seuil.

Sagredo Fernández, F., & Izquierdo Arroyo, J. M. (1983). *Concepción lógico-lingüística de la documentación*. Madrid: Universidad Complutense de Madrid, Departamento de Documentación.

Ségal, J., & Danchin, A. (2003). *Le zéro et le un: histoire de la notion scientifique d'information au 20e siècle*. Paris: Syllepse.

Shannon, C., & Weaver, W. (1949). *The matematical theory of communication*. Urbana: The University of Illinois.

KEY TERMS AND DEFINITIONS

Information Science: A science related to the design and maintenance of external social memories and the process of referring their contents to relevant personal and social activities. The focus of Information Science is the optimization of the processes of social memory, and, more specifically, the methodologies and technologies (social or technical) that exist to optimize its functioning by means of external memories, references (metadata) and systems of metadata (ontologies).

ENDNOTES

1. There are several groups and institutions working on a science of information and the transdisciplinary clarification of the concept of information. See, for example, the classic conferences on the Foundations of Information Science, or the very interesting project and network Bitrum.
2. A new revolution is on the march, biotechnology or genomics, that uses the concept of information to control the genetic and physiological processes of life, with the purpose of systematically transforming living organisms into factories and bio-robots and also of improving and controlling human physiology.
3. Of course, this sense of informationism must be distinguished from other uses of this word, as a self-actualization philosophy, for example. Perhaps, a less-contested word

in English would be informationalism, as an anonymous author assumed in Wikipedia.

4 In another chapter in this book, professor Nafria (2012) examines this topic in detail.

5 A very discussed topic about information is that it can revert, at least *locally*, the effects of entropy. This is the reason because it has been proposed as negentropy (Brillouin, 1956), a sort of reciprocal process to entropy. Such an approach has been strongly opposed by many authors when applied as a general law.

6 Human scientists normally use the concept of second-order communication for meta-communication, or reflections about communication. In our own counting, meta-communication would be a fourth-order communication process, being the first one interaction, the second one reproduction, and the third one message-based communication.

7 The medium is not only the external medium, but also the own system and, inside it, the representations that it stores.

8 As all the memories are interconnected in memory, and the memory is also linked with the rest of the functions that make representation possible — reasoning, imagining… —, they are all also considered to be a system, e. g. the cognitive system.

9 From a strictly physical point of view, information implies, in some way, a new dimension over the one of time and the three of space.

10 Artificial communication — communication among machines or machines and humans — should be considered human, at least regarding its purpose, because it consists in the delegation of processes in a machine by human agents.

11 A discussion of the evolution of documents can be found in chapter 2 of Pinto, Garcia y Agustin (2002).

12 This vision of a world of nature, a world of knowledge and a world of human creations — including documents — was formalized by Karl Popper in his theory of the three worlds (1972, 1978).

13 It has been recursively present in modern writers, and one example in a field as diverse form ours as human resources management can be found in the theory of the two creations of Stephen R. Covey (1989).

14 It is a well-known fact that one of the precedents of both the systemic approach and computer science is Cybernetics, the science of control, from the Old Greek word κυβερνήτης (kybernētēs, pilot). In this sense our set of "Information Matryoshkas" must be understood as a hierarchical chain of control tools: each level is a device for governing the inferior.

Chapter 3
Information:
A Multidimensional Reality

José María Díaz Nafría
Universidad de León, Spain & Science of Information Institute, USA

ABSTRACT

Making an incursion in the forest of problems and theories of information, beyond observing a lack of mutual understanding among information theorists, we find out that information can be understood as a multifaceted reality. The variety of theories is in itself a reflection of the complex nature of information. A systematic approach to these theories, looking for common and divergent understandings render– so to speak – a cubist picture of what information really is, showing for instance its multi-dimensionality. In other words, when we say there is information in cables and organisms, in antennas and societies, in robots and mental states, we do not have to be mistaken: information is considered in each case in different aspects.

Delving into the nature of observation, we will find a solid ground to pose information as a bridge between objects and subjects, therefore providing the possibility to overcome the inveterate segregation of the objectivist and subjectivist understandings. As we will see, such vision also provides the possibility to articulate an understanding of information in its multifaceted reality.

1. INTRODUCTION

"It is hardly to be expected that a single concept of information would satisfactorily account for the numerous possible applications of this general field." (Shannon, 1993, p. 180)

DOI: 10.4018/978-1-61350-201-3.ch003

"And just as the same town when seen from different sides will seem quite different – as though it were multiplied perspectivally – the same thing happens here: because of the infinite multitude of simple substances it's as though there were that many different universes; but they are all perspectives on the same one, differing according to the different points of view of the monads." (Leibniz, Monadology, §57)

In the "information age," finding the current variety of meanings of information is surprising. What is understood by information in the streets, in the industry, in courts, in physics, biology, psychology, sociology, technology or philosophy is so diverse that we could hardly find a common understanding among all these points of view. In contrast to this current situation, in the "age of iron," it was very clear what iron was – probably not regarding its nature, but concerning its usage. The iron brought about a whole spectrum of new possibilities with respect to previous materials: its hardness with respect to cupper and its facility to find the raw material determined a clear difference that caused a change in the technical possibilities evolving in new tools, larger production, greater resourcing and subsequently a cultural and social change. The techniques for producing implements or the understanding about its cosmological origin could differ among different peoples, but the basic properties of hardness and abundance in addition to others common features of metals constituted a common point for any understanding of iron. On the other hand, the materiality of iron provided an ontological toehold for its apprehension, a sure reference – especially from an antique worldview – for the semantics of iron. However concerning information, neither a common understanding, nor a fixed ontological support can be found in the allegedly age of information.

Historically, the usage of information evolves from Greek and Latin roots embracing the fundamental beliefs of each epoch: the objectivist aspects in antiquity, the subjectivist ones in modernity (Peters, 1988; Capurro and Hjørland, 2003). In a bird's eye view, the ontological senses of antiquity (related, for instance, to the *corporaliter* – bodily – values of the Latin information; and coexistent with some epistemological uses in moral or pedagogical contexts) were superseded by the dominancy of pure epistemological senses in modernity. However, since the second half of the XX century this usage started to differentiate, driven by the particular visions of each discipline –either professional or scientific –, at the same time that the objectivist and ontological values of antiquity were recovered, mixed with the subjectivist and epistemological ones still dominant in the ordinary usage (Capurro, 1979, 2009; Segal, 2003; Díaz, 2010a). This differentiation in the use of "information" led to the following consequences: (i) scattering of the different understandings of information and the subsequent gaps among each use, (ii) the belief that information can be useful for anything, (iii) the possibility to bridge between apparently irreconcilable disciplines by means of delving into the common roots among each usage.

These three consequences, which can be observed by means of a detailed scrutiny in the evolution of the concerned scientific disciplines (Segal, 2003; Lyre, 2002), represent extreme positions. The two first poles could be metaphorically branded by the bible images of the Babel tower (complete misunderstanding of multifaceted usages: information for each) and Pentecost (perfect understanding by means of a too general abstraction equidistant from any position, though endangered by empty content: information for all). A third pole corresponds to a midterm mediating between the detailed specificity of the multifaceted usage and the complete abstraction of a general understanding too broad to be useful.

If we intend to vertebrate our information societies around the backbone of information, as the new culture of iron did with respect to the well recognizable new material, we also need a clearer and common understanding of information. Since we have to solve the many problems arisen in our societies and we allege to use information as a new means for bringing about a change in our cultures: we need a clear understanding of information for handling, managing producing and using information in order to meet social needs. If we pursue a *Babel* approach, cooperation, communication and knowing will enter a dissolving path; if we pursue a *Pentecost* approach, we will loss the possibility to come into the specific problems arisen in personal and social life. Therefore, we need the previously pointed out intermediate via in which different domains can bridge their particular endeavors with a common and articulated understanding of information in different realms.

For providing the necessary bridges between different professional and scientific domains, we must satisfy the following requirements:

1. The nature of information has to be clarified. First, because – according to the aforementioned duality in the historical uses of "information" (material/immaterial or objectivist/subjectivist) – we do not have a sure support for our semantics of information as in the case of iron. Second, because we use science for solving our technical problems, and science seeks for the nature of its investigated objects.
2. The multifaceted dimensionality of information has to be clarified in order to articulate the different uses in each professional or scientific domain, because the complexity of our technical and scientific system cannot be resumed in a holistic approach of everything capable to address the specificity of each realm.

2. THE NEED OF A NEW ORGANIZATION OF SCIENCES FOR THE UNDERSTANDING OF INFORMATION

2.1 Analyticity and the Historical Evolution of Modern Sciences

From the viewpoint of the positivistic organization of sciences, the crucial requisite to beware for a good division of the scientific labor concerns the fulfillment of the adequate methodology in the search of knowledge. This assumption is rooted in the very foundations of modernity, which seeks "the true Method to bring me to the knowledge of all [...] things, of which my understanding was capable." As Descartes realizes, such method needs "to divide every [difficulty], which I was to examine into as many parcels as could be, and, as was requisite the better to resolve them." (Descartes, 2008, pp. 27, 30). Thus, the analyticity of reality (in the sense that it can be divided for its independent scrutiny and the subsequent addition of partial results) constitutes the cornerstone of the scientific method of modernity and the positivistic division of the scientific labor from XIXth century onwards. However, such division of scientific labor also depends on: (ii) the increase of observation means, (iii) the complexity of the observed reality and (iv) the complexity of the involved theories (Solis & Selles, 2005, §23).

If we inquire into the historical support to the philosophical *positivism* and its more radical beliefs, we observe a quite intricate evolution. Its foundations were refused since the beginning of the 20th century, then revitalized in a refined manner in the so-called *neopositivism*, which after the critiques of Popper and Kuhn – among others – lead to the development of the *postpositivism*. Finally, in our days, the basic stance of a non-radical positivism might be identified in a wide variety of forms supported in confrontation with other anti-positivistic stances (Bullock et al, 1999; Comte 1844; Kuhn, 1962; Rorty, 1988). However just focusing on the classical or positivistic division of sciences, we observe that in the articulation of the academic and scientific system such division has been deepened throughout the 20th Century until our days, crystallized in the current countless division of scientific domains. In contrast to this fact, the vanguard discoveries of the early 20th century in physics and mathematics (i.e. the two pillars of modern science) showed: (i) the non-analyticity of the simplest reality and (ii) the non-analytical verifiability of the most elementary mathematical theories (Calude 2005).

Highlighting these facts of the historical development of sciences, and stressing the non-analyticity of reality or thought, we are not pursuing to withdraw the validity of the very analytical method, but rather to underscore its limits and to mark off its domain of application. Thus, it is not that the analytical method is invalid in the inquiry of the investigated reality; simply, it does not suffice to support a valuable account of reality. If – in our inquiries – we analyze reality considering its parts, its properties, its relations among parts, its organization in structures, etc., we should right after come back to the actual manifestation of reality, being ready to refuse our previous analysis, to find new models and maintaining a critical stance among the theories devoted to explain each domain of reality. The circularity or non-analyticity of the scientific method, and even of the mathematical method, is paradigmatically expressed by the Quine-Duhem thesis (Duhem, 1962; Quine, 1953) and Gödel's theorem of incompleteness (1931). Such non-analyticity puts forwards that a critical stance is needed, that theories are not only analytically supported but also synthetically adopted and rejected, and therefore the scientific method is properly a combination of analysis and synthesis, evolving in endless cycles of analysis, theory building and confrontation with reality (Popper, 1959; Kuhn, 1962; Lakatos, 1978; Laudan, 1977). This is the sense we will adopt when referring to the non-analyticity of reality or theories.

2.2 Methodological Quest (The Articulation of Disciplines)

Despite the non-analyticity of our confronted reality, we cannot achieve a theory of all. As we mentioned above, that is because the division of sciences is not only grounded in the analyticity principle, but also in: the increase of concerned problems linked to the rise of observation means, the complexity of the attended reality and even the complexity of the set of accepted theories. All this is just too much to put in the same box. Therefore it defies the purpose of reconciling the diversity of problems of the social and scientific life with the necessary unity of the different approaches as to make them converge into the non-analytical challenge of our time (be it concern with the organization of matter, with the complexity of biological life, or the complexity of society). To this end, we need a proper articulation of disciplines into an inter- or trans-disciplinary framework capable to delve into the very complexity of our problems, and particularly into the multifaceted reality of information.

The multidisciplinarity, frequently claimed for the solution of complex problems, is not enough since it corresponds to the belief in the analyticity of reality that is to be overcome. On the other hand, transdiciplinarity might be seen as a long-term objective which feasibility is not proven – i.e. the integrative, abstract and united vision for all the involved disciplines. Therefore, interdisciplinarity is the intermediate via that seems to be more reasonable to pursue. Since no unified vision is beforehand assumed, it is methodologically feasible and furthermore it might asymptotically converge towards the erection of a unified vision – namely, the basic objective of the transdisciplinarity. Recalling the aforementioned poles of Babel and Pentecost: multidisciplinarity might be branded as a "disciplined Babel"; transdiciplinarity as an "articulated and moderated Pentecost".

2.3 Bridging Cultural Gaps

But not only among scientific disciplines, the evolution of science has built incommunicable walls, also between the science system as a whole and social life, what makes the incommunicability among disciplines deeper since the social level does not serve to bridge among sciences (Ortega, 1932, §12). This segregation of scopes brings about an allegedly irreducible difference among "the *manifest* and the *scientific* images of man-in-the-world" (Sellars, 1962, §I). While the former describes the way the world stands as grasped in the language commonly used in our interaction with it (therefore including: intentions, conventions, appearances, etc); the scientific image describes the world in terms of causality, regularities and theories, usually leaving apart moral claims. This presence or absence of normative vs truthful aspects might be regarded as a basis for the complementarity –as Sellars argued (1962)-. However, such complementarity is hindered by the reference to incommensurable realities.

This lack of understanding, pointed out by Sellars, is also close related to "the gap between the two cultures of (natural) science and social and human sciences that has to be considered in approaching information – a gap between the natural and the engineering sciences (including formal sciences) on the one hand and the arts and humanities (including the social sciences) on the other hand that dates back to the 17th century" (Hofkirchner, 2009). This cleft is often referred as the Snow's dilemma in terms of the opposition among these two cultures – of sciences and humanities – that this scientist and writer regretted in 1959 (Snow, 1998). Thus, the dilemma can also be translated into the relevance of objectivity – of the science image – vs the relevance of subjectivity – in which the manifest image and the humanities are rooted.

To this respect, the aforementioned blurred position of information between objectivity and subjectivity or material and non-material aspects – argued as a problem for a good understanding of information – might create the conditions for bridging this gap as we will see below. On the other hand, as Weaver pointed out at the early scientific development of the information concept, information is actually being "found when the parts are viewed in association", and it is in the assembly of the parts that other human and social values (for instance, ethical or aesthetical values) are discerned (Shannon and Weaver, 1949, p.28). Moreover, as Lyre (2002) argued, information might also serve for bridging over physical, biological and cognitive sciences. Hence, information might offer the possibility for interweaving the scientific and social fields, overcoming the traditional segregation of scopes, which has hindered the confrontation to the non-analytical challenges of our social life. However, to this end, information must be properly understood with respect to its nature, to its different dimensions, and to how it relates to the other realities, grasped by our system of scientific visions.

3. AN OVERVIEW ON INFORMATION VISIONS

For delving into the manifold understanding of information, let us start considering a historical common ground. Being the 1950s the period in which information science properly emerges as to acquire an active and notorious presence in science and society, Shannon's seminal work of 1948 ("A Mathematical Theory of Communication", in short MTC), undoubtedly represents a landmark in the development of the information understanding, or more properly, understandings. In this early formulation of MTC (which has also been branded as "information theory"), Shannon curiously starts referring to the common use of information with its semantic aspects (to which Weaver later adds the pragmatic ones). However, he immediately after redefines the concept within an engineering framework, losing these basic dimensions, and paying exclusive attention on the *syntactical* aspects of *information* (Shannon & Weaver, 1949; Floridi 2005a-c, Capurro 2009).

MTC focuses its efforts on the quantitative determination of information, deepening into those features of information that are indeed intuitively quantitative, especially in the contexts of encoding, storing and transmitting information. For instance, it is prima facie admitted that information may be additive, non-negative, depending on the number of distinctions that it permits to do, etc. (Floridi 2005a). Despite of this devotion to the syntactic aspects of information, Weaver admits that "the concept of information developed in this theory at first seems disappointing [...] because it has nothing to do with meaning", however he considers both semantics and pragmatics as strongly constrained by the syntactical analysis. Furthermore, "this analysis is so penetratingly cleared the air that one is now, perhaps for the first time, ready for a real theory of meaning." However, regardless of several attempts to clarify semantics and pragmatics of information, this does not seem to be the case (Floridi, 2005c), at least in a generally agreed sense.

Any qualitative approach to information shows the relevance of both its *semantic* dimension (whereby the signals or symbols considered by the MTC are necessarily referred to something) and its *pragmatic* one (whereby information is the foundation for action, either by intentional actors, living beings or automatic systems). This does not simply mean broadening the attributes or details of what we refer as information, but also an important negative limitation driving to exclude what could not be discriminated at a merely syntactical level, in which – going beyond Weaver's distinctions – we can even include more levels or aspect of information (Gitt 1996; Collier 2011).

As pointed out by Machlup and Mansfield (1983), this negative limitation can be illustrated by considering the requirements that human contexts normally impose on the legitimate meaning of information, i.e. need for truth, value, innovation, surprise or reduction of uncertainty. This would classify as non-informative those messages that – even complying with all syntactic requirements – were false, incorrect, useless, redundant, expected or promoters of uncertainty. To this regard, the MTC could not say much; neither could any other just syntactical approach. As Burgin stated, although MTC provided effective means for measuring information in some contexts, "without understanding the phenomenon of information, these formulas bring misleading results when applied to irrelevant domains" (2003, p.147). Thus, the multifaceted aspects of information had to be deepened as well as analyzed their respective constrains.

To this end, each discipline – after accounting the syntax in their particular fields – had to delve into the aspects of information beyond the syntactical ones. However, constrained to the objective of theoretical coherence at each discipline, this brought about a panoply of alternatives and criticisms since the MTC was formulated (often in a vague, limited and confusing manner). Such alternatives can be systematically overviewed considering: (i) what stance they take up concerning the objective-subjective dilemma; (ii) what dimensionality is being covered (particularly concerning how they cover the syntactical, semantic and pragmatic aspects of information); (iii) what disciplines has contributed to its development.

3.1 How Is the Nature of Information Conceived in the Information Theories?

The fact of being considered as something *objective* or not is perhaps the main distinction that can be made concerning what is understood by *information* (Capurro & Hjorland, 2003). If it is objective, it will be independent from mental states or user's intentions; if it is *subjective*, it will necessarily depend on the interpretation of a cognitive or intentional agent. Between both poles, an intermediate approach might be adopted, according to which information does not need to be considered as something having its own entity or something belonging to subjectivity, but rather in terms of a *relationship*. This may enable an action to be executed, an order to be obeyed, a structure to be established, or simply it allows a behavior, adaptation or an interpretation – even though it might be referred to some type of intentionality.

Objectivistic pole. In the extreme position of *objectivist* categorization, information is deemed as a third metaphysical principle, in the sense expressed by the popular Wiener's adage: "Information is information, not matter or energy" (Wiener 1948, p. 132; Günther 1963). This principle is sometimes associated with a teleological description of the universe as it happens in Teilhard de Chardin's "noosphere", to which also Stonier refers (1991), or in an openly theological "cosmovision", as in Gitt (1996). Regarding the MTC, it remains unclear if the authors consider information as objective, substantial (as sometimes interpreted) or by the contrary it refers to the uncertainty concerning the identification of the received signals by the recipient. This second interpretation seems closer to the interests in which the theory was developed (Shannon 1948, 1949).

Figure 1 shows in a bird's eye view – without attempting to be exhaustive – a significant number of theoretical viewpoints. These theories are collected in groups labeled not always as the authors do, but referred to some key and common elements of the approaches, grouped together. This taxonomy arranges different information concepts with respect to its greater or lesser subjective nature. On the left, the most objectivist theories are placed; on the right, the most subjectivist ones, and centered, a range of intermediate theories that normally adopt a two-fold approach. This is, for instance, the case of Weizsäcker's dual concept of his *objectivised semantics*, in which information is defined as: (1) what might be understood (even if it is done by an abstract intentionality) and (2) what generates information (Weizsäcker 1974, p. 351).

Relational pole. As shown in Figure 1 for those visions in which information is conceived as a *relational* or mediating concept, the kind of relation that mediates between objects and subjects (considering the later in a broad sense) can be multifarious. Following the differences referred to in Figure 1, information might be dependent on:

- *Reception probability or uncertainty* of recipients as in MTC (Shannon, 1948).
- *Measurement* processes, as in the general theory of measurement (Neuman, 1932; Brillouin, 1956; Mähler, 1996);
- The *complexity of a referred object* to be reconstructed, or complexity of a process to be carried out, as in the "Algorithmic Information Theory" (Solomonoff, 1964; Kolmogorov, 1965; Chaitin, 1966; 1982a). Despite the apparently objective definition of "information content" within this theory, it has been branded as relational because, since it is actually referred to a non-calculable value, what is in fact calculable dependent on the actually available semantics (Lyre, 2003, pp. 38-40).
- The *understanding potentials and generating facts* of the mentioned "objectivised semantics" (Weizsäcker, 1974) and other related or similar approaches as Lyre's information-theoretic atomismus (1998) or Matsuno's informational diachronism of evolution (1998);
- The *evolutionary adaptation ability* of self-organizing systems as in the "Unified Theory of Information" (Hofkirchner, 1999);
- The *ability to change recipients* as in the General Theory of Information proposed by Mark Burgin, whose formal model provides a framework for the articulation of most points of view on information (2003, 2010) or in Karpatschof's *activity theory*, in which information is also regarded in its ability to cause changes in what the author names a *release mechanism* (2007).

As illustrated in Figure 1, this relational character implies sometimes the reference to a certain kind of subjectivity or intentionality. This is, for instance, the case of the *Unified Theory of Information* (UTI) which is frequently presented as a mediator of all points of views without falling into reductionism (bottom-up approaches) or holism (top-down approaches) (Fenzl & Hofkirchner, 1997). The UTI appeals to a certain degree of intentionality, not necessarily human, that we call *general*. The complexity may present different de-

Figure 1. Taxonomy of theories based on information as something objective, relational or subjective

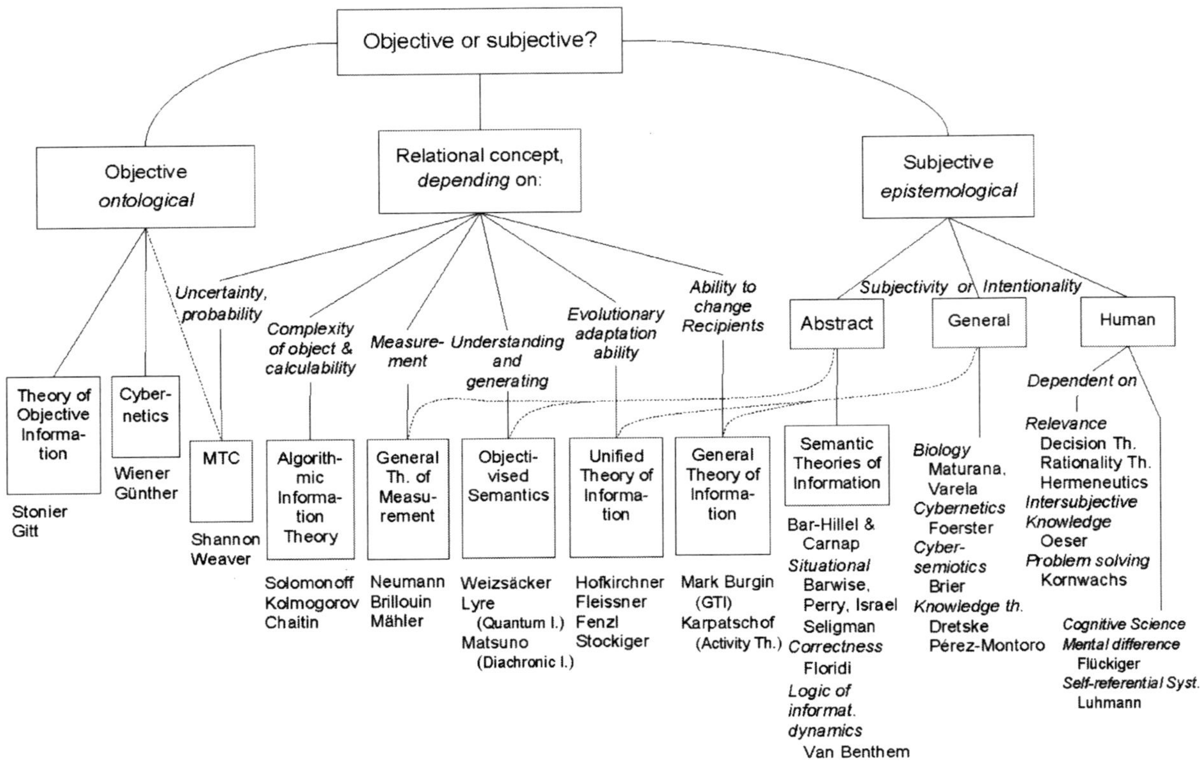

grees depending on the process this theory refers to (i.e. adaptation of systems with a greater or lesser complexity, which is also related to the degree of intentionality achieved). Nevertheless, trying to give account of all processes and to explain the emergence of more complex auto-organizing systems, this approach also refers to the organization of physical systems without intentionality. Thus, intentionality belongs to the realm of the most complex systems (normally human or social) aiming to harmonize with diachronic structuring and organization from the most simple elements.

This kind of generality with respect to the complexity level of the system receiving information can be observed in the *General Theory of Information* (GTI). Here the recipient is modeled as a non-specific *info-logical system* that can be potentially changed by information. Such system may correspond to "a person, community, class of students, audience in a theater, animal, bird, fish, computer, network, database and so on", and therefore it is accordingly referred to different degrees of intentionality – even empty – (Burgin, 2010). If the recipient were just a physical system, information – as what represents potential changes in the system – coincides with energy, i.e., energy can be here envisaged as a kind of information in a broad sense, what does not represent a monist position. The embodiment principle stating that "there is always a carrier C" for information, which can be interpreted as a substance (2010) makes clear that monism is not the case of GTI.

Subjectivist pole. In case an *epistemological* point of view is fundamentally used (namely, information is considered as *subjective* or concerning some kind of intentionality – in a broad sense), the objective qualities of signals are left in a second plane, focusing on those regarded as relevant by subjects (interpreters). However, this does not mean that information is only interpreted from an anthropocentric point of view, or something just occurring inside minds. Sometimes indeed, an *externalist* viewpoint is adopted, reducing the role of intentionality with respect to information to a kind of correlation between facts, signals and behavior; or even as a reservoir in which previous received information is stored (Drestske, 1981; Díaz & Pérez-Montoro 2011a). In this broad sense, subjectivity is referred to an intentionality that can be:

1. **Abstract,** or formal, in the sense of a series of general conditions of representation and intellection of reality, as it happens in most of the semantic theories of information (Bar-Hillel & Carnap, 1953; Barwise & Perry, 1983; Barwise & Seligman, 1997; Israel & Perry, 1990; Floridi, 2004-2005c);
2. **General,** in the case of information as a construct of an observer (whether human or not), who finds differences in its circumstance, as suggested by Maturana and Varela (1980) from a biological approach, or by Heinz von Foerster (1981) from a cybernetic perspective (Brier, 2008; Dretske, 1981; Pérez-Montoro, 2007);
3. **Human,** in whose case the consideration of language (Wilson & Sperber, 1993), interpretation (Capurro, 2009), action (Benthem, 2003; 2008; Floridi 2005d), cognitive mechanisms (Flückiger, 2005) or social systems (Luhmann, 1987) become essential, while the quest for *relevance,* whether social or individual, *veracity* or relationship with *knowledge* turn into articulating aspects (Kornwachs, 1996, Oeser, 1976, Habermas, 1981).

If we intend to evaluate the epistemic relevance of each perspective, it is clearly neutral for objectivist conceptions (the value of information lies in itself and it is meaningless to speak of truth), while it can be considered subjectivist or not for those conceptions depending on intentionality, especially if they are linked to knowledge or semantic issues. To some extend when moving from left to right in Figure 1, we move from ontological to epistemological questions. The particular epistemic relevance will also depend on the attention paid to syntactical, semantic and pragmatic aspects.

3.2 What Aspects of Information Are Considered in the Information Theories?

3.2.1 Aspects, Dimensions and Levels of Information

The aspects or dimensions of information that each approach considers are also illustrative of their respective scopes and intentions. As mentioned above, both epistemological and ontological consequences will result from the aspects of information being covered by each specific information vision. For instance, if just the syntactical level is considered (as it was Shannon's intention in 1948), the question about the truth of the content is meaningless, whereas the way toward the objectification of information is maximally feasible. On the other hand, when pragmatics comes on stage, other issues, such as value or utility, substitute the question of truth.

For the sake of simplicity, we will just compare how different information theories cover the three fundamental aspects of information referred to by Shannon and Weaver (1949). These fundamental aspects comes from the disciplinary division proposed by Morris, following Peirce's definition of sign as what is linked to the sign itself, to the object, and to the subject respectively (Morris 1938). Nonetheless, we could broaden the dimensions of information as to consider in a hierarchical vision other levels, enriching the distinctions introduced by Morris' categories. For instance, Gitt (1996) proposes a *statistical* level under the syntactical one, and an *apobetic* level above the pragmatic one. The former is conceived as exclusively referring to stochastic properties of signals, without any consideration of syntactical rules or structures as used in our linguistic communications, i.e. not distinguishing grammatical correctness. On the other hand, the apobetic level (from the greek *apobeinon*, purpose) is concerned with the fact that the result of the information reception is based on the purposes, objectives, plans… of the partakers. However and despite the relevance of distinguishing these aspects, these and other distinctions can be subsumed within the limiting levels (the statistical aspects in the syntactic one; the apobetical aspects in the pragmatic ones).

Hence, we will here just consider the *syntactic*, *semantic* and *pragmatic* dimensions, which can be characterized by means of three major questions: 1) concerning the *syntactical* content, "How is it expressed?"; 2) for the *semantic* content, "What does it represent?" as well as "with which truth value?"; and, 3) for the *pragmatic* content, "What value and utility has it?".

Although in communicative or information-transmission processes, speaking about transmission of semantic contents without expression is clearly meaningless, and such contents are in turn necessary to identify the pragmatic contents, it is still unclear to what extent each question determines the other two. Although the three regarded dimensions are usually regarded hierarchically (being the syntactical aspects at the lowest level and the pragmatic aspects at the highest level), such hierarchy will not be considered here for comparison because different positions are held to this concern. On the one hand, the degree of freedom that each aspect lets the others depends on the adopted point of view; on the other hand, usually some of the mentioned levels are not considered at all, and furthermore, sometimes the levelism is simply avoided.

Thereby, whereas the MTC is only related to the syntactic dimension – regarding the other two beside the point –, some semantic approaches consider the semantic question strongly restricted by Shannon's information – such as in Weaver (Shannon & Weaver 1949) – and others consider it as a weak restriction that allows a larger margin of freedom (Sloman 1978, Floridi 2005c, §4). To this respect, it is worth mentioning there are good reasons to consider that a simple noise (for instance, due to the thermal erratic movement of electrons in a resistor) does not meet the requirements commonly attributed to information, though it were maximally pondered by the MTC in terms of entropy or amount of information. On the other hand, a single bit might tell us if the Ptolemaic universe is or not the case or if a war has begun, which might drastically change our worldview or our expectations, i.e. with mostly significant syntactic or pragmatic consequences at each case. Weizsäcker's distinction between *potential* and *actual* information might provide –as we will later argue– some clarity to this confusion (1974).

3.2.2 The Coverage over Syntactic, Semantic and Pragmatic Aspects

In Figure 2 (which, as Figure 1, does not intent to be exhaustive), the extent to which each concept answers to the posed questions about the multi-dimensionality of information is shown.

Syntactic dimension. Shannon's information and those developments trying to supersede the inconsistencies with respect to modern physics epistemology are chiefly located at the syntactical plane (e.g. quantum information theory, or information according to the holographic principle). The last-mentioned cases are represented as partially covering semantic aspects, since – contrary to the classical MTC concept – there is a certain degree of indeterminacy in the description of reality by means of data, implying that information is necessarily mediated by theory. However, this consideration rather belongs to an epistemological level concerning the observation and measurement of reality, therefore not referring to

Figure 2. Aspects of qualitative content, covered by different information concepts. To facilitate the representation of inclusion/exclusion of dimensions for each theory, the syntactical one is located both on the left and on the right.

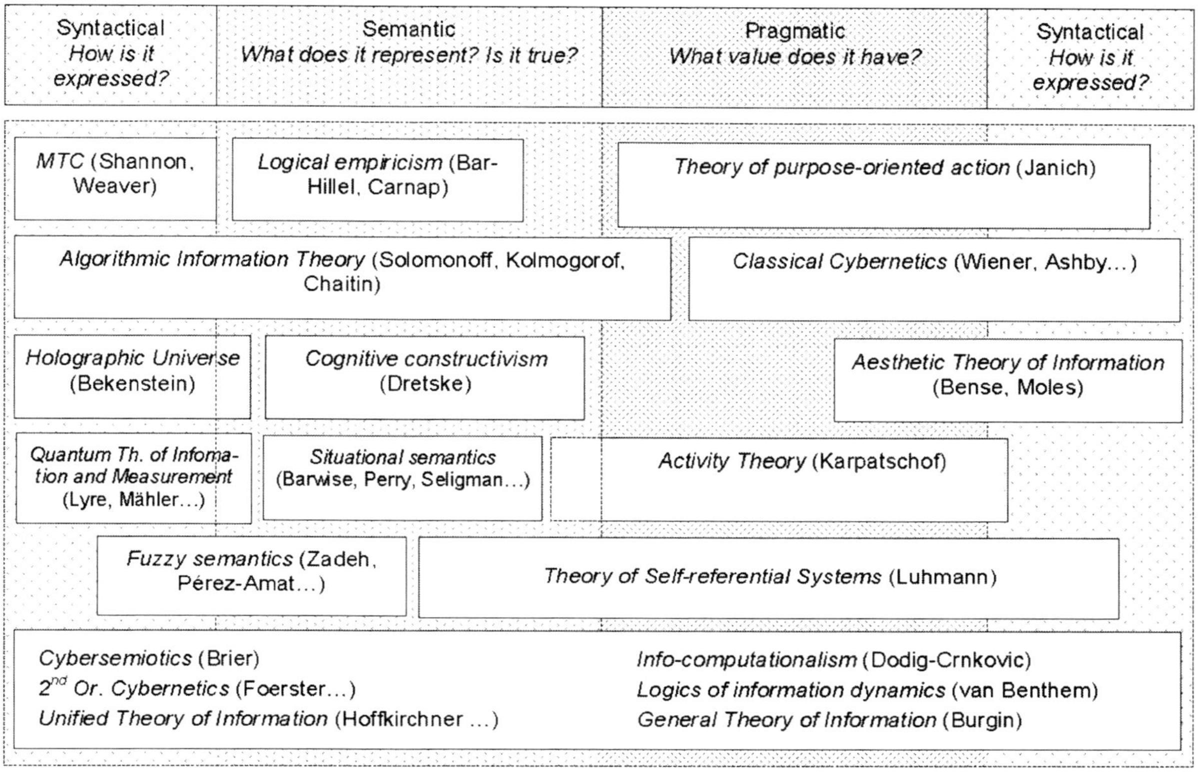

what is commonly understood as semantic aspects of information. To some extent, it can be regarded as an additional limitation at the syntactical level with respect to MTC assumptions. For instance, the fact that Von Neumann's entropy, related to quantum states, is smaller than Shannon's entropy, since the latter assumes the possibility of independency among the parts of a system, namely the analyticity of reality previously discussed (Neumann 1932).

Semantic dimension. If only semantic questions are to be accounted – in many cases intending to complete Shannon's programmatic neglect to this question –, there are a significant number of proposals. These semantic approaches present important internal differences hardly reconcilable, as they are rooted in atavistically opposed assumptions, such as empiricist, constructivist or rationalist positions. Thus, although the semantic value of a proposition – assumed as informative – is usually referred to probabilistic computations (inspired by Shannon's quantification model) and the "Inverse Relationship Principle" is followed, linking the increase in information to the decrease in possibilities (Barwise, 1997), a different probabilistic approach can be found in each case:

- For Bar-Hillel's and Carnap's *logical empiricism* (1953), the probability space is based on the result of a logical construction of atomic propositions in a formal language;

- In Dretske's *cognitive constructivism*, the probability of the observed state of affairs is accounted (Dretske, 1981);
- In *situational semantics*, the probability of the space of states and the consistency from a certain contextual situation are accounted (Barwise & Seligman 1997);
- In Zadeh's *fuzzy semantics*, the categories used to define descriptors are associated to elastic constraints and fuzzy quantifiers (Zadeh 1986).

In a more integrated framework (i.e., bringing together several information dimensions) and differing from combinatory and probabilistic approaches, the *algorithmic information theory* conceives *information content* in terms of the minimal resources to reproduce (compute) something, whether a mere binary structure, an object, or the development of a certain operation (Somolonoff 1964, Kolmogorov 1965, Chaitin 1966, 1982a). Hence, by referring to the expressive resources required to perform something, this approach covers both the syntactic and the semantic issues. But, on the other hand, taking into account that certain codes are just aimed at doing something – purpose oriented – the pragmatic questions may also arise. Indeed, the complexity limit studied by Chaitin in relation to Gödel's incompleteness theorem and Turing's halting theorem can be interpreted as having a practical scope, since the knowledge background or the used/selected semantic frame actually limits what can be done, and therefore what can be pursued (Chaitin 1982a, 1982b, Lyre 2002, §1.4.2).

Pragmatic dimension. In an explicitly pragmatic sense, Janich's theory of information (1998) refers to purpose-oriented human actions seeking the replicability of such actions through artificial anthropomorphic devices articulated by standard interrogative dialogues, qualified by information predicates. Hence, a two-fold attention to pragmatic and syntactical dimensions is here found.

In a higher degree of abstraction regarding informative pragmatics, *Karpatschof's activity theory* (2007) reduces the syntactical field to that of qualities of signals with regard to a "release mechanism" which – so to speak – rules the roost. Thus, Karpatschof's approach focuses on the characteristics of this mechanism as a system containing potential and stored energy that can be released in a specific way, whenever trigged by a signal fulfilling certain conditions. One of the benefits of this proposal, concerning the possibility of finding an integrative framework for the understanding of information, is the lability of the signals requirements and the characteristics of the release mechanism. For instance, if the imposed requirements concern the satisfaction of certain truth or veracity constrains, the model will be linked to the knowledge problem, ready to delve into the semantic dimension of information. On the other hand, if the requirements are of aesthetic nature, the model will be linked to the problem of artistic information; and analogously, it could be adapted to the investigation of information in biological contexts (evolution or adaptation to the environment), social coexistence, etc. However, this model – though heuristically valuable – provides not enough theoretical resources to articulate such a framework as we can find in other integrative perspectives. However the complexity of our awareness, as well as the communication and interactions processes shows that this requires a detailed inspection and a subtle frame to give account of them, as it has been studied in the binding problem (Treisman, 1996), the perception-cognition-action cycle (Bruni, 2008), semiotics (Brier, 2008), hermeneutics (Díaz & Capurro, 2010), the complexity of social systems (Luhman, 1987).

Integrative perspectives. One of these – though biased towards the pragmatic pole – is Luhmann's *theory of self-referential systems* (1987). In this vision, information is conceived as a mediating instance between the "meaning offer" (typical of the cultural circumstance) and "understanding". Thus, semantic and pragmatic dimensions are closely related here, whereas social systems can be considered as both worlds of meanings or problem-solving worlds. This interrelation of pragmatic and semantic dimensions constitutes in Lyre's Quantum Theory of Information (1998) or Weizsäcker's semantic theory (1974) the condition for the possibility of the objectivisation of semantics. These theories address and unify the three fundamental dimensions of information (Lyre, 2002), while solving for the syntactical one the aforementioned epistemological defects of the MTC –especially in relation to the certitudes of quantum mechanics.

In a more hierarchical sense of the three dimensions of information, the *unified theory of information* intends to cover all problems related to information, such as physical-, organic- or social phenomena, by means of the self-organizing paradigm (Hofkirchner 1997, Fenzl & Hofkirchner 1997). In this approach, the three referred dimensions are considered as levels: the constitution of the syntactical level is the condition and substratum for the articulation of a semantic level, and this one is, in turn, the condition and substratum for the self-re-creation of a pragmatic level (Hofkirchner 1999a, 1999b). Such hierarchical approach is also shared by the objectivised information theories of Stonier (1999) and Gitt (1996) or in Collier's nested hierarchies of information (2011). For the latter, who arranges different kinds of information in a hierarchical or nested relation from the physical substratum to a kernel, represented by intentional information, each level imposes a restriction on the preceding levels; being such restrictions "created by the formation of cohesion through self-organization within the preceding level" (p. 8).

In the so-called *first order* or *classical cybernetics*, the pragmatic paradigm of achieving a proper behavior to cope with the surrounding reality, worked out as a fertile frame in which many different scientific visions could fit into a transdisciplinary approach. The results obtained, for instance, in control theory and the development of automatic systems speak by themselves. However, the posed outer vision, which meta-scientifically entails an epistemological anachronism, implies that the proper semantic dimension of information shall be sacrificed, what is understandable if animal or human intentionality had to be jostled with the motion of automata (Wiener, 1948; Díaz & Aguado, 2010). Considering the necessity to surpass this epistemological voids, von Foerster proposed a *second order cybernetics*, in which (reviewing the basic model of cybernetics, i.e., a system pursuing some goals and being observed from the outside) now the observer is an effective part of the system, asserting his own goals and his own role within the system. Although the semantic dimension was gained, this stance also branded as radical constructivism has been criticized as providing a cognitive closure in which objectivity is denied.

Related to this radical constructivist position, Søren Brier (2008) considers that information is not enough to account the reality of communication and cognition proposes, proposes a cybersemiotical approach to information connecting Peirce's semiotics (*sign*) with the *cybernetics of the second order*. Brier defines *cybersemiotics* in terms of a dynamic and contextually adaptive relationship between a sign, an object and an interpreter; while Capurro (2007) argues that Brier's approach can be regarded as a "hermeneutics of the second order that extends the concept of interpretation beyond human knowledge, relating it to all kinds of selective processes".

In the *info-computationalism*, proposed by Gordana Dodig-Crnkovic (2010) as a means to supersede the traditional mechanistic worldview, information is conceived as the ontological basis of the universe (its structure), whereas computation – in a broadened sense – represents its dynamics. This approach intends to cover from the physical, to the ethical domains going through biological and cognitive realms by means of levelism on the complexity of information. Dodig-Crnkovic argues that this frame opens a space for logical, epistemological and ethical pluralism. However, van Benthem and Martínez (2008) considers – regarding this pluralism – that "having several complementary stances in a field is fruitful itself" (§9), therefore instead of unification, they propose *dynamics of logics* for a wide inquiry of information in its variety of aspects (Benthem, 2003).

Finally, the *general theory of information*, proposed by Burgin (2003, 2005, 2010) – aware of the irreducible variety of information kinds –, instead of pursuing a unitary definition of information, seeks for a parametric definition in which information stands for a capacity to cause changes in an infological system. Thereby, this class of systems plays the role of a parameter, which allows embracing any kind of information from the most elementary, namely energy – as previously discussed – to cognitive and social changes. As Burguin argues (2003), this frame enables to integrate the syntactical, semantic and pragmatic aspect, as well as other significant distinctions involved in information phenomena, by means of refined definitions of the infological systems, at the same time that it provides a flexible means to measure and evaluate information (2003).

3.2.3 Dialogical vs. Syncronical Understanding of the Information Multidimensionality

As we have seen in the integrative approaches, delving into the reality of information requires crossing its multifaceted manifestation and finding the interrelation of its different aspects. However, we can distinguish two kinds of approaches according to the role played by the evolution of systems in the emergence of new properties of information. This dichotomy can be branded as diachronic vs synchronic, representing a dissimilar endeavor in different explanation domains.

In a *diachronic* account of information as in the UTI – considering here several strives in the same direction –, understanding is sought on how the manifold reality of information phenomena can evolve from the most simple to the most complex cases. On the other hand, an account as the GTI provides a framework for representing any kind of information synchronically. Although GTI refers to systems dynamics, and even in a very detailed way, it does not focus on how the systems evolve in order to make, for instance, new properties emerge. In both cases, crossing through the many aspects of information – namely being able to cover its multidimensional reality – is a toehold of the complete theoretical building.

In diachronic accounts, information phenomena can evolve from the very simple organization of matter to higher organization of more and more complex structures. Here, the effects of information are dependent – in a decreasing deterministic way – of subsystems that interact with each other and manifest the many aspects of information. Let us for instance consider three cases: cognition, communication and cooperation. In case of *cognition*, the involved subsystems can be regarded – in the syntactical level – as the sensitive structures that arrange sensation in different modalities of perception. By means of interaction, these modalities allow to grasp a sensed reality – in a semantic level –, which bring about some kind of change in the system state depending on the pragmatic situation. Here, it is the pragmatic situation what mainly opens the system to its environment. In case of *communicative* processes, one of the fundamental subsystems is the symbolic system shared by a community, which represents an openness of the system at the semiotic level, or just the necessity to be chiefly referred to social systems. In case of *cooperative* processes, the system of goals, means and agents become essential.

Nevertheless, such diachronic accounts – as in the case of biological evolution – are hindered by circularity: the changes that are produced are those been produced. We do not have a path to predict them. In other words, the footprints left by the evolution in the complexity of the involved systems are not enough to distinguish what path the systems really followed. However, it heuristically provides a ground for understanding the dynamics of the system evolution, as well as a simple hypothetical ground that avoids the necessity to maintain a more complex system of assumptions.

On the other hand, in the synchronic account pole, the flexibility of the framework provided by the GTI allows us to adapt the different types of information (unfolded in its multifaceted dimensions) into an explanatory system. This perhaps does not give account on the long-term evolution of complex systems in its interaction with information, but it is suited to provide a perspective on its short and mid-term dynamics as well as on "how to measure or, at least, to evaluate information" (Burgin 2003, p. 148), which in the age of information is a major concern.

4. NATURE OF INFORMATION: IN THE INTERFACE BETWEEN OBJECTS AND SUBJECTS

As we argued in section 2, it is the blurred position of information between objects and subjects – instead of a problem – a privileged standpoint for bridging over the traditional gap between the objectivist and subjectivist stances, and moreover among specialized sciences. For deepening into this radical position of information, let us consider the problem of observation.

4.1 Observation Scenarios

When a subject is confronting an object of observation, this scenario can be modeled in different ways concerning the relevance and nature of the interaction between them. As we know from the quantum mechanics, the interaction is actually inherent to the nature of observation (Lyre, 1999). However, such interaction can be minimized as to consider the classical picture of neutral observation as approximate enough (model 1: ideal observation), and we can even develop a model of interaction in which a classical approach can be followed to delve into the complexity of observation (model 2: classical interaction). Nonetheless, as we know, quantum interaction provides a more proper and exact account on the real interaction process (model 3: quantum interaction).

An exact account on what is really happening is strictly out of reach since the non-locality of quantum theory might bring us to the extreme consequence that we should consider the Universe as the collection of all physical objects into one and the same wave-function. Regarding this theoretical extreme stance, Heisenberg said: "if the whole Universe were included into the system, the physics would disappear, leaving only a mathematical schema" (Heisenberg, 1930, p.44 –my translation).

For the sake of simplicity, we have restricted here our scope regarding a very simplified universe constituted by an object and a subject of observation. Figure 3 represents this simplified situation for the aforementioned three models of interaction. Although, the ideal observation (Figure 3.a) is not exact, the model might be accurate enough when the intensity of the interaction is so weak that it makes no significant difference, for instance, when the observer is far apart and its dimension is small with respect to the distance between relevant differences of the wave phenomena. In this case, the structure of the wave phenomena Ψ occurring in the allegedly homogeneous space surrounding the sources is described by the wave equation as represented in the figure, and the changes produced in the observation means are in direct relation to this phenomenon. We will later on delve into this case to inquire into the limits of the manifestation of the object, since – being this an ideal case of observation – the other models add even more limitation to the knowledge that can be achieved from the information, provided by the observation (§4.2). But before going into these details, let us glance into the other models.

Figure 3. Three models of observation: a) ideal (valid for too weak interaction); b) classical interaction in which the energy detected by the observation system acts as a new source that affects the object; c) quantum interaction

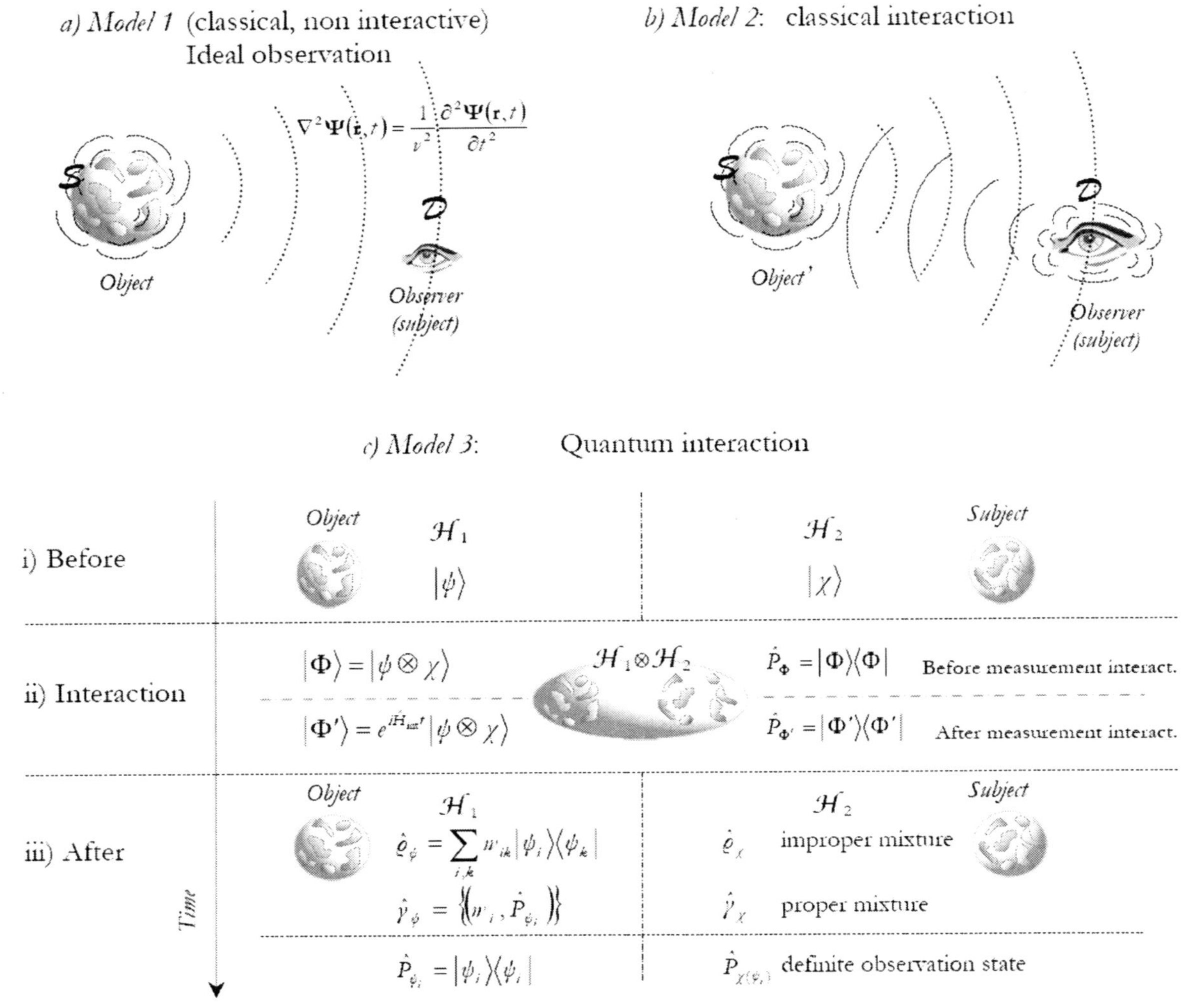

Classical interaction. For the classical interaction (Figure 3.b), the relation between the object and observation system can be interpreted in a recursive way, by using a linear relation as the one that will be used below to describe the ideal observation. Such relation shall be determined between a set of equivalent sources properly distributed over the surface surrounding the object S and the phenomena, represented by another set of equivalent sources over the observation domain D. In a first step, the set of equivalent sources at D is modified by the particular distribution of equivalent sources at S. Subsequently, the equivalent sources at D affect the object sources by means of a new wave phenomenon – weaker than the former one –, producing a transformed set of sources – slightly different to the original ones. In subsequent iterations the sets of phenomena at the observation domain, and the set of sources will asymptotically tend respectively to what has been observed and to the modified object. To some extent, the observed phenomena is directly related to the modified object, not to the observed object, as it was before being observed, although this can be figured out. Concerning the interaction and despite of this invertibility, what matters is that the object has changed, and the fact that the object at this moment is something indivisible from such interaction. However, it is also true that from this classical point of view the initial state could be recovered.

Quantum interaction. Something else happens with the quantum interaction (Lyre, 1998; Vedral 2006). Here the object and the observing systems – formerly at an original state in their respective Hilbert spaces k_1 and k_2 – mix into a new quantum system at the product Hilbert space. The state of this mixture $|\Phi\rangle$ (a pure state with a projection operator $\hat{P}_\Phi$) is changed by the measurement interaction into another pure state $|\Phi\rangle$ by means of the Hermitian operator corresponding to the observable being sought. Right after and to make the observation possible, both systems must be separated again. After this separation, the states of both systems are not any more pure, but improper mixtures that can be described by density operators. These mixed states $\hat{\rho}_\psi$ allow an infinite number of decomposition into states $\left|\psi_i\right\rangle$. Selecting one of these decompositions, the improper mixture turns into a proper mixture described by $\hat{\gamma}_\psi$, i.e. the collection of possible pure states and the corresponding probabilities. Finally, one of these possible pure states is determined by observation at the subject system, linked to the value of the observable object (for which the observation system was prepared, i.e. some observable can be determined while other observables are left apart).

In this process, it is worth mentioning two relevant features: i) by observing the object, it is changed in an irreversible way; ii) some characteristics of the former states get to be scarcely known or completely unknown. In other words, as in classical observation (model 1 in which we will delve below and model 2) the object can not be completely determined; but unlike classical observation, the object is here irremediably changed as to intend a further inquiry. We can also say that the subject has got materially "informed" about some features of the object, which in turn has also been "informed" by the interaction. Neither of them will get to be the same after observation. Before the observation, the wave function of the object system represents a catalog of what can be potentially measured (i.e. changed) in the subject, thus we can speak here – following Weizsäcker – of "*potential information*". After the observation, the subject has been changed according to how the object was, i.e., it has been actually informed; it has received "*actual information*" (Weizsäcker, 1985).

4.2 Ideal Observation

The aforementioned model 1 of observation, though may not suffice to give a proper account on the "actual information", it will be very useful to deepen into the limits of the potential information and to probe the indetermination of the object, even in a classical interpretation.

Under the circumstances and approximations already mentioned when an observer pays attention into the manifestations of an object (no matter whether they are due to mechanical or electromagnetic interactions with the environment, as in the case of sound or light respectively), the observing properties of such an environment respond – where the observer is located – to the well-known wave equation:

$$\nabla^2\Psi\left(r,t\right)=\frac{1}{v^2}\frac{\partial^2\Psi\left(r,t\right)}{\partial t^2} \tag{1}$$

where $\boldsymbol{\Psi}$ represents the properties of the environment to which the observed is allegedly sensitive (e.g. the air pressure or the light), $\mathbf{r}$ is the position vector, t the temporal variable, and v a constant depending on the environment characteristics and corresponding to the propagation speed of the wave phenomenon. The pertinence of (1) implies that the observation domain (or domain of manifestation of the object) is homogeneous and isotropic (i.e., the interactions independent of either the direction or the position in which the parts are located).

The relative complexity of (1) may be smoothed if any temporal variation is expressed – by means of the Fourier theorem – as a linear combination of harmonic variations. Thus, we can separate a relation for each involved frequency, f (a subsequent combination of single-frequency variations may render the full temporal evolution), namely the Helmholtz equation:

$$\nabla^2\Psi\left(r\right) + k^2\Psi\left(r\right) = 0 \tag{2}$$

where the wave number $k = 2\pi f/v = 2\pi/\lambda$, being λ the wavelength for the involved frequency, and $\boldsymbol{\Psi} \in \leq$ reflects the amplitude and phase of the f component of the temporal phenomenon

$$\Psi\left(r,t\right) = \int_{\forall f \in B} \Re\left\{\Psi_f\left(r\right)e^{-i2\pi ft}\right\}df$$

In other words, though for the sake of simplicity, we delve into the Helmholtz equation (2) instead of the wave equation (1) in which the dynamics are explicit, the reference to time variations are implicitly reflected in the frequency parameter, or the inversely related wave length λ. On the other hand, due to the symmetry shown by the wave equation regarding space and time, the conclusions that will be derived for the space dimensions can be easily translated into any set of space-time dimensions, i.e. the actual problem is four dimensional, but we analyse any three dimensions at the same time.

If we now apply the Fourier Theorem in the spatial dimensions for the phenomenon $\boldsymbol{\Psi}$ described by the Helmholtz equation (2), we can find a linear combination of harmonic variations in each of the spatial directions which allow us to represent any spatial distribution of the observed property $\boldsymbol{\Psi}$. Thus, it can be expressed as a linear combination of distributions of the following type:

$$\begin{aligned}&\Psi\left(r\right) = \Psi_x\left(r\right)\cdot\Psi_y\left(r\right)\cdot\Psi_z\left(r\right)\\ &with \quad \Psi_u = A_u e^{-ik_u u} + A_{-u}e^{ik_u u}\quad .\end{aligned} \tag{3}$$

where u represents any spatial direction, and k_u its corresponding spatial frequency or the wave-number in the direction u.

By limiting k_u to real values, it can be easily noticed that a valid type of solution for equation (2) has not been considered, namely the one corresponding to exponentially decaying distributions, which are named evanescent modes. Thus, (3) and the following discussion just refer to harmonic distributions. However, we should stress that although the absence of evanescent modes is not strictly the case (i.e. there are indeed evanescent waves around the object) in a practical sense such waves do not go beyond the very vicinity of the object in an observable level. That is, its actual level may be underneath noise level, or even under the sensibility of the observer.

Now applying (3) to equation (2), we obtain:

$$k_x^2 + k_y^2 + k_z^2 = k^2 \tag{4}$$

These wave-numbers for each spatial direction might be interpreted in terms of spatial frequency components (i.e. sinusoidal distributions in the corresponding spatial direction). Hence, relation (4) implies that the harmonic variations that may be expected in each direction are limited to a fundamental constraint, which may be geometrically expressed as a spherical surface or radius k in a space of three spatial frequencies.

4.2.1 Inquiry into the Dimensionality of Ideal Observation

Considering the previous analysis of the wave phenomenon according to its structural constraints, particularly the constraints referring to spatial variations, we can straightforward arrive – by means of the sampling theorem (e.g., Shannon, 1949, p.11) – to the *general discretizability theorem for radiation fields* (T1):

The minimal distance between independent intensity values of a field generated by an arbitrary object is λ/2. (Díaz & Pérez-Montoro, 2011b, §2.1)

If based on this theorem we now consider the spatial limitation of the object within the boundary S, the validity of the Helmholtz equation at the interface (i.e. right besides the object), as well as the uniqueness theorem of this equation, we immediately arrive to the *theorem of the essential dimensionality of the radiation problem* for a bounded object (T2):

The maximum number of details of an object, inscribed in an sphere of radius a, which is causing an observed field distribution, is $16\pi(a\chi/\lambda)^2$. This is the essential dimension of the observation problem. (Díaz & Pérez-Montoro, 2011b, §2.2)

If we now add the restriction of an observation located at a minimal distance with respect to the object of observation (more explicitly, at a distance d from the centre of a ball containing the object), it can easily be demonstrated – appealing to the features of the spherical harmonics – *the special discretizability theorem for distant radiation* (T3):

The minimal distance between independent values of the field corresponding to the manifestation of an object inscribed in a sphere of radius a, whose centre is at a distance d, is:$\lambda d/2a\chi$. (Díaz & Pérez-Montoro, 2011b, §2.3)

4.2.2 Reframing the Ideal Information Problem

Using these theorems, the relation between the sources of radiation (object) and the observed field can be expressed by means of a linear transformation:

$$\begin{pmatrix} \Psi(u_1, v_1) \\ \vdots \\ \Psi(u_M, v_M) \end{pmatrix} = \begin{pmatrix} G(u_1, v_1, x_1', y_1', z_1') & \cdots & G(u_1, v_1, x_N', y_N', z_N') \\ \vdots & \ddots & \vdots \\ G(u_M, v_M, x_1', y_1', z_1') & \cdots & G(u_M, v_M, x_N', y_N', z_N') \end{pmatrix} \times \begin{pmatrix} f(x_1', y_1', z_1') \\ \vdots \\ f(x_N', y_N', z_N') \end{pmatrix} \quad (5)$$

where (u, v) represent curvilinear coordinates over the observation space; 1… N the cardinals of the samples over the observation domain; (x', y', z') the locations of the founts or sources – i.e. the object –, properly discretized; 1…M the cardinals of these samples; and $G(u,v,x',y',z')$ the Green function, which at the same time satisfies the wave equation (2) in the homogeneous space and establishes a direct relation to the non-homogeneity, to which the presence of the object (or one of its infinitesimal parts) intrinsically responds: between the location (x',y',z') at the sources and (u,v) at the observation domain.

More densely, the relation between field and its corresponding sources can be expressed grouping the field distribution into an M-dimensional vector Ψ, the sources into an N-dimensional vector f, and representing the transformation among them through a matrix operator T:

$$\Psi = \begin{pmatrix} \Psi_1 \\ \vdots \\ \Psi_M \end{pmatrix} = \sum_{n=1}^{N} \begin{pmatrix} \psi_1 \\ \vdots \\ \psi_M \end{pmatrix} \cdot f_n = \sum_{n=1}^{N} \psi_n \cdot f_n = T \cdot f$$

$$\text{where } \psi_n = \begin{pmatrix} G(u_1, v_1, x'_n, y'_n, z'_n) \\ \vdots \\ G(u_M, v_M, x'_n, y'_n, z'_n) \end{pmatrix} \tag{6}$$

which can be interpreted as the wave function for each discrete source of unitary amplitude, located at (x'_n, y'_n, z'_n).

Considering this formulation, the forward problem (namely, the prediction of the field when the sources distribution – namely the object – is known) does not have any difficulty: if we indeed knew the distribution of sources, described in terms of f, it would suffice to apply the former relations to know how actually the manifestations are in terms of Ψ. We do not care if N is bigger or smaller. However, this is – so to speak – a pseudo-problem if we give for granted the way the environment transmits the changes in one part of the space (in our case, the validity of the wave equation in our real environment), and of course, it does not correspond to the observation problem as we have stated it.

Generally, our knowledge about the objects is not *a priori* but *a posteriori*, that is, reckoning with its manifestation. This is the so-called *inverse problem*, which in our formulation implies obtaining f from Ψ. In this case, it is evident that the dimension N is important, since we would never invert the relation if $N>M$. It is also important the independency of the wave functions ψ_n, or at least, that the dimensionality (or complexity) of the space developed by an arbitrary set of N sources corresponds to the dimensionality (or complexity) of an arbitrary observation.

Theorems T2 and T3 establish fundamental limits which enable a proper arrangement of our problem: according to T3, the actual dimension of the observed phenomenon does not depend on how detailed the observation is, since we often have to move quite distant to find some independent value of the considered phenomenon. The number of spatial details that we can perceive can never be higher than the essential dimension predicted by theorem 2. Thus, it is also the maximal number of details that might be specified concerning the object. It is here relevant to remind that such dimension does not depend on the volume ($\propto a^3$) but on the bounding surface ($\propto a^2$). Thus, since the complexity of volumetric distribution may wroth with the volume, whereas the complexity of the field only grows with the surface, this leads us to a fundamental conclusion: the volumetric distribution of the object is inscrutable. In this case, what might we know about the object?

At this point, it is worth remembering the Huygens principle (1690). It establishes that "each point on a primary wavefront can be considered to be a new source of a secondary spherical wave and that a secondary wavefront can be constructed as the envelope of these secondary spherical waves." This principle can be justified by means of the aforementioned uniqueness theorem of the Helmholtz equation, which for the electromagnetic problem was rigorously stated by Schelkunoff in terms of the equivalence theorem (Schelkunoff, 1936). Thus, it suffices to refer to the secondary sources (or *equivalent sources*) distributed on the surface bounding the object, which is properly located at the homogeneous space. As we have just shown, the dimensionality of the observation and that of the radiated field around the object implies that we can only obtain from the object a superficial knowledge, which can be interpreted as a projection of what is inside. But coming into such "inside" is forbidden solely based on *a posteriori* knowledge.

To clarify this last condition, we must take into account that if the inner complexity of the object structure is smaller than the essential dimension N, then the observer could grasp an idea of the volumetric distribution. However, such 'idea' would be achieved based on an assumption of the inner structure, since there is in principle an unlimited number of inner structures whose projections over a bounding surface are equal.

Considering the separation required for the independence of the equivalent sources at the bounding surface (here translated into the independence of the fields generated over the observation domain, D), a good way to make our problem well-posed is by locating punctual equivalent sources over S regularly spaced at a distance $\lambda/2\chi$. The space of radiated fields that shall be generated by this discrete distribution of equivalent punctual sources over S is equivalent to the one that might be generated by any inner (discrete or continuous) volumetric distribution. It can be shown (Díaz, 2003, §3.2.1) that if a quadratic norm is defined for the mentioned space of radiated fields, as well as a distance between field distributions based on such norm, $d(\psi_i, \psi_j)$, then there will only be a unique distribution of equivalent punctual sources over S that optimally matches the observed phenomena. This distribution can be understood as an orthogonal projection of the observed field Ψ on the source domain f:

$$\Psi = \begin{Bmatrix} \Psi_{OBSERVED} \\ T \cdot f_{projection} \end{Bmatrix} \Rightarrow \exists f_{projection}$$
$$= [T^{+} \cdot T]^{-1} T^{+} \cdot \Psi_{OBS.} \Big/ \min_{f} \left\{ d\left(T \cdot f_{projection}, \Psi_{OBS.}\right) \right\} \quad (7)$$

where T^{+} represents the adjoint matrix of T.

4.2.3 Observational Limits and Perception

Based upon the previous analysis of the ideal observation problem, the following fundamental conclusions can be forward extracted concerning what can be maximally known about the object causing an observed wave phenomenon. In other words, how much can be the subject informed about the object from its very manifestation:

1. The number of details to be found in the environment due to the presence of the object is finite.
2. Such number depends on the surface bounding the object and not on its volume.
3. The volumetric distribution of an object cannot be known only based on its manifestations on the environment.
4. The description of the object that can be achieved corresponds to a projection of the inner inhomogeneities over a bounding surface.

These four conclusions establish fundamental limits to the observation problem, not attached to the specificity of our organs of animal or human sensibility, but to the differences that can merely be found in the environment and the maximal knowledge that might be derived about the object causing these differences. Using Kantian terminology, these are the limits in the determination of an object of knowledge by means of a transcendental subject, to which the intimate knowledge of the object is withheld – as we previously showed. In other words, in spite of the actual complexity of the object, the complexity of the manifestations in the space surrounding the object – due to its presence – is constitutively smaller than the complexity of the object. We could argue that this is the case unless the object is completely described by its projection over the bounding surface. But even in this case, observation does not suffice to conclude that this completeness is the case, we must also know, for instance, that the inner part is empty, since there is a whole set of possibilities regarding the inner configuration. As previously pointed out, another possibility for a complete determination is that the observer intends to find out the specific configuration of a structure whose degrees of freedom are equal or smaller than the complexity of the field in the surrounding space, which obviously implies an important amount of previous knowledge.

Our analysis might be considered trivial if we just think in its correspondence to the visual problem, since there is a danger to confuse the limits to acknowledge the inner part of an object with its opacity. Even if some degree of transparency were ascribed to all the inner parts, the limit concerning the complexity of the field generated by the object leads us to the same conclusion: the three dimensionality of the inner distribution cannot be determined by the two-dimensionality of the object manifestation, which is also coherent with the *holographic principle*. According to this, the maximal entropy contained in a limited space depends on the bounding surface and not on its volume (Susskind, 1997, Díaz, 2010b). As a corollary of the holographic principle, Bekenstein proposes that if the physics of our real (tetra-dimensional) universe were holographic, there would be an arbitrary set of physical laws which could be applied to some tri-dimensional space-time boundary. Therefore, there is a radical indeterminacy between this *holographic universe* – as he names it – and the physics, used to interpret it. (Bekenstein, 2003). Concerning the determination of the object, we arrive to the same conclusion.

4.3 Sensation, Perception, Intellection and Nature of Information

Sensation and Perception. If we now reckon the specificity of the animal sensitivity, we would encounter further limits concerning the amount of differences that a perceiving subject can acknowledge about the object. The more complex its sensitive organs are, the closer it can reach the stated limits. For instance, the eagle vision is closer to this boundary than what the human vision is (Díaz, 2008). But in the impression of the reality gathered by the subject there is an essential element which is consistent with our former conclusions: the differences encountered in sensation points to a radical incompleteness in relation to the reality which is being felt. As we have seen, there is an essential ambiguity regarding the possible volumetric configurations of the objects, as there is ambiguity in many illusory images considered in theory of perception (Rock 1984). Although there is some kind of autonomy in perception with respect to the whole act of apprehending reality, this seems to be a unitary act in which different sensitive structures take part (synchronic or diachronically) together with an intellective moment.

To illustrate this, let us consider a simple example. In Figure 4, we try to deal with the ambiguity of the visual image of an object. In Figure 4a, it is normally perceived a big square bump in whose middle there is a regular hole. Both the geometrical regularity and the shadowing drive us to perceive the bump with a hole. However, Figure 4b brings us about the sensation of a more ambiguous object: the geometrical properties drive us to see again a hole that is differently colored than the rest. However, the shadowing invites us to see a smaller but irregular protuberance into the bump. According to an externalist interpretation of perception – for instance in Dretske (1981; Díaz & Pérez-Montoro, 2011a) –, if we only assume informational relations holding a deterministic condition (i.e. the related parts are linked with probability p=1), we might say that we perceive in Figure 3b a bump with {(a regular hole) or (an irregular protuberance)}. But this is not the case of what we really perceive. We can alternatively perceive either an irregular protuberance or a regular and colored hole (different intellectual moments are taking part at each time, understood as different intellectual apprehensions of the object).

Moreover, a different percept can also be obtained from Figure 3a: a colored and irregular protuberance. Although this last percept is much lesser probable, it has been experimentally shown that, in spite of geometrical and color visual

Figure 4. Perception of ambiguous figures. It illustrates the dependence of complexity of percepts in perception. In (a) the simplest corresponding figure is perceived: a regular hole. However, in (b) because of geometrical regularity we may perceive a hole, but shading tends us to perceive an irregular protuberance.

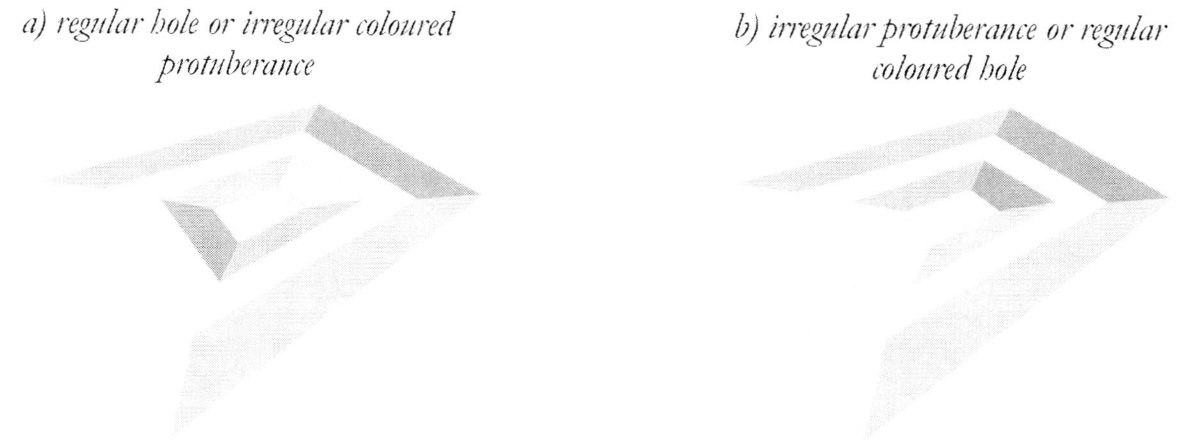

properties, the preferred visual percept might turn to be an irregular protuberance if the subject has the tactile sensation that something juts out (Robles-de-la-Torre et al. 2001, 2006). Furthermore, even when the object is touched and the ambiguity – so to speak – is solved, the subject can visually perceive it as a hole, although (s)he is aware that a protuberance exists. This property allows us to speak of the aforementioned relative autonomy of perception (Rock 1984), at the time that the awareness and intellection of reality forms some kind of unitary act in which different notes of reality, as well as different modes and structures of sensing take part.

As different experiments, carried out in the study of perception, have shown: the preferred perceptions tend to be those corresponding to the simplest configurations. For instance, in the previous example, a symmetrical bump, a homogeneous colored object, etc. In other words, perception seems to apply Ockam's razor: if something admits a simpler description, then this is preferred. To this respect, it is relevant to mention that the mathematical regularization methods to solve inverse problems also appeal to this same principle.

Complexity of sensation vs. ambiguity of perception. The more complex the sensitive structure, the greater the ambiguity of its perception and the more accurate the determination of the object. For instance, if we consider the simplest case of a cell, it has several means to sense the environment and to adapt to those variations that are relevant for its survival. More specifically, the unicellular organism *Euglena viridis* (among others of the same genus) has an eyespot apparatus, which filters sunlight into the light-detecting, photo-sensitive structures at the base of its flagellum. This eyespot enables the cell to sense the strength and direction of light, and straightforward to move accordingly towards a medium of moderate light (away from darkness and bright light). In the Euglena the afferent structures of the cell – sensing the environment – are directly connected to the efferent ones – the flagellum which causes the necessary movement towards a more suitable environment (Lemmermann, 1913, PEET 2010). The ambiguity of perception is here very low: the strength of light is high or low, and it comes from this or that direction. In addition, it is also low the accuracy in the determination of the environmental state. In the animal vision, as we have shown before, the ambiguity can be much higher as it is the accuracy in the determination of the observed reality. Grasping more notes of reality, especially if they have different modality (e.g. visual and tactile notes) the ambiguity left by some partial perceptions (e.g. a visual percept) can decrease although new kinds of ambiguity may appear. Reality is more accurately sensed, feeling at the same time that the non-felt part of reality is bigger. In our previous analysis of observation, sensation may grow in two dimensions, whereas the non-observed part is three-dimensional.

Intellection. The constitutive indeterminacy of the manifestation of reality and the ambiguity of sensation (both closed related but not the same) might bring about, on the one hand, the feeling that there is a part of reality beyond its manifestation; on the other hand, an invitation to find further notes to delve into the sensed reality. Probably, if sensation were sufficient for a particular being in its interaction with its world, this invitation might not be felt. But in this case some kind of deterministic relation should provide univocal perceptions of what is being sensed allowing it to successfully deal with the perceived objects. This relation can be interpreted as a fixed assumed solution to the ambiguity of sensation. The Spanish philosopher Xabier Zubiri refers to this kind of apprehension as "apprehension of stimulation", characterized by a "formality of signitivity", which in evolutionary sense precedes the "formality of reality". Here formality is conceived as what allows the apprehension of anything, therefore being independent of the content. In the formality of signitivity, the act of signing is in question, and this is in turn linked to a particular reaction of the subject – in a broad sense – (Zubiri, 1999); but in the formality of reality, the hypercomplexity of the intellectual-sensitivity allows to go beyond the limits of the given notes, i.e. the "informed" sensitivity. Such formality of reality, rooted in the hypercomplexity of the broaden sensitivity (intellectual sensitivity), permits the apprehension of the reality itself, including the transcendence of such information, i.e. the insufficiency to determine what the sensed reality really is.

Human sensation is clearly characterized by feeling the necessity of searching beyond the given sensations. The history of science as a whole might be interpreted in this sense, including deep changes in the sensed realities, as when the dawn star is beginning to be perceived as Venus, human as an evolved primate, atoms as something particularly empty, etc.

In a lower level of intellection, the "formality of reality" can be conceived as linked to the necessity of dealing with the world when the system of signs and reactions is not enough to cope with the environmental dynamics. In an evolutionary sense, we might say that the structures of sensation evolved bringing about such formality of reality.

Information. Considering the aforementioned constraints in the manifestation of an object, information can be understood as a relational entity between the objective world and the subjective one that brings about some changes in the subject. Here subject is understood in a broad sense, in which simple systems can be included, as well as complex organism or individuals, immersed in even more complex environments.

A paradigmatic case of information is the one considered above of a field through which an object manifests to a subject, namely the observation problem. Such understanding of information requires broaden the concept of subject, just as what is being subject to the changes coming from an object (which in turn might become also subject to the changes due to the interaction). From this point of view and as we advanced in section 2, information represents a bridge between the object and the subject; between the ὄντος and the ἐπιστήμη; between the scientific world driven towards the objective world and the manifest world oriented to the subjective one.

However, according to our analysis of the nature of the manifestation of the object in its surroundings and the way this manifestation can be reflected in the subject: information is not enough to explain the changes produced; that is, there is not a causal determination chain in general. We can use the aforementioned distinction of Weizsäcker between potential and actual information to distinguish respectively the ability to cause changes and the changes already caused.

Despite the general non-deterministic causation of information, in the simplest systems, a more direct causation can be founded out. At this elementary level of system complexity, there is no difference between syntactic, semantic and pragmatic aspects (if we deal with physical systems, energy is a kind of potential information). However, in more complex systems, as the biotic ones, the syntactic aspects differentiate from the semantic-pragmatic ones, which remain together (observing a light is equivalent to beat the flagellum as to advance towards brightness). In the most evolved systems, the semantics and the semantics aspects differentiate: some kind of autonomy allows the subject to decide upon the grasped information (including the inherent ambiguity) in its epistemic realm, though in relation to some pragmatic commitments (Díaz & Pérez-Montoro, 2011a, §2.5). Due to the ambiguity of the manifestation of reality, a *heterarchical* process drives the course of causing higher-level changes under particular constraints determined by a particular pragmatic situation. Besides the concept of heterarchical systems – which allows the approach to open and adaptative systems of high complexity as biological, nervous systems and cultural systems (Bondarenko, 2007) –, this process can be understood using the concept of *analogical-digital consensus* proposed by Luis Bruni (2008). According to this concept, a determined amount of information qualified by the heterarchical structure in relation to the given situation, shall be grasped as to satisfy some threshold for a change in the higher level, for instance, 'what I am seeing is bump', or 'I will start to run to get away of a danger'. The information, grasped before the change is produced, is interpreted as analogical because it is not yet associated to a digital change. The information can be qualified as digital when the change at the higher level is produced. However the set of conditions that defines such quality is not given once and for all, but dependent of the given situation.

Such an understanding of information permits on the, one hand, to delve into the syntactic, semantic and pragmatic dimensions, on the other hand, to focus on the physical, chemical, biological, psychological, social, technical, ethical and philosophical aspects of information.

FUTURE RESEARCH DIRECTIONS

Among the scientific approaches mentioned in section 3, several of them are in progress (e.g., GTI, UTI, cybersemiotics, infocomputationalism, logical dynamics of information, situational theory…), other has the potentiality to be continued in specific fields or generalized to other fields (e.g., the objectivised semantics, the theory of measurement…).

A major pitfall for the development of a general understanding of information concerns how to articulate the relation among different theoretical frameworks in order to delve into the many aspects of information and to gain the insight provided by each approach. In the 4th International Conference on the Foundations of Information Science (celebrated in Beijin, August 2010), several proposals for reconciling the diversity of informational approaches were offered. Among them, the author (Díaz & Salto, 2011) has proposed a transversal coordination between research domains (understood as objects of investigation) and different theoretical frameworks (understood as points of view in the research of information) aimed at furthering an effective interdisciplinary in study of information. Figure 5, synthesize this proposal – showing some relevant frameworks. As complement, the creation of a virtual research community is proposed based upon electronic-

Figure 5. Articulation of research domains and theoretical frameworks in the author's proposal for interweaving the field of information studies (Díaz & Salto, 2011)

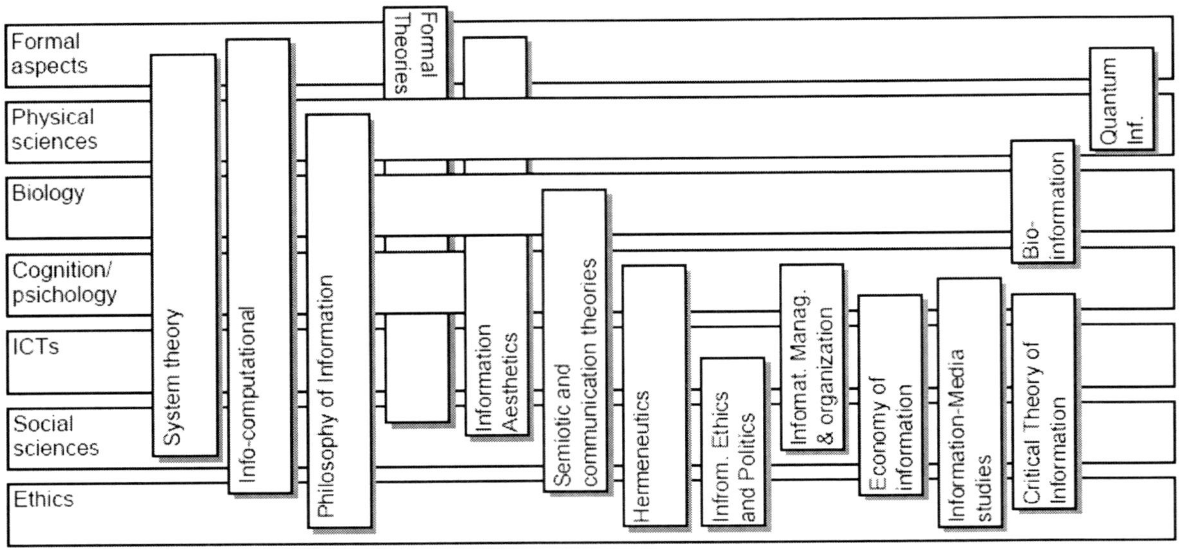

infrastructures, aimed at avoiding the problem of scientific and geographical divides.

CONCLUSION

We have posed the necessity to achieve a common understanding of information as a must in the allegedly age of information, and we have stressed the dual usage of information connected to the cultural divide of objectivist *vs* subjectivist understanding. We have also argued the necessity to supersede the methodological positivism or specialism of sciences, particularly in information concerns, since it manifests in a rich variety of fields and aspects (referred to as multi-dimensionality of information).

Seeking a comprehensive view in the forest of information theories, we have seen the variety of scopes concerning their stance with respect to: (1) the nature of information (especially in the dichotomy: objective-subjective), and (2) their coverage over the multifaceted aspects of information. Beyond the differences – which prima facie seems to be in many cases irreducible –, on the one hand, some common points has been highlighted; on the other hand, some insights on several approaches or trends has been given, which could provide a good ground for a common understanding of information.

Finally, through an inquiry in the reality of observation, we have essayed an answer to the nature of information that might provide the bridge between the objectivist and the subjectivist realms, formerly posed as a must. From the perspective achieved, information corresponds to the 'real' manifestation of the object interacting with the subject (both understood in a broader sense). Information is fundamentally characterized by its potentiality to produce changes in the subject, but it is not enough – in the general case – to understand causally the derived consequences, especially in the semantic and pragmatic dimensions. Neither is information enough to provide the intentional values, related to the object – in the case of high complexity subjects. Nonetheless, it provides a 'real' link between objects and subjects.

AUTHOR NOTE

José María Díaz Nafría, Department of Psychology, Sociology and Philosophy, Universidad de León, Spain; Director of Communications, Science of Information Institute, USA.

The matters discussed within this chapter proposal are framed into an interdisciplinary and international project aimed at the elucidation of the information concept that I coordinate since 2008 under the name BITrum (http://www.en.bitrum.unileon.es). Its name allegorically refers to the conjunction of the information unit "BIT" and *vitrum* (Latin name for the stained-glass windows in which a multiplicity of colors and nuances are assembled into a common picture). BITrum gathers over 60 European and American scholars representing a wide variety of scientific disciplines from telecommunications to philosophy, from biology to sociology, from mathematics to ethics... To date, the project has been materially supported by Spanish institutions as the Ministry of Science, the University of León and others, but it promotes several initiatives to be supported by international institutions in the European Union and abroad.

Correspondence concerning this chapter should be addressed to José María Díaz Nafría, Department of Psychology, Sociology and Philosophy, Dcho. 254, Facultad de Educación, Campus de Vegazana s/n, 24071 León, SPAIN. E-mail: jdian@unileon.es.

REFERENCES

Bar-Hillel, Y., & Carnap, R. (1953). Semantic information. *British Journal of Science*, *4*, 147–157. doi:10.1093/bjps/IV.14.147

Barwise, J., & Perry, J. (1983). *Situations and Attitudes*. Cambridge, MA: MIT Press.

Barwise, J., & Seligman, J. (1997). *Information Flows: The Logic of Distributed Systems*. Cambridge, RU: Cambridge University Press.

Bekenstein, J. D. (2003). Information in the Holographic Universe. *Scientific American Magazine*, *289*(2), 58–65.doi:10.1038/scientificamerican0803-58

Bondarenko, D. M. (2007). Approaching "complexity" in anthropology and complexity studies: The principles of sociopolitical organization and the prospects for bridging the interdisciplinary gap. *E:CO, 9(3)*, 62-74. Retrieved January 22, 2011, from http://emergentpublications.com/eco/ECO_papers/Issue_9_3_6_PH.pdf

Brier, S. (2008). *Cybersemiotics: why information is not enough*. Toronto: University of Toronto Press.

Brillouin, L. (1956). *Science and Information Theory*. New York: Academic Press.

Bruni, L. E. (2008). Hierarchical Categorical Perception in Sensing and Cognitive Processes. *Biosemiotics*, *1*(1), 113–130. doi:10.1007/s12304-008-9001-9

Bullock, A., & Trombley, S. (1999). *The Fontana Dictionary of Modern Thought* (pp. 669–737). London: Harper-Collins.

Burgin, M. (2003). Information Theory: a Multifaceted Model of Information. *Enthropy*, *5*, 146–160. doi:10.3390/e5020146

Burgin, M. (2010). *Theory of Information: Fundamentality, Diversity and Unification*. Singapore: World Scientific Publishing.

Calude C.S. and M.A. Stay (2005). From Heisenberg to Gödel via Chaitin. *Int. J. Th. Phys.*, *44*(7). 2005. pp. 1053-1065.

Capurro, R. (1978). *Information. Ein Beitrag zur etymologischen und ideengeschichtlichen Begründung des Informationsbegriffs* [Information: A contribution to the foundation of the concept of information based on its etymology and in the history of ideas]. Munich, Germany: Saur. Retrieved September 3, 2010, from http://www.capurro.de/info.html

Capurro, R. (2007). Epistemologia y ciencia de la información. *Enl@ace: Revista Venezolana de Información, Tecnología y Conocimiento, 4(1)*, pp. 11-29. Retrieved December 29, 2010, from http://www.capurro.de/enancib.htm

Capurro, R. (2009). Past, present, and future of the concept of information. *TripleC*, *7*(2), 125–141.

Capurro, R., & Hjørland, B. (2003). The Concept of Information. Retrieved September 3, 2010, from http://www.capurro.de/infoconcept.html. *Annual Review of Information Science & Technology*, *37*(8), 343–411.

Chaitin, G. J. (1966). On the length of programs for computing finite binary sequences. *Journal of the Association for Computing Machinery*, *13*, 547–569.

Chaitin, G. J. (1982a). Algorithmic Information Theory. In *Encyclopedia of Statistical Sciences*, 1, 38-41. New York: Wiley.

Chaitin, G. J. (1982b). Gödel's theorem and information. *International Journal of Theoretical Physics*, *22*, 941–954. doi:10.1007/BF02084159

Collier, J. (2011). Kinds of Information is Scientific Use. *Triple*, *C*, 9.

Comte, A. (1844). *Discours sur l'Esprit positif.* [*A general view of positivism*]. London, 1856. Retrieved September 3, 2010, from Google Books: http://books.google.com

Descartes, R. (1649). *A discourse of a method for the well guiding of reason, and the discovery of truth in the sciences*. London: Thomas Newcombe. Retrieved September 3, 2010, from Guttemberg Project: http://www.gutenberg.org/files/25830

Díaz Nafría, J. M. (2003). *Contribución en métodos inversos para la caracterización de sistemas radiantes* ("Contributions in inverse methods for the characterization of radiant systems" in Spanish). Madrid: Universidad Politécnica de Madrid. Retrieved May 2010 from Novatores: http://www.novatores.org/html/es/eprint/show.html?ePrintId=119

Díaz Nafría, J. M. (2008). The interminacy of observation. In Díaz & Salto (eds.) *¿Qué es información?* (What is information? Proceedings of the I International Meeting of Experts in Information theories. An interdisciplinar approach). León: Universidad de León, pp. 489-502. Retrieved September, 2010 from http://wp.me/pzKNC-58

Díaz Nafría, J. M. (2010a). What is information? A multidimensional concern. *TripleC*, *8*(1), 77–108.

Díaz Nafría, J. M. (2010b). Holographic principle. In Díaz, Salto and Pérez-Montoro (eds.) *Glossarium BITri: Glossary of concepts, metaphors, theories and problems regarding information.* León: Universidad de León. Retrieved September, 2010 from http://glossarium.bitrum.unileon.es

Díaz Nafría, J. M., & Aguado, J. M. (2010). Cybernetics. In Díaz, Salto, & Pérez-Montoro (Eds.). *Glossarium BITri, op. cit.*

Díaz Nafría, J. M., & Capurro, R. (2010). Hermeneitics. In Díaz, Salto, & Pérez-Montoro (Eds.). *Glossarium BITri, op. cit.*

Díaz Nafría, J. M., & Pérez-Montoro, M. (2011a). Is information a sufficient basis for cognition? (Part 1: Critique on Dretske's vision). *Triple*, *C*, 9.

Díaz Nafría, J. M., & Pérez-Montoro, M. (2011b). Is information a sufficient basis for cognition? (Part 2: physical foundations). *Triple, C*, 9.

Díaz Nafría, J. M., & Salto Alemany, F. (2011). Towards a transdisciplinary frame: Bridging domains, a multidimentsional approach to information. *Triple, C*, 9.

Dodig-Crnkovic, G., & Stuart, S. (2010). *Computation, Information, Cognition – The Nexus and The Liminal*. Cambridge, UK: Cambridge Scholars Publishing.

Dretske, F. I. (1981). *Knowledge and the flow of information*. Cambridge, MA: MIT Press.

Duhem, P. (1962). *The aim ans structure of physical theory*. New York: Atheneum.

Fenzl, N., & Hofkirchner, W. (1997). Information Processing in Evolutionary Systems. An Outline Conceptual Framework for a Unified Information Theory. In Schweitzer, F. (Ed.), *Self-Organization of Complex Structures: From Individual to Collective Dynamics* (pp. 59–70). London: Gordon and Breach.

Floridi, L. (2004). Outline of a theory of strongly semantic information. *Minds and Machines*, *14*(2), 197–221. doi:10.1023/B:MIND.0000021684.50925.c9

Floridi, L. (2005a). Information. In Mitcham, C. (Ed.), *Encyclopedia of Science, Technology and Ethics*. New York: Macmillan.

Floridi, L. (2005b). Is Semantic Information Meaningful Data? *Philosophy and Phenomenological Research*, *70*(2), 351–370. doi:10.1111/j.1933-1592.2005.tb00531.x

Floridi, L. (2005c). Semantic Conceptions of Information. In E. N. Zahlta (Ed.) *Stanford Encyclopedia of Philisophy*. Stanford: The Metaphysics Research Lab. Retrieved September 3, 2010, from http://plato.stanford.edu/entries/information-semantic/

Floridi, L. (2005d). Consciousness, Agents and the Knowledge Game. *Minds and Machines*, *15*(3-4), 415–444. doi:10.1007/s11023-005-9005-z

Flückiger, F. (2005). Mathematical Foundation of Information Theory. A Set Theoretical Approach. In Michel Petitjean (ed.) *Proceedings of FIS2005, The Third Conference on the Foundations of Information Science*.

Gitt, W. (1996). Information, Science and Biology. *Technical Journal*, *10*(2), 181–187.

Gödel, K. (1931). Über formal unentscheidbare Sätze der Principia Mathematica und verwandter Systeme. *Monatshefte für Mathematik und Physik*, *38*, 173–198. doi:10.1007/BF01700692

Günther, G. (1963). *Das Bewußtsein der Maschinen. Eine Metaphysik der Kybernetik. Krefeld/Baden-Baden*. Germany: Agis Verlag.

Heisenberg, W. (1930). *Die physikalische Prizipien der Quantentheorie*. Leipzig: Hirzel.

Hofkirchner, W. (1999a). Towards a Unified Theory of Information. The Merging of Second-Order Cybernetics and Semiotics into a Single and Comprehensive Information Science. In: *15e Congrès International de Cybernétique, Namur 1998*, Namur, pp. 175-180.

Hofkirchner, W. (2009). How to achieve a unified theory of information. *TripleC*, *7*(2), 357–368.

Huygens, C. (1690). *Traite de la Lumiere*. Leyenden. Translated to English by Thompson, S.P., London, 1912. Retrieved July, 2010 from Project Gutemberg: http://www.gutenberg.org/etext/14725

Israel, D., & Perry, J. (1990a). What is information? In Hanson, P. (Ed.), *Information, language and cognition* (pp. 1–19). Vancouver, Canada: University of British Columbia Press.

Janich, P. (1998). Informationsbegriff und methodisch-kulturalistische Philosophie. *Ethik und Sozialwissenschaften*, *2*, 169–182.

Karpatschof, B. (2007). *Human activity. Contributions to the anthropological sciences from a perspective of activity theory.* Lund, Sweden: InformationR.net. Retrieved in 12/11/09 from http://informationr.net/ir/12-3/Karpatschof/Karp00.html

Kolmogorov, A. N. (1965). Three approaches to the quantitative definition of 'information'. *Problems of Information Transmission, 1*(1), 3–11.

Kornwachs, K. (1996). Pragmatic information and System surface. In Kornwachs, K., & Jacoby, K. (Eds.), *Information. New questions to a multidisciplinary concept* (pp. 103–118). Berlin: Akademie Verlag.

Kuhn, T. S. (1962). *The Structure of Scientific Revolutions*. Chicago: University of Chicago Press.

Lakatos, I. (1978). *The methodology of scientific research.* Cambridge: Cambridge University Press.

Laudan, L. (1977). *Progress and its problems.* Berkley: University of California Press.

Leibniz, W. (orig. 1714, trans. 2007). *Monadology*. Trans. J. Bennett. Retrieved September 6, 2010 from http://www.earlymoderntexts.com/pdf/leibmon.pdf

Lemmermann, E. (1913). In Pascher, A. (Ed.), *Eugleninae* (pp. 115–174). Jena: G. Fischer.

Luhmann, N. (1987). *Soziale Systeme*. Frankfurt am Main: Suhrkamp.

Lyre, H. (1998). *Quantentheorie der Information. Zur Naturphilosophie der Theorie der Ur-Alternativen und einer abstrakten Theorie der Information. Viena*. Springer.

Lyre, H. (2002). *Informationstheorie. Eine philosophisch-naturwissenschftliche Einführung* [Theory of information. A philosophical and scientific introduction]. Munich, W.: Fink Verlag.

Mähler, G. (1996). Quantum Information. In Kornwachs, K., & Jacoby, K. (Eds.), *Information. New questions to a multidisciplinary concept* (pp. 103–118). Berlin: Akademie Verlag.

Matsuno, K. (1998). Dynamics of time and information in a dynamic time. *Bio Systems, 46*, 57–71. doi:10.1016/S0303-2647(97)00081-6

Maturana, H. R., & Varela, F. J. (1980). *Autopoiesis and congnition: the realization of the living*. Dordrecht, Netherlands: Reídle.

Morris, C. W. (1938). *Foundations of the theory of signs*. Chicago: International Encyclopaedia of Unified Science.

Oeser, E. (1976). *Wissenschaft und Information*. Vienna, Austria: Oldenbourg.

Ortega y Gasset, J. (1932). *The revolt of the masses*. New York: Norton.

PEET. (2010). The Euglenoid Project (web). Partnership for Enhancing Expertise in Taxonomy-National Science Foundation. Retrieved September, 2010 from http://euglena.msu.edu

Pérez-Montoro, M. (2007). *The Phenomenon of Information. A Conceptual Approach to Information Flow*. Lanham, Maryland: Scarecrow Press.

Quine, W. O. (1953). Two dogmas of empiricism. In *From a logical point of view*. Cambridge: Harvard University Press.

Robles-De-La-Torre G. (2006). The Importance of the Sense of Touch in Virtual and Real Environments. *IEEE Multimedia 13(3)*, Special issue on Haptic User Interfaces for Multimedia Systems: 24–30.

Robles-De-La-Torre, G., & Hayward, V. (2001). Force Can Overcome Object Geometry In the perception of Shape Through Active Touch. *Nature, 412*(6845), 445–448. doi:10.1038/35086588

Rock, I. (1984). *Perception*. New York: Scientific American Library.

Rorty, R. (1982). *Consequences of Pragmatism*. Minneapolis: University of Minnesota Press.

Schelkunoff, S. A. (1936). Some equivalence theorems of electromagnetics and their application to radiation problems. *The Bell System Technical Journal*, *15*, 92–112.

Segal, J. (2003). *Le Zéro et le Un. Histoire de la notion scientifique d'information*. Paris: Syllepse.

Sellars, W. (1962). Philosophy and the scientific image of man. In Colodny, R. (Ed.), *Frontiers of Science and Philosophy* (pp. 35–78). Pittsburgh: University of Pittsburgh Press. [Also online. Retrieved September 3, 2010, http://www.ditext.com/sellars/psim.html]

Shannon, C. E. (1949). Communication in the presence of noise. *Proc. IRE, 37(1)*, 10-21.

Shannon, C. E. (1993). *Collected Papers*. New York: IEEE Press.

Shannon, C. E., & Weaver, W. (1949). *The Mathematical Theory of Communication*. Urbana: The University of Illinois Press.

Snow, P. C. (1998). *The Two Cultures. A Second Look*. Cambridge: Cambridge University Press.

Solomonoff, R. J. (1964). A formal theory of inductive inference. *Inf. Control, (7)*, 1-22 (I part), 224-254 (II part).

Stonier, T. (1991). Towards a new theory of information. *Journal of Information Science*, *17*, 257–263. doi:10.1177/016555159101700501

Stonier, T. (1999). The Emerging Global Brain. In Hofkirchner, W. (Ed.). *The quest for a unified theory of information. Proceedings of the Second International Conference on the Foundations of Information Science*. Amsterdam: Gordon and Breach. pp. 561-578.

Susskind, Leonard (1997). Black holes and the information paradox. *Scientific American*, Special Issue "The edge of physics", April 1997, 52-57.

Treisman, A. (1996). The binding problem. *Current Opinion in Neurobiology*, *6*(2), 171–178. doi:10.1016/S0959-4388(96)80070-5

van Benthem, J. (2003). Logic and the Dynamics of Information. *Minds and Machines*, *13*(4), 503–519. doi:10.1023/A:1026296600182

van Benthem, J. (2008). Tell It Like It Is: Information Flow in Logic. *Journal of Peking University*, *1*, 80–90.

Vedral, V. (2006). *Introduction to quantum information*. Oxford, UK: Oxford University Press. doi:10.1093/acprof:oso/9780199215706.001.0001

von Foerster, H. (1981). *Observing systems*. Seaside, CA: Intersystems Publications.

Von Neumann, J. (1932). *Mathematische Grundlagen der Quantenmechanik*. Berlin: Springer.

von Weizsäcker, C. F. (1974). *Die Einheit der Natur*. Munich: Deutscher Taschenbuch Verlag.

von Weizsäcker, C. F. (1985). *Aufbau der Physik*. Munich: Hanser.

Wiener, N. (1948). *Cybernetics: Or Control and Communication in the Animal and the Machine*. Cambridge, MA: MIT Press.

Wilson, D., & Sperber, D. (1993). Linguistic form and relevance. *Lingua*, *90*, 1–25. doi:10.1016/0024-3841(93)90058-5

Zadeh, L. A. (1986). Test-Score Semantics and a Basis for a Computational Approach to the Representation of Meaning. *Literary and Linguistic Computing*, *1*(1), 24–35. doi:10.1093/llc/1.1.24

Zubiri, X. (1999). *Sentient Intelligence. Tr. by Thomas B. Fowler*. Washington: Xavier Zubiri Foundation of North America.

ADDITIONAL READING

For an introductory reading to the many aspects of information, the books of Luciano Floridi and Holger Lyre are recommended:

Floridi, L. (2010). *Information: A very short introduction*. Oxford: Oxford University Press.

Lyre, H. (2002). *Informationstheorie. Eine philosophisch-naturwissenschftliche Einführung* [Theory of information. A philosophical and scientific introduction]. Munich, W.: Fink Verlag.

Some other concise reviews of information visions in a broaden perspective can be found in the following contributions:

Capurro, R., & Hjørland, B. (2003). The Concept of Information. *Annual Review of Information Science and Technology*, Ed. B. Cronin, *37*(8), 343-411. Retrieved November 12, 2009, from http://www.capurro.de/infoconcept.html

Floridi, L. (2005). Information. In Mitcham, C. (Ed.), *Encyclopedia of Science, Technology and Ethics*. New York: Macmillan.

Probably the best historical perspectives in the evolution of the information understanding are the books of Rafael Capurro, who delve into the evolution of the information concept throughout western history of thought, and Jèrôme Segal, who explores the evolution of the scientific notion of information in the twenty century:

Capurro, R. (1978). *Information. Ein Beitrag zur etymologischen und ideengeschichtlichen Begründung des Informationsbegriffs* [Information: A contribution to the foundation of the concept of information based on its etymology and in the history of ideas]. Munich: Saur.

Segal, J. (2003). *Le Zéro et le Un. Histoire de la notion scientifique d'information* [Zero and One. History of the scientific notion of information]. Paris: Syllepse.

For deepening into the diversity of information theories, as well as in the potentiality to unite these perspectives it is highly recommended the book of Mark Burgin, where further references can be found:

Burgin, M. (2010). *Theory of Information: Fundamentality, Diversity and Unification*. Singapore: World Scientific Publishing.

Concrete overviews of the different theoretical proposals have been referenced throughout the text of this chapter. Another valuable resource for deepening into the manifold understanding of information is the *Glossarium BITri: glossary of concepts, metaphors, theories and problems concerning information*, conceived as a tool in constant growth to reflect the different points of view in information research. It has book and online editions:

Díaz Nafría, J. M., Salto, F., & Pérez-Montoro, M. (Eds.). *Glossarium BITri: Glossary of concepts, metaphors, theories and problems regarding information*. León: Universidad de León. Retrieved September, 2010, from http://glossarium.bitrum.unileon.es

KEY TERMS AND DEFINITIONS

Cybernetics: The name of this well settled scientific discipline derives from the Greek word Κυβερνήτης, which means the art of steering a ship and was used by Plato in the sense of guiding or governing men. In coherence with this Greek sense, Cybernetics nowadays refers to the study of the control and communication of complex systems, whether they are living organisms, machines or organizations, paying special attention to the feedback as the main way of regulation.

Cybernetics of the First order or Classical vs Cybernetics of the Second Order: In 1958, Heinz von Foerster conducted a critical review of

Wiener's cybernetic theory. He argued that, though this theory was introducing significant changes regarding previous conceptions of regulation and control, it did not involve an epistemological break with the traditional conception of science. As Foester criticized, the model in which the observer is able to contemplate the object or the system from outside – without perturbing it and achieving an objective knowledge of it – continued to be applied, whereas cybernetics of the fist order can be synthetized through the question: "What and how are the mechanisms of feedback of the studied system?," cybernetics of the second order raise the question: "How are we able to control, maintain and generate this system through feedback?" In the last case epistemology plays a central role, which was absent in the classical approach.

Cybersemiotics: By means of connecting Peirce's semiotics (*sign*) with the *cybernetics of the second order*, Søren Brier defines *cybersemiotics* in terms of a dynamic and contextually adaptive relationship between a sign, an object and an interpreter (Brier 2008).

General Theory of Information: In this approach proposed by Mark Burgin under the awareness of the irreducible variety of information kinds, instead of pursuing a unitary definition of information, a parametric definition is offered. By this means, information stands in a very flexible way for a capacity to cause changes in an infological system. The flexibility of these infological systems enables the adaptation of this approach to the multifaceted reality of information by means of formal models. On the other hand, this approach provides tools for measuring and evaluating information.

Infocomputionalism: In this approach proposed by Gordana Dodig-Crnkovic (2010), information is conceived as the ontological basis of the universe (its structure) whereas computation – in a broadened sense – represents its dynamics.

Interdisciplinarity: articulation of different disciplines into a common objective (scientific, technical or social), providing each one its particular point of view, contrasted with the others and therefore pursuing a mutual understanding of their respective points of view (especially concerning shared fields of interest). It does not intend to provide an integrative and unitary theoretical perspective, but (i) a good and useful articulation of perspectives to broaden the scope of the common objective; (ii) smoothing any phenomenological discrepancy at shared fields of observation; (iii) maintaining a critical stance among perspectives. It may also pursue the objective of seeking for a minimal set of primitive abstract theories (eventually one), each of them being consistent with different sets of disciplinary theories, which also contain specific components to grasp the particular reality being attended and not covered by the corresponding primitive theory. If just one unitary theory were feasible, the interdisciplinarity might converge into transdisciplinarity.

Multidisciplinarity: Articulation of different disciplines into a common objective (scientific, technical or social) through division of tasks/objectives among the partaking disciplines. The interplay between different participants must be carefully coordinated through protocols for the mutual understanding of the partial results provided by other parties. A key factor in the work division, which follows the scheme of modularity, concerns the specification of the requirements that each party must satisfy for meeting the global objective. It intends neither the mutual understanding among partaker's visions, methods or theories, nor the critical stand among parties. It just considers that the addition of the "positive" results (i.e. satisfying the validity requirements) of each discipline converge into the common objective. From this point of view, it can be branded as a "positivistic" approach to the integration of knowledge, rather pragmatically than epistemologically oriented. Interdisciplinarity and transdisciplinarity can be regarded as different levels of integration of knowledge beyond multidisciplinarity, in which the later represents the most integrative level.

Positivism: In a very wide sense, it can be understood as a doctrine attained to the relevance of the positive, i.e., what is certain, effective, true, etc. It can also be regarded as attained to what is given, in opposition to what is supposed, assumed. Thus, positivism represents a fundamental rejection of metaphysics. Although historically a wide variety of schools has been branded as positivism, two main stances can be highlighted. The first related to *Auguste Comte* who understood "positive" as a last evolutionary stage after the metaphysical one, in which the praxis is rooted on the predictions provided by a knowledge based on facts. The second referred to as *logical positivism* (also branded as empirical positivism and neopositivism) which sprang up in the Vienna Circle, and later developed within the Anglo-American philosophy as well as in the analytical tradition. This later is chiefly characterized by an anti-metaphysical inclination and the development of verification thesis.

Transdisciplinarity: Articulation of different disciplines into a common objective (scientific, technical or social), gathering each discipline into an integrative, abstract and united vision, being consistent with all the involved disciplinary theories, which are completed with specific components to grasp the particular reality being attended and not covered by the united theory. As in the case of interdisciplinarity, a critical stance among disciplines is a basis for its articulation, but in this case aiming a common theoretical frame for the smoothing of phenomenological discrepancies. The transdiciplinarity can be regarded as a principle for the unity of knowledge beyond disciplines.

Unified Theory of Information (UTI): This approach aims at a theoretical articulation embracing all processes and structures related to the creation, transformation and the crystallizing out of information in cognitive, communicative and cooperative contexts, by means of (a supposedly feasible) blending of the concepts of self-organization and semiosis. This approach has been mainly advanced by Peter Fleissner, Wolfgang Hofkirchner, Norbert Fenzl, Gottfried Stockinger and Christian Fuchs.

Chapter 4
Informationism, Information and Its Neuronal Theories

Emilia Currás
Autonomous University Madrid, Spain

ABSTRACT

In this chapter an epistemology, based in the information, as the paradigm, that rules our lives, is stated - Informationism -. Information, or perhaps the message, reaches the brain as tiny impulses - quanta or useful information -, hitting and activating the neurones; as a consequence becoming quanta of useful information which produce knowledge, science and wisdom. Some definitions of information are quoted, as well as its connotations and peculiarities. The physical, psychic and pragmatic, etc. connotations of information are studied, including its energetic aspect; within a Cosmovision of it. Some neuronal theories are also studied.

INTRODUCTION

A transmutation process is taking place in these historical times of changes in social structures, which affects all human manifestations. Considered as a whole, as an essential element, information is also affected by the transmutations that are currently taking place. The concept of information is changed and widened. For instance, Lutz Herrschaft (2000) states, in 1996, that information is an attribute, a quality from the object, an added value. Some are warned about its incoherence and the mirage it can turn out to be. However, underlying information there is a whole process typical of living beings, to adapt their existential passing to the environment in which they live; also to adapt the environment to their natural living condition. Among human beings, this process acquires very special connotations; it is an ontological process involving intelligence. Therefore intelligence, as a human faculty, plays an essential role, directly affecting information.

DOI: 10.4018/978-1-61350-201-3.ch004

Considered both as a natural phenomenon and as a dynamic and evolutionary process (Curras, 1998), information acquires a new dimension, going from the being to the environment and from the environment to the being. It is therefore an unavoidable means for the integrating process which builds up society. Alexander I. Mikhailov (1982) pointed out that society exists because information does. Without information there would be no link between individuals. These individuals are, on the other hand, doomed in fact to coexist, in an unlimited unity of universal destiny, thus articulating society (Curras, 2008).

The number of studies about information, its nature, its idiosyncrasy, its intrinsic values, its applications and economic repercussions, is increasing lately. These studies have always been carried out taking into account the essential characteristic of information, which provides its reason for being: its usefulness. Authors such as Norbert Henrichs (1997), Rafael Capurro (2000), Peter Ingwersen (1996), Jiri Cejpek (1998), J. Zeman(1994), D. Katuscák (1998), and the author of this article (Curras, 2008), have mainly based their information theory on how to make information attainable for whomever it is necessary. There is research on means and methods, either manual or computerized, to make the data present in documents accessible and useful. In all this is shown the fact that information is considered as a process; a process involving a theoretical and industrial evolution. Most of the bibliography found refers to information from this point of view. However, information includes a phenomenological connotation which has an impact on the development of individuals and on their scientific and social actions as well.

Historic Evolution

It is refer to its evolution with time, in order to place it within a historical context and be able to consider its evolution throughout the years. In the last 60 to 70 years, great changes have been observed regarding "information" as an entity of general and particular usefulness; changes in which there has been a major shift towards computerization. Information is considered to be the first link in any human activity, and even the basis to formulate an "Information Society". Bear in mind that information, as an essential element to the development of human beings, is inherent to them (McCrank, 2001) and their coexistence on Planet Earth in an associated way of life. Information society has therefore always existed; since the beginning of times. Babylonians and Egyptians, as well as later Greeks and Romans, already knew how important an adequate spreading of ideas (information) is to the development of their corresponding civilizations; holding back information sometimes, in order to manipulate their people at will. Likewise, information was considered a crucial link in wars.

Not wanting to go too far back in time, and to mention only some relevant authors, we notice Plato (427-347 BC) (Capurro, 2000) who included information in his Poetica, as part of philosophy. Poetica entails a connotation of usefulness - *note of the author: first written reference on the usefulness of information that has ever been found* -. Poetica also refers to its pedagogical aspect. Around the same period of time, as far as Aristotle (384-322 BC) (Capurro, 2000) is concerned, the soul and intelligence can be formed through information; thus granting it an ontological nuance: "life comes from life". He also states that the concept of "information" comes from in-form which is equivalent to give-form - "morphe" in Greek means form -; con-form. This derivation of the concept passed on later to the Roman world: "Information is and is not, but it allows it to be" (Titus Lucretius Carus, s. I b.C, "La Naturaleza"(Lucrecio, 2003)). From Roman it has been taken for Romance languages like Castilian (Spanish).

The influence of Greek philosophy can be seen on Saint Augustine (354-430 AD) (Cappuro, 2000), and later on Saint Tomas D'Aquino (1225-1275 AD)(Cappuro, 2000). They both emphasize the ontological value of information, giving the first priority to the soul. There is a great deal of references to the concept of information coming from learned authors from the Middle Age, such as San Isidoro de Sevilla, Albert Magnus, Maimónides, Santo Toribio de Liébana, Alfonso X the Wise and many others that should be discussed in another paper. Moving on to the Modern Era now, one must quote Descartes (1596-1650 AD) (Curras, 1993). In his famous statement "I think, therefore I am", he grants an absolute value to human thinking, valid by itself; which confers nature to the being. This "thinking" is reached through a process of assimilation of information producing knowledge. The point of view of Cristoph Martin Wieland (1733-1813 AD) (Capurro, 2000) which deals with information, with the understanding and the information of the heart, is also interesting.

In the Oxford English Dictionary, there is a great deal of definitions for information, dating from the XIV century. Apart from pointing out information as an element to form the mind, to teach and to learn, it mentions its function as an advice, as a warning; as well as in legal terms. The "Diccionario Enciclopédico Abreviado", published by Espasa Calpe, gives the same characteristics and attributes to the concept.

Evolution in the XIX, XX and XXI Centuries

Going up to the XIX and XX centurian, authors such as Dewey, Paul Otlet, Henri La Fontaine, Husserl, etc. come up. These authors mainly focussed on "documentation", considering information as a subsidiary, auxiliary element; as a consequence of the "documentary" process. There was even a period, already in the XX century, during which information was mistaken with knowledge. Jason Farradane (Curras, 1998), already a classic amongst them, marked the difference between knowledge, information and information science. Still in 1997, Greame Johannson (Curras, 1990) made a distinction between information, knowledge and research. It has been discussed how the first is the driving force to the rest. Likewise, during the XX century, data was mistaken with message and information. I have dealt with clarifying this subject in various papers (Curras, 1990) myself. It is very interesting to consider the authors from former Czechoslovakia, who have been pioneer in some aspects. (Cejpek, 1995)

The truth is that the amount of studies about information has been increasing throughout the XX century, sometimes arousing controversy about whom, when and how these have been carried out. Important debates have even arisen about the origins of the word "information". It has even been said that it was created by a columnist from New York. One of the most recent works treating the concept of information is the one whose authors are R. Capurro and B. Hjorland (2003). In a general sense, it may be pointed out that, once information was seen as an entity in itself, around the 60's of the XX century, studies started to be carried out about its nature, properties, influences and uses. Information is being granted an aim, as a way to know and provide the contents of the documents. Also at these times, its physical and ontological components started to be discussed, which implies carrying out studies related to psychology, pragmatic, sociology, ontogeny, phylogeny, philosophy, metaphysics... It may have been the end of the 80's of the XX century - one has to be cautious with these statements -, when its neurological connotations started to be studied as such - neuronal assimilation -, along with its connection with theology (Henrichs, 1994) and hermeneutics (Capurro, 1989).

Perhaps a little earlier, at the end of the 70's of the same century, a relationship is established, in the context of information sciences (Curras, 1998), between information and the inscrutable theories of Hermes Trismegisto, the ones by Karl Popper, the Pensática, and the philosophic theories of knowledge themselves. This is also the period in which the impact of information in subsequent attitudes and activities was studied in detail. For instance, it was added to it a connotation of intentionality (Wersig, 1971), of receiver's will for understanding and, obviously, of its value for the industrial and economical world, as well as for business organization. All these studies are carried out at the same time as the development of computerized communication techniques, the computer science, and all that is related to computational science (Capurro, 2000).

"INFORMATION", WHAT IS IT?

I start by saying that it is both "everything" and "nothing" at the same time. On the one hand, it is indeed "everything", due to the fact that, through its mental or physical use, one can reach knowledge; and from that, taking as an example its most pragmatic sense, research, science, wisdom and the truth - objective, relative and conditioned truth -. From this reasoning, it can be concluded that information has a transcendental connotation, given that, following the same line of thought; from truth one can reach evidence and certainty. Finally, wisdom would be reached. Information will also be "everything", when its use in the fields of economy or industry is considered. On the other hand, with the idea that information is "nothing", one refers to its properties: intangible, abstract, inexhaustible, non contaminant and recyclable. It cannot be touched; however, it is there. It is there, as a result of a human process, carried out within human brains, and composed of the following stages: seizure, comprehension, storage, adaptation, perception, understanding, response capacity. The response takes shape into ideas production. Through a new process of development, of new assimilation, where conscious or perhaps unconscious reasoning takes place; knowledge production is finally reached, knowledge that may be useful or not.

However, the logical question would be to ask oneself what this "human process" may be (Curras, 1983). According to Krumholz (2004), the internal brain mechanisms capable of assimilating external impulses, and producing the subsequent information, are not yet known. There seem to exist "dark regions", impossible to reach with the current research methods. Nevertheless, many authors have conceived different theories. On the one hand, we are told that, first, the meaning is reached; and then, through a sensory transformation within our brain, we reach knowledge. On the other hand, it is mentioned that, from stimulus from the outside world reaching the brain, an inner world is elaborated. An ontogenic principle is assumed, since the resulting inner world is subjective, depends on receiver's idiosyncrasy, and on his cultural, environmental and social background. In several of his papers, Professor Kaula (2002) states that information has a human nature as well as an influential one, regarding the building of its knowledge, which is also human. Many other points of view could be quoted on the subject.

Information in Its Definitions

Throughout the years, there has always been a need and concern for knowing what we refer to by information. There are many definitions in the bibliography of all times. In certain definitions, one can notice an anthropological and ontogenic sense, involving a characteristic that affects the influence of information on human beings, as well as its connotations and behaviours. In other definitions is stated its practical and pragmatic nature, which results in proceedings for information processing, mainly by computerized methods, to supply the information - maybe the message - to whoever needs it.

Hereafter, the definitions given by some information specialists are quoted. Through them can be deduced what information "may be", in its primary nature. In the Oxford English Dictionary one reads that information is the communication of knowledge, as an informative "thing", and it gives the example of a newspaper, which produces information. Similarly, Michael Buckland (1991) states information must be considered as a "thing" to generate informative data - note of the author -; that is, it refers to "information processing, or data processing". As far as Fred I. Dretske (1987) is concerned, information includes a perceptive, sensory process on the one hand; and a cognitive process on the other hand. Sensory information is an analogical phenomenon, and conscious information is a digital phenomenon. Michael Hill (Curras, 1998) defines information through its causes, given that it is through information that we perceive and receive the outside world, giving us the chance of making decisions and expressing judgements. To Rafael Capurro (2003), there is a controversy between the definition coming from cybernetics, and another coming from the field of sociology (language, culture). He also writes (Capurro, 2000) that information has an anthropological nature, as a non-human process of being.

Norbert Henrichs (1994) relates information technology to human beings when he mentions that, because of its use, the human being discovers he is somehow an information processing system... Human intellectual activity will be influenced by machines... Also, this author defines information as an exchangeable knowledge and as a process through which, starting from an informative base, one can obtain raw material on the one hand, and energy on the other hand (synonymous of usefulness). To Lawrence McCrank (2001), information is a compound data structured for its interpretation; but it can also be seen as something apart from interpretation in itself. The Slovakian authors D. Katuscák, M. Matthaeidesová and M. Nováková (Krumholz, 2004), consider information from a realistic point of view. They consider it is a reflection of reality, both in its conventional sense, and in the scope of its use. As far as Silveira Zaragoça is concerned (1980), information is a physical act, followed by psychical act. The physical act is supposed to be the message, whereas the psychical act corresponds to the perception and assimilation activities of the mind. Many more definitions could be quoted here, since every researcher priding himself on being a scientist and specialist formulates some definition of information.

Information as a Phenomenon, and as a Process

When the definitions above are examined thoroughly, one can notice, on the one hand the tendency of considering information as a process (phenomenon) that often modifies, or has an influence, in the state of knowledge of the human being. On the other hand, a (physical) process is mentioned, in which take part its usefulness and its use, applying processes that are most of the times computerized and high-tech related. In other words, information is some times presented as a "phenomenon" and others as a "process". Therefore, the difference between both can be established considering:

- Information as a *phenomenon*
  - Which is takes place around us, independently of ourselves, and which we receive conscious or unconsciously.
  - Produced by the environment of our noosphere, which surrounds us and gives shape to the development of our daily activities.
- Information as a *process*
  - Developed by us, from some documents, for its subsequent use.
  - As a consequence of an information science process that consciously affects the activities of human intellect; and which reverberates in the development of mankind, in its scientific, technical, or artistic aspects.

Data and Message

Let us now move on to the level of real and tangible things. It must be admitted that, for knowledge to have a given consistency, it needs to be supported by something also real and tangible, such as a sheet of paper, a floppy disk, a hertz wave, etc., forming thus a document which can also, nowadays, take many different formats. If we consider the idea as the first product of the brain activity, at a practical level this concept will also need to have a tangible support in order to become a "useful knowledge", which is itself composed by small portions forming a whole. These portions have come to be called "*data*".

The data therefore corresponds to a quantum (Curras, 1990) of knowledge, which is coherent, objective, neutral and without value. In a different level, L. McCrank (2001) thinks that "data" is what is given by the unit itself, from the digit to the line, forming a compound of lines and bits. They cannot be counted or collected. They are not acts, and they do not constitute any evidence by themselves. They are the raw material to build a piece of information.

When a given value, scientific, economic or artistic, etc, is added to the data, it becomes a "*message*". This is the definition adopted in this paper for the concept of message, because it is in agreement with the text that is written and discussed. There are obviously other definitions for the concept of message, considered from different points of view, such as linguistic, semiotic, philosophic, economic, and several others.

From this we deduce that, in order to have useful information, either the data or the message need to leave the document, and then be put at the disposal of whoever may need it. In general and wide terms, this would be the duty of "information science": "ciencias de la información"; o "ciencias de la documentación" ("documentation science"), terminology coined by the author and used in Spain.

Important Characteristics

There is a basic attribute for information to be considered as such, that has not been explicitly mentioned so far, although indirectly it has been. That is its usefulness. It has been said that Plato included information in his "Poetica", precisely where this characteristic was granted to it. Therefore, information must be useful; it has to get out from wherever it is, and reach a receiver... It can be deduced from this that information cannot be innate, intangible, imperceptible and endless... or can it?

When the empirical-practical value of information is studied, the concept is granted with a linguistic, philosophical and neuronal origin. To Alwin Diemer (1975), information is the vehicle for the circulation, transfer, evaluation and application of knowledge. In this sense, we consider it is an element of transmission of culture (Curras, 1985), bringing peoples together, in a globalizing and universalizing sense. However, in order to have information it is not sufficient with the data leaving the document, and one expecting it to be used. It also needs to be emitted, transmitted, perceived, understood and interpreted (Curras, 1998; Wersig, 1971)To Harm Glashof(Curras, 1998), there is a difference between the processes of understanding, comprehending and knowing. Each of them involves a higher complexity in the corresponding brain processes. To this author, the simplest, easiest one is the concept of knowing something, an object or idea... In a more complex state of reasoning one gets to understand; and adding one more stage of higher complexity, the capacity of comprehending is reached.

Nowadays, in the economic and industrial fields, information has acquired a great relevance. It is not considered anymore as something secondary, marginal, and insignificant. Economical principles are used today, in which information is considered to be a raw material, an added value, a consumer good, a currency producer, a form of energy (driving force, in the mechanical, intellectual and social senses), and even as grey gold (Curras, 1998). Norbert Henrichs (1994) gives also a social value to information, when he considers it is crucial to the education of peoples, especially the least developed ones, to the elimination of cultural barriers, to establish a bridge between cultures and eliminate the barbaric behaviour of peoples. Also (Henrichs, 2001), this author considers information can have an effect on production; on the one hand creating work, and on the other giving rise to capitalism. Acting on knowledge, information creates raw materials and energy. L. McCrank (2001) grants information a positive attribute, and a value he assumes as true.

Ontological Aspects

Thus, information is inherent to human beings. It is necessary for their development, both at individual and at species level. It is thought that there is an innate genetic information, which is brought at birth by the individual itself - note of the author - and is therefore naïve, and unintentional (Curras, 1984). According to the argument that information has an influence in human development, John McHale (McHale, 1981) mentions it is information that will give us the opportunity of learning how to become human beings. Along this same line of thought, information is supposed to be neutral, without value. It is the individual who, depending on his set of values, chooses certain behavioural criteria.

I also granted information an ontogenic connotation, including it in the same category as vital elements such as water, earth, etc; given that it is considered the fourth vital element (Curras, 1985). An "information route" is outlined, in parallel with the silk route, silver route, gold route, black gold route and so on. Throughout the centuries, such route has turned out to be cyclic; given that it had its origin in the East, continued towards the West and, after going around the world, it has come back to the East. Things have changed, nowadays. Due to communication technologies, the World has become smaller and, in a way, more homogeneous. As a result of this, information does not have a circular motion anymore, but a translational one; horizontal, vertical and multidirectional and global.

Cosmic Information and Its Energy Aspects

Human beings are at the same time on Planet Earth, and immerse in a complex, scattered and changing Universe, from which it constantly receives influxes; which in turn means receiving information. One can therefore speak about *cosmic information*, within the Omnicosmos (Curras, 2008). So far, this cosmic information is quite unknown of, although indeed known by intuition, due to its influence both physical and on the state of mind. One can predict it can be perceived in an imperceptible way. Its effects and peculiarities are also unknown and unappreciable, except from in so-called cases of intuition and foretelling.

Information is therefore being considered as a form of energy (Curras, 1998). Its energetic nature is interesting, deduced for instance from papers by N. Henrichs (2001), which get to the conclusion that information is a property of Universe. To Paulo Manzelli (1991), there is a matter-energy-information relationship. It is known that matter is a "condensed" form of energy, which gradually breaks down into a lighter, more manageable form of "energy". At the same time energy breaks down into something more scattered, subtle, manageable, which is supposed to be information. Naturally, through consecutive breaks down of matter into energy, and then into information, a time would come when the World and the Universe would only consist of information and... it would obviously die. This will never become true, given that there is also an inverse motion, such as: matter-energy-information-matter... and then start all over again, although not at the same level. This level could in fact be either higher or lower. A cosmic connotation of information is observed as well. In this sense, information can even be considered as a *catalyst* (Cobos, Alaman, Esquivel, 2001) for evolutionary processes. With respect to the cosmic dimension of information, within the Omni cosmos it belongs to the *meso cosmos* (Curras, 1981), which is between the macro and micro cosmos. Regarding the point of view of information as a human product, it is included in the *noosystems* (Curras, 1993).

In the end, "nothing without information, and everything because of it".

Quanta of Useful Information

From what is written above, it can be deduced that these opinions and points of view are somewhat imprecise and incoherent, since they do not get to the core of the matter... it is said that... there is a process... caused by... The explanation occurred to me when the neuropsychologist José Manuel Rodríguez Delgado (Curras, 2008) returned to Madrid with his neurological theories. In these theories was stated the fact that impulses from the outside are received by neurones, which thus start their activity. In other words, neurones are activated, giving the individual – the human being – a higher reasoning capacity and intelligence. Each generation will be more intelligent than the previous one, given that it is receiving a continuous and abundant flow of information. This seems to hold true, if we take into account the discoveries and inventions that continually follow one another. The famous sentence of Rodriguez Delgado "knowledge does take up space" has gone around the world.

Everything became clear. The signals coming from outside the brain formed small "*quanta of information*", which were immediately followed by the *processes mentioned* above, to develop knowledge; and subsequently, ideas becoming "quanta of useful information". And this is a phenomenon that has been occurring since Man became Man, or maybe even before that. Helmut Anntz (1983) affirms hominid became human exactly due to the consecutive reception and assimilation of information, reaching its brain from the outside, from its environment.

Neuronal Theories of Information

Therefore, we know information is processed - neuronal assimilation - when certain impulses, or quanta of useful information, reach the brain; thus giving rise to knowledge: a useable product. Several authors have done research on this significant subject, and have developed different theories which I can today describe as "neuronal theories of information".

In order to study some neuronal theories, one has to go back to the middle of the XX century, when C. E. Shannon published his Theory of Information (Shanon & Weaver, 1949), which can be considered as the starting point. Somewhat later, in 1988, I had the satisfaction of releasing my theory of the quanta of useful information (Curras, 1988). Since then, many different theories, of many different kinds, have been developed. Most of them try to find some parallelism between the processes occurring in the brain and the mechanisms carried out by computers; in accordance with some programmes prepared beforehand, in order to have the machine carrying out the function for which it is manufactured – by human beings – note of the author. Some authors think the process has been carried out the other way round; i. e. it was the machines operation that induced the thought of a similar operation in the brain. In any case, these theories have been developed by different specialists and researchers of the field of information science.

In order to study the mentioned process of neuronal assimilation, we will expound some relevant opinions, considered as the starting point of subsequent researches. On the one hand, John McHale (1981) considers information is a consumer good, which humans should use in their benefit and to obtain better living standards. He assumes living beings use their senses to collect information from the environment, and the difference between human beings and the other living beings is that man can "process" information consciously; humans use a system of symbols to communicate with fellow men. The author also mentions the changing and changeable environment of information - note of the author -, since he assumes that it is due to its influence and use that our life conditions, basic principles, cultural manifestations and so on vary. The use of information to a greater or lesser extent measures the level of evolution of human race. More informed societies will have more possibilities for choice.

On the other hand, Fred I. Dretske (1987) grants information a holistic, primal and basic nature. He states that, in the beginning, there was information; and the world came after it. The transition, perhaps better transmutation – note of the author –, was carried out through the development of organisms with the ability of exploiting information in a selective way, with the purpose of being able to survive and endure as a species. Information reaches the brain and affects and activates the neurones. For a reaction to happen, the brain needs a reference scale; which is built through consecutive information reaching it from the outside world. These theories seem somehow incoherent to me, since the question about the origin of information arises. If the world has risen from information, perhaps the idea of an all-embracing creator loses strength... or is information then the creator?

Another interesting researcher is Thomas J. Froelich (1988), who deals with information as an element to develop knowledge, subsequently studying the latter. He states thought is not absolute; it depends on the nature of each individual, on its reference system and on its set of values. Nothing new so far; but he carries on with the statement that thought can always and only be valid from the point of view of the individual thinking it. Therefore the famous sentence of Descartes needs to be inverted, thus considering: "I am, therefore I think". Thinking is a human activity, and it implies information as an element, cause and effect. This activity grants a social function to thinking. Each society - social group - creates a different form of knowledge and thought.

Some Outstanding Theories

Similarly, the theories of R. M Bergstrom (1988) are interesting. According to him, humans behave as a communication system, at the centre of which is the brain. Here, the signals are received from the outside and emitted to the outside. Information is supposed to be the raw material to develop these abilities. The author also states one needs to make the difference between information and the processing of it. There is a reference to this above, when the difference between considering information as a "phenomenon" or as a "process" has been mentioned. Through subsequent reasoning, the difference between "information" and "information science" can be established. As several other authors maintain, Bergstom compares the brain with the machine - perhaps the computer -, stating that information is the raw material driving both, and thus comparing information with energy. The informative capacity of the brain, within the brain structure, is estimated to be generated at approximately $10^9_{\text{bits/sec}}$. However, when it reaches the conscious level it is only about 100 $_{\text{bits/sec}}$, which means there is a loss of $10^7_{\text{bits/sec}}$ when going from the physiological to the psychological level. Human beings have the capacity for a higher brain development; to be more intelligent. The mechanism to go from the sphere of the "unconscious" to the sphere of the "conscious" (Krumholz, 2004) is missing.

The theories of Brier (1996) will now be considered. He deals with the interpretation of the message, different from the information; in order to make it understandable and comprehensible by the receiver. The brain, together with the machine, is responsible for this comprehension, in which a cognitive process is included. Brier, together with M. Leupolt (1978, 1981) and other researchers, within whom I am included, (Curras, 1984) is of the opinion that this cognitive process should be extended to every living being, i. e. plants and animals.

Alexander King (1989) assumes there is a series of phenomena, events and stages of understanding, each of them at a higher and more complex level of abstraction, in order to reach the "knowledge" of the world we live in, and to adapt our acts to this world. Information is in every one of these stages, either as a base or as a vehicle to pass from one level to the other. These theories are actually shared nowadays by several specialists and researchers. What was new about them was the historic moment in which they appeared. Alexander King was one of the pioneers, and he is well known for his many works and papers.

The principal theories of Norbert Henrich (1994) have been discussed earlier. It is worth mentioning here his interest in the creative ability of human beings, which enables them to reach science, and therefore wisdom. This author also focuses on the spiritual attributes of information and, to a certain degree, grants it theological connotations. Another of his research interests is the study of the sensory, visual, tactile, acoustic information and so on, as opposed to textual information (Henrichs, 2001). Rafael Capurro (2000) has published a paper about the introduction to the concept of information. It actually is an essay about information in itself. It is understood that he is concerned about the origin, meaning, transcription and representation of the concept of information. His theory on "Hermeneutics" (Capurro, 1989), which has been widely spread and known, should be taken into account.

Amongst other opinions and research are the ones from the theories of Peter Ingwersen (1995), we could stress those in which research is considered as the result of a modification of the structures of knowledge of whom receives the information - supposedly a human being -. He also deals with the concept of information, which he considers is limited by the influence of linguistics, pedagogy, sociology, psychology and computer science.

From either point of view, neuronal theories are based on the same principles and follow almost identical reasoning. Perhaps A. N. Leontiev (Curras, 1983) contributes with something new, by relating information with conscience, and assuming information is in fact the way in which conscience exist for the others. Apart from that, information is the link between individuals; obviously in a process of communication.

Informationism: Primary Theories

After what has been written until now, it would seem unnecessary to continue justifying the possibility to formulate a new epistemology or a theory of knowledge based on *information* as *paradigm*: *informationism*. However, it may be convenient to establish relationships with other theories on knowledge organization, in order to observe perhaps the parallelism between these and information, taken now as a mental process.

On the one hand, information arrives into the brain, and activates a mental process which starts with the seizure, reaching the knowledge and then the comprehension, to end up with a total understanding of whatever was involved by the information in the origin. All this implies a process of organization of knowledge itself. On the other hand, information is considered to be the connecting thread which affects the brain of human beings, helping them to form their intelligence. Each historical period has based its knowledge theories (Curras, 1981) on a different principle, which is itself influenced by the stage of mankind evolution. Similarly, the philosophical trends being studied by men through different viewpoints have had an influence; different theories have thus risen, such as causalism, empiricalism, positivism, historicism, physicism and so on.

The relationships that may be applied between some of these known theories and information are now considered. Firstly, "causalism" which states there is no effect without a cause: effect = quanta of useful information reaching the brain; cause = knowledge. *Realism* states that real objects are the base for knowledge. Here, and idea corresponds to an object, and the former has its origin in information, which will thus become the object. *Positivism* is the theory which matches the best. It was devised by August Comte (Curras, 1993), and based on the concept that only the facts, immediately received by the senses and quantitatively verified, can generate knowledge. This author also allows for a social attitude, given that the perception of the outside world may condition our behaviour.

In the past times, perhaps since 1980 to mention a guiding date, the chemical and spiritual components of human beings have been being considered; this implies a change in the postulation of such theories. A modern theory of knowledge has subsequently risen, based on the principle of "get to know yourself", which has lately gained great importance. Such principle studies and examines within human beings, both physical and psychologically, in a neo-realistic attempt to turn the activities of the spirit into mere equations, and chemical and physical formulae; arguing that human being is formed by chemical elements and compounds.

More recently, a turn towards a more humanizing position is being observed. Let us for instance quote Fernando de Elzaburu (1987), whom bases his theory of knowledge organization on the change of paradigm of his new "vision of reality". We live in a transmutation period, and therefore old reference parameters are no longer valid. Other more highly abstracted parameters, based on systems theory, should be accepted. Norbert Henrichs (1994) also develops his theory from a change of paradigm, by adding a phylo-theological connotation to information, based on obtaining "wisdom" - more complex than "knowledge" -; subjective and relative knowledge, since it is human, but objective and absolute with respect to its relationship with science - note of the author -. Jirî Cejpek's (1998) sets his paradigm on human conscience, as a psycho-physical phenomenon carried out in the brain when it receives information. Many other formulations, by many other authors, and deducible from the ones already mentioned, could be quoted here.

Informationism: A New Theory of Knowledge

Even though it is widely admitted that we are currently living in the Age of Communication, given that information flows back and forth through communication; it is obvious that information surrounds and invades us. Not even on a desert island could we escape its influence. Information is the basis for any human activity, for all our reasoning, the origin of any social attitude; it is the base... It is the base to formulate a theory of knowledge, which takes *information* as fundamental *paradigm*, and which I call *"Informationism"*.

On the one hand, Informationism (Curras, 1981 & 1983) entails an *optimistic viewpoint,* through the belief that a more equal and homogeneous world can be achieved, if its paradigms are correctly applied. On the other hand it implies a *waiting* and *hoping* attitude, given that it implies an *uncertainty* before *the truth* is revealed. Informationism also assumes a functional principle for thinking, *philosophic* and *scientific* activity, with its repercussion on scientific development. Moreover, it affects daily activities, such as *trade* and *industry*. Its influence can be observed in *moral* and *cultural* behaviours. It also has an effect on *pragmatic* activities such as *decision-making*, for instance. Having an attitude based on Informationism means perceiving the world from a higher level, on which a broader range of concepts is observed; a *higher level of abstraction*.

Informationism is an *objective* in itself. It relies, in each particular case, on real and objective reasoning, based on the existence of also real and objective information, hence true information. Therefore, Informationism is also *true* and *real*. These rather deterministic attitudes; stating a totalitarian view of information as the seed of "all" that happens in the Universe, within which is Planet Earth and the rest of the Cosmos, leads one to consider Informationism from its *pantheistic* aspect, of *globalizing* connotations, considering this as a positive view. Informationism can thus be considered to have *positivistic attributes*.

It is deduced that Informationism can be described as *human, objective, realistic, optimistic, globalizing, philosophical, scientific, pragmatic, real, terrestrial, cosmic... pantheistic*; all "good" qualities anyway.

In any case, it can be stated that the *Informationism era* has arrived.

CONCLUSION

We live in a constantly evolving world, which leads to a continuous transmutation as well. In the past forty years or so, to set some date, there have been greater transmutations than in the fifty previous years. Information technology has been the cause of all this change. What an amazing change in the way we do some research, write some conference, or send a letter to a friend! Machines and electronic devices would not have gained such importance in our lives... if it was not for the influence of a driving force... towards change. Here is just where information has its place, exactly in this driving force, which is mainly determined by two specific factors: quantity on the one hand, and speed on the other, in which human beings are immersed. We are in a hurry to do everything; even, or maybe due to that, to control the amount of information surrounding us.

Ours is a changing world, influenced by information. It is information itself which leads us to understand that our fields of consideration; our points of view must be broadened. Everything is related to everything; and to be able to distinguish what captures the relevance, the attention or the interest, a higher degree of abstraction needs to be reached. Things need to be looked upon from higher above; a higher level of thought needs to be reached... till a cosmovision... with higher level of abstraction.

Information is a term that is used for everything; for nearly everything that is related to something, mainly in communication processes, whichever these are. In a few words, information is a term used by everyone. But is it really known what it stands for? In this paper there is an attempt to clarify some concepts and opinions. There is also an attempt to discuss about information from different points of view, such as its nature, its social connotations, its influence on the philosophical theories about knowledge organization, etc. Only few studies have considered information in itself. Its application in order to process messages, documents, reports and so on has much greater relevance. It is the so called "information science" that attracts all the attention of both pragmatic and technical specialists and researchers. And... what information is remains unknown.

In order to carry out a somewhat detailed study on what information may be, I have searched opinions from some researchers and specialists. Going back in time, there are very many and varied definitions to be found. In the first periods, information is granted a philosophical, moral and practical value, which has social and cultural influences. Later, studies on its nature, psychological and ontological connotations, etc, appeared; all of them significant. Likewise, its social, cultural, economical, industrial aspects are studied.

Since the appearance of information was shown up: due to the influence on the brain of impulses coming from the outside - quanta of useful information -, thus reaching the neurones and activating them, nearly all definitions found consider this aspect; appearing then the anthropological, neurological, biological, ontogenical, epistemological, and theological connotations. Regarding this, our colleague A. García Gutiérrez

(1990) mentions *"bioinformation"*. We are warned that human beings have a right to information. Yet, we are also warned about its illusion and incoherence. Throughout this paper, all this is shown up.

The influence of information on the cultural development of societies can be noticed in several sections here examined. The reflection of reality within our mind is mentioned, and some Slovakian authors (Krumholz, 2004) are quoted, due to the novelty and progress involved in the incorporation of other ways of thinking in these countries. Information, as an all-times route of civilization (Currás, 1985), is also analyzed. It is supposed to belong to the mesosystem, within the noosystems. And there is also here an induction to consider the validity of *Informationism*: a new *epistemological theory*, based on the *paradigm of the universality of information*.

A *new area of Knowledge* is emerging, independent in itself, but systemic and vertically related to the rest of the scientific areas of knowledge; that is to say, Information itself as a science in itself.

Finally, it is deduced that information is a science for science, and a science of science ; that is, it acquires the characteristic of an *Aristoscience* (Curras, 1998).

REFERENCES

Arntz, H. (1983). *Information und Hominisation: Grenzlinie der Entwicklung. Vorstudie zu einer Paläologie der Information*. The Hague: FID 627.

Bergstrom, R. M. (1988). Man as an Information Processor. In P. Hämäläinen, B. Koskkiala, & A.J. Repo (Eds.), *44th FID Conference and Congress records book* (pp. 7-9). Helsinki: FID.

Brier, S. (1996). Cybersemiotics. A New Interdisciplinary Development Applied to the Problems of Knowledge Organization and Document Retrieval in Information Science. *The Journal of Documentation*, *52*(3), 296–344. doi:10.1108/eb026970

Buckland, M. (1991). Information as Thing. *Journal of the American Society for Information Science American Society for Information Science*, *42*(5), 351–360. doi:10.1002/(SICI)1097-4571(199106)42:5<351::AID-ASI5>3.0.CO;2-3

Capurro, R. (1989). *Hermeneutik der Fachinformation*. Freiburg: Alber.

Capurro, R. (2000) *Einführung In Den Informationsbegriff. I Kapitel: Der Informationsbegriff in den Informationswirtschaft*. Retrieved July 5, 2011, from http://www.capurro.de/infovorl-kap1.htm

Capurro, R. (2000). *Einführung In Den Informationsbegriff. II Kapitel: Der Informationsbegriff in der Informationswissenschaft*. Retrieved July 5, 2011, from http://www.capurro.de/infovorl-kap2.htm

Capurro, R. (2000): *Einführung In Den Informationsbegriff. IV Kapitel: Zur Geschichte des Informationsbegriffe*. Retrieved July 5, 2011, from http://www.capurro.de/infovorl-kap4.htm

Capurro, R., & Hjørland, B. (2003). The concept of information. [ARIST]. *Annual Review of Information Science & Technology*, *37*, 343–411. doi:10.1002/aris.1440370109

Cejpek, J. (1995). Aportaciones checas a la ciencia de la información. *AABADOM*, *2*(April-June), 4–7.

Cejpek, J. (1998). *Informace, komunikace a mysleni: Uvod do informacni vedy*. Prague: Karolinum.

Cobos, R., Alamán, X., & Esquivel, J.A. (2001). KnowCat: Catalizador de conocimiento. KnowCat: Knowledge Catalyser. *RedIRIS, Boletín de la red nacional de I+D. Nº 58-59 (December 2001 - January 2002)*, 7-10.

Currás, E. (1981). ¿Estaremos en la Época del Informacionismo? *Rev. Univ. Complutense*, *2*, 186–188.

Currás, E. (1983). Ciertos Principios Científico-Filosóficos de las Ciencias de la Documentación. *Rev. Univ. Complutense, 1*(4), 83–88.

Currás, E. (1984). Moral and Social Implications of the New Technologies in Information Science. In Van Der Laan, A., & Winters, A. (Eds.), *The Use of Information in a Changing World* (pp. 417–432). Amsterdam: FID Publications.

Currás, E. (1985) La Información como Cuarto Elemento Vital y su Influencia en la Cultura de los Pueblos. *Toletum. Año LXIX, 2ª época, 20,* 27-46.

Currás, E. (1988). *Aktuell Probleme der Information. Inst. für Informationswissenschaft, Erfindungwesen und Patentrechts. Technische Universität, Ilmenau.* Typed text.

Currás, E. (1990). *El Dato Informativo en la Industria Alimentaria.* Paper presented at Congreso Internacional de Tecnología y Desarrollo Alimentario, Murcia, Spain.

Currás, E. (1993). The influence of System Science on the concept of Information. *ICS Innovazione, Comunicazione, Sviluppo, anno V, 3,* 5-6.

Currás, E. (1998). *La información en sus nuevos aspectos*. Madrid: Paraninfo.

Currás, E. (2008). *Ciencia de la información bajo postulados sistémicos y sistemáticos*. Madrid: edición personal.

Currás, E. (2008). Interacción Dialéctica en la Ciencia. In E. Currás (Ed.), *Ciencia de la información bajo postulados sistémicos y sistemáticos* (pp. 37-50). Madrid: edición personal.

Diemer, A. (1975). Information Science: a new science. *Problems of Information Science*, 192-203.

Dretske, F. (1987). *Conocimiento e información*. Barcelona: Salvat.

Elzaburu, F., & Martintegui, J. (1987). *De la incertidumbre a la esperanza*. Madrid: AINPA.

Froehlich, T. (1988). Relevance and the relevance of social epistemology. In P. Hämäläinen, B. Koskkiala, & A.J. Repo (Eds.), *44th FID Conference and Congress records book* (pp. 9-19). Helsinki: FID.

García Gutiérrez, A. (1990). *La estructura lingüística de la documentación*. Murcia: Universidad de Murcia.

Henrichs, N. (1994). Informationswissenschaft als angewandte Antropologie: Der Düsseldorfer Ansetz. In Saur, K. G. (Ed.), *Bucher für die Wissenschaft* (pp. 445–461). Munchen: Festschrift für Günter Gattermann.

Henrichs, N. (1997). Informationswissenschaft. Grundlage des praktischen Information und Dokumentation. *4 Aufl. Munchen*, 945-957.

Henrichs, N. (2001). *Einführung in die Informationswissenschaft. Gegenstand, Erkenntnisinteresse Und Zielsetzung Der Informationswissenschaft*. Düsseldorf: Universität Düsseldorf.

Herrschaft, L. (2000). II Kapitel: Der Informationsbegriff in der Informationswissenschaft. In R. Capurro (Ed.), *Einführung In Den Informationsbegriff.* Retrieved July 5, 2011, from http://www.capurro.de/infovorl-kap2.htm

Ingwersen, P. (1995). Information and Information Science. *Enciclopedia of Library and Information Science, 56*(Suppl.), 137–174.

Ingwersen, P., & Borlund, P. (1996) Information transfer viewed as interactive cognitive processes. In P. Ingwersen, P., & N. Pors, N. (Ed.), *Information Science: Integration in Perspective. Proceedings of the 2nd. International Conference on Conceptions of Library and Information Science (CoLIS 2), Oct. 13-16, 1996*. Copenhagen: The Royal School of Librarianship.

Katuščák, D., & Matthaeidesová, M., & Nováková, M. (1998). Informačná výchova. Terminologický a Výkladový slovník. Odbor knižničná a informačná veda. *Slovenské pedagogické nakladatelstvo. 1. vyd.*, 375 s.

Kaula, P. N. (2002). Reflections on the Organisation and Working of the National Library and the Efforts at the Establishment of the National Central Library. *Herald of Library Science*, *41*(1-2), 37–47.

King, A. (1989). The Great Transition. *Int. Forum Inf. Docum*, *14*(2), 3–8.

Krumholz, W. (2004). Grenzen der physiologischen Informationsverarbeitúng des Menschen. *Information Wissenchaft und Praxis*, *55*(5), 283–287.

Leupolt, M. (1978). Some considerations on the nature of information. *Int. Forum Inform. Docum*, *3*(3), 29–34.

Leupolt, M. (1981). Information Science. Its Object and Termonology. *Int. Forum Inform. Docum*, *6*(2), 19–21.

Lucrecio. (2003). *La naturaleza*. Madrid: Editorial Gredos.

Manzelli, P. (1991). *Nueva Química para la Vida. Speech made at ATENEO in Madrid*. Typed text.

McCrank, L. (2001). *Historical Information Science: An Emerging Undiscipline. Medford*. New Jersey: Information Today, Inc.

McHale, J. (1981). *El entorno cambiante de la información*. Madrid: Técnos.

Mikhailov, A. I. (1982). Science As A System Of Cyclic Process of Generation, Processing, Accumulation and Transfer of Scientific Information. *Theoretical Problems of Informatics: Place of Information in the Global Problems of the World, FID 659*.

Shanon, C. E., & Weaver, W. (1949). *The Mathematical Theory of communication*. Urbana, IL: Univ. of Illinois Press.

Silveira Zaragoça, F. J. (1980). Consideraçoes generais sobre a Problematica en Informaçao. *Revista Espanola la de Documentacion Cientifica*, *3*(2), 159–168.

Wersig, G. (1971). *Information-Kommunication-Dokumentation*. München; Berlin.

Subsection

Information, in Collaborative Information Systems, as a Science in Itself

Chapter 5
The Complexity of Finding Information in Collaborative Information Systems:
Cognitive Needs

Aida Varela
Universidade Federal da Bahia, Brazil

Marilene Lobo Abreu Barbosa
Universidade Federal da Bahia, Brazil

ABSTRACT

This chapter reflects objective and subjective principles to organize and disseminate information. It presents the human condition in the dynamic of searching and using information by making explicit the informational need of the user with learning theories, information organization, and user studies as subsidies. This is done in order to increase the development of cognitive trajectories to search, select, and use information, bearing in mind the permanent process of modifiability to face new environments. Finally, the text focuses on the social and economic development promoted by the science and technology advances, pointing out the social gap that has emerged from this reality.

INTRODUCTION

Libraries and files were the first systems of information organized by knowledgeable persons to allow information access. The contemporary information systems for scientific, technological, economic, cultural, et cetera, though they absorbed the finest information technology, have taken the role of globalizing the knowledge produced and accumulated by humanity transmitting it to other generations. Actually, what is evident is the constant demand for knowledge accessibil-

DOI: 10.4018/978-1-61350-201-3.ch005

ity from the traditional libraries to the modern information systems.

The insertion of collaborative technologies in information systems since the creation of web 2.0 makes changes in the relations of production/creation, dissemination, and accessing to information; for example, the all-to-all communication process is based on the "from many to many" participatory philosophy, in which all sorts of communication are hybrids and dynamical to make records, while the documents become, many times, socially recognized collective products.

Although this rearrangement in the flow of information has become more effective, the communication process between the groups, with the intermediation of this technological display, can be done in real time and in a shared and interactive way. Increasingly, the autonomy of the user to seek information is the objective in the movement of globalization of knowledge, and it requires the application of more complex cognitive trajectories to make effective the search process and use of information. The answer given by TICs was to create friendly and interactive solutions, and by libraries, an action to enable the user with information literacy. It also implicates mediation and application of cognitive theories and establishes services oriented by the philosophy of the interactivity between the parties and the simultaneous collaboration that have been identified as Library 2.0.

The tendencies of the contemporary systems are to integrate collaborative technologies with free access, to increase the information access, seeking to obtain knowledge. It demands further studies on user cognitive maneuvers at the moment of capture, processing, and transcendence of information, and the impact of using of this new knowledge of society. Future studies should also be conducted on the role of mediator and the librarian in this context, as well as of sophisticated mechanisms and search tools for the multiple syntaxes.

Consistent with the nature of the presented phenomenon, this chapter reflects, based on a context of constant changes in virtual environments of organizing and propagating of information, about the principles to make the human condition objective and subjective in the dynamic of searching and use of information. It does so by making explicit the informational need of the user, having the reading as subsidy, the informational competencies and the mediation of the information professionals, creating and offering interactive services that answer the user's questions, making effective the propagation, and improving signification and usability of the information.

Finally, the text presents considerations about economic development and social well-being promoted by the advancement of science and technology. It also considers the appropriation of the scientific knowledge for the privileged stratum of society, anywhere in the world, and the social gap that has emerged from this reality of high technology in the social classes in higher classes and social strata sidelined for several socioeconomic reasons.

COGNITION AS SUPPORT TO BUILD THE PROCESSES OF SEARCHING, RETRIEVING AND USING OF THE INFORMATION

The theoretical and experimental studies from the 1950's aim to solve the issues of and information recording and retrieval, made clear by Saracevic:

"[...] the nature of information, the knowledge structure, and its records (including Bibliometrics), the use and the users, leading to studies of human behavior with information; the interaction man-computer, with emphasis on the human side of the equation; relevance, utility, obsolescence and other attributes of the information use along with methods and measures to assess the information retrieval systems; economy, impact and value of the information, among others". (Saracevic, 1996)

Within these studies, Mooers (1951 apud Saracevic, 1996), brought up the expression "Information Retrieval," and he sought answers to the following questions:

1. How can people intellectually describe the information?
2. How can people intellectually specify the search?
3. Which systems, techniques or machines must be used?

These questions are based on finding theoretical and practical solution regarding information retrieval; therefore it has created many concepts and theoretical, empirical, and pragmatic constructs, as well as many practical achievements. This has created impressive evolutions of systems, techniques, and/or machines for information retrieval, which were built from the most rudimentary means, and have been transformed into intelligent interfaces and the highly interactive processes of the present day.

Dynamics to Search and Use Information

The process of the information retrieval is, in essence, the answer to a cognitive act, which expresses itself in the action to search information to meet the user's need. So it justifies the interrelation of the CI with the Cognitive Psychology, a knowledge area that studies the way people realize, learn, remind, and think about information (Sternberg, 2000), aiming to elucidate the cognitive trajectory of the actors who interact to access and search information.

Knowledge representation takes the many ways our minds create and transform mental structures that represent what we know about the outside world. The declarative way (know what) is as involved as the non-declarative way (know how) of knowledge. (Sternberg, 2000).

Feurstein (1980), in his studies about the human mind functioning, recorded trajectories that would reach a mental processing more efficientlu, identifying, also, existing factors that interfere in this process. In his opinion, the human being has three basic functions: the *psychological*, that is the internal biological, chemical, and psychological processes; the *cognitive*, that is the processes of learning, reasoning, perception, and intelligence; and the *affective*, or *connotative*, that is the emotional aspects and feelings. The author states that there are some structured and dynamic processes that combine and organize to operate the cognitive structure, called cognitive functions (Souza; Depresbiteris; Machado, 2004).

The fundamental components of a cognitive function, according to Feuerstein (1980), are: *capacity, necessity,* and *orientation*. Together, they create mental operation. The capacity, characterized by its dynamics, makes acting possible in its many levels of complexity, and it is influenced by genetics, endogenous, and external factors. The necessity stimulates or inhibits the action, according to its intensity level, to move the cognitive function. The necessity is closely related to the world requirements. The orientation manages the cognitive function, by defining individual choices, methods, and strategies to deal with the problem; it also guides someone's choices about the content domain, the environment, or the structure to which go the efforts to solve problems.

As Choo (2006) pointed out, information needs do not come fully developed, but they are clarified and defined during a period of time. They come from uncertainty, and it decreases as the information need becomes questions or aware themes and, later, they are formalized. The more constant questions are about what one wants to know, why someone needs to know it, what the matter is, what knows already, what is expected to find, how it will help, how one needs to know it, and which way one needs to know it, (Choo, 2006).

Since the informational need is defined, the next step is the pursuit of information to meet it. In his studies about the searching process, Kuhlthau (1993) decided that it is made by some personal choices that will determine efficiency of the use of sources and strategies. The beliefs and expectations about which sources must be used and about the relevance or irrelevance of the selected sources, are based on the experience, as well as on the potential and cognitive style of the individual.

Kuhlthau (1993) divides the process of information searching into six phases: initiation, selection, exploration, planning, collection, and presentation. Each phase is characterized by user behavior in three fields of experience: the emotional (feelings), the cognitive (thought), and the physical (action).

To reinforce Kuhlthan ideas, Figure 1 shows the instances of human interactions, where the generative poles start from the person who learns. The person is composed by organism, body, intelligence, and desire. Organism means the collection of organs that characterize the human being, individualized by the genetic load. The intelligence, the desire, and the body are situated in the organism. The intelligence and the desire should be the unconscious structures that are expressed by language. People build their structuring systems, incorporated in level of representations on two pillars: the logical and the dramatic. Desire lies in the logic articulation, product of representations, and products of significant experiences that constitute knowledge. One learns, therefore, in the dialectical web of contacts, the objective world (the social world) interacting with the epistemic structures by that who learns. In this schema, a topological language is used, which makes the inclusion of regions, represents the society as people learning together. The cultural universe and the scientific universe are also part of reality. Language and action are considered approach vehicles.

According to Choo (2006), the pursuit of information makes the following trajectory: start, interlink, search, compare, select, pull, verify, and finish. Starting, interlinking, and searching help the individual focus on the research object and strategies to perform. As Choo observed (2006), the 'cognitive gap' stimulates the searching process, which increases the process the search ant has in its different emotional states. The first stages of information searching are characterized by anxiety, confusion, frustration, and doubt. As the process succeeds, the confidence grows and a feeling of satisfaction arises. The emotional states influence: a) how the individual processes and uses the information; b) the user's capacity of making significance; c) how to focus on the search; d) the capacity of distinguishing relevant and irrelevant information; e) how to deal with the emotional and the expectations; f) the level of interest in researching (Choo, 2006).

Feuerstein (1980) says that the mental act is the result of mental operations and cognitive functions; they can be understood as many internalized, organized, and coordinate actions, regarding the information from external and internal sources. The mental operations, according to Feurstein (1980) are: identification, comparison, analysis, summary, classification, codification, decoding, projecting a virtual link, differentiation, mental representation, mental transformation, divergent reasoning, hypothetical reasoning, transitive reasoning, analogical reasoning, logical reasoning, syllogistic reasoning, and inferential reasoning.

In an analogy with the processing of computer information, Feuerstein classified the cognitive functions in the human mind into three phases: entrance, elaboration, and exit. However, this classification cannot be seen in a stagnant way. The total of the phases is the mental act, in which each phase is related to other. At the beginning, the problem is identified and analyzed, and the elaboration phase occurs in the information process while trying to solve the problem. At the end the appropriate answer to the problem presented at the entrance stage is shown, which requires accurate skills of communication.

Figure 1. Instances of human interactions (Source: Varela A. & Barbosa M.)

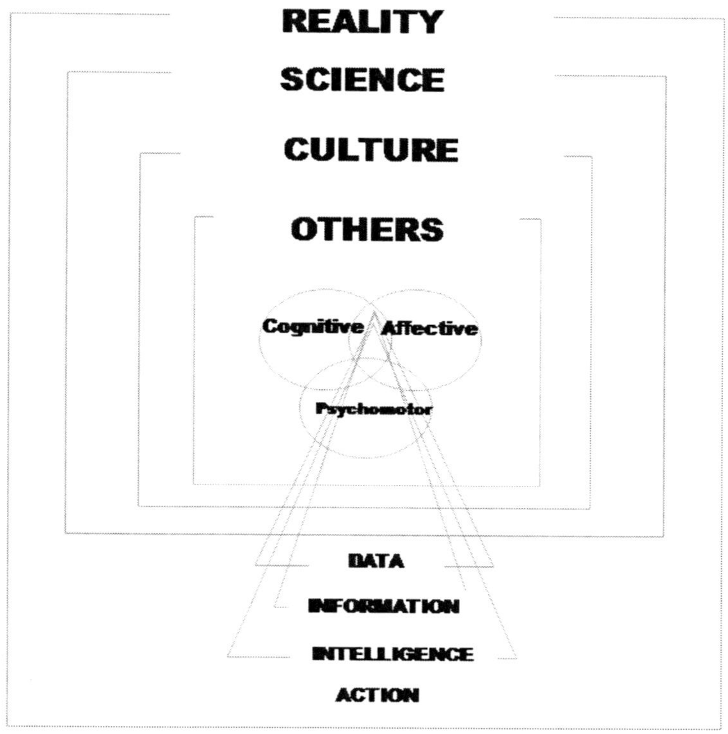

Based on the exposed problems, it concludes that the search and use of information in all its dimensions – access, analysis, interpretation, assessment, production, et cetera – subtend the power competencies and skills to search information, in agreement with this text, but reading and understanding are also related to cognition.

Competencies to Search and Use the Information

Contemporary experts have asserted that social and technological changes make a new culture appear and change the ways of production and appropriation of knowledge. The end of the limits among the knowledge areas, the new methodological and epistemological suggestion give special importance to the reflections about reading and the process of obtaining information. The reading and its understanding are an activity of processing of the accomplished information by the human mind.

The use of information by the user requires the capture of the information and turning it into knowledge, with intellectual skills like decoding, interpretation, knowledge control, and organization. Decoding and interpretation of new information includes reading skills, previous knowledge, determining relations, comparing many points of views, and assessment. The control and organization relate properly to the mental organization of information by using cognitive tools, for example schema, conceptual maps, and text preparation.

The 70s assumed the importance of information to society and the necessity of new competencies and skills of the professionals of many knowledge areas to use the information and communication technologies and to use and propagate the information in an efficient and effective way.

In the 80s, the concept of competence in information had instrumental emphasis, by enabling professionals to use technologies, especially the computer. In 1987 the work of Karol Kuhlthau stands out, on the topic of searching and using information. Kuhlthau suggests the integration of informational competences to the school curriculum, intending to give students the technologies to access information. Kuhlthau (1996) defined the competence in information as a way to learn, emphasizing the idea of cognitive process, creating what is conventionally called the alternative model, centered on user. Gaining competence in information includes lifelong learning and the applying informational skills daily.

In 1989, the Presidential Committee on Information Literacy, from American Library Association (ALA) observed that the development of informational competences is associated to the skills to localize, assess, and practically use the information based on a need. Actually, informational competence is realized in "the internalization of the trajectory of the knowing how to learn, how the knowledge is organized, how to find the information, and how to use it" in a clear way, so that everyone can learn from it.

Searching and using information are decisive competences in the learning society, involving the active pursuit of information, planning, strategies, and motivation to reach the point. This also includes monitoring strategies, knowledge, and definition of sources of potential in information, competences to use information technologies, and assessment of these processes.

Competence, according to Teixeira (2008), is the capacity of moving knowledge, values, and decisions to act in a pertinent way in a situation. These competences can only be constituted by practicing. It is not only knowing, but the know-how. Learning is by doing, in a situation that would require this specialized doing, and skill comes after getting competence.

For Guy Le Boterf (2003), competence is how to move and combine resources. The professional has double tools: personal resources and resources from his environment. The first one consists of knowing, knowing to do, aptitude, or qualities and accumulated experiences. The second one consists of machines, material installations, information, and related networks.

The idea of competence for Perrenoud (2000, p. 26) is the capacity of moving cognitive resources to face different situations and dealing with the characteristics of the today's society. That includes, as a fundamental basis, information and the knowledge, so professionals who deals with information have to have responsibility to seek new tolls to prepare and integrate people to technology and to virtual environments, and it requires new learning and strategies, to get two kinds of competences:

1. **Technological competence** – the theory and practice of the shape, development, selection, and using assessment and management of technological resources, meeting the following aspects: theoretical scientific knowledge of the TICs and media, management skill, audio visual education, telematics and computer education; valorize the impact of the TICs and media for all in society and education; know available materials on the market: media for all, videos, software, web space, and assessment of the technical, pedagogic and functional quality; know the possible applications in education; planning, management and assessment of educational activities with technological support; development design of educational materials in technological support; organization of central pedagogic resources (Alfin/EEES, 2005).
2. **Informational competence**, also called education in information or informational literacy, is a learning process centered on three moments: *information search* – skills to localize and regain documents and to manage technological equipment; *Information*

use – skills to investigate, think and study I; *Dissemination of information* – skills to produce and to represent (Alfin/EEES, 2005).

The informational and technological competences require a minimum skill level to succeed in education by using internet, such as: Use the main internet tolls; know the basic characteristics of equipments and informatics infrastructures necessary to access the internet; Verify which information is necessary; Find the sought information and retrieve it with agility; Evaluate the quality, authenticity, and the actuality of the information that is wanted; Evaluate the information identity obtained to be used in each concrete situation; Take advantage of the possibilities of communication the internet offers; Evaluate the effectiveness and efficiency of the methodology used to seek information and to communicate through the internet. (Alfin/EEES, 2005).

In this expectation to develop the informational competences, the Alfin/EEES represents the movement of Informational Pedagogy on its site: teach to learn in the Information Society, centered in the educational hypothesis – teach to learn, and, especially, by appropriately using the information in the teaching and learning process, demand new planning strategies focused on lifelong learning.

The purpose of the Informational Pedagogy is to prepare educators and students to play the role of mediators of information, seeking reciprocity, meaning, and transcendence of this information, traversing the flow of a cognitive process in access dimensions, analysis, interpretation, assessment, production, et cetera, closing the cycle of information and pedagogy – the information as exit and entrance point. It is worth emphasizing the meaning given to particular phenomena in this process; in this perspective the information to be treated requires knowledge or epistemological capacity, which allows for its finding and interpretation.

The Informational Pedagogy aims to establish true dialogue between the reader-user and the informational environment and make meaningful learning, by innovator methodologies, such as informational thematic segments (portfolio), specialized search, thematic web work, data micro basic by subscriber, alternative digital reading, a virtual discussion forum with digital readings, Iconic conception with digital images, and use of digital media, among others.

Thus, the model of library 2.0 would have an expressive function in the context of the Informational Pedagogy, regarding the application of the web tools to create shared, dynamic, and interactive informational services and to enable users to seek and use information, constituting a social network that potentiates of the user active participation, the collective intelligence, and the collaborative work, fortifying the mission of the library and of the professionals who work there.

In contrast to the demands of the informational and digital competences, the document of the Alfin/EEES emphasizes that, from Paulo Freire until now, the advancement and the innovation in pedagogy have been relatively slow, considering the scientific dynamicity in other areas. The Alfin/EEES (2005) represents Paulo Freire's concept of literacy, for whom literacy means "learn[ing] to write his life, as author and as witness of his history;" in other words, "alphabetizing is to raise awareness," to comment that at present, the same happens. There is an imperious need of getting awareness of the coordinates of the society of the knowledge, besides the task of creating, managing, selecting, processing, and propagating the information, as a fundamental tool to the human development.

Behaviors Search and Their Implications in Information Organization and Knowledge Processes

The access to knowledge has become matter of survival, constituting a factor of competitiveness in any social system. The changing dynamic of reality puts the individuals facing diversity of processes, instability, contingency, and permanent change, realizing that flexibility is a tendency of present day (Dias Villa, 2002). In the field of organization, information retrieval, and propagation, everything has been to search new procedures and resources to represent the information and quickly make it accessible and useful to the user.

The information retrieval systems were made to expand the possibility of accessing the document. Therefore, their primary function is to order information in a logical way. This makes it possible to localize information for an interested user. In this part, the big challenge is to design and apply means to organize this information, making the systems to interact with the user; thus, it is necessary to articulate the user interest with system of search and retrieval.

The first SRI appeared early in the 20th century, and always acted as the interface between the user and the informational items (Lancaster & Warner (1993 p. 4-5), so for Chowdhury (1999, p.1), the SRIs are mediating tools that put the information producers and those that need them in interaction. One may also consider SRIs as conceptual products and technical tools. From the conceptual point of view, the SRI should be classified as a system that previously organized the knowledge in expectation of the user's search, allowing information retrieval and transfer to the user. In this sense, the SRI is a communication channel. In the excerpt below, Novellino explains the concept of transfer in the area of Information Science and its overlapping with the communication actions that involve the indexer, the system, and user.

"The concept of information transfer is understood as an intervention performed realized by systems of knowledge organization and information retrieval in certain communicative actions, which are those that take place between producers and knowledge users. The communicative actions, which have language as a tool, can be realized through the relationships as: (a) between speaker and listener, (b) between image and one that assists (c) between text and reader. Information Science turns mainly for communicative action between text and reader, having as main objective to create conditions for its realization. It takes part in textual communicative action to ensure that it really occurs, it means that information becomes accessible to those that need it." (Novellino, 1996)

The procedures and techniques that will verify the information transfer to the user are based on two actions: first, it must represent the content of the informational item – it is the access point; second, it is necessary to create searching tools - the indexes. At this confluence point, people need to use cognitive and learning theories, because to represent information content, it is necessary to simulate user behavior to search information.

At this point of the system, the focus is on the ways to exit the system, because it is desirable to develop user-friendly interfaces that facilitate the understanding of the user, with respect to the system's structuring and modeling, even allowing that it interferes with the language of the system (user-modeling) (Novellino, 1996, p.37). With the development of computerized systems, knowledge and resources of artificial intelligence and computational linguistics have been applied in an attempt to approximate the user's mental strategy to syntax strategies applied by the machine, and thus, to maximize the chances of recovering the user's object of desire.

The other side of the system is the informational representation items, and, therefore the focus is how the data came into the system, to be retrieved later by the user. In this field, Information Science had invested in studies and research and established theories and methodologies, aiming to develop models and tools to represent the contents with more accurately representation of the contents contained in the informational items enrolled at SRI. Novellino, evaluating the performance of the Information Science, in this particular field, had this to say:

"The researches developed in this area focalize the system access entrance. They develop homologatly nearby the scientific understanding of knowledge structure, designing methodologies for the analysis of the matter, to the generation of classification systems and indexing languages". (Novellino, 1996)

In the process of information representation, procedures are created that focus on the thematic essence of the document, which means it is necessary to summarize the contents, which can be done by the preparation of summaries, or by indexing content through descriptors and keywords. This summary is not done by the impossibility of storing the entire document in the computerized system, because this restriction has been already resolved technically, but because the summarization of the document, with the emphasis in the matter, will allow greater recall and precision in information retrieval, increasing the possibility of success in the search. In terms of representation versus information retrieval, is still "the ideal solution for the organization and use of information" (Novellino, 1996, p.38), although contemporary information systems are, naturally, full text.

The investment and the advancement of C&T in research has increased the knowledge specialization and has demonstrated, since the last century, that in SRIs, one should emphasize the scientific and technological thematic organization of information. The great challenge that was set was how to represent knowledge, because several times, there are a multiplicity of terms to represent the same concept. This creates the risk of decontextualization of the indexer's terms in the search process, increasing the recall, but impairing its accuracy. Problems than can happen. From these problems, CI has put its focus in finding solutions to issues of representation of subject and then possible inconsistencies establishing models and tools.

In view of the CI, information representations consists of two phases: 1) analysis of the document content, with the linguistic representation of this analysis, 2) to impute concepts to the content of the document review; in this point, in order to standardize the indexing, avoiding the indiscriminate use of synonymous terms, for example, that come to disturb the harmony of the system hampering the precision of search, people have recourse to utilize some control features. For example, indexing language is now also a language interaction between the user and the system, and indirectly, among users and indexers. The lists of subject headings were the first documentary languages, and at first they had the function to standardize the subject entrances of library catalogs and indexes, fulfilling, as a consequence, the role of indexing and to facilitate information retrieval. To this end, the indexer chose the list of subject headings as the terms allowed. The thesaurus, however, has already been created as a tool for information retrieval, because it can demonstrate the logic of the organizational structure of knowledge to the users. This allows it to repeat the same logic in the search; thus the structure of the representational language can create faceted and classified thesauri.

The combination of the principles of the content classification with the verbal documentary languages established the organization of concepts, led them to transcend the limitations of verbal arrangement (Novellino, 1996). At the same time, as classification is no longer a co-ordinated instrument, it becomes the theory that underlies analysis, representation, and information seeking. This integration comes closer and closer to verbal languages, or perhaps to classifying, symbolic, or coded languages.

The first documentary languages were pre-coordinated, as the subject heading lists, however, still at the mechanics stage and analogic information systems were applied to these free languages, planned for post-coordinated information systems. For example the Unitermo system, the first with this principle, processed into the dossier. These post-coordinated systems were characterized by not setting the main subject, and neither its hierarchical network, the contextualization of terms and descriptors in indexing time, when they were assigned to the content document memberless isolated terms that the indexer deemed necessary.

The conceptual and contextual web was woven by the user mental strategy in the search moment; at the same time the coordination was built among the representing terms of the content (subject). The post-coordinated systems have gained notoriety and wider application with the use of computers in automated indexing, because computer systems began to offer the possibility of extracting the representing terms from the concepts in the texts on their own. They did so by applying appropriate syntactic schemes.

In the 1960s, the computer entered extensively in the processes of control, representation, and retrieval of information. From the publishing of the publications, especially periodicals, and their contents, numerous databases have emerged as byproducts of the process of generating indices and/or printed bibliographies.

"Since the publication of the article written Williams about the impact of Databases in Libraries and Information Services in 1977, the growth of these files readable by computer has continued to occur steadily. Each month brings the context new data bases, in various areas of Science and Technology." (Lopes, 1985)

Since then the computer has become an indispensable tool in the processes of representation search and retrieval of information, especially by introducing innovations almost always in a perspective to facilitating the search and promoting the direct interaction between the user and the information retrieval system. In the accessibility logic and in the user autonomy in search of information, the great invention was the World Wide Web or simply Web. Structured as a hypertext, the web establishes relations among the network content, linking words or phrases on the disposable addresses electronics. The network is structured as a relational web, which enables the intertwining of content, maximizing the chances of search and retrieval. For example, the results of Internet searches done through the mediation of engines such as Yahoo, Google, et cetera may return precious data, but also answers without any meaning to the user.

It happens because documents on the Internet are not classified according to a pattern, affecting the relevance of the revoked informational items during the search in relation to user interest. The efficiency of a system of information retrieval is closely related to the rates of recall and precision, which ensures the tracking of the largest possible number of relevant documents, ideally, those who agree more strongly with the user's interest.

On the Web, however, the user is put in front of a huge mass of documents, but without any organization, and to find the information needed will depend on the user's ability and efficiency of the search tools (also called search engines), which are specialized systems, generated in order to retrieve information on the Internet. They operate by collecting information in the sites, after they are being stored in databases to be disposed at the user community. The web 2.0 platform is the latest implementation of scientific and technological information to promote client autonomy in the management of digital tools.

In this direction, people can find digital repositories, tools increased by the policy of free access to scientific knowledge and by the technology open archives, which were also increased by the acceptance of scientific institutions aiming to collect, to preserve, to provide access and disseminate knowledge produced by the scientific community of a particular institution, contributing to the recognition and visibility of the researcher and its institution of origin, as to accelerate the science advancement.

The network represents the web that Ptolemy tried to build representing at the same time, the library of Alexandria and Paul Otlet's Mundaneum, fulfilling the desire of man, in a perspective to gather and share, now collaboratively, the knowledge produced by all, considering that the technological tools allow this prowess.

One must consider however, that in a scientific information environment, one of the priorities of the search tools should be to ensure the relevance of the results from literature search, to ensure to the researcher the delivery of significant documents in the area of interest. Renowned scholars in the field of indexing and retrieval of information, such as Lancaster (2004) and Saracevic (2009) have projected this point: principles such as relevance and accuracy are always used in scientific information retrieval systems in order to preserve the quality in the research literature.

The web 2.0 should be considered as an alternative resource that stimulates the colloquial conversation between the network of actors, but not an accredited and endorsed model to store and retrieve scientific and technological information as in major information retrieval systems such as the Index Medicus, Chemical Abstracts Services, and countless others with a scientific nature. The information retrieval systems devoted to scientific and technological information permit the user: to access information through the representation of information contents, using the description of documents and indexing; storing and managing physical and logical items such documentary and their representations; and retrieval of information represented and the documents themselves represented, leading the user to find the represented items in the system. For this, the system should provide an interface in which users describe their needs and issues.

In other words it means that the SRI must produce an informational, affective, cognitive and social trajectory to the user, as demonstrated in Figure 2, created from the Bloom's taxonomy (1974-1979).

The cognitive area varies from simple evocation of material up to highly original and creative ways to combine and synthesize new ideas and materials in the following gradation: know, understand, implement, analyze, synthesize, and evaluate. The affective area integrates changes expected in interests, attitudes, values, and assessments in the following gradation: responsiveness, reaction, valuation, organization, and characterization. The categories of training of the individual are objectification and ownership (subjectivity), humanization or disposal, and humankind (becoming a person) and individuality for a person as part of a collective.

There is, therefore, that the process of cognitive operations in information retrieval requires self-awareness, demanding the establishment of search strategies that allow recovery of what really matters, quickly, and in trusted sources. From this perspective, it can be inferred that, to reach the knowledge, not just physical access to technologies is necessary, but above all, it is important to stimulate multiple cognitive processes, mediation, and contextualization. This constitutes prerequisites to grasp and understand content and information. Understanding phenomena means competence to formulate hypotheses or ideas about the causal relationships. For this, it is important to establish relationships and inferences, product analyses, and reflections essential to the learning process.

In this sense, there already exists in the field of information science, a consensus among scholars as to the contribution of cognitive science in the process of representation and retrieval of information and referral service, specifically in user interaction with the information worker.

Scholars of CI, such as HjØrland (1998), Beghtol (1986), and Pinto Molina (1994), have highlighted the implementation of a cognitive indexing approach based on understanding of the text and the representation of the document. The research identifies three steps in indexing activity: understanding content, textual representation (creation of indexing languages), and generation of text (summary).

By way of strengthening the presence of cognition in the process of indexing, the studies of Lancaster (2004) and Guinchat and Menou (1994) on the relationship that keeps the content

Figure 2. Information transfer (Source: Varela A. & Barbosa M.)

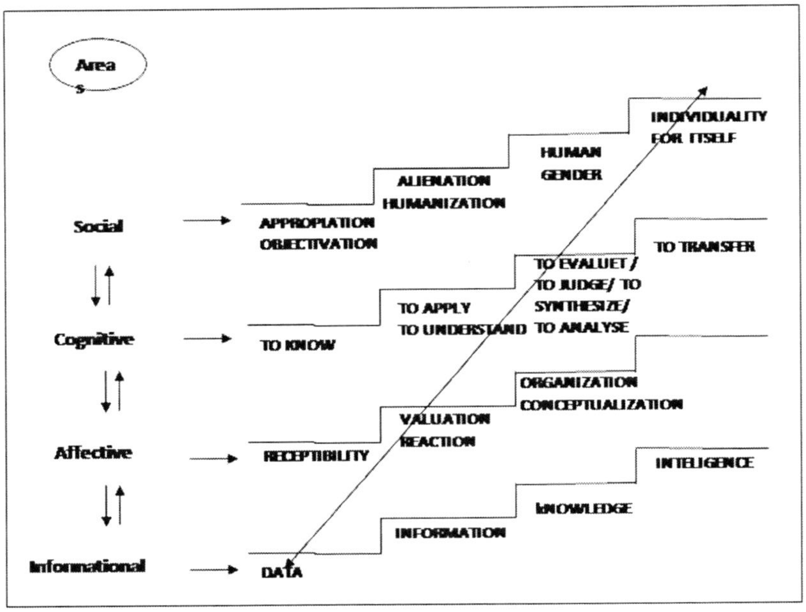

indexing with the user's interest, leads the indexer to consider the interest that led them to search information at the time of the choice of terms in the representation of content. Therefore, the same source of information can be indexed in different ways, focusing on diversified interests of users.

The chart illustrates particularly the existence of the convergence of cognitive paths between who draws up the indexing scheme and the subject that encodes/decodes at the time of search of information, showing that the recovery only becomes possible when the strategies of indexing and search. This route is closely related to the categories/cognition, knowledge elements that permeate the stock course content indexing/information retrieval. This is insofar as the logical path indexer is in the construction of the instrument of search and user in the elaboration of the strategy.

Additionally, Fujita studies (1999) characterize the indexing process, identified using metacognitive skills in conducting reading held informational for impersonation purposes. In this same line of thought, Neves (2004) suggests that the indexer could be instructed, during his training, in using reading strategies and metacognitive abilities in order to get more efficiency in their performance during the indexing process.

THE INEVITABLE PRESENCE OF INTERSECTIONS: CROSSING CONCEPTS AND METHODOLOGIES

Substantiated in the line of the development of thought, humans are in permanent motion, learning through construction and transformations, modifying their informational needs, their way of knowing, reflection, and behavior in relation to the world around them.

With cognitive psychology, the thought, its processes, and ways of thinking have predominant resonance. Multiple processes tend to relate or combine ideas, concepts, emotions, situations, facts, et cetera with a view to a decision or finding a solution.

Based on these considerations, it can be noted that there are a variety of processes and topics to think about. The process of weaving senses or thinking brings together the implementation of processes such as analysis, synthesis, identification, comparison, and grouping, among others. Thinking and reflection aren't unique activities. Every person has enough potential to think.

According to Piaget (1971) and Vygotsky (1991), the knowledge base is the constructive mental activity of the subject, and the learning process is seen as a relationship of objectification, which establishes itself in a given spatio-temporal context between the subject and the object (or between a subject and a set of objects), the most publicized interaction.

This way, teaching to seek information and research, and developing an investigative spirit and autonomy are aspects which arise not only from cognitive understanding, but also the development of skills and attitudes that promote ownership of information and its transformation into knowledge.

CI cognitivism took place in the 1980s, with authors such as Belkin (1984) who built his concept of information based on the concept of mental representation. This cognitivist orientation submits arguments about the intelligibility of information to shift the object of studies of information retrieval toward user studies. Belkin (1984) assigns the development of the cognitivist approach in CI, as support for the information system modeling with artificial intelligence resources. This indicates that the design of information, such as entity or substance, shall be replaced by the concept that the meaning and interpretation, and in this case, the information, is seen as a factor of cognitive structures.

Physics and Neuroscience, in recent decades, are challenging disseminating studies, which cause changes of behaviour, i.e. people change, modify, improve, progress, and evolve. Transformation will lead to structural changes, not only individually, arising from future historical, social, economic, political, and cultural settings, changes that are influencing the way of feeling, thinking, and cognitive science.

Based on consensus among the main theoretical psychology, as Piaget (1977), Wallon (1963), Vygotsky (1979), George Mead (1992) and Bakhtin (1981), and Bourdieu (1982), Barthes (1992), Bruner (1990), Lotman (1988), and Moscovici (1988), Fávero (2005, 2008) supports the psychology of knowledge, registering that, in view of these authors, the human being is built from the dialectical interaction with the socio-cultural context, sustained by internalizing and externalizing, which breed awareness – outsourcing as a re-scheduling of internalization – for which the system of signs is especially important, as they are of the representation. Regarding this theme, Fávero (2005, 2008) outlines four conceptual aspects:

The first refers to the evidence of the interaction between the dictates of cognitive and social norms, shifting the emphasis dyad subject-object to the triad subject-object-the other. From the point of view of Psychology, knowledge is a consensus that considers human interaction as a reciprocal exchange of meanings, undoing the classic dichotomy between body and mind, individual and environment, language and thought, emotion and cognition (Fávero, 2005).

The second focuses on the role of semiotic mediation on human psychological development process, what it means to understand that the objects, as well as the human actions, have socio-cultural meanings. Social practices and integrated educational practices take place in a context that gives them meaning.

The third, assuming the existence of mediation in human activities, are the effects of systems of signs on the psychological development of individual cognition, communication, and shapes as the practice of social institutions interact with the individual's mental functioning (Fávero, 2005).

The fourth assumes the awareness that human actions are social practices, reasoned knowledge. Both objects as actions include social representations of knowledge areas and act as mediators of meanings, which interact between the institutional and personal paradigms. Creating a new discourse and a new social practice should be based on the industrial processing of meanings, the possibilities of re-scheduling (Fávero, 2005).

In consonance with the aforementioned ideas and with the necessity of substantiating the study about the application of cognitive theories in the knowledge apprehension, it is proposed by some theorists, firstly to study the teaching and process of learning and, and next to that study the interaction between the information professional and the user.

Learning Theories in the Perspective of Knowledge Building

Each person in a society is part of the whole that it represents. The society intervenes in the life of the person since birth, in language, in standards, prohibitions in culture, knowledge, but in the dialogue of these interventions, obstacles emerge from transferred information, in the majority of the cases, by the participants' asymmetry. Those are on the poles of information transmission and reception, in relationship to the generations pragmatic conditions, use of information, and especially, by the lack of common criteria for acceptance and value assigned to information.

So scientists seek for the ideal – equity for those who give and receive information with pragmatic conditions: social frameworks of transfer, communication conditions, criteria of value, and acceptance. The relationship and coding potential will increase the interference from different paradigms, becoming a multiplied environment of information.

The true learning happens when a person reaches a modified fleeting or long-term behaviour, by the individual's own action or in conjunction with other individuals. According to Reboul (1982), learning is: an act that the subject holds about itself, not simply a record to be reproduced, and therefore, should be used to resolve situations and, in some cases, create and reinvent solutions.

Several classifications can be used as a reference to categorize the psychological theories and their diverse influences in the field of cognition and education. Currently, constructivism represents the most developed and sustained position of contemporary pedagogical vanguards by reaching an emerging consensus between the pedagogical and psychological academic community. Without a doubt, pedagogical constructivism has its pillars epistemology and psychology during the 20th century, when considering the construction of knowledge as a human being and not as a copy of reality and when considering science as builder and not as "discoverer" of realities.

One of the greatest contributions of constructivism is the active role of the subject in the process of conceptualizing and recognizing the existence of personal elements, hues, and meanings in individual representation. To substantiate the reflection on the theme under consideration in this chapter, some scholars sought theoretical subsidies.

Piaget

Piaget's studies and his followers register that cognitive structures are the result of reflection and elaboration stages, as well as personal action in the world and of his interaction with his interlocutors. Thus, information search and use are transformed in strategies of exploring the information universe, represented by the variety of texts that circulate socially.

According to Piaget (1971), cognitive structure is constructed in stages and each stage incorporates the previous, occurring in the construction of knowledge for the reciprocal and interactive action of subject with the objects (environment). The organization of reality occurs by means of the structured thought, expressed by means of the adaptation process. Thus, the mental structure and knowledge are constructed in a dialectic relation between biologic maturation and the environment.

Piaget's Genetic Psychology is centralized in the cognitive operativity of person, according to Logic and Physics laws, of formal natural laws, therefore, Piaget's logicism allows a description of mental structures implicit in the resolution of problems.

Genetic structuralism is concerned with the genetic process (contingent and necessary) of structures, seeking the rationality of structuration processes. The starting point is that all human beings, individually or socially, seek equilibrium in their relationships with nature and with other human beings or social groups. It occurs when there is an accommodation of their awareness and praxis, or rather, when they consider themselves able to face and solve problems and challenges regarding those relations.

Lucien Goldmann (1973, p. 39) developed the concepts of comprehension and explanation, understood as necessary and additional steps of knowledge process, with basis in the dialectic reason, expressed by Piaget (1971),emphasizing the fundamental transformation of"knowledge-state" in "knowledge-process." Thus, to understanding information means to consider it as a structure or a relative totality and to submit it to an intellectual operation that verifies the function of their internal dependencies or constitutive parts. According to that theoretical position it's clear that if there aren't structures, but structuration processes, the researcher should verify the equilibrium states for the social processes and, in what refers to the visions of the world, the corresponding moments of ideological normality. On account of the totality relativity, it is also a constitutive part of wider structures that integrate them, or rather, explaining information means introducing it to a wider reality. This second process moment of knowing has the same nature of understanding and constitutes an element of explanation, and it becomes evident in a dialectic and not static perspective. (Goldman, 1973)

To understand the process of reality apprehension by means of the cognitive structure, that organizes the world of stimuli, Piaget (1971) developed and defined the two pillars of his theory: assimilation and accommodation. The concept of assimilation refers to the capacity of individual cognitive structure to actuate in its environment. The organism assimilates reality according to the capacity of its internal cognitive structure. In rebuttal, the cognitive structure is mobilized and changed in terms of the reality, adapting to it. The adaptation is justified as a state of equilibrium between the accommodation and the assimilation.

Thus, learning is conceptualized as modifying behavior, because of the acquisitions from experience. Knowledge is constructed in a continuous movement, stimulated by the mediator that gives space to create and/or discover solutions, from the effort of the problem. It is important to register that Piaget was influenced by Kant, as well as Vygotsky and Marx. Kant gave Piaget the array to the Genesis of structuring categorical (schemas and aftercare) thought. Piaget rebuilt the basics of Kant: time and space, intuition, quantity, quality, respect, and understanding.

Vygotsky

Vygotsky's sociohistorical approach(1991) is based in the central idea that the human beings develop by social interaction, when cognitive development maintains a narrow relation with an apprenticeship. Individual psychic functions interact continuously with the apprenticeship, with the appropriation of knowledge produced by the humanity, and the relationship it establishes with its environment.

For Vygotsky (1991), development and apprenticeship constitute a unit. An apprenticeship, when significant, stimulates and unleashes the advance for a level of greater complexity that, in its turn, should be a basis for new apprenticeships.

To explain the relationship established between development and learning, Vygotsky formulated the concepts of the real development zone, the zone of proximal development, and the potential development zone. The actual development zone is the level of development of mental functions of the individual established as a result of certain cycles of development already completed, or a specific development process. The zone of proximal development is the distance between the actual level of development, which tends to determine with the solution of problems independently, and the potential determined development zone, with troubleshooting under the guidance of another individual or in collaboration with people more capable.

The area of proximal development comprises mental functions or operations in the process of maturing, or processes that are in a state of formation. Second, to Vygotsky, all knowledge is a cultural production directly related to language. It is language that gives the internalization of content, because it causes the social nature of people to become the psychological nature. Vygotsky gives importance to the development of language, the word being a rich tool to convey the historical experience of humanity.

All human beings, inserted into a socio-historic reality, only acquire the human condition if, in its relationship with the world, it is mediated by the instrument of its culture – sign, word, and symbol. Knowledge is, therefore, a cultural production, directly related to the language and social interaction. Mediation is the action which interposes between subject and object of learning, being the word of fundamental importance. If Vygotsky applied psychology, Hegel defined mediation philosophically.

The concept of mediation was invested in its broadest meaning by Hegel, who saw in it a characteristic aspect of human reason. For him, "reason is as ingenious as it is powerful." This ingenuity is primarily an activity mediator, causing objects to act and react with each other, respecting their own nature and thus without any direct interference in the process, performing the intentions of reason.

Learning to communicate, understanding others, understanding rules, understanding that another can have a different point of view, and understanding facial expressions or other expressions of emotion requires higher cognitive functions, such as: decoding signs, gestures, sounds, words, combining information sources, and lifting and examining hypotheses, among other cognitive functions.

Vygotsky asserts that knowledge building stems from a shared action, implying a process of mediation between subjects. In this perspective, social interaction is a prerequisite for learning. The heterogeneity of the group, cooperation, and information enrich dialogue, consequently extending individual capacities.

Vygotsky underscores cultural relations in mediation with psychological structures. The decisive factor in the development does not lie with the individual, subject to the intellectual construction processes, but in mediation processes of cognitive and linguistic structures. The theory of Vygotsky de-emphasizes only stand-alone epistemological subject action, but emphasizes the cultural mediation or the action of other subjects in individual psychological construction.

Paulo Freire

The work of Paulo Freire (1980) is an attempt to retrieve and provide methodological concepts and tools of genetic structuralism and reason dialectics, showing its applicability to the pedagogical process. In his work, some ontological epistemological-elements can be highlighted, among them, the concept of factual education versus Bank education. In the "Bank" two education issues confront structures – the educator who knows and communicates, and educating that doesn't know and learn. In factual education, two processes structuring epistemology interact: teaching and learning from each other, and knowledge of the world.

In an effort to highlight the importance of the concept of awareness for science and its relevance to political activities, Freire distinguishes awareness from "awareness," in the light of reason dialectics. He argues:

[I am of the] belief that education as the practice of freedom, is an act of critical knowledge, an approximation of reality [...]; awareness is not to "be against reality" leading intellectual falsely. Awareness cannot exist outside of Praxis, or better, without the Act action-reflection. This unit dialectics is permanently, be mode or turn the world featuring men.(Freire, 1980, p. 25)

Freire (1979, 2002) underscores the importance and the need to understand the human existence from its substantiality, i.e. the recognition of all men as real historical subjects. The attributes of human beings cannot therefore override the recognition of human existence as its presence in the world as subject. It is necessary to recognize the humanization not just as ontological viability, but as historical reality. Humanization and dehumanization are inserted into the story, in a real, concrete context, and are possibilities of men as inconclusive and conscious of their inclusion.

For Freire, dialogue takes a key role in the formation of consciousness, because this is essentially factual relations established as each other and with the world. In dialogue, awareness turns into awareness. For Freire, it is through dialogue and communion that men and women become aware. Dialogue is the key to the awareness of men, women, and the world.

According to Freire (1985), awareness is the first moment of apprehending reality. This knowledge exists because human beings are "situated" and "dated," and men are spectators "with" and "in the world." This awareness does not mean critical consciousness when there is greater intensity of critical development. For this reason, the critical consciousness implies overcoming the spontaneous seizure sphere of reality to a critical position. Through this critical lens, reality becomes recognized as an object on which the man takes an epistemological position: man in pursuit of knowledge.

Feuerstein

The Structural theory of Cognitive Modifiability (TMCE) is based on an approach that is active and optimistic: for the changes that today's society requires, the human being must have capacity for modifiability, enabling integration. A disciple of Piaget, Feuerstein's TMCE, proposes revolutionary concepts in the field of cognition, with a focus on learning and human development. Feuerstein examines how the subject arrives to the solution of the problem, using the analogy of computer – input, process, and output – and proposes the cognitive map as a tool for analysis of mental act. This map shows how the taxable learns and, most importantly, allows you to learn to learn. The theory has as a central conceptual intake of the assumption that man is endowed with a plastic, flexible mind, open to change, as well as a potential and a natural propensity for learning.

The TMCE became a theoretically plausible hypothesis from three major assumptions. The first assumption is related to the design of the ontogeny of human body double – the biological ontogeny and sociocultural ontogeny. The biological ontogeny consists of realizing the human being as a community is made up of cells linking with the environment, becoming a subject. The sociocultural ontogeny is responsible for social structure, moral and human communication, giving the body the true nature of human entity. The second assumption reinforces the concept of cognitive modifiability, setting modal human behavior as a State and not as something fixed and immutable. The third assumption, considered as a great source of support for the concept of Modifiability, is the new neuroscientific conception of the human brain as a highly flexible and elastic body (Feuerstein, 2002).

Explained thus, human learning, not only by the biological integrity of genes and chromosomes or direct exposure by simple objects, event, attitudes and situations, emerges from an individual. That individual is publicized by others more experienced, whose practices and cultural beliefs are transmitted, promoting wider areas of critical and creative development – development of higher psychological processes – towards autonomy; so derives cognitive learning mediated.

To explain how human interaction drives the development of cognitive structure and promotes the human capacity to modifiability, Feuerstein develops the central conceptual contribution of his theory: the Mediated learning experience (EAM), noting that underpins all human interaction by communication. The EAM is focused not on the content of information, but in the factual intentional methodological strategy when sender and receiver are responsible for built knowledge, interacting constantly, giving importance to the exchange of views, the feelings about the world, and the exchange of forms of understanding of reality.

The EAM, in its dual role, the explanatory and the heuristic (which affirms the universality of human modifiability and the role it plays in the quality of intervention, depending on the cognitive modifiability structure), causes it to be the master-key throughout the process, since it is the factor for the development of basic cognitive functions and the transformation of cognitive, communicative, and affective structure. Among the main criteria of EAM, there are three universals Feuerstein considered in any learning experience: mediation of intentionality/reciprocity, mediation of meaning, and mediation of transcendence.

The modifiability refers not to a specific behavior change (for example, the passage of spelling read), but to changes of a structural nature that alter the course of cognitive development, how the Agency interacts, acts, or responds to information sources. What the individual experiences is a modified structural cognition, which occurs through a program of intentional intervention, making it more sensitive to internal and external sources of stimulation (Feuerstein, 1980).

So, it seems consistent with the concept of adaptation in a generic sense, when referring to changes that the body suffers in response to the emergence of a new situation. This is a dynamic process which represents a process of change from one State to another. This adaptability of the body (the individual or group) is named Modifiability, which can vary, differing from individual to individual, the State, and the State of the situation. It is a phenomenon that, although observed with reasonable frequency, requires elaboration.

It can be said that the approach of Feuerstein tie is (paradoxically) based on two important epistemological assumptions resulting in the following summary: the subject is *cognoscente* of Piaget, the constructor of knowledge, with a qualified cognitive activity through the intervention of the mediator, a subject of a Vygotsky approach.

For Feuerstein, the modifiability is a factor that is both biological and cultural, which refers to Vygotsky. The concept of cognitive modifiability means it is permeable to cultural stimuli and makes each individual unique, unpredictable, and able to overcome its current conditions. Feuerstein takes ownership of cultural mediation Vygotskian emphasis of psychological processes, emphasizing the need and importance of mediated action epistemologically in cases of intellectual construction, because it is self-sufficient in regulating processes of cognitive development; however, this autonomy lacks, for its solidification and structuring, sociointeractive experiences.

In summary, Feuerstein and Vygotsky developed their theories under strong influence of Piaget. However, they began to realize that certain aspects of Piagetian guidelines could be enriched. For Vygotsky, dissatisfaction was in epistemological individualism of Piaget's theory and negligence of social mediation. For Feuerstein, there was the question of practical learning mechanisms in relation to mediation of another human being.

Morin

Morin (1986) declares that the ability to learn is connected with the development of individual innate competences to acquire knowledge, associated with external stimuli, influences, and culture. The act of knowing is present in biological actions, brain, spiritual, cultural, linguistic, historical, and social policies. Thus, the being regulates the knowing; at the same time the knowing regulates the being.

According to Morin (2000), relevant knowledge must face complexity. Complexus means "what has been woven together". There is complexity when different elements constituting the whole are inseparable (such as the economic, political, sociological, psychological, affective, the mythological); there is an interactive and interdependent tissue of inter-retroactive knowledge object with its context – parts to a whole, the whole and the parties, the parties between themselves. Complexity, therefore, is the union of the unit with the multiplicity, knowing beforehand that there will always be uncertainty in complex thought, which allows it to escape from dogmatism that prevails in thoughts that aren't complex.

According to Morin, the notion of individual/subject integrates autonomy and dependence, without, however, being reduced to this. It is necessary to understand what it is, fundamentally, the living organization. Molecular biology and genetics gave us all elements to understand this organization. First and foremost, identity enables the treatment goal of all operations of molecules, the cells of a multicellular organism. However, this objective also has a subjective dimension, allowing the self-reference.

The individual/subject can realize itself via the objectification instrument that is language. Consciousness arises, then, by being conscious and aware of yourself and clearly inseparable from self-reference and reflection. It is the man with consciousness, says Morin, who is himself to subjectivize a recursive, unremitting circle. In subjectivity, man has the freedom to choose between several alternatives. Freedom assumes two conditions: the domestic conditions (cerebral, mental capacities, intellectual), necessary for the review of a particular situation and the establishment of one's own choices and responses, and external conditions (the world), through which these choices are possible.

There exists also in human subjectivity, the concept of soul, spirit, animus, animation, manifesting itself in a deep feeling of inadequacy that can only be satisfied with "the other." According to Morin "it is the feeling of love that is present the idea that the other restores ourselves the fullness of our own soul, staying totally different from ourselves" (2000).

Studies on the Behavior of the User in Search Information

The Royal Society Scientific Information Conference of 1948 stimulated the rise of thousands of papers and research reports on the information needs of users and user behavior in search of information. Currently, with the introduction of ethnographic methods being applied in design and architecture of information systems, the organisation of information studies are seeking answers to how people are using the system and how the behavior of search of information relates to other task oriented behaviors (Garcia, 2007).

Informational behavior models are generally presented as diagrams that try to represent the activity search associating it with the causes and consequences produced, in addition to the relationships between stages or phases in search of information behavior (Wilson, 1999). The contents of these models can take diverse perspectives, such as: cognitive, social, organizational and socio-cognitive or cognitive approaches (users processing information) and the holistic (contains aspects such as: cognitive, physical, emotional, social, and behavioral).

Focus is a model of information behavior assuming prior knowledge of the user, who uses the information search and interacting with the informational system, and how the brain processes this information, i.e. how the brain processes information from the user to browse and use the information in their interaction with the informational system. Some scholars have been dedicated to understanding the information behavior of the user, with the prospect of making more efficient the information retrieval systems.

Bertran Brookes

Bertran Brookes (1980), considered the initiator of the cognitive approach in CI, in the 1970s, proposed the cognitive equation for information science: K (S) + D (I) = K (S + DS). In this equation, K (S) represents the structures of knowledge; (d) (I), the person who gives the other conditions for modifying the knowledge structures; and K (S + DS) represents the product, i.e. the modification in the structures of knowledge of people. The author thus proves that the information is something that modifies the cognitive structure of someone.

Wilson

Wilson (1996) proposed a new model, based on the structure of the model in 1981 where the data context remains in focus the need for information, while barriers are represented by "interfering " with variables and the behavior (s) to search for information is (are) identified (s).

The first model of Wilson (1981) is based on two main propositions: first, that the need for information is not the first necessity, but a need that arises beyond secondary needs as a most basic type; and second, that in an effort to discover the information to meet the requirement, it is likely that the individual find barriers of different kinds. Using definitions from psychology, Wilson (1981) proposes that the basic necessity can be defined as psychological, cognitive, or affective.

The revised model by Wilson (1996) presents the information cycle of activities, from the urgent need for information to the stage where the information is being used, using the following: context of information need, mechanism to activate, interfering variables, mechanism to assess, and behavior of information search. The model includes multiple interfering variables that have significant influences on behavior informational, beyond the mechanisms that activate.

Carol Kuhlthau

Carol Kuhlthau (1991) studied search process standards and use of information by exploring the Constructivist Learning vision, under a phenomenological perspective. By approaching of meaning of Kuhlthau (1991), the information search process is an activity of construction from the user to find meaning, from the information in order to expand their knowledge about a particular issue or subject.

Using the ISP model – Information Search Process (Kuhlthau 1993), this work associates the many phases of the process of information search of feelings, thought, and actions, besides the appropriate informational tasks (behaviors). So, Kuhlthau (1991) points out that her theoretical bases to substantiate her model of ISP are in Kelly's work (1963), which

"[...]described the construction process happening in stages tried by individuals and how they construct their visions of the world through the assimilation of new information. The constructions phases, as characterized by Kelly, formed the base of the original hypothesis that leaded to the exam of feelings as well as the cognitive aspects of ISP." (Kuhlthau, 1991)

According to Kuhlthau (1991) people have a limited capacity to assimilate new information, that way, they on purposely construct meanings by assisted selectivity and connect them to what they already know. The active process to elaborate the information meaning is the task of the user in the ISP. Thus, searching information is a process of construction that involves all the experience of the person's feelings, and also thoughts and actions.

The new information is assimilated in many phases and it begins with the confusion (uncertainty) in which increases the inconsistencies and, the incompatibilities are confronted between the information and the present constructs. The new idea can become so threatening that it can be discarded and the construction abandoned. At this moment, there is another alternative: to form a hypothesis that can be tested and assessed to incorporate the new construct in the system of personal constructs. Forming an attempt of hypothesis is a decisive point to construct and reconstruct (Kuhlthau 1991).

The Kuhlthau studies (1991, 1993) revealed common patterns of experiences of the user in the process of information search that can be described in many stages or phases: initiation, selection, exploration, formulation, collection, and presentation. Each stage requires appropriated tasks to move to the next stage. The ISP model incorporates three aspects: the affective (feelings), the cognitive (thoughts), and the physical (actions) common to each stage. (Kuhlthau 1991)

Ingwersen

Human cognition research made by Ingwersen (1982, 1996) in their interaction with information retrieval systems, indicate the steps that lead to information retrieval. The need for information takes the user to formulate questions to the system, which are traded between user and librarian. To answer the questions, the information worker establishes a search strategy, either alphabetically or systematically, which will lead to choose which tools to use. The librarian will provide the user with the description of documents and evidence-based summaries, aiming toward evaluation by the user. This improves the interaction between user and librarian, both in the indexing step versus recovery, and in attendance in the referral service, through a process of learning management.

Ingwersen (1996) said that the science of information can be seen as a cognitive science, and also highlighted its relationship with artificial intelligence, knowledge that gained influence from the 80s, when cognitive sciences were understood as the intersection of artificial intelligence, linguistics, and psychology. Deserving of mention is the direct influence of those fields at the time of recovery of information.

The cognitive model of information retrieval process of Ingwersen (2002), focuses on identifying cognition processes that can occur on all elements of information processing involved. The variables proposed by Ingwersen (2002) show the influence of the extensive variety of factors such as the social environment, the system of information retrieval, informational objects, the intermediary, and the user. Ingwersen (2002) incorporates these variables to the notion of poly-representation, i.e. the combination of methods of representation of "potential" textual information (extraction of text for the inverted file creation, as well as the use of controlled vocabulary, for example) that may result in: redundancy, which is inherent in information retrieval processes, and learning that overlap is the term used for different informational objects, but with similar ideas.

Second, Ingwersen (2002) discussed how the user's cognitive space is divided into four components: information needs, space problem, current cognitive state, and area of interest/work task.

The need for information is characterized by the user's ability to express what they wish to retrieve during a search of information; the space problem is the gap, which characterizes the uncertainty of the user with respect to its search; the cognitive state is defined by the user's knowledge in a given time; the social and environmental conditions offered to users are the domain of interest/work task.

So the author points to the need for such cognitive structures (user, the author, and developers/maintainers of information retrieval system), and its transformations are effectively transmitted along the system.

Hjørland

In the 1990s, cognitive hegemony is questioned by Birger Hjørland (1995), to raise questions about the exclusion of cognition of social and cultural contexts in which the individual participates, declaring the need to incorporate, in psychological research, cultural and social perspectives, historically and with a broader reach, arguing:

The sociocognitive trend isn't just a criticism of the Orthodox cognitivism, and, Yes, a new way to take the cognitivist vision, integrating this focus to the sociological and cultural universe, drawing the attention of individual knowledge structure (areas of speech), for the communities that produce, share and consume knowledge. (Hjørland, 1995).

The field of speech or of knowledge is a scientific or professional space with unique communication structures, unique types of informational documents and specific combinations. For both, to identify the domain of discourse and the professional community of knowledge, focusing the context that produces it. (Hjørland, 1995).

Indexing is an intellectual processing that depends on cognition and the domain of physical, psychological and sociocognitive context, assuming that the indexer will need to perform the identification and selection of concepts in the design and content oriented to the demand. The basic premise of the theoretical-methodological proposal of Hjørland (2002; Fujita, 2006), based on the analysis of domain, noting that the content is irrelevant to the analysis of an area specific domain knowledge, transcending the speciality in librarianship or information science. (Apud Fujita Hjørland, 2002, 2006).

Hjørland (2002 apud Fujita, 2006) notes that the science of Information needs to understand and interact with different knowledge areas and groups of users, under humanistic and sociological approaches, reinforcing the socio-cognitivist vision.

Dervin

The theory of sense-making stands out as important cognitive approach in the study of users. Brenda Dervin (2003), author of this theory, offers a theoretical and methodological proposal prepared by separating humans by information systems. Sense-making understands how a given incomplete information, to which the individual assigns sense from the intervention of its interior mental schemes. The search for information is driven by a gap, a failure in the structure of the user's knowledge, which requires changes in strategies seeking answers, by the user, to the problem, i.e. the need that led to their informational search.

Sense-making is made up of four elements: the situation in time and space; the gap that identifies the desired situation; the use, or the result; the bridge as a means to fill the gap, i.e. the user's need.

The sense-making theory of Dervin (1983 1986) has been developed for many years. According to it, the "reality" (the contexts) is neither complete nor constant, instead, it is permeated with fundamental and diffused discontinuities called gaps. In this way, the human being is seen as a set of tools that assumes a supposed reality to make/create sense of this reality that is at the same time chaotic and ordered. It is about a methodology model to use and study the information, and it cannot be seen only as a model of information search. However, in the sense-making theory, the individuals are recognized with different behavior to search and use information, even though they are within an environment of common work, or a group of common interests (Ferreira 1997).

The value of Dervin's model (1983 1986) is a part in its methodological consequences regarding informational behavior, leading to a way of questioning that can reveal the nature of a problematic situation (the problem or the uncertainty), to the extent that the information will serve to cross the gap of uncertainty, confusion, et cetera and to reach the nature of the results with the information use.

Ellis

The behavioral model of enquiry Ellis (1989) is not fused in diagrammatic form and makes no requirement to the effect that the various behaviors (when searching for information) constitute themselves into a single set of phases/stages; actually he uses the term "features" instead of "phases." These characteristics are:

- **Tutorial:** means employed by the user to begin seeking information;
- **Link:** following a network of citations or other forms of referential connection;
- **Navigation:** seeks casual by information in areas of potential interest;
- **Differentiation:** using known differences between the sources found, as a way to filter the amount of information collected;
- **Monitoring:** keep up to date regularly monitor the sources of information;
- **Extraction:** selecting relevant sources;
- **Checklist:** checking of the accuracy of information;
- **Finalization:** a final attempt for information search.

Such behaviors do not necessarily happen in a specific sequence and can be started in different sequences and in different time in the process of global search. It means, from the start, man can go to browse, go to a link, come back to the start, make the monitoring, come back to a link, et cetera.

It should be noted that the search of information models presented are derived from surveys and studies in the area of information science. They differ in vocabulary, emphases, approaches, and theoretical and methodological assumptions; however, they all bring significant contributions to submit potential variables involved in the user's search behavior, and thus, contribute templates with subsidies for thematic information treatment, provoking reflections and challenges towards developing methods for organizing inventory information, in order to increase access, incorporating the users' perspective.

It is recognized, through these studies on models, the existence of differences in the various search styles, with its many variables involved in the user's search behavior, suggesting to information professionals better attention in how to organize and represent information, especially in the digital environment. Starting from the detection of these behaviors and the motivation of users, information workers can develop systems of organization and representation of information that promotes multiple approaches in representation, organization, and presentation of information, facilitating human behavior, search, and retrieval of information in this way.

GAP IN ACCESS TO KNOWLEDGE: BRAZILIAN SITUATION

Given the emerging situation – advanced development of science and technology – the question is whether the school and library are ensuring the acquisition of skills needed to understand the complexity of the reality that exist in the contemporary world, with respect to socio-political–economic aspects: scientific, technological, cognitive, et cetera. With this concern, the United Nations Educational, Scientific and Cultural Organization (UNESCO) is insisting on discussing and finding out solutions to a number of issues of utmost importance (UNESCO, 1998; PROJECT CIRET-UNESCO, 1997), among which are the following statements: developing countries will only achieve development with qualified and competent preparation of their professionals; global changes happen in a accelerated rhythm; classical logic and using only one way of thinking generates poverty; it's impossible to continue knowledge fragmentation; there needs to be a transdisciplinary approach in culture, politics, economics, and religious areas.

The text gives us a series of reflections about science and technology's mission as human development tools. It's clear that the world is divided between those that produce and appropriate themselves with the benefits from advancements of C&T and those who ignore the degree of development of science, for not having critical condition at least evaluate or assess it, much less appropriate it.

In finding strategies to achieve quality in education, surveys are made to establish cause and effects, taking as an example the international Student Assessment (PISA) made by the Organisation for Economic Co-operation and Development (OECD). PISA was created to measure the empowerment of young people who are about to complete compulsory education to meet the challenges of today's societies, dependent on knowledge, focusing on abilities of reflection, applying knowledge and face challenges.

According to authors cited in PISA (2000), an important factor that allows you to predict the comprehension in reading is the amount of time students spend reading. If students read well, they tend to read more, and consequently gain more knowledge in all areas. Students with disabilities often find that reading material is too difficult, and therefore, they develop a negative attitude towards reading, and end up entering a vicious circle, since, by reading less, they have less opportunity to develop reading comprehension strategies, and thus are lagged in all disciplines because reading is required for all academic areas.

Levels of literacy proficiency in reading are determined by the structure and complexity of the text itself. However, notice also that, in most readers, questions or instructions vary along the scale of literacy in reading. This means that, although the structure of a text contributes to the difficulty of an item, what the reader needs to do with the text, defined by question or statement affects the overall difficulty of the task (PISA 2000).

Currently, the concept of literacy demystifies the division of readers and non-readers, questioning the readings given legitimacy by cultural tradition associated with certain objects, shapes, places, and reader models and brings in underlying searches that thematize reading. Literacy has thus been within the academic production, a term which now replaces, or extends, but opposed to the concept of reading.

In Brazil, the results of Exame Nacional do Ensino Médio (ENEM), disseminated by MEC/SAEB, reinforce the need for studies and attitudes that optimize the informational literacy for reading, thus strengthening in higher education, the act of reading. Also, the differences related to public school and the private school, the latter scores higher than the public school. Averages are associated with schooling of father and mother and to the family income. Lower averages, located in public school, are articulated to the absence of parental education and on lower household income ranges from a minimum wage, inferring that inequality of family literacy and the consequent lack of access to information are reflected in the degree of cognitive proficiency of students.

According to the pedagogical considerations about the ENEM 2001 and 2002,

"The absence of comprehensive reading domain was the main cause of lie the performance of the participants of ENEM between insufficient and regular, comprehensive visa that reading is a global process, linked intrinsically fuzzy intentions of participant (reader), teachers authors of problem situations, and context-sensitive socio-historical where both the author and the reader are immersed. To understand the text of problem situations of ENEM, the participant needs to build

a mental model of the situation described above, and this requires a series of previous skills: word recognition, understanding of grammatical and semantic relationships between words and the integration of ideas and concepts through inferences. The inferences intra-sentences require membership information contained in the text of the situation-problem; the pragmatic need inferences previously constructed knowledge; and the inferences avaliativas require personal placements and involve values. The comprehensive reading is, therefore, an integration process and construction of meanings. "(Source: ENEM final reports, 2001, 2002 and 2003)

More recently, the INAF/2007, created and implemented by Instituto Paulo Montenegro, shedding innovative educational practices, and by NGOS, Educational Action comes being held since 2001 and implemented by sampling of 2000 people, between 15 and 64 years who reside in urban and rural areas in all regions of Brazil. The INAF works with the term "literacy," corresponding to the term in English literacy on condition of persons or social groups in making use of written language. The term Literacy considers the two domains: *literacy* (verbal information processing in various formats; written comprehension and expression) and *numeracy*, ability to understand and operate with mathematical representations and concepts involved in everyday situations.

Based on the analysis of the tasks, the INAF has defined four levels of literacy:

1. Illiteracy;
2. Literacy in rudimentary level;
3. Literacy in basic level;
4. Literacy in full level.

The results show that the level of schooling does not always provide the level of skill that is expected, since 64% of Brazilians between 15 and 64 years old that studied up to fourth grade get the literacy in rudimentary level, 12% from the 64% are considered to have absolute illiteracy on skills of reading/writing; they do not decode words and phrases and show difficulties dealing with numbers in daily situations, despite they studied for four years in the Elementary School. Those who studied the fifth to eighth grade, just 20% can be considered fully literate, while most of them are in the basic level of literacy.

We can note that 26% of those who studied between the fifth and eighth grade are still in the rudimentary level; whereas 47% of those who studied or are studying secondary school reach the literacy in full level (it is expected 100% of this group) and practically 45% remain in the basic level; only the ones who reach the high school (74%) are the individuals that have full mastery of reading/writing skills and of mathematic skills.

INAF shows, also, the distribution of different levels of literacy throughout Brazil, emphasizing regional contrasts and differences: people from the South have a higher level of literacy, with 71% of functionally literate, with 1/3 of full power; the northeast has the largest contingent of functionally illiterate, representing 46% of people between 15 and 64 years old; there is similarity in the profile of the South and Southeast population (more people in the basic level, a small amount of illiterate and equivalent proportions in the full and rudimentary levels).

Confirming the indicators of INAF, the Brazilian Institute of Geographic and Statistics (IBGE) states that 11.4% of people older than 15 years old are illiterate and 23.5% are functionally illiterate, which means they are considered literate but they cannot read and interpret information. Of people older than 10 years old, 11.3% are not instructed or studied less than one year, and just 26% studied for 11 years or longer than that (IBGE 2004-2005). IBGE shows that, generally, the Brazilian people do not have high level of instruction and, probably do not dominate information technologies.

INAF shows that most literate people in the rudimentary and basic level do not read books (29% and 16%) or they read only a type of book

(42%), normally, the Bible or religious books. The reading of the literate people in the full level is diversified (33% read two kinds and 34% three or more). To enrich the data, in the 2003 and 2005 editions, INAF asked the interviewees if they had been to a library and where. The results show that there was a decrease in the number of people who had already been to a public library (from 59% to 49%), but it the people who had already been to a school library increased a little (from 45% to 49%). The multivariate analysis of the INAF's data has showed that going in many libraries is an important differential in literacy levels.

The results of INAF from 2001-2007 show that it needs to invest in the quality, so that the schooling can provide the necessary learning and the citizens can insert in a autonomous and responsible way in contemporary society. It is also very important to analyze the library function to subsidize the process of literacy/illiteracy that has happened in the Brazilian Education.

A new quality must be constructed, by considering demands of using the reading, writing, and mathematics, it is not only to keep studying, but also to insert in a efficient and autonomous way in the world of work and to practice the citizenship.

How, then, is it possible to form new generations prepared for the self-government of learn, if these people don't have developed thinking skills to anticipate, to find alternatives and strategies to resolve problems and to make decisions? How is it possible to expand the professional and personal opportunities without providing flexible thinking that allows changes?

Ideologically society is aware that it is necessary to produce a more harmonious development, hence the discussions, on the other hand, that technology has already produced the conditions for bringing knowledge to everyone. However, social differences are created, especially by the income gap.

A new quality needs to be built, considering the demands of reading, writing, and math not only for the continuity of studies, but to give the subject conditions of insertion, efficiently and unattended in the world of work and in the exercise of citizenship. There is the need to draft and implement policies that can extend the socialization of information and promote more intensely the dissemination of knowledge.

CONCLUSION

Ideologically society is aware that it is necessary to produce a more harmonious development; for this reason, discussions and the establishment of social and educational goals are presented in supranational social forums. Governments and society are focused on the integration and social development of the human being; science and technology have already produced the physical conditions, such as computers networks, which can spread knowledge to all corners of the planet, however actions have been accomplished very slowly, and the strategies adopted don't consider the global and local political interests.

It's important, however, that a new concrete and objective quality is built urgently, especially considering the historical delay to which is afforded the population of certain parts of the planet, and also by the obstacle that such a situation creates the in the developing world.

Information and communication technologies have brought the belief that they would make possible the universalization of knowledge; there is to consider, however, that many searches demonstrate this fact, and not just the existence of physical network and the possibility of handling equipment. It's necessary to promote, on the subject, the conditions for the acquisition of intellectual knowledge, through the developing of instrumental natural skills and fundamental and applied skills, which can raise knowledge, giving subsidy to citizens, to participate with autonomy and responsibility in the contemporary society.

Brazil, for example, a country of many contrasts, is today the thirteenth in the ranking of scientific knowledge production, a consequence of a post-graduation system of high quality, legitimized by the local and international scientific community, coordinated under the rigor of monitoring and evaluation by Coordenação de Aperfeiçoamento de Pessoal de Nível Superior, CAPES. However, the indicators of INAF presented here demonstrate the fragility of teaching in primary and secondary levels, which will compromise the quality of science education later.

Libraries integrate educational-cultural segment of a country and have the mission to contribute to the formation of an infrastructural intelligence in society. In this sense, the government, the community librarian, and cultured society have a responsibility to promote policies and actions that foster the emergence structuring this cultural base.

In this direction the Brazilian Government imposed some measures, such as the law (n° 10,753, 30 October 2003) laying down National Book Policy, aiming to ensure access to and use of the book, promoting the transfer of knowledge, the dissemination of culture, promoting social and scientific research, as well as to promote and encourage the habit of reading and empower people to use the book as an essential factor for economic, social, and political progress, to promote the fair distribution of knowledge and income. Already another law (n° 12,244/2010) determines that each public or private school should have, obligatorily, a library under conditions sufficient to meet the number of students enrolled, considering that the book is a means of dissemination of culture and transmission of knowledge.

About professional assistance, the Conselho Federal de Biblioteconomia created the project Construction of an Information network for Public Education, which proposes the establishment of a comprehensive national effort aimed at promoting higher quality in public education through the provision of quality information, which contributes to the formation of critical autonomy of Brazilian citizen and the development of informational competence that instrumentalizes the subject for research and for life.

In summary, the supranational institutions, constitutive governments, and society, those devising development projects should consider in the foreground the valorization of the human being, and apply Morin's maximum.

REFERENCES

ALFIN/EEES. (2005). *Habilidades e competencias de gestión da información para aprender a aprender en el marco del espacio europeo de enseñanza superior*. Espanha: Universidade de Granada. Retrieved October 15, 2009, from: www.um.es/dp-lengua-espa/.../habilidades-competencias.pdf.

American Library Association. (1989, January). *Report of the presidential Committee on information literacy: final report.* Retrieved October 3, 2009, from: http://www.ala.org/ala/mgrps//divs/acrl/publications/whitepapersreports.cfm

Bakhtin, M. (1981). *Marxismo e filosofia da linguagem*. (6Th Ed.). Translated by Michel Lahud e Yara F. Vieira (da edição de Paris: Les Éditions de Minuit, 1977), São Paulo: Hucitec.

Barthes, R. (1992). *Elementos de semiologia*. Translated by de Izidoro Bilkstein (do original Élements de Sémiologie, Paris: Seuil, 1964). São Paulo: Editora Cultrix.

Beghtol, C. (1986, June). Bibliographic classification theory and text linguistics: aboutness analysis, intertextuality and the cognitive act classifying documents. *The Journal of Documentation, 42*(2), 84–113. doi:10.1108/eb026788

Bloom, B. S. (1979). *Taxionomia de Objetivos Educacionais, domínio cognitivo 1*. (7Th Ed.). Translated by Flávia Maria Sant'Anna, Porto Alegre: Editora Globo.

Bloom, B. S., & Krathwohl, D. R, Masia, Bertran B. (1974). *Taxionomia de Objetivos Educacionais, domínio afetivo 2*. Translated by Jurema Alcides Cunha. 3ª impressão. Porto Alegre: Editora Globo.

Boterf, G. L. (2003). *Desenvolvendo a competência dos profissionais*. Porto Alegre: Artmed.

Bourdieu, P. (1982). *Ce que parler veut dire*. Paris: Fayard.

Branski, R. M. (2004, January/June). Recuperação de informações na Web. *Perspectiva Ciência Informação*, *9*(1), 70–87.

Brookes, Bertram C. (1980, October). The forms of information science: part 1. Philosophical aspets. *Journal of Information Science*, 2, (3/3), 125-133.

Bruner, J. (1990). *Acts of meaning*. Cambridge, Massachusetts: Harvard University Press.

Choo, C. W. (2006). *A organização do conhecimento: como as organizações usam a informação para criar significado, construir conhecimento e tomar decisões* (2nd ed.). São Paulo: Editora do Senac.

Chowdhury, G. (1999). *Introduction to modern information retrieval*. London: Library Association Publishing.

Dervin, B. NILAN, M. (1986). Information needs and uses. *Annual Review of Information Science and Technology, 21*, (pp. 03-33). NY: Knowledge industry publications

Dervin, B. (2003). *Sense-making methodology reader: selected writings of Brenda Dervin Cresskill*. NJ: Harupton Press.

Duarte, Newton. (1993). *A Individualidade para SI: contribuição a uma teoria histórico-social da formação do indivíduo*. Campinas, S.P: Editora Autores Associados.

Ellis, D. (1989). Behavioural approach to information retrieval system design. *The Journal of Documentation*, *45*(3), 171–212. doi:10.1108/eb026843

Ellis, David; Haugan, M. (1997). Modelling the information-seeking patterns of engineers and research scientists in an industrial environment. *The Journal of Documentation*, *53*(4), 384–403. doi:10.1108/EUM0000000007204

Fávero, M. H. (2005). *Psicologia e Conhecimento. Subsídios para a análise do ensinar e aprender*. Brasília: EDUnB.

Fávero, M. H. Os fundamentos teóricos e metodológicos da Psicologia do Conhecimento. In M. H. Fávero & C. Cunha (Coord.) (2008). *Psicologia do Conhecimento. O diálogo entre as ciências e a cidadania*. Brasília: UNESCO.

Ferreira, S. M. S. P. (1997). *Estudo de necessidades de informação: dos paradigmas tradicionais à abordagem Sense-Making*. Porto Alegre: ABEBD.

Feuerstein, R. (1980). *Instrumental enrichment: an intervention program for cognitive modifiability*. Baltimore: University Park Press.

Freire, P. (1979). *Educação e mudança*. Rio de Janeiro: Paz & Terra.

Freire, P. (1980). *Conscientização*. São Paulo: Moraes.

Freire, P. (1985). *Educación y concientización*. Salamanca: Sigüeme.

Freire, P. (2002). *Pedagogia do oprimido* (32nd ed.). Rio de Janeiro: Paz & Terra.

Fujita, M. S. L. (1999, January/June). A leitura do indexador: estudo de observação. *Perspectiva em Ciência da Informação*, *4*(1), 101–116.

Fujita, M. S. L. (2006). Abordagem cognitiva e sócio-cognitiva da leitura documentária na formação inicial do indexador: análise da perspectiva individual em contexto sociocultural. In UNESP (Ed), *ENANCIB, 7, Encontro Nacional de Pesquisa em Ciência da Informação,* Anais. Marília, SP: UNESP.

Goldman, L. (1973). *Lukács et Heidegger* (p. 39). Paris: Denoël/Gonthier.

Hjørland, B. (1995). Toward a new horizon in information science: domain analysis. *Journal of the American Society for Information Science American Society for Information Science, 46*(6), 400–425. doi:10.1002/(SICI)1097-4571(199507)46:6<400::AID-ASI2>3.0.CO;2-Y

Hjørland, B. (1998). Theory and metatheory of information science: a new interpretation. *The Journal of Documentation, 54*, 606–621. doi:10.1108/EUM0000000007183

Hjørland, B. (2003). Fundaments of knowledge organization. *Knowledge Organization, 30*(2), 87–111.

Ingwersen, P. (1982, September). Search procedures in the library: analyzed from the cognitive point of view. *The Journal of Documentation, 38*(3), 165–191. doi:10.1108/eb026727

Ingwersen, P. (1996, March). Cognitive Perspective of Informaction Retrieval Interaction: elements of a Cognitive IR Theory. *The Journal of Documentation, 42*(1), 3–50. doi:10.1108/eb026960

Ingwersen, P. (1996). Cognitive perspectives of information retrieval. *Journal of Documentation, 52*(1), 03-50.

Ingwersen, P. (2002). *Information retrieval interaction*. London: Taylor Graham. 246 p. ISBN: 0-947568-54-9. PDF Version. Retrieved December 13, 2005, from: www.db.dk/pi/iri

Instituto Paulo Montengro (IPM). (2007). *Indicador de Alfabetismo Funcional (INAF); relatório*. São Paulo: IPM.

Kuhlthau, C. C. (1991). Inside the search process: information searching from the user's perspective. *Journal of the American Society for Information Science American Society for Information Science, 42*(5). doi:10.1002/(SICI)1097-4571(199106)42:5<361::AID-ASI6>3.0.CO;2-#

Kuhlthau, C. C. (1993). A principle of uncertainty for information seeking. *The Journal of Documentation, 49*(4), 339–355. doi:10.1108/eb026918

Kuhlthau, C. C. (1993). *Seeking Meaning: process approach to Library and information services*. Norwood: Ablex Publishing.

Kuhlthau, C. C. (1996). *The Concept of a zone of intervention for identifying the role of intermediaries in the information search process*. New Brunswick, NJ: Rutgers University. Retrieved March 30, 2010, from: http://mail.asis.org/annual-96/electronic proceedings/kuhlthau.html.

Lancaster, F. W. (2004). *Indexação e resumos: teoria e prática* (2nd ed.). Brasília: Briquet de Lemos Livros.

Lancaster, F. W., & Warner, A. J. (1993). *Information Retrieval Today*. Information Resources Press.

Lopes, I. L. (1985, January/June)... *Ciência da Informação, 14*(1), 55–60.

Lotman, Y. M. (1998). The semiotics of culture and the concept of a text. *Social Psychology, 26*(3), 52–58.

Mead, G. (1992). *Mind, Self, and Society* (Morris, C. W., Ed.). Chicago: University, Chicago Press.

Morin, E. (1986). *La Connaissance de la connaissance (Vol. 3)*. Paris: Le Seuil.

Morin, E. (1995). *A educação e a complexidade do ser e do saber*. Petrópolis, Rio de Janeiro: Vozes.

Morin, E. (1996). A noção de sujeito. In *Schnitman, Dora Fried (Org.). Novos paradigmas, cultura e subjetividade*. Porto Alegre: Artes Médicas.

Morin, E. (1998). *Ciência com consciência*. (2nd ed.) Translated by Maria D. Alexandre e Maria Alice Sampaio Dória. Rio de Janeiro: Bertrand.

Morin, E. (2000). *Os sete saberes necessários à educação do futuro. Translated by Catarina Eleonora F. da Silva e Jeanne Sawaya. São Paulo: Cortez*. Brasilia: Unesco.

Morin, E. (2005). *O Método 3: Conhecimento do Conhecimento* (3rd ed.). Porto Alegre: Sulina.

Moscovici, S. (1988). Notes towards a description of Social Representations. *European Journal of Social Psychology, 18*, 211–250. doi:10.1002/ejsp.2420180303

Novellino, Maria Salet Ferreira. (1996, july/december) *Instrumentos e metodologias de representação da informação, 1*(2), 37-45.

Perrenoud, P. (2000). *Dez novas competências para ensinar* (Ramos, P. C., Trans.). Porto Alegre: Artes Médicas Sul.

Piaget, J. (1971). *A epistemologia genética*. Petrópolis: Vozes.

Piaget, J. (1977). *A tomada de consciência*. São Paulo: Edições Melhoramentos/Editora de São Paulo.

Pinto Molina, M. (1994, June). Intedisciplinary approaches to the concept and practice of written text documentary content text. *The Journal of Documentation, 50*(2), 111–133. doi:10.1108/eb026927

Saracevic, T. (1996, January/February). Ciência da Informação: origem, evolução e relações. *Perspectivas em Ciência da Informação, 1*(1), 41–62.

Saracevic, T. (1996, January/June). Ciência da informação: origem, evolução e relações. *Perspectivas em Ciência da Informação, 1*(1), 41–62.

Souza, Ana Maria Martins de; Despresbiteris, Lea; Machado, Osny Telles Marcondes. (2004). *A mediação como princípio educacional* – bases teóricas de Reuven Feuerstein. São Paulo: Editora do Senac.

Sternberg, R. J. (2000). *Psicologia cognitiva*. Porto Alegre: Artes Médicas.

Teixeira, G. (2008). *Significado de competência. Ensino e aprendizagem. Ser professor universitário*. Retrieved September 28, 2009, from: http://www.serprofessoruniversitario.pro.br/ler.php?modulo=12&texto=728

UNESCO. (1998, October 5-9). Declaración Mundial sobre la Educación Superior en el siglo XXI: Visión y Acción. *Conferencia Mundial sobre la Educación Superior*. Paris. Dervin, B. (1983). An overview of sense-making research: concepts, methods and results to date. In *International Communications Association Annual Meeting*. Dallas, Texas.

UNESCO – CIRET. (1998, April). Que Universidade para o Amanhã? Em busca de uma evolução transdisciplinar da Universidade. *Congresso Internacional de Locarno*. Retrieved August 15, 2010, from: http://perso.club-internet.fr/nicol/ciret/.

Urdaneta, I. P. (1992). *Gestión de la Inteligência. Aprendizaje Tecnológico y Modernización del Trabajo Informacional. Retos y oportunidades*. Caracas, Venezuela: Instituto de Estúdios del Conocimento de la UniversidadSimon Bolívar / Consejo Nacional de Investigaciones Científicas Y Tecnológicas.

Díaz Villa, Mario. (2002). *Flexibilidad y educación superior en Colômbia*. Bogotá: Série Calidad de la Educación, n. 02. ICFES-MEN.

Vygotsky, LS. (1979). *Consciousness as a Problem in the Psychology of Behavior Soviet Psychology*, Summer 1979/vol. XVII, no. 4, p. 35.

Vygotsky, L. S. (1991). *A formação social da mente*. São Paulo: Martins Fontes.

Wallon, H. (1963). "Psychologie et matérialisme dialectique" *Enfance, Numero special*. In *Henri Wallon, buts et méthodes de la psychologie* (pp. 31–34). Janvrier-avril.

Wilson, T. D. (1981). *On user studies and information needs. Journal of Documentation, 37*, (1), 03–15. Retrieved April 23, 2007, from: http://informationr.net/ir/9-1/paper164.html

Wilson, T. D. (1996). *Information behaviour, an interdisciplinary perspective*. Retrieved April 23, 2007, from: http://informationr.net/tdw/publ/infbehav/

Wilson, T. D. (1999). Models in information behaviour research. *The Journal of Documentation, 55*(3), 249–270. doi:10.1108/EUM0000000007145

ADDITIONAL READING

Albrechtsen, H. (1993). Domain analysis in Information Science: investigations into the nature and structure of knowledge domains for classification and retrieval. In *Proceedings of the 56th ASIS Annual Meeting, 30*, p.290-291.

Albrechtsen, H. (1993, October). Subject analysis and indexing: from automated indexing to domain analysis. *The Indexer, 18*(4), 219–224.

Alvarenga, L. (2003). Representação do conhecimento na perspectiva da Ciência da Informação em tempo e espaço digitais. *Encontros Bibli: Revista Eletrônica de Biblioteconomia e Ciência da Informação*, (15).

April 18, 2006 from http://mariner.rutgers.edu/tipster3/iirs.html

Authier, M., & Lévy, P. (1993). *Les arbres des connaissances*. Paris: La Découverte.

Baeza-Yates, R., & Ribeiro-Neto, B. (1999). *Modern information retrieval*. New York, NY: Addison Wesley.

Barclay, R. O., & Murray, P. C. (1997). *What is knowledge management?* Retrieved March 15, 2009, from http://www.media-access.com/whats.html

Bardin, L. (1977). *Análise de conteúdo*. Lisboa: Edições 70.

Barreto, Aldo de Albuquerque. (2001, August). A informação em seus momentos de passagem. *DataGramaZero: revista de Ciência da Informação, 2*(4). Retrieved August 27, 2001, from: http://www.degzero.org/Atual/Art_01.htm.

Bateson, G. (1986). *Mente e natureza*. Translated by Claudia Gerpe. Rio de Janeiro: Francisco Alves. (Translation of the original: Mind and nature: a necessary unity, 1979).

Belkin, N. J. (2004). *Intelligent information retrieval: whose intelligence?* Retrieved.

Buckland, M. K. (1991). Information as think. *Journal of the American Society for Information Science American Society for Information Science, 45*(5), 351–360. doi:10.1002/(SICI)1097-4571(199106)42:5<351::AID-ASI5>3.0.CO;2-3

Carlos, H. (2005). *Bibliotecas digitais: saberes e práticas, Salvador: EDUFBA* (pp. 55–75). Brasília: IBICT.

Cintra, A. M. (2002). *Para entender as linguagens documentárias* (2nd ed.). São Paulo: Polis.

Cristine, B. A. R. R. Y. (1997). A. Information skills for an electronic world: training doctoral research students. *Journal of Information Science, 23*(3), 225–238. doi:10.1177/016555159702300306

Dudziak, E. A. (2001). *A information literacy e o papel educacional das bibliotecas*. Unpublished Master's degree dissertation. Escola de Comunicações e Artes da Universidade de São Paulo. São Paulo.

Dudziak, Elisabeth Adriana. (2007). O bibliotecário como agente de transformação em uma sociedade complexa: integração entre ciência, tecnologia, desenvolvimento e inclusão social. *Ponto de Acesso: Revista do Instituto de Ciência da Informação da UFBA, 1*, (1).

Ellis, D. (1989). Behavioural approach to information retrieval system design. *The Journal of Documentation, 45*(3), 171–212. doi:10.1108/eb026843

Ellis, David; HAUGAN, M. (1997). Modelling the information-seeking patterns of engineers and research scientists in an industrial environment. *The Journal of Documentation, 53*(4), 384–403. doi:10.1108/EUM0000000007204

Ferneda, E. (2003). *Recuperação de informação: análise sobre a contribuição da Ciência da Computação para a Ciência da Informação*. 137 p. Unpublished doctoral degree thesis. Escola de Comunicações e Artes, Universidade de São Paulo, São Paulo.

Fugmann, R. (1990). An interactive classaurus on the PC. *International Classification, 17*(3/4), 133–137.

Garrick, J., & Clegg, S. (2000). Knowledge work and the new demand of learning. *Journal of Knowledge Management, Bradford, 4*(4), 279–286. doi:10.1108/13673270010379821

Grossi, E. P. (1992). Ser a Aprender em Nova Síntese. In *Grossi, Esther Pillar; Freire, Madalena. (1992). Paixão de Aprender. Petrópolis, Rj: Vozes*. Construtivismo Pós-Piagetiano.

Hjorland, B. (1992, June). The concept of 'subject' in Information Science. *The Journal of Documentation, 48*(2), 172–200. doi:10.1108/eb026895

Imbert, M. (1998). Neurociências e Ciências Cognitivas. In ANDLER, Daniel. (ed). *Introdução às Ciências Cognitivas*. São Leopoldo: Ed. Unisinos.

Japiassú, H. (1975). *Interdisciplinaridade e patologia do saber*. Rio de Janeiro: Imago.

Japiassu, H. (1993, September/December). A representação do conhecimento e o conhecimento da representação: algumas questões epistemológicas. *Ciência da Informação, 22*(3), 217–222.

Järvelin, K., & Wilson, T. D. (2003). On conceptual models for information seeking and retrieval research. *Information Research, 9*(1), Retrieved April 12, 2007, from http://InformationR.net/ir/9-1/paper163.html

Johnson-Laird, P. (1983). *Mental models*. Cambridge, UK: Cambridge University Press.

Katiachedid. (2008). *Cognição. Cognitio?* Núcleo de Ciência Cognitiva da USP. Retrieved July 12, 2008, from http://cognitio.incubadora.fapesp.br/portal/espaco aberto/Cogni_c3_a7_c3_a3o

Kent, A. (1972). *Manual da recuperação mecânica da informação* (Berrini, B., Trans.). São Paulo: Polígono.

Luria, A. R. (1976). *Cognitive development: as cultural and social foundation. Org. by M. Cole*. Cambridge, MA: Harvard University Press.

Mai, J.-E. (2000). Deconstructing the indexing process. *Advances in Librarianship, 23*, 269–298. doi:10.1108/S0065-2830(1999)0000023013

Manis, M. (1973). *Processos cognitivos*. São Paulo: Herder.

MEHO, Lokman I.& TIBBO, Helen R. (2003). Modeling the information-seeking behavior of social scientists: Ellis's study revisited. *Journal of the American Society for Information Science and Technology, 54*(6), 570–587. doi:10.1002/asi.10244

Mooers, C. N. (1951). Zatacoding applied to mechanical organization of knowledge. *American Documentation, 2*, 20–32. doi:10.1002/asi.5090020107

Morin, E. (1991). *O paradigma perdido: a natureza humana* (5th ed.). Lisboa: Europa-América.

Nerlich, B.& Clarcke. (2000). D. *Semantics fields and frames*. *Pragmatics*, 32.

Novak, J. D. Gowin, D. B. (1988). A*prendiendo a aprender*, Barcelona, Martínez Roca.

Olmi, A., & Perkoski, N. (2005). *Leitura e cognição: uma abordagem transdisciplinar*. Santa Cruz do Sul: EDUNISC, 256p.

UNESCO. (1998). Declaración Mundial sobre la Educación Superior en el siglo XXI: visión y acción. In: *Conferencia Mundial sobre la Educación Superior*. Paris. Retrieved April 10, 2009, from http://www.unesco.org/education/educprog/wche/declaration_spa.htm

Varela, A. V. (2007). *Informação e Autonomia: a mediação segundo Feuerstein*. São Paulo: Editora. *SENAC*, *1*, 368.

Varela, A. V. (2007). Informação e Construção da Cidadania. Brasilia. *Thesaurus*, *1*, 167.

Varela, A. V. (2008). Sistema informacional, lectura y conocimiento: gerenciando el flujo de una herramienta cognitiva hacia la albatización informacional. *Investigación Bibliotecólogia*, *22*, 89–102.

Varela, A. V. (2008). Informação, cognição e mediação: vertentes, contextos e pretextos. *Revista Ibero-americana de Ciência da Informação*, *1*, 21–45.

KEY TERMS AND DEFINITIONS

Interactive Communication Process: This process involves the information professional and users to search, to select and to use information. It's a dialectic process in which both learn how to improve and create new knowledge.

Information Competence: The informational competence is realized in the internalization of the trajectory of the 'knowing how to learn, how the knowledge is organized, how to find the information and how to use it' in a clear way, so that everyone can learn from it.

Information Needs: The needs comes from questions, uncertainties, answers that someone needs to solve problems.

Information Retrieval System: Information system constituted by interactive process involving, searching, finding, and presentation of potential information desired by a human user. The systems organize, store, manage and make accessible the documentary information that are represented in these item.

Learning Theories: They explain the mental structures and how knowledge is constructed to modify behaviors by acquisitions from experiences.

Search and Recuperation Models: Models are presented as diagrams that try to represent the activity of searching. Models have contents taking diverse perspectives (cognitive, social, organizational etc.). Cognitive models demonstrate how the information transfer and IR interaction happen.

User's Studies: They present how the user's brain process information and use information in their interactions with a informational system. In the information search process multiples variables interfer on behaviour informational.

Subsection
Vertical Integration of Collaborative Information Systems

Chapter 6
Understanding User Attitudes toward Information Systems:
A Grounded Theory Approach

David A. Jank
Long Island University, USA

ABSTRACT

People develop attitudes toward things in many ways. While direct experience can be the foundation of permanent attitude formation, both indirect experience and referential input from others are strong influences on both attitude development and changes in personal attitude. The psychological factors that govern attitude are varied. They are documented in the scholarly literature of many fields, and frequently reference the study of people and technology. Research in the use of information systems (IS), however, does not typically aggregate the psychological factors influencing user attitude. The purpose of this chapter is to bring together the divergent empirical evidence of IS user attitude formation. A grounded theory approach is used to formally identify and analyze this evidence. Such analysis can provide a more cohesive understanding of what is known about user attitudes toward information systems, and can offer an ontological framework for more formalized study of the relationship between people and information systems.

INTRODUCTION

Psychological research tells us that even though attitude development can seem capricious at times, attitudes themselves are not easily changed once they have been established. This is true not only when referential experience is accurate, but when it is inaccurate as well. This phenomenon has implications for both developers and managers of information systems (IS). Words such as "trust," "dependability," "like," "hate," "confusing," "easy to use," and even "love" all appear in the published literature addressing people's feelings about information systems. But what do such labels actually mean? How believable are they?

DOI: 10.4018/978-1-61350-201-3.ch006

And do they really have any strong relationship to how information systems can be developed, launched, and managed?

Whether or not IS engineers pay heed to the emotional or psychological reactions of users toward information systems is of less importance than is having a clear understanding of how such reactions can impact the successful launch and acceptance of information systems. A failure to comprehend the attitudes of users toward specific IS platforms, whether in the enterprise or on the Internet, can result in rejection of a system by the audience it is intended to serve. Such rejection is particularly painful when the system is intended to make life easier for users in a certain information environment. Conversely, attention to what users have to say about information systems can enhance both the level of use and the marketability of them. Appreciation of user attitude, if modeled within an empirical framework, can ensure both meaningful product development and successful product launch.

This chapter documents the many ways in which IS users develop attitudes toward information systems in order to provide a framework for studying this phenomenon. It offers a detailed breakdown of the manner in which attitudes toward IS are discussed across cognate disciplines. The tools of discourse analysis and bibliometrics are utilized to document a number of characteristics of user attitude study. These include a taxonomic representation of the components of user attitude, and a survey of epistemological views evident in the literature on user attitudes toward information systems across disciplines. Qualitative analysis of the published research on user attitude is provided as a framework that can continually inform the development of information systems theory. Such grounded techniques can provide a reliable understanding of what the phrase "user attitudes toward information systems" actually means across all domains that inform information systems scholarship.

BACKGROUND

Users of information systems develop personalized attitudes toward IS in much the same way they develop attitudes toward other things (Jank, 2010b; Hjørland, 2007; Hemingway, 1998). These attitudes result from neurocognitive reactions to situations and things, and mental assignments of personal feelings constructed within emotional and relational paradigms (Salzer & Burks, 2003; Bhattacherjee, 2001). Such attitude formation with respect to information systems is discussed in the scholarly literature across disciplines. Examples include research on systems analysis and design (Fidel, 2006; Stone & Stone, 2005), human-computer interaction (Pantic & Rothkrantz, 2003; Schmidt, 2000), human-information interaction (Jank, 2010b; Albers, 2008), medical information systems (Miller & Sim, 2004; Moehr, 2002; Cork, Detmer, & Friedman, 1998), and social computing (Wang, Carley, Zeng, & Mao, 2007; Bradley, 2006). This discourse provides convergent epistemological views that frame human attitude development toward information systems largely in terms of activity-based interaction with technology, and functionality of systems.

More divergent scholarship documenting attitude formation on a personal and emotional level is evident in domain-specific discourse. This scholarship can beneficially inform the development of grounded theory in IS. In these communities of discourse, emphasis is less on the interactive nature of information systems and more on the behaviors exhibited by users of these systems in ways that are particular to their spheres of activity. Topics found within this sort of scholarly discourse include feelings of trust (Griffiths, 2007; Nicolaou & McKnight, 2006), affect (Nicholas, Huntington, Williams, & Dobrowolski, 2004; Wagner & Flannery, 2004), and willingness to use information systems (Zviran, Glezer, & Avni, 2006; Santosa, Wei, & Chan, 2005).

The study of attitude formation toward "things" shows that people tend to ascribe personalized attributes toward many non-human entities. Scholars have been able to model people's attitudes toward animals, plants, historical artifacts, images and symbols, words and phrases, and political institutions (Jank, 2010b). Related models document the attitudes people hold toward computer systems and other technology products. These include such things as feelings, moods, and opinions that relate to people's perceptions of IS usability and interface design, as well as certain associated attitudes such as trust (McKnight & Chervany, 2002), believability (Kelton, Fleischmann, & Wallace, 2008), anxiety (Barki & Hartwick, 2001), comfort level (Gal-Or & Ghose, 2004), and satisfaction (Liang, Lai, & Ku, 2007).

When looked at ontologically, all research on attitude development toward information systems can be valuable to systems designers and developers. Epistemologically, however, these varied approaches to the study of people and IS have rarely been quantitatively or qualitatively analyzed, and their multidisciplinary facets are not properly established as foundational components of information systems theory. This can make it difficult for scholars studying theories of information systems development because summary data is rarely available concerning the personalized feelings about information systems that users are known to possess. This can be exacerbated by the fact that, with respect to technology, such scholarship is spread throughout many different academic domains, and rarely unified. Methods for documenting and analyzing related scholarship in divergent communities of discourse are well established. They offer scholars a number of approaches to bringing related areas of scholarship together in a way that more uniformly informs a particular discipline.

Chen and Chen (2005) demonstrated that it is possible to create ontological frameworks for areas of study that cross multiple domains, yet are not uniquely domains of their own. Jank (2010b) and White and McCain (1998) demonstrated that such an approach to domain analysis is particularly valuable for identifying key areas of research that are cognate to a specific field of study. This technique can inform the study of interdisciplinary discourse by examining characteristics of data emergent in its empirical research. This chapter offers a grounded view of IS user attitude formation that provides:

- A taxonomic depiction of the conceptual components of "user attitudes" as documented in the literature;
- A contextual analysis of those areas of scholarship that provide a home for the scholarly discourse of IS user attitudes, and that identifies specific discursive communities as "homes" to user attitudes research ; and
- An ontological framework of current and emergent discourse found in user attitude research that can contribute to the development of information systems theory.

UNDERSTANDING USER ATTITUDES IN THE IS ENVIRONMENT

Grounded Theory and Domain Analysis

In this chapter, I summarize the results of discourse analysis performed on published scholarly literature covering a fifteen year period of time. The charts, tables, and figures presented here were constructed following data mining, filtering, and bibliometric analyses of this literature across scholarly disciplines from 1995-2010. In this section, I attempt to define what is "meant" by the phrase "user attitudes" toward information systems by way of content and discourse analyses of the prominent literature identified for this time period. Grounded theory principles are followed in analyzing these data in order to establish a more cohesive view of user attitudes, framed entirely in terms of how scholars and practitioners interpret or use this phrase within their own communities of discourse.

Glaser and Strauss (1967) established four stages of grounded theory analysis for identifying and understanding areas of scholarly study that are not definitively linked to a particular domain of discourse. These are: categories, concepts, codes, and theory. Based to a large degree on qualitative analysis of documented research findings, these processes allow for identification and analysis of component pieces of knowledge for one concept that may be spread across a variety of cognate disciplines that address that concept. In the field of information science, this practice can be seen in the use of bibliometrics (White & McCain, 1998) and domain analysis (Hjørland, 2002) where quantitative analyses of published literature can be qualitatively coded to reflect underlying meaning in the use of terminology not formally defined for a particular field of study. In this chapter, grounded theory is applied as follows:

- Categories are constructed via taxonomic classification of scholarly discourse where research focuses on user attitudes
- Concepts are extracted thematically based on data mining performed on the terminology that is prominent within the scholarly literature of these disciplines
- Codes are constructed axially based on content analysis of the texts contributive to this literature
- Theory is explored via summative description of topical themes and research agendas emergent in these data

Taxonomic classification offers the ability to relationally define categories for concepts whose meanings are emergent within unique communities of discourse. Beghtol (2003) presents two methods of taxonomy construction: professional classification, in which pre-established authenticated terminology is used; and naïve classification, in which authenticated terminology is emergent across multiple communities of discourse. Jank used naïve classification to construct interdisciplinary definitions of human-information interaction (2010b) and collaborative systems (2010a). Such an approach is valuable when attempting to construct a definitive representation of user attitudes toward information systems, as the essence of this phenomenon is best understood when considered across the environments in which they are manifest. Before such classification can begin, however, it is necessary to identify appropriate sources of information from which the concepts emerge; in this instance, the areas of scholarly discourse that most strongly identify the cognate components of user attitudes toward information systems.

Figure 1 provides an overview of those communities of discourse in which user attitude formation is most typically discussed. The figure identifies and ranks these areas in terms of where this formation is documented and explored. Such identification allows for proper grounding of data extraction (Sugimoto, Pratt, & Hauser, 2008) and qualitative coding of that data (Terenziani, 2002).

The most prominent research on user attitudes toward information systems can be found in the field of Psychology, and in particular, in the research on individual behavior, socio-cognition, and social neuroscience. The fields of Information Science and Education offer similar levels of emphasis on the study of IS user attitudes. Whereas the latter discipline often defines user attitude in terms of support for curriculum and instruction, and ease of use for students, the former includes operational definitions focusing on systems analysis and design, human-computer interaction, and library and information science (the latter particularly so with respect to Internet usage patterns). Literature in the contributive areas of Sociology tends to frame user attitude in terms of social relationships and group behavior, while the scholarship in Business and Health Care

Figure 1. Areas of research most contributive to an understanding of IS user attitudes

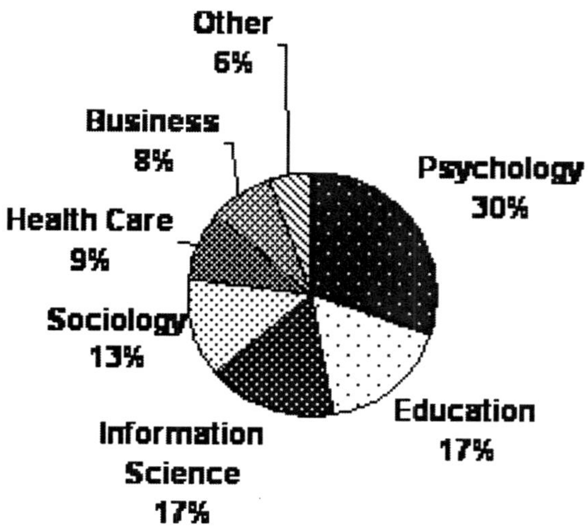

frames user attitudes in terms of effectiveness in the enterprise, or believability of medical information.

Whereas Figure 1 offers a proportional depiction of research genres that contribute to an understanding of IS user attitudes, the taxonomy in Table 1 provides a compilation of epistemological views of IS user attitudes. The categories in this Table were identified by conceptually grouping codes that were assigned to text data mined from the literature identified in the scholarly domains illustrated in Figure 1. This taxonomic approach is important for two reasons. First, it identifies what is "meant" by the term "user attitudes" with respect to information systems when employed by scholars who are engaged in such study. Second, it identifies frameworks in which the topic is studied so as to more fully understand the contexts in which this term is used.

More than 15,000 pieces of scholarly research from 1995-2010 were filtered through data mining software, and categorized using online thesauri and data dictionaries. Keywords, titles, and author supplied abstracts were parsed in order to reflect the authoritative usage of terms supplied by scholars in the fields contributive to user attitude research. The categories of user attitude discourse documented in the Table 1 taxonomy reflect thematic foci, or epistemological views, of how user attitude can be interpreted and studied. Each category in Table 1 is accompanied by contextual codes indicating prominent themes of scholarly study related to the category, and by conceptual frameworks documenting prominent research agendas evident within these themes. Discussion of these categories of discourse follows.

Behavioral Analysis: The Individual

Discussion of user attitudes toward information systems can be framed in terms of analysis of human behavior. Such examination focuses on what individuals do when utilizing IS, and how they do it. Patterns of IS use by individuals can be viewed attitudinally in terms of repetitive practices of access, personalization of system interfaces and artifacts, and individualized methods of information seeking. The published research in these areas provides a view of user attitude as something that can be measured empirically in such settings as usability labs, or examined via observational analysis of online information behavior. At the individual level, attitudes are manifest in terms of what users say they want, and what they say they like to do.

Behavioral Analysis: The Group

Unlike individual development of attitude toward IS, attitudes at the group level are strongly influenced by referential behavior, or, the tendency among members of groups (both large and small) to influence the attitudes of group members. In this venue, user attitudes toward IS are sometimes studied online, via chat rooms or virtual meeting spaces, or by the use of focus groups. More importantly, it is at the group level where scholars have documented the unpredictable aspects of

Table 1. Naïve classification of communities of discourse examining user attitudes toward information systems

Categories of User Attitude Discourse	Contextual Coding of User Attitude Research	Conceptual Frameworks of Research and Discourse
Behavioral Analysis: The Individual	• Usage patterns • Collaboration • Information seeking	• Frequency of system use • Interaction practices • Personalization techniques
Behavioral Analysis: The Group	• Information sharing • Social computing • Friendships • Relationship formation • Organizational behavior, domain-specific needs, problems, etc.	• Online networking and social media • Small/large group study • Virtual communities • Recommendations and usage needs within specific domains
Task Completion	• Work performance • Computer mediation • Application design • Training and support	• Human-computer interaction • Systems analysis and design • Knowledge management • Systems administration
Psychological Health	• Attitude development • Social neuroscience • Pathologies	• Emotions and expressions • Cognition and understanding • Effects of illness on ability to use information systems • Clinical studies of attitude

user attitudes. Input from friends, colleagues, and co-workers has been shown to influence the attitudes of individuals. It is at the group level where IS attitude is viewed as fluid, and often tied to variation in relationships among and between individuals.

Task Completion

User attitude can also be considered in terms of how well an information system is able to meet the needs of users engaged in completing specific tasks. From a research perspective, task completion is viewed both as informal (such as a person's desire to track down financial, medical, or recreational information) and formal (such as job requirements or collaborative work activities). User attitude in these venues is discussed in terms of how efficient a system is considered to be, how welcoming systems interfaces are perceived to be, and how quickly users can accomplish tasks at hand. This epistemological view of user attitudes toward IS places an emphasis on the importance of system support, help desks, training, and consulting in influencing user attitudes toward information systems.

Psychological Health

Information systems specialists can learn a great deal by understanding how user attitudes are influenced at a physiological level. A large portion of scholarship on user attitudes toward IS highlights the role played by cognition in the development of these attitudes. It focuses on how an understanding of systems operations contributes to attitudes toward them, and how attitudes are largely shaped by initial experiences with IS more so than by subsequent experiences. The emergent field of social neuroscience has shed light on how methods of learning in IS can impact the cognitive behavior of a system user, and how operational environment can directly influence attitude. Further, research in the clinical sciences has helped us to understand how pathology and overall mental health can relate to attitudes toward IS in ways that might have nothing to do with IS functionality.

An Ontological Framework for User Attitudes Toward Information Systems

Meaningful ontology construction depends upon accurately identifying distinctive terminology, and properly framing the contexts in which this terminology is used (Weng, Tsai, & Liu, 2006). Content analysis on authoritative terminology, using bibliometric techniques, allows for theory building in the study of phenomena that necessarily span multiple disciplines of study (White & McCain, 1998). Word co-occurrence analysis is used here to identify the most authoritative terminology for inclusion in an ontology, while theme co-occurrence is used to reveal the most accurate contexts in which to understand relevant usage of that terminology. The ontological framework presented allows for an understanding of the most prominent ontological themes extracted from the published literature contributive to the classification in Table 1. It also offers a ranking of these themes in terms of the most common environments in which the scholarly study of user attitudes toward IS can be found.

Such frameworks are best established by first documenting how terms are used together within communities of discourse (Hjørland, 2002). Dendrograms can be used to represent thematic partnering of terminology use, as they provide evidence of linked relationships found via word co-occurrence. Figure 2 depicts thematic linking of key terminology in IS user attitude research, as extracted from the published literature.

The benefit of dendrogram representations of word or theme co-occurrence is that concepts are

Figure 2. Thematic linking of terminology use in communities of discourse involved in the study of user attitude development toward information systems

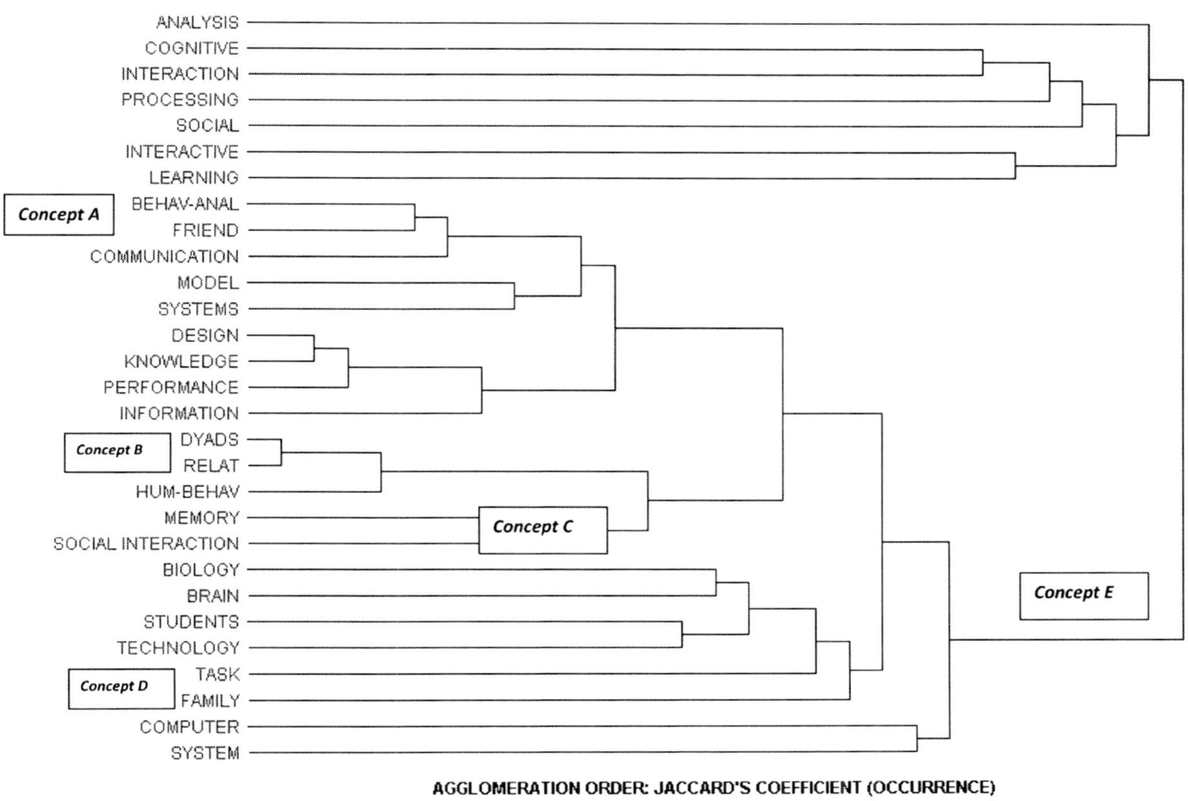

depicted both in terms of their prominence and in terms of their topical "partnering" with other concepts. In the case of discourse analysis, dendrograms reflect both the commonality of terminology use, and the contextual nature of that use, thus offering a more precise representation of words and terms that could otherwise suggest alternative meanings. The data in Figure 2 were empirically determined as most prominently occurring within the scholarly literature on user attitude development toward IS. Both terms and themes are linked conceptually, based upon the naïve classification categories in the taxonomy in Table 1.

An example of dendrogram interpretation is provided here. For example, in Figure 2, words and themes are linked by way of grid lines that represent both strength of co-occurrence and taxonomic grouping of themes. In the dendrogram, the closer the grid lines join two words or terms, the more frequently those words or terms are used together in the scholarly discourse on user attitude development. As the gridlines extend to the right, thematic grouping of words and terms become evident. For example, the dendrogram arrived at from this analysis of discourse over the time period mentioned suggests that:

- Behavioral analysis techniques seem to be regularly used when studying the role played by interpersonal communication and friendship in user attitude development toward IS [Concept A];

Figure 3. Euclidean Distance Model of term and theme co-occurrence within the published scholarship on IS user attitude development following multivariate analysis

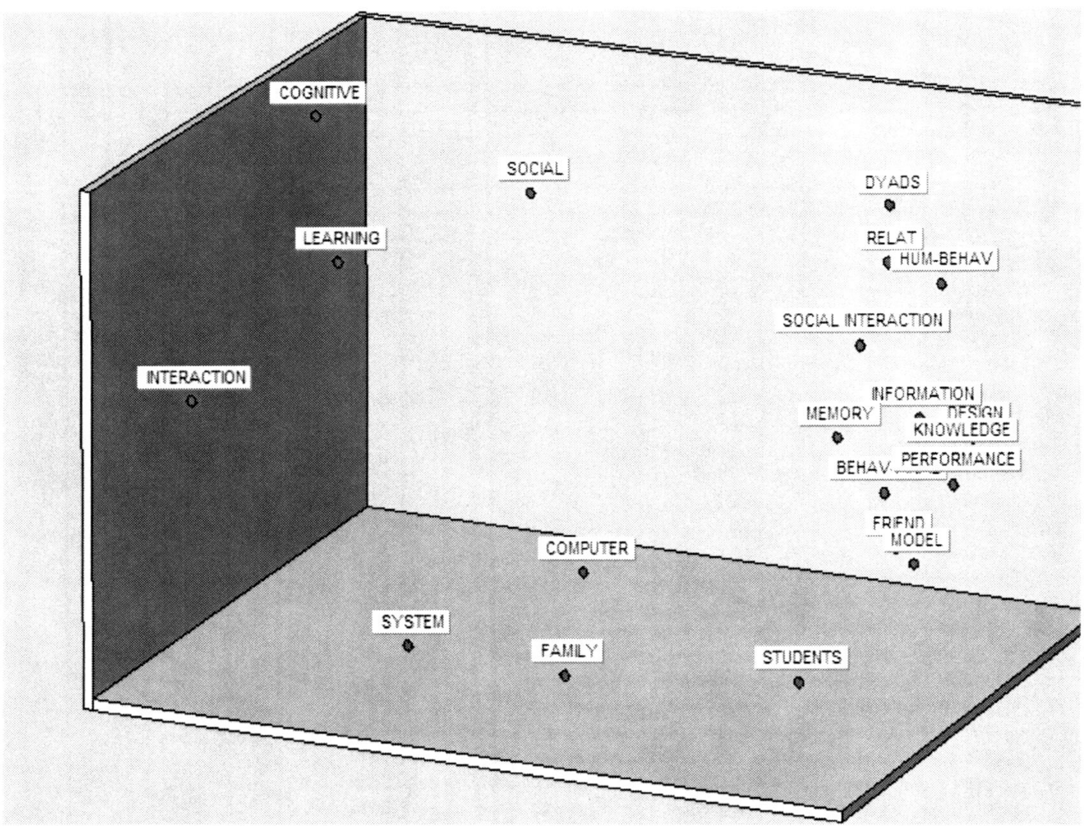

S = .12   J = .93

- The process of dyad formation between and among users of IS are discussed in terms of relationship theory [Concept B];
- The role of an individual's memory in the formation of attitudes toward IS can be discussed in the examination of social interactions between and among information systems users [Concept C];
- IS user attitude formation is studied both in terms of student groups and familial interactions, especially with respect to the use of technology for task completion [Concept D]; and
- The study of human biology (in particular, brain function) is common to several areas of research on IS user attitude formation [Concept E].

This method of dendrogram analysis can be used to uncover many patterns in the discussion of IS attitude formation. In research on information systems development, it can be especially useful because the terminology and themes presented in the dendrogram might otherwise be misinterpreted if researchers relied on their vernacular meaning alone. The relationships uncovered here allow for a more precise, and more empirically sound, interpretation of interdisciplinary scholarship during theory building.

A complement to discourse analysis as a bibliometric tool for theory building is the study of agglomeration order of topical themes evident in scholarly publishing (Jank, 2010b). Whereas the study of word co-occurrence can reveal the extent and proprietary meaning of terminology and themes within individual pieces of scholarly research, use of the Jaccard coefficient of agglomeration helps to determine how strongly these meanings permeate an entire body of scholarly discourse (in this case, within the published literature on user attitude research examined from the period 1995-2010). The Jaccard coefficient demonstrates how representative, or "believable," a depiction of discourse patterns within a body of scholarship can be.

One use of the Jaccard coefficient is to depict, by way of Euclidian distance modeling, a multivariate analysis of term and theme co-occurrence within a body of literature. Figure 3 offers a three-dimensional scaling of the most prominently occurring themes in the IS user attitude research examined here, based upon the taxonomic classification in Table 1.

In multivariate analysis, Jaccard coefficients are typically paired with stress levels as a means of empirically validating graphical representations of co-occurrence. While the Jaccard ("*J*") value indicates the validity of data representation in terms of its believability in "real life," the stress value ("*S*") signifies at what level of "shakiness" the representation might be. Jaccard coefficients greater than *.70* are thought to be acceptably representative of the thematic focus of discursive content in interdisciplinary research, while stress levels lower than *.20* are thought to indicate stability for a body of scholarship as a whole, over time (White, 2003). The multivariate analysis in Figure 3 seems to suggest that, at $J=.93$ and $S=.12$, the taxonomic classification derived from the content analysis of research literature on IS user attitude formation may well be an acceptable one.

The Jaccard coefficient may also be used to identify how prominently the validated terminology and themes established during multivariate analysis can be found throughout a body of scholarly literature. While three-dimensional scaling serves to validate the identification of key themes in terms of appropriate taxonomic classification, this additional use of Jaccard suggests just how often these themes actually occur in scholarly discourse. Table 2 provides the results of this further analysis performed on the data extracted from the relevant bodies of research literature. All words and terms included in the published scholarship were filtered through online dictionaries and thesauri, and axially coded using topical themes emergent in the Table 1 taxonomy. Table 2

Table 2. Jaccard analysis of the prominence of topical themes throughout the entire body of literature on IS user attitude formation

Discursive Themes	Jaccard	Coefficient
Input from personal friends	0.82	•••••••••••••••••••••••••••••••••••••
System performance* (*both real and perceived*)	0.82	•••••••••••••••••••••••••••••••••••••
Knowledge of system functions	0.80	••••••••••••••••••••••••••••••••••••
System design	0.78	•••••••••••••••••••••••••••••••••••
Modeling of system use	0.75	••••••••••••••••••••••••••••••••••
Availability of information on system features	0.74	•••••••••••••••••••••••••••••••••
Cognitive memory function of users	0.73	••••••••••••••••••••••••••••••••
Social interactions among users	0.69	••••••••••••••••••••••••••••••
Human behavioral analysis projects	0.63	•••••••••••••••••••••••••••••
Functioning of relationships (both person and "thing")	0.57	••••••••••••••••••••••••••••
Opinions of students	0.56	••••••••••••••••••••••••••••
Formation of dyadic relationships	0.46	•••••••••••••••••••••••
Input from family members	0.35	••••••••••••••••••
Successful/Accurate functioning of systems	0.20	••••••••••
Familiarity with computer technology (*training, experience, etc.*)	0.18	•••••••••
Individualized learning processes	0.08	••••
Levels of cognitive and neurological function of individual users	0.05	••
Awareness of human-computer interaction principles	0.04	••
Awareness of social or popular trends	0.02	•

features a "break" at the level of *J*=.50, in order to distinguish discursive themes that occur in either more or less than 50% of the published scholarship examined here.

Once a clearer understanding is established regarding proper terminology usage and epistemological themes, discourse analysis allows for empirically sound ontology construction in areas of study that do not have clearly established parameters (Hjørland, 2002). The ontology provided in Table 3 represents a merging of the taxonomic themes listed in Table 1 and the ranked prominence of topics provided in Table 2. Whereas Tables 1 and 2 offer documented categories of IS user attitude research, Table 3 provides validated groupings of the terminology most typically used in the scholarly discourse within this research.

The purpose of the ontological framework provided in Table 3 is to offer researchers in information systems development a window into how, and under what conditions, users develop attitudes toward information systems and their use. It can be helpful to IS developers to understand that many factors influencing user attitudes toward IS appear to have less to do with the functional

Table 3. An ontological framework for the study of user attitudes toward information systems as documented in the scholarly literature

Categories of User Attitude Discourse	Topical Themes (or, Research Agendas) in User Attitude Research	Prominent Terminology Groupings of Scholarly Discourse in the Study of IS Attitude Formation
Behavioral Analysis: The Individual	• Expressions/reactions • Help seeking • Motor behavior • Memory recall • Attitude formation • Dyadic relationships	• Vocalized opinions • Use of cognitive artifacts • Personalization practices • Reliance on habit/dyads • Interactive learning • Levels of cognition
Behavioral Analysis: The Group	• Within-group sharing (friends) • Within-group sharing (family members) • Shared tasks/work • Social networking • Classroom activities	• Online discussion groups • Role of "gossip" and referential input regarding system functions • Design of online classrooms • Social neuroscience and group cognition
Task Completion	• Systems analysis and design • Human-computer interaction • Automation of work functions • Quality of technical support • Availability of support tools	• Cognitive work analysis • Computer supported cooperative work • User support services/help desks • Quality/accuracy of online content • Development of online tutorials
Psychological Health	• Personal health (biological) • Personal health (neurological) • Attitudes and opinions toward IS providers • Pathologies	• Influence of emotions and feelings on IS use • Influence of illness, brain injuries, addiction, etc., on ability to understand IS • Formation of attitude, affect, trust, likes/dislikes, etc.

efficiencies of systems, and more to do with the behavioral patterns and cognitive abilities of IS users themselves. Table 3 is presented as an ontological framework rather than as an ontology for two reasons. First, it provides an empirically documented breakdown of categories of discourse, which is valuable when conducting discourse analysis of interdisciplinary fields (Hjørland, 2002). Further, it helps to establish valid parameters within which future ontology construction can occur (Tillett, 1991).

FUTURE RESEARCH DIRECTIONS

It is possible to consider future research implications for interdisciplinary scholarship by documenting epistemological stances as ontological frameworks. This allows for appropriate grounding of communities of discourse and legitimate identification of research agendas (Jank, 2010b). With respect to the development of user attitudes toward information systems, the communities of discourse examined in Tables 1 through 3 seem to be acceptable environments in which to suggest future trends in research.

Behavioral Analysis (Individuals)

It is likely that empirical study of individual behavior during information systems use will continue to be strong. Studies of information seeking behavior, personalization of IS functionality and parameters, and reliance on habit or dyadic relationships as determinants of attitude toward IS continually permeate the literature. Increasingly, clinical studies of cognitive ability and the role of memory during information systems use are topics of interest in user attitude research. This seems to be especially true in research documenting individualized learning styles, social tagging, folksonomy, and online training.

Behavioral Analysis (Group)

The study of both small and large group behavior is found in many areas of scholarly discourse. As distinctive from that of individual behavioral analysis, it continually provides new paradigms for the study of IS user attitude formation. This is particularly true in online settings such as Web-based classrooms and interactive learning environments. There appears to be an increasing number of empirical studies of user behavior in groups online; with respect to IS attitude research, the study of opinion sharing about information system features and functionality is evident in this scholarship. It is reasonable to assume, as Web-based environments continue to expand, that attitude formation toward IS (as is now the case in other areas of scholarship) may be studied in terms of what some consider a shared reality; and that the role of online reputation, credit, blame, gossip, affection, and other contributors toward group-based attitude formation will come to play an ever greater role in explaining the development of user attitudes toward IS.

Task Completion

Research on IS user attitude development is regularly found in the scholarship of human-computer interaction. In particular, scholarship on computer-supported cooperative work, activity theory, and cognitive work analysis all contribute to the study of how attitudes are developed toward information systems. In recent years, research on group-based behavioral study, such as common ground theory, has contributed to further understanding of how attitudes toward systems are influenced during task completion. In the study of organizational behavior, continued research allows for greater understanding of how group-based behavioral analysis can be applied to the study of work performance of teams. Throughout this scholarship is evidence of the role of technical support, help desks, and online tutorials for the support of individual and group work. It is likely that further research on group behavior specifically as it relates to online completion of work tasks will contribute to a broader understanding of user attitudes toward information systems.

Psychological Health

Whereas psychological research has been prominent in the study of attitude formation toward information systems for some time, this body of scholarship in recent years has expanded to reflect the impact of physiology on attitude development. Typically, this research has demonstrated how personal health, neurological function, and various pathologies can affect both attitude formation and cognitive ability of users when interacting with information systems. In recent years, research in the emergent field of social neuroscience has shown that cognitive ability is also influenced during social interaction and relationship development processes. This trend will likely have implications for research on information systems development in the future as we develop a greater understanding of the role social interaction plays in the development of attitudes toward information systems.

CONCLUSION

What at times has been lacking in the study of user attitudes toward information systems is an awareness of both how and where this scholarship takes place. Historically, various sectors within the information technology industry have addressed this issue tangentially. User attitudes frequently were acknowledged as important, but at times were not discussed in depth, or were heavily concentrated in one or two areas of research (such as the various subdisciplines of human-computer interaction). In this chapter, I have attempted to document the divergent scholarship on user attitude formation during information systems use by empirically investigating those scholarly disciplines in which it is often discussed.

Today, scholarship related to information systems development and use is not limited to the literature of information science. In research focusing on, for example, digital environments, what is known about IS attitude formation is often discussed in the contributive literature addressing applications in specific industry sectors. Consequently, by identifying how user attitudes toward IS have been empirically examined across the varied disciplines that contribute to information systems research, it is possible for scholars to further explore such research questions as:

- How might information systems in the health sciences better address the needs of patients in the health care environment?
- How can an understanding of pathology (in particular, mental illness or addictive behavior) assist IS developers in designing information systems that will be positively received?
- Might it be useful to more scientifically examine within-group behavior patterns in order to develop information systems that are well received by targeted user groups?
- Can information systems be tailored to better serve specific work teams or learning environments?
- How can consideration of the cognitive functions and learning patterns of students in both traditional and distance classroom settings contribute to more effective online learning products?
- Can collaborative product development between computer scientists and scholars outside of the IS world result in stronger acceptance of information systems in specific product environments?
- How much should developers consider such user characteristics as moods, feelings, opinions, or gossiping when designing or enhancing information systems and products?
- Is it useful for researchers in IS to be aware of the social interaction behaviors that can influence user attitudes, such as friendships, familial ties, and other relationship formation?

While user attitudes toward information systems may historically have emanated from the scholarship of information and computer science, this is no longer the case. The prominence of online networked environments, and the emerging role of social media in the information industry requires that a proper understanding of the relationship between people and information systems include consideration of the many human factors that drive attitude formation. By empirically documenting the divergent areas of scholarship where IS user attitudes are studied, it is possible to complement the user attitude scholarship that originates from within the field of information systems research. This can ultimately provide a more convergent view of IS user attitude formation, and thus inform theory building in information systems development.

REFERENCES

Albers, M. J. (2008). Human-information interaction. In C. J. Costa, A. Protopsaltis, M. Aparicio, & H. O'Neill (Eds.), *Proceedings of the 26th Annual ACM International Conference on Design of Communication* (pp. 117-124). New York, NY: Association for Computing Machinery.

Barki, H., & Hartwick, J. (2001). Interpersonal conflict and its management in information system development. *Management Information Systems Quarterly*, *25*(2), 195–228. doi:10.2307/3250929

Beghtol, C. (2003). Classification for information retrieval and classification for knowledge discovery: Relationships between "professional" and "naïve" classification. *Knowledge Organization*, *30*(2), 64–73.

Bhattacherjee, A. (2001). Understanding information systems continuance: An expectation-confirmation model. *Management Information Systems Quarterly*, *25*(3), 351–370. doi:10.2307/3250921

Bradley, G. (2006). *Social and community informatics: Humans on the Net*. New York, NY: Taylor & Francis.

Chen, A. P., & Chen, M. Y. (2005). A unifying ontology modeling for knowledge management. *Lecture Notes in Computer Science*, *3681*, 318–324. doi:10.1007/11552413_46

Cork, R. D., Detmer, W. M., & Friedman, C. P. (1998). Development and initial validation of an instrument to measure physicians' use of, knowledge about, and attitudes toward computers. *Journal of the American Medical Informatics Association*, *5*(2), 164–176. doi:10.1136/jamia.1998.0050164

Fidel, R. (2006). An ecological approach to the design of information systems. *Bulletin of the American Society for Information Science and Technology*, *33*(1), 6–8. doi:10.1002/bult.2006.1720330103

Gal-Or, E., & Ghose, A. (2004). The economic consequences of sharing security information. In Camp, L. J., & Lewis, S. (Eds.), *Economics of Information Security* (pp. 95–104). New York, NY: Springer. doi:10.1007/1-4020-8090-5_8

Glaser, B. G., & Strauss, A. (1967). *Discovery of Grounded Theory: Strategies for qualitative research*. Mill Valley, CA: Sociology Press.

Griffiths, J. R. (2007). User satisfaction as a measure of system performance. *Journal of Librarianship and Information Science*, *39*(3), 142–152. doi:10.1177/0961000607080417

Hemingway, C. J. (1998). Toward a socio-cognitive theory of information systems: An analysis of key philosophical and conceptual issues. In T. J. Larsen, L. Levine, & J. I. DeGross (Eds.), *Information systems: Current issues and future changes, Proceedings of the International Federation for Information Processing, 10-13 December 1998, Helsinki, Finland* (pp. 275-286). Helsinki, Finland: Kluwer.

Hjørland, B. (2002). Domain analysis in information science: Eleven approaches – traditional as well as innovative. *The Journal of Documentation*, *58*(4), 422–462. doi:10.1108/00220410210431136

Hjørland, B. (2007). Information: Objective or subjective/situational? *Journal of the American Society for Information Science and Technology*, *58*(10), 1448–1456. doi:10.1002/asi.20620

Jank, D. (2010a). Collaborative systems and groupware. In Bates, M. J. (Ed.), *Encyclopedia of Library and Information Sciences* (3rd ed., pp. 1088–1096). New York, NY: Taylor & Francis.

Jank, D. (2010b). Toward a unifying ontology for human-information interaction. *Canadian Journal of Information and Library Science*, *34*(4), 403–432.

Kelton, K., Fleischmann, K. R., & Wallace, W. A. (2008). Trust in digital information. *Journal of the American Society for Information Science and Technology*, *59*(3), 363–374. doi:10.1002/asi.20722

Liang, T. P., Lai, H. J., & Ku, Y. C. (2007). Personalized content recommendation and user satisfaction: Theoretical synthesis and empirical findings. *Journal of Management Information Systems*, *23*(3), 45–70. doi:10.2753/MIS0742-1222230303

McKnight, D. H., & Chervany, N. L. (2002). What trust means in e-commerce customer relationships: An interdisciplinary conceptual typology. *International Journal of Electronic Commerce*, *6*(2), 35–59.

Miller, R. H., & Sim, I. (2004). Physicians' use of electronic medical records: Barriers and solutions. *Health Affairs*, *23*(2), 116–126. doi:10.1377/hlthaff.23.2.116

Moehr, J. R. (2002). Evaluation: Salvation or nemesis of medical informatics? *Computers in Biology and Medicine*, *32*(3), 113–125. doi:10.1016/S0010-4825(02)00009-4

Nicholas, D., Huntington, P., Williams, P., & Dobrowolski, T. (2004). Re-appraising information seeking behaviour in a digital environment: Bouncers, checkers, returnees and the like. *The Journal of Documentation*, *60*(1), 24–43. doi:10.1108/00220410410516635

Nicolaou, A. I., & McKnight, D. H. (2006). Perceived information quality in data exchanges: Effects on risk, trust, and intention to use. *Information Systems Research*, *17*(4), 332–351. doi:10.1287/isre.1060.0103

Pantic, M., & Rothkrantz, L. J. M. (2003). Toward an affect-sensitive multimodal human-computer interaction. *Proceedings of the IEEE*, *91*(9), 1370–1390. doi:10.1109/JPROC.2003.817122

Salzer, M. S., & Burks, V. (2003). A mediational study of computer attitudes, experience, and training interests among people with severe mental illness. *Computers in Human Behavior*, *19*(5), 511–521. doi:10.1016/S0747-5632(03)00020-7

Santosa, P. I., Wei, K. K., & Chan, H. C. (2005). User involvement and user satisfaction with information-seeking activity. *European Journal of Information Systems*, *14*(4), 361–370. doi:10.1057/palgrave.ejis.3000545

Schmidt, A. (2000). Implicit human-computer interaction through context. *Personal and Ubiquitous Computing*, *4*(2-3), 191–199. doi:10.1007/BF01324126

Stone, D. L., & Stone, D. (2005). *User interface design and evaluation*. San Francisco, CA: Morgan Kaufmann.

Sugimoto, C. R., Pratt, J. A., & Hauser, K. (2008). Using field cocitation analysis to assess reciprocal and shared impact of LIS/MIS fields. *Journal of the American Society for Information Science and Technology*, *59*(9), 1441–1453. doi:10.1002/asi.20863

Terenziani, P. (2002). Toward a unifying ontology dealing with both user-defined periodicity and temporal constraints about repeated events. *Computational Intelligence*, *18*(3), 336–385. doi:10.1111/1467-8640.00194

Tillett, B. (1991). A taxonomy of bibliographic relationships. *Library Resources & Technical Services*, *35*(2), 150–158.

Wagner, G. D., & Flannery, D. D. (2004). A quantitative study of factors affecting learner acceptance of a computer-based training support tool. *Journal of European Industrial Training*, *28*(5), 383–399. doi:10.1108/03090590410533071

Wang, F. Y., Carley, K. M., Zeng, D., & Mao, W. (2007). Social computing: From social informatics to social intelligence. *Intelligent Systems, IEEE*, *22*(2), 79–83. doi:10.1109/MIS.2007.41

Weng, S. S., Tsai, H. J., & Liu, S. C. (2006). Ontology construction for information classification. *Expert Systems with Applications*, *31*(1), 1–12. doi:10.1016/j.eswa.2005.09.007

White, H. D. (2003). Author cocitation analysis and *Pearson's r*. *Journal of the American Society for Information Science and Technology*, *54*(13), 1250–1259. doi:10.1002/asi.10325

White, H. D., & McCain, K. W. (1998). Visualizing a discipline: An author co-citation analysis of information science, 1972-1995. *Journal of the American Society for Information Science American Society for Information Science*, *49*(4), 327–355.

Zviran, M., Glezer, C., & Avni, I. (2006). User satisfaction from commercial web sites: The effect of design and use. *Information & Management*, *43*(2), 157–178. doi:10.1016/j.im.2005.04.002

ADDITIONAL READING

Albers, M. J. (2008). Human-information interaction. In C. J. Costa, A. Protopsaltis, M. Aparicio, & H. O'Neill (Eds.), *Proceedings of the 26th Annual ACM International Conference on Design of Communication* (pp. 117-124). New York, NY: Association for Computing Machinery.

Baecker, R. M. (1993). *Readings in groupware and computer-supported cooperative work: Assisting human-human collaboration*. San Mateo, CA: Morgan Kaufmann.

Bates, M. J. (1990). Where should the person stop and the information search interface start? *Information Processing & Management*, *25*(5), 575–591. doi:10.1016/0306-4573(90)90103-9

Belkin, N. J. (1987). Discourse analysis of human information interaction for specification of human-computer information interaction. *Canadian Journal of Information Science*, *12*(3/4), 31–42.

Bernard, S., & Cong, C. (2007). Designing interactive learning environments: An approach from first principles. *Campus-Wide Information Systems*, *24*(3), 174–186. doi:10.1108/10650740710762211

Bhatt, G. D. (2001). Knowledge management in organizations: Examining the interaction between technologies, techniques, and people. *Journal of Knowledge Management*, *5*(1), 68–75. doi:10.1108/13673270110384419

Bickmore, T. W., & Picard, R. W. (2004). Establishing and maintaining long-term human-computer relationships. *Transactions on Computer-Human Interaction*, *12*(2), 293–327. doi:10.1145/1067860.1067867

Carroll, J. M. (Ed.). (2003). *HCI models, theories, and frameworks: toward a multidisciplinary science*. San Francisco, CA: Morgan Kaufmann.

Case, D. O. (2002). *Looking for information: A survey of research on information seeking, needs, and behavior*. New York: Academic Press.

Case, D. O., Andrews, J. E., Johnson, J. D., & Allard, S. L. (2005). Avoiding versus seeking: The relationship of information seeking to avoidance, blunting, coping, dissonance, and related concepts. *Journal of the Medical Library Association*, *93*(3), 353–362.

Claver, E., Llopis, J., González, M. R., & Gascó, J. L. (2001). The performance of information systems through organizational culture. *Information Technology & People*, *14*(3), 247–260. doi:10.1108/09593840110402149

Dai, P., Di, H., Dong, L., Tao, L., & Xu, G. (2009). Group interaction analysis in dynamic context. *IEEE Transactions on Systems. Man & Cybernetics: Part B*, *39*(1), 275–282.

Fisher, K. E., Erdelez, S., & McKechnie, L. E. F. (2005). *Theories of information behavior*. Medford, NJ: Information Today.

Green, W. S., & Jordan, P. W. (2002). *Pleasure with products: Beyond usability*. Boca Raton, FL: CRC Press.

Griffiths, J. R. (2007). User satisfaction as a measure of system performance. *Journal of Librarianship and Information Science*, *39*(3), 142–152. doi:10.1177/0961000607080417

Hemingway, C. J. (1998). Toward a socio-cognitive theory of information systems: An analysis of key philosophical and conceptual issues. In T. J. Larsen, L. Levine, & J. I. DeGross (Eds.), *Information systems: Current issues and future changes, Proceedings of the International Federation for Information Processing, 10-13 December 1998, Helsinki, Finland* (pp. 275-286). Helsinki, Finland: Kluwer.

Jank, D. (2010). Toward a unifying ontology for human-information interaction. *Canadian Journal of Information and Library Science*, *34*(4), 403–432.

Karahanna, E., & Straub, D. W. (1999). The psychological origins of perceived usefulness and ease-of-use. *Information & Management, 35*(4), 237–250. doi:10.1016/S0378-7206(98)00096-2

Koenig, M. E. D., & Srikantaiah, T. (2004). *Knowledge management: Lessons learned*. Medford, NJ: Information Today.

Landauer, T. K. (1995). Let's get real: A position paper on the role of cognitive psychology in the design of humanly useful and usable systems. In Baecker, R. M. (Ed.), *Readings in human-computer interaction: Toward the year 2000* (2nd ed.). San Francisco, CA: Morgan Kaufmann.

Nahl, D., & Bilal, D. (2007). *Information and emotion: The emergent affective paradigm in information behavior research and theory*. Medford, NJ: Information Today.

Nicolaou, A. I., & McKnight, D. H. (2006). Perceived information quality in data exchanges: Effects on risk, trust, and intention to use. *Information Systems Research, 17*(4), 332–351. doi:10.1287/isre.1060.0103

Norman, D. A. (1990). *The design of everyday things*. New York: Basic Books.

Norman, D. A. (2004). *Emotional design: Why we love or hate everyday things*. New York, NY: Basic Books.

Pantic, M., & Rothkrantz, L. J. M. (2003). Toward an affect-sensitive multimodal human-computer interaction. *Proceedings of the IEEE, 91*(9), 1370–1390. doi:10.1109/JPROC.2003.817122

Pejtersen, A. M., & Rasmussen, J. (1997). Ecological information systems: Coupling work domain information to user characteristics. In Helander, M., Landauer, T. K., & Prabhu, P. V. (Eds.), *Handbook of human-computer interaction*. Amsterdam: Elsevier.

Pyoria, P. (2005). Information technology, human relations and knowledge work teams. *Team Performance Management, 11*(3/4), 104–112. doi:10.1108/13527590510606307

Salzer, M. S., & Burks, V. (2003). A mediational study of computer attitudes, experience, and training interests among people with severe mental illness. *Computers in Human Behavior, 19*(5), 511–521. doi:10.1016/S0747-5632(03)00020-7

Schmidt, A. (2000). Implicit human-computer interaction through context. *Personal and Ubiquitous Computing, 4*(2-3), 191–199. doi:10.1007/BF01324126

Spink, A., & Cole, C. (2006). *New directions in human information behavior*. Dordrecht, The Netherlands: Springer Verlag. doi:10.1007/1-4020-3670-1

Szewczak, E. (2009). *Selected readings on the human side of information technology*. Hershey, PA: Information Science Reference.

Szewczak, E., & Khosrowpour, M. (1996). *The human side of information technology management*. Hershey, PA: Idea Group.

Szewczak, E., & Snodgrass, C. (2002). *Human factors in information systems*. Hershey, PA: IRM Press.

Thong, J. Y. L., & Yap, C. S. (1996). Information systems effectiveness: A user satisfaction approach. *Information Processing & Management, 32*(5), 601–610. doi:10.1016/0306-4573(96)00004-0

Vicente, K. J. (2004). *The human factor: Revolutionizing the way people live with technology*. New York: Routledge.

Wang, F. Y., Carley, K. M., Zeng, D., & Mao, W. (2007). Social computing: From social informatics to social intelligence. *Intelligent Systems, IEEE, 22*(2), 79–83. doi:10.1109/MIS.2007.41

Section 2
Technology in Collaborative Information Systems

Chapter 7
Review and Brief History of Collaborative Systems:
Taxonomy, Services and Classification

Nuria Lloret Romero
Universitat Politècnica de València, Spain

ABSTRACT

E-collaboration and collaborative systems bring geographically dispersed teams together, supporting communication, coordination and cooperation. From the scientific perspective, the development of theories and mechanisms to enable building collaborative systems presents exciting research challenges across information subfields. From the applications perspective, the capability to collaborate with users and other systems is essential if large-scale information systems of the future are to assist users in finding the information they need and solving the problems they have. This chapter presents a review of research in the area of creating collaborative applications and taxonomies. The author analyzes previous literature, and examines some practice cases and research prototypes in the domain of collaborative computing. Finally the chapter provides a list of basic collaboration services, and tools are presented relating to the services they provide. All surveyed tools are then classified under categories of functional services. In conclusion, the chapter highlights a number of areas for consideration and improvement that arise when studying collaborative applications.

INTRODUCTION

The history of collaborative systems is not recent. Its beginnings stem from various studies and previous software developments, ranging from the so-called HCI (Human Computer Interface Studies) to current network systems resulting from the development and evolution of the technology involved, herein called groupware or groupware systems, which have gone through many different phases.

In this paper a study is proposed on the different aspects associated with these systems, which are

DOI: 10.4018/978-1-61350-201-3.ch007

based on the integration of participation in a single project by many geographically dispersed users connected via a network. Typically, collaborative systems were designed to share information and coordinate related activities in a project. Some of the basic characteristics of groupware systems are a shared calendar for sharing events, a mailing list for accessing shared information, a space for sharing files and communication tools such as a chat or forum to communicate with a group.

To better understand collaborative systems, the state of the art in fields that most directly affect research on collaborative systems have to be studied:

1. Human-Computer Interaction (HCI), collaborative systems,
2. Online social networks.

We considered it appropriate to present the state of the art in a phased manner, starting from the beginnings of human-computer interaction, which is the field of research that in turn includes collaborative systems. The greatest focus was placed on the latter since online social networks are among them (being a particularity thereof).

Additionally, in order to thoroughly understand the development of collaborative systems, it is important to know all the areas that are directly or indirectly related to our study.

Some of the following studies can be broken down by area:

1. Computation
    a. Human-computer interaction
    b. Group and "awareness" interfaces
2. Databases
    a. Organizational or group memory
3. Networks
    a. Geographically distributed cooperation
4. Hypermedia
    a. Web Environment
5. Multimedia
    a. Improved means of communication
6. Artificial intelligence
    a. Agents
7. Social Sciences
    a. Groups
    b. Administration

1. DEFINITIONS AND BASIC CONCEPTS

The origins of Groupware and CSCW date back to 1968, when they were specifically presented in the Online System. Later in 1975 the same author, Douglas Engelbart, presented a prototype with the following features: shared screen collaboration, telepointing and tele-conference with video. Also at this same time writers such as M. Turoff and S. Hiltz, began researching this subject, studying the potential of conferencing systems and comparing these with similar systems in their work.

The term Groupware came into use in 1981 before the term CSCW, based on the article [26] by the authors P. Johnson-Lenz and T. Johnson-Lenz. It was a little later, in 1988, when I. Grief coined the term CSCW, a term referring to a new area of research which uses technology to provide people with support at work.

Groupware: This is an application or set of tools that covers needs such as communication, cooperation and coordination. These are all needs arising in collaborative work between two or more people, and groupware provides them with a common interface.

CSCW: This is a term which combines the understanding of how people work in groups with the potential of computer network technologies associated with software, hardware, services and techniques.

The difference between CSCW and groupware can be seen clearly from the definitions above. It can be observed that the term groupware refers to commercial technologies, whereas the term CSCW refers to research and experimental systems.

Although some authors consider the terms collaboration and cooperation to be synonymous, others such as P. Dillenbourg conclude that there are certain differences between these terms. They differ with respect to the division of labor: in the collaborative process tasks can be divided inter-hierarchically in layers. However, in cooperation tasks are divided into independent sub-tasks. Coordination is required in cooperation when assembling partial results and collaboration is a coordinated and synchronous activity resulting from the continued attempt to solve a particular problem.

Collaboration Role: Role is understood to be a set of properties, knowledge and responsibilities that a user will have at a given time. It allows for an understanding of the user at all times when interacting with other users in the system. Users can dynamically change this role and this change will be managed by the protocols of collaboration.

User: This represents a user within the system. Each will have a set of identifying properties.

Shared Objects: These are items created by users themselves which can be managed in a shared manner using the supporting collaboration tools. This allows users to use items created by other users. The most common collaborative objects in groupware environments are text documents, drawings, websites and chat logs.

Workspace: This is the place where collaboration takes place and in part, it defines the style of collaboration to be implemented. Generally, a workspace or group of workspaces is not sufficient for defining a collaborative application. Usually a workspace is defined within a larger environment containing it which we call a collaborative setting.

Session: A session is a period of interaction supported by a system. In general, a user logs in to the session by identifying himself with a username and password and later explicitly logs out.

Tool: These are programs which, unlike single-user applications, provide for use by a group of people. Naturally, the group manipulates items which we call shared objects. These are the products obtained as a result of the collaboration. Examples of collaboration tools are as follows:

- Chat
- Shared blackboard
- Collaborative editors
- Graphical tools

Collaborative Setting: This is the integration of a set of workspaces. Often, complex groupware applications need more than one workspace in a way similar to a virtual university, which will be composed of different workspaces and classrooms, the library, etc. The settings also contain protocols that structure access to and use of different workspaces by the various existing roles. For example, it should be taken into consideration that some roles may not be able to log in to some workspaces or that changing workspaces will lead to a change in role. Collaborative settings are a special kind of Workspace that can contain other workspaces thereby creating a more complex sharing environment.

CollaborativeAssociation: It allows elements of design to be associated. With this association the tools available in a workspace and the roles that participate in a session, etc. are linked. There are several associations between these elements.

These elements will be expressed in the method through collaborative associations. For example, LocationRelationship will model the location of objects and roles within the spaces, UseRelationship will model the use of collaborative objects by users, ParticipationRelationship will model user participation in the sessions, and SessionRelationship will model the relationship of the sessions with the spaces. All of these will subsequently be described in the metamodel.

SharedRepository: This is the repository where collaborative objects are hosted. Users will have access to this repository to create, read and modify collaborative objects and according to the policy of each collaborative system the shared repository may be unique (i.e., all users of the application share all collaborative objects in a single place). In other cases, there may be multiple shared contexts associated to a specific system component.

Telepointer: This is each user's mouse cursor, which is connected to a collaborative object and moved by each user. In some cases the users' cursors can all be viewed at once. In other cases, only one cursor can be viewed at a time, but in view of the collaboration protocol users are able to change control over the cursor. This feature allows a user to point to a certain part of the collaborative object in the course of the collaboration. The movement of the telepointer is shown on the screens of the users who are connected to the collaborative object.

Protocol: An important factor in group work is the social process undergone. Without people interacting, the groupware system is dead. The protocols are used to model, guide and structure the social process carried out within the group. Protocols define how collaborative tools and objects can be used by the different roles or users. An important aspect defining a protocol is at what time each user can participate.

View: This is the portion of the shared repository that can be viewed by a user. In some cases, users can view the entire shared repository, and in this case the view is a representation of the shared repository. In other cases, due to the limitations of the devices, the view represents a portion of the information.

Meta-Protocol: Sometimes it is necessary to provide a way to change the protocol. In short, the meta-protocol is the protocol that manages the protocol changes. As previously mentioned, elements in a workspace can be shared using different protocols. Such is the case of the virtual classroom which is used to teach class and to make queries. The class and consultations naturally have different protocols. A possible meta-protocol for a virtual classroom would be one enabling students to make queries following a class. Meta-protocols control the change and the transition between protocols and provide a way to make workspaces more flexible.

Coupling: Coupling is a measure which determines a single component's degree of assembly in the workplaces of a groupware system. The components may or may not be coupled, and coupling will be referred to as either strong or loose coupling. If the system is said to have a strongly coupled view, it means that users have the same view. If the workspace is said to be loosely coupled (the term decoupling can also be used), this means that users can be in different workspaces.

Awareness: This is the information the system provides on the state of collaboration. At in-person meetings staying aware of others is natural. You can observe where each person is located, their state, the activity they are carrying out and for what purpose. However, keeping this information updated in groupware systems is somewhat difficult. For this reason, the first groupware systems, which did not maintain this information efficiently, were confusing and inefficient compared to working face to face. Workspace awareness involves keeping the information from other users in relation to the shared space up-to-date, and indicating at least the identity and the presence of users. Along with this information other awareness information usually appears such as the activities being carried out, their location within the system, their state, the actions to be taken, the changes to be made and the items to be used, etc.

Avatar: This represents a user within the system. It may be a small image, graphic or icon. In some cases, such as virtual environments, the avatar moves within the area and serves to initiate collaborations with that user. The avatar can serve as basic awareness information and in many collaborative systems, indicates the presence and location of users within workspaces.

2. HISTORY OF COLLABORATIVE SYSTEMS

As mentioned in the first section, before focusing on the state of the art in collaborative systems, it is important to discuss the area encompassing HCI. Following is a brief introduction to this discipline subsequent to which the collaborative systems and finally, the network systems they encompass, will be dealt with specifically.

2.1 Human-Computer Interaction (HCI)

Research in HCI (Human-Computer Interaction) has been the basis of what is now called usability studies and has made possible many of the changes in software development today. The study by Meyers, which is based on other works of great relevance to the field, has enabled us to provide a brief history of this discipline. The first demonstration of the direct manipulation of objects was carried out by I. Sutherland in his study called Sketchpad in 1963. This system supported the direct manipulation of objects using a "light pen", including the grabbing, moving and resizing of objects.

In 1968 W. Newman introduced "Light Handles", which allowed for the direct manipulation of graphics, in what was one of the first "widgets." Other important terms in HCI such as "WYSIWYG (what you see is what you get)" were also researched at Xerox PARC in the 70's.

Among the first commercial systems that used direct manipulation were Xerox Star, Apple Lisa and Apple Macintosh. As can be observed, these projects were carried out by companies that have pioneered the development of products which were much more user friendly for end users.

The term direct manipulation was coined by Ben Shneiderman in 1982. According to Myers, the so-called "mouse" was developed at the Stanford Research Laboratory in 1965.

The reason for developing this new input device was that it was sought to be a cheaper device than "light pens". Many of the current uses of the mouse were demonstrated by D. Engelbart in 1968 in his study "Display selection techniques for text manipulation". As in previous cases, its use was made extensive with the advent of Xerox Star, Apple Lisa and Apple Macintosh. The so called windows by Windows were first used by D. Engelbart, who worked with multiple windows in 1968. But it was the early 80's when Andrew J. Play developed the Andrew system and Xereox PARC developed the Cedar system. As in the cases of the mouse and direct manipulation of objects, their popularity and use became extensive in the Xerox Star, Apple Lisa and Apple Macintosh systems. The X Window System, which became an international standard, was developed at MIT in 1984.

With respect to the main applications of HCI studies, reference can be made, above all, to applications for gesture recognition, which can now be recognized in developments for video consoles like the Wii and the Microsoft Natal project, whose origins date back to the work undertaken by Sutherland on the Sketchpad system in 1963. In 1964 Teitelman developed the first trainable gesture recognizer. Another example of a gesture recognition system was GRAIL by Tom Ellis.

With respect to multimedia environments, the FRESS project (1968) at Brown University used multiple windows and integrated text and graphics. The first hypermedia system in which text and graphics were used, but not video, was also researched at Brown University. However, video and computer graphics were truly integrated in 1983 by the research group "Movie Manual at the Architecture Machine".

Another area where HCI has been vital is in the development of 3D applications. One of the first systems to use three dimensions was the Sketch-pad 3 system created by Larry Roberts, who developed an ultrasonic 3D location sensing system in 1966. 3D gave way to studies on virtual reality which are now on the rise with the development of so-called Augmented Reality systems. The beginnings of such applications date back to Ivan Sutherland's work on virtual reality at Harvard (1965-1968), which was funded by the U.S. Air Force, CIA, and Bell Labs. Subsequently, in his study "Responsive environments" in 1977, Myron Krueger worked on an interface system that incorporated and played a video in which the user had some kind of interaction. Finally, those closest to the collaborative systems which are the focus of our study would be called CSCW (Computer Supported Cooperative Work). The CSCW emerged as the result of the development of applications for individuals and small groups of users. CSCW conferences began to be offered in 1986.

Although historically HCI's mission was to understand the relationship between humans and computers, this relationship has been radically altered in recent times as a result of large changes in the social and technological environment. These changes are so profound that they have led experts in the field to question where this field is currently headed. Based on the work of Abigail Sellen it can be seen that studies on the transformations of interaction are currently the focus of studies on HCI. Specifically, they are focused on the current end to the stability of the interface, stemming from the change from one to multiple interfaces and even their disappearance, followed by a more personal relationship with these interfaces given that they have become more mobile and as a result of our wearing them or even having them implanted, which implies an increased dependency on technology and a need for increased connectivity anywhere and at any time. This dependence has been exponentially increased with the emergence of Web 2.0 and all network systems.

2.2 A Brief History on Collaborative Systems

As discussed earlier collaborative systems are encompassed within HCI studies. However, in this case, a distinction must be made above all between systems which are collaborative and those which are not. Systems are found where the user interacts only with the system, either by accessing a database, preparing a document or interacting with a video game. These are not what we call collaborative systems. Hence, it should be noted that the main requirement of collaborative systems is precisely that they support the interaction between system users as part of a group activity rather than activities in an individual context. To meet this requirement, collaborative systems will have to cover three core areas: communication, coordination and collaboration.

Computer-based communication has improved greatly in recent years. Initially there were asynchronous tools such as mail and news. Today there are a large variety of tools which make it possible to communicate with a group of users in a synchronous manner and to send different types of text information, sound, images and more. Large advances have also been made due to the integration in mobile devices of all Web 2.0 applications. On the other hand, effective collaboration requires users to be able to access shared information. Many systems (database systems in general) tend to isolate users, allowing them to access a common database. However, none of them have the perception that there are other users in the same system. For example, they do not receive notification of changes or activities being carried out by other users in the system. Finally, effective collaboration and communication can be improved with good coordination. Without coordination, group members may come into conflict with other users accessing the same shared resources, or users may have to make an extra to communicate for the purpose of organizing their activities.

The implementation stage of Collaborative Systems is usually supported by various tools and object oriented frameworks but there is no unified way to specify and design applications on these frameworks.

Douglas Engelbart, who was ahead of his time, surprised his audience at a session of a conference in San Francisco with a demonstration of a system called NLS (Online System, later marketed as Augmented) consisting of a prototype video conference system for sharing the screen and a "telepointer." The demonstration was an online communication between Engelbart at the podium in the conference and Bill Paxton from the SRI laboratory in Menlo Park. Furthermore, Engelbart pioneered other innovations, such as the use of the mouse, the 2D editor, Windows and Hypermedia, as discussed earlier.

At the same time, at the Institute of Technology in New Jersey, Murray Turoff developed the first computer conferencing system, called EMISARI (Emergency Management Information System and Reference Index). Later in 1976, some modifications were made to the system and it was called EIES (Electronic Information Exchange System). For several years Turoff and Hiltz studied the potential of computer conferencing systems and how to use these systems regularly, comparing them with other media.

In the early eighties with the advent of personal computers, the computer world was revolutionized by the "user friendly" interface introduced by Apple Macintosh. While timeshared computers invented to give the user the feeling that they were the only ones in the system provided basic communication service (basically chats), the era of personal computers seemed further away than ever from the use of computers in collaborative work. Only in 1984, Engelbart's ideas were introduced in a workshop at MIT, organized by Irene Grief and Paul Cashman. Grief was working at MIT on RTCAL and MBlink systems inspired by NLS, and Cashman was working at Digital Equipment Corporation on the XCP system, a tool to support administrative processes forming part of the workflow system (Workflow Management System). Together, Grief and Cashman coined the term Computer Supported Cooperative Work (CSCW) to unify a new area of research. Thereafter, major CSCW (Computer Support Cooperative Work) conferences were held on this new field of development.

It was considered important to introduce a classification of collaborative systems in this state of the art system, this sub-section being initiated with the work carried out by R. Johansen, who created a classification of collaborative systems serving as the basis for other subsequent classifications.

In Johansen's space-time matrix, the tools (and/or applications) are classified according to the time and space in which the interaction occurs. In terms of space two distinctions were made: either the users that interact are in the same physical location or are in different physical locations. In terms of the classification with respect to time, whether the interaction takes place in real time or at different times is taken into account. Accordingly, the classification presented in Table 1.

Although this classification is very important, and was the first stepping stone for classifying CSCW systems, it has become somewhat obsolete for classifying certain types of applications, since the development of such applications has not stopped since then. An example of the need for other types of classifiers for this type of systems is the BSCW knowledge management system, a tool that enables different members of a team to work synchronously or asynchronously. The BSCW system allows both synchronous and asynchronous interactions either face to face or remotely, and accordingly, it can be asserted that the classification of this application with Johansen's space-time matrix is not applicable.

Table 1. Johansen's space-time matrix

	Real Time	Different Times
Same physical location	Face to face	Asynchronous
Different physical location	Distributed Synchronous	Distributed Asynchronous

In 1994 J. Grudin presented an improvement in R. Johansen's space-time matrix. This classification takes into account the possibility of performing an activity in the same space or in different spaces. Likewise, with respect to tome, it is taken into account that activities can be carried out at different times or simultaneously. The main difference from its predecessor relates to whether the user knows the space and time in which the action is performed. Therefore, this matrix can be called "Grudin's space-time matrix with awareness of space and time".

Table 2 shows the way this matrix makes classifications and some examples of applications.

Another extension of Johansen's initial classification is proposed by J. Andriessen, and hereafter will be referred to as Andriessen's matrix. In this case the extension is based on combining the old with the five possible groups of processes in ICTs (Information and Communications Technologies). These are as follows: exchange processes between people (communication) group-oriented processes (social interactions) and group-oriented processes (cooperation, coordination and information sharing).

The current communication tools allow for contact and communication between people located in different physical points of the planet, usually quickly and economically. As for tools which enable information to be shared, they equip the user with large amounts of storage to store and share large amounts of data of all types in a fast and reliable way. For group coordination purposes, coordination tools enable users to work in groups (especially those distributed) by means of synchronizer elements, such as timetables, benchmarks in process control systems, workflows and so on. Collaboration tools can improve the ways in which a group works especially when working on a number of files that are required to be the same version for all members of the team. A clear example is co-authoring tools that allow for joint management and participation in creation and / or modification by users. Version control tools in software developments are also another example. The social interaction provided by tools allowing virtual meetings to be held with different types of hardware (cameras, monitors, mobile devices) and software, have gradually made this type of virtual meetings more and more similar to face to face meetings. As in the case of the WallShare system, work is being performed on a system that allows multi-pointer interaction (on a common work area, such as a screen) using the mobile devices of each of the meeting participants.

This table shows how Andriessen combines Johanssen's matrix and the previously listed process types:

Table 2. Grudin's space-time matrix with awareness of space and time

	Same time	Different time but known	Different Time and unknown
Same place	Meeting	Work shifts	Meeting room
Different place but known	Videoconferencing-Teleconferencing	E-mail	Collaborative writing
Different place and unknown	Multicast	Interactive whiteboards	Workflow

Table 3. Andriessen's matrix table

	Asynchronous communication and different sites	Synchronous electronic meetings and different sites	Synchronous face to face meetings
Communication systems	Email and its variants	Chats, mobile phone	
Information sharing systems	Share documents Forums	Teleconsultation	Remote display systems
Cooperation Systems	Co-authored tools with version management	Shared whiteboards	Group decision systems
Coordination systems	Agenda Group timetables Shared planning	Notification systems	Central control support systems and commands
Social interaction systems		Virtual reality Media spaces	

2.3 Types of Groupware-Based Applications

Both in academia and industry groupware applications have been developed to support one of the collaborative situations described in the previous sections. Collaborative settings are defined in terms of tasks performed by the group, the duration of these tasks and the organization of the group from a social and cultural standpoint. Lastly, it is important to consider whether the group manages a common language, for example, whether they are colleagues of a certain discipline, or whether the group is open to connection by any type of user, and to try to collaborate where communication may be hindered. Imagine, on the other hand, a setting where the protagonists of the collaboration are of different nationalities.

In the following table, there is a list of categories of groupware applications and some equivalent names by which they are known on the market. The order of this list is similar to the order in which the tools were made known.

Conferencing Systems

These systems can be considered to be very similar to email. However, while email allows for interpersonal communication by sending messages to one or more persons, conferencing systems allow a number of messages to be sent to an online location to deal with a particular topic. In the beginning, these systems relied on text messages, acting as an information panel, where users could post messages on a particular topic and check their own messages as well as those posted by other users. One of the first conferencing systems which not only supported text messages, but also allowed other types of documents to be sent was TeamTalk [49]. One of the first commercial products to appear was LotusNotes (the conferencing system is one of its components). The main advantage of LotusNotes is that it gives users the option of programming custom groupware applications. Currently, Thunderbird and Outlook Express are the applications of this type which are most used.

Chat Systems

They are similar to e-mail and conferencing systems as they provide for communication between users based primarily on text. The main difference in chat messages is the instant appearance of messages written by a user on the screens of other users who are chatting with them at that time. Following are some of the most important chat systems:

Table 4. Table of collaborative systems and synonyms according to H. Hofte

Categories	Synonyms
Computer conferencing systems	Bulletin board systems, News-groups
Chat systems	Forums
Electronic meeting systems	Group (Decision) Support Systems (G(D)SS), Electronic meeting rooms
Application sharing systems	Screen / window sharing systems, desktop / data conferencing systems
Shared whiteboards	Shared drawing systems
Coauthoring systems	Collaborative/ joint / shared editing Systems
Multiuser hypermedia systems	
Collaborative virtual environments	Multiplayer games, virtual worlds
Group scheduling systems	Group calendaring systems
Audio conferencing systems	
Videoconferencing systems	Multimedia conferencing systems
Collaborative software engineering systems Document management systems	

The IRC (Internet Relay Chat) system provides communication between users connected to a specific address on the network. One of the most popular implementations is MIRC. In this case, personal messages can be sent as well as messages to the full group of connected users by writing in the general chat area (conference style). ICQ is another chat system that was quite popular, the interface of this application being divided into two main parts: the list of contacts and the media. One of the main new features was that the list of contacts had to be added by the user. In the contact list you could see whether or not contacts were connected so as to establish communication with them, and in the case that the contacts were offline a message could be sent to them (although of a limited length). Systems very similar to ICQ are Microsoft Messenger and Yahoo Messenger. Today, the chat systems integrated into online social networks have to be taken into account, such as Facebook or Tuenti. In both cases, since they are not the main part of these web sites the user has the option to disable them.

Electronic Meeting Systems

Electronic meeting systems allow the effectiveness and efficiency of meetings to be increased (before such systems were only face to face). The electronic voting system used in parliaments is one of the simplest electronic meeting systems. In these systems, each participant can vote quickly and anonymously. Other examples in which the application of electronic meeting systems is beneficial are: brainstorming, and the evaluation and organization thereof; the early stages of projects; milestones in projects and so on. An example of these system applications is the Colab system, consisting of a room with large shared screens, connected to a set of interconnected terminals or personal computers. Another system which can also be added to this type of systems is the Wallshare system currently under development, which can also be considered to be an improvement with respect to Colab given its series of additional features relating to human-computer interaction at meetings.

Application Sharing Systems

Such systems allow for the use of single-user applications by multiple users, and the same application may be used by more than one person at a time. This is accomplished through multicasting as an output of the application and data is entered separately by each of the users who are currently using it. Once all entries have been input, the system includes them in the application, making it possible to visualize the user actions immediately on the screens of users who are currently online. Such systems are also known as shared windows systems. D. Engelbart was one of the pioneers in developing such systems in his work, both applications having a shared area for all users and no private place. Subsequently, work was undertaken on systems in which instead of sharing the entire screen, only the application window was shared, as in the case of X Windows and similar systems such as Microsoft Windows and Xerox Start (the first to appear). Currently the most popular applications are as follows: audio and / or video systems in which this functionality is integrated and the VCN (Virtual Network Computing) system which allows desktop sharing with another person and also allows the desktop to be remotely controlled.

Shared Whiteboards

Such systems support meetings in which it is necessary to share, use and modify certain ideas or designs based on drawings, prototypes, or anything that can be represented graphically. The main reasoning behind such whiteboards lies in the importance of a shared graphic space at meetings in which participants are not in the same physical location, where whatever is drawn by the participants is available to other users who can add to or modify it. Currently, this type of systems also integrate audio or video conferencing as part of their functions, as in the cases of Microsoft NetMeeting and Messenger.

Co-Authoring Systems

At the same time as all types of applications changed from single-user to multi-user, document creation, which is one of the most important tasks, also gave way to this change. Taking into account that many documents are the result of the work of several people, they evidence the importance of this type of co-authoring systems. Such systems are created to support the creation of documents by multiple users.

Such systems have to support the following:

- Simple, rich or multimedia texts.
- The different phases in authorship.
- Notes, versions and revisions.
- Simultaneous and / or sequential editing of the document.
- Communication between authors.
- Coordination of the authoring process.

Currently office suites are available that support some of these characteristics, such as OpenOffice, Microsoft Office, Google Docs etc.

Multiuser Hypermedia Systems

Internet can be considered to be a co-authoring system, where each user writes a part of a hypermedia document. Updates of these documents are available for consultation as soon as the user uploads changes, and users can work simultaneously on certain parts of a website. However, at times if users are working on the same part, their work can be overwritten by the other user. Some of the co-authoring systems can also be classified as multiuser hypermedia systems given that they enable and support links between different parts of the documents.

Collaborative Virtual Environments

Collaborative virtual environments range from virtual worlds such as SecondLife to multi-player games of all kinds. In strategy games it can be clearly seen how collaboration, coordination and communication (basic features in collaborative systems) are bases for meeting group objectives. They are also used in many cases for informal learning given the high interest they generate (mainly because they are fun).

Group Planning Systems

This type of systems is used to improve group planning. Specifically, it is possible to more efficiently find free time for a meeting in several diaries using a computer application. Currently, systems such as Google Calendar allow us to conduct this type of planning although multiple applications were previously launched such as: Lotus Calendar, Novel Groupware, Microsoft Schedule+ etc.

Audio Conferencing Systems

Telephony may be considered as the oldest groupware system, allowing communication between people in different geographical locations. Some of the systems appearing under certain of the above classifications also implement part of communication by means of audio (such as NetMetting). Currently the best representative of this type of system is IP telephony. One of the most popular applications is Skype, which allows communication with other computers, landlines and mobile phones. Such systems also allow for multi-audio conferencing.

Some of the most important characteristics of such systems are as follows:

- Management of contacts.
- File Transfer.
- Audio conferences.
- Profile, status and personalization options.

One of the main disadvantages of this system over the chat system is that only you can hold only one audio conference at a time, while communication via chat systems allows you to have a number of communications open at once. Additionally, the main chat applications have integrated audio conferencing.

Video-Conferencing Systems

The origins of communications via video date back to 1964 when the Picturephone prototype was developed. Following are cases where video has been applied to groupware applications:

- CRUISER, which makes it possible to look at the offices of the people who you want to talk to see if they are there or not.
- VideoWindows [whose main feature is the use of permanent giant screens to facilitate communication.
- ClearBoard, which integrates video with shared work spaces. In the case of this system, in addition to seeing the other user, each one can draw on the surface on which the other user is seen as if it were a board and see what the other in turn draws. In other words, on the same screen there is a space for video and a shared workspace.
- Nowadays there are systems which allow three-dimension video conferencing. In the case of [20] an attempt is made to obtain an approximate view using a generic webcam. Additionally, the main chat applications currently have integrated video conferencing.

The main types of video conferencing systems are as follows:

- Mobile video-conferencing systems.
- Desktop video-conferencing systems.
- Room-based video-conferencing systems (with rooms for this purpose).

Document Management Systems

For any business document management is key. Also the more people working on these documents, the more complicated their management. Two clear examples of document management systems are BSCW (Basic Support for Collaborative Work) and the Microsoft SharePoint Portal Server. BSCW facilitates the exchange of information between shared workspaces at any time and from any location based on self-managed and flexible work spaces. Users of this system can store, transfer and manage documents, organize meetings with others in their work group and store all information in a structured way. Some of the most important features of BSCW are: authentication, version management, document locking mechanism, discussion forums, event notification, customized access rights, search facilities, document delivery, online surveys, integrated HTML editor, contact lists, etc. Sharepoint Portal Server allows you to develop a portal that connects users, teams and knowledge. It allows users to share information that enables them to work more efficiently by integrating information from several different systems into one. This integration of information is achieved through application integration and a single sign-on for all applications. A site created with SharePoint facilitates collaboration using capabilities such as adding, organizing and searching for people, equipment and information. Its main objectives are: information, the connection of spaces and people and targeted and customized information. As with the other types of systems viewed, the Google Docs package can also be included within document management systems. There are many document management systems on the market but only those specifically dedicated to the management of office have been included, leaving aside other types of software dedicated to e-government, library or industry-specific document management

In this section the most well-known applications in the Windows environment are discussed. Additionally, there are multiple solutions for each of these types of applications in the open source environment and ever more initiatives are emerging, but these extend beyond the scope of the topics studied in this chapter.

2.4 Online Social Networks

This chapter on collaborative systems would not be complete without a discussion of the latest developments in online networking sites. Online social networks or OSNs can be considered a specific and prolific example of systems included within other broader areas such as human-computer interaction (HCI) and the collaborative systems already discussed in above sections. One of the latest developments in human-computer-human interaction is provided by the field of OSNs where this interaction between people and groups of people reaches its peak. These applications are not developed which are developed for a certain purpose and happen to incorporate mechanisms allowing for interaction between people via machines, but rather applications designed for such interactions. Internet social networks are continuously gaining in strength. Today many people have included the use of OSNs in their daily lives. Another important term relating to OSNs is social network site, hereinafter SNS. Currently there are hundreds of SNSs, supported by different types of web technologies and encompassing a variety of interests and practices. Some of these sites help to maintain and / or strengthen existing social relationships, and also promote (some SNSs more than others) meeting strangers based on shared interests, activities, views, etc. Some SNSs base their growth and therefore have among their users, a particular type of audience with common characteristics, such as age, race, sexual aspects, religion, etc. However, there are also general SNSs whose target users do not have a specific profile. Another important feature of SNSs is the tools available to their users for the purpose of adding and sharing new information on the site and how this is done (wireless connectivity).

To end the introduction of this section a couple of terms relating to OSNs should be explored. These are terms which in turn are closely related to each other and can also be considered to form part of the research field of collaborative systems.

OSNs can be classified as "social software". The term "social software", emerged in 2002 to describe the software systems that supported interaction between groups of people and allowed data sharing.

Some examples of highly popular websites which can be considered social software are as follows:

- Some SNSs such as MySpace, Facebook, Myspace and Bebo.
- Sites more focused on image and video such as YouTube Flickr and Instagram
- Commercial websites such as Amazon and eBay.

Another important term is Web 2.0, which can also be used to describe social software, although it encompasses much more than this. Web 2.0 is supposedly a second generation of internet-based services. These services enable people to collaborate, communicate and share information online in a way that was not possible prior to the emergence of these services. In addition to the above, another important feature of Web 2.0 is a richer user experience, with interfaces which are increasingly more similar to equivalent desktop applications. One of the technologies that enable such applications to be created is AJAX (Asynchronous JavaScript and XML).

2.4.1 Definition

Danah Boyd's article provides a possible definition of SNSs:

Web-based services that allow individuals to:

- Construct a public or semi-public profile with a system of relationships.
- Have a list of other users with whom you share a connection.
- View and traverse their list of connections and those made by others within the system.

The nature and nomenclature of these connections may vary from one social network to another. What makes SNSs unique is not that they allow individuals to meet strangers, but rather that they enable users to articulate and make visible their social network. Connections on SNSs are normally made between "latent ties" (Haythornthwaite) who share some offline connection. On many of the SNSs, users are not necessarily "networking" (as in the case of linkedIn). Instead, they are communicating with people who they already knew prior to entering in this SNS. While SNSs offer a wide variety of possibilities, their main features consist of the following (possibilities which almost all the SNSs have in common):

Profiles, through which users can see a list of friends who are also users of the system. Profiles are unique pages where users include certain information about themselves Typical descriptors that usually appear in them are the name, age, place of residence, interests and a section called "about me" in which the user describes himself in a few lines. Most SNSs encourage users to upload a profile photo so that other users can view and/or recognize them (recognition is especially important when adding new connections). Some sites like Facebook even offer users the ability to enhance their profiles by adding modules (applications).

The visibility of the profile varies depending on the SNS and the settings that each site allows according to user discretion. Normally, by default profiles within some SNSs are crawled by search engines, making them public profiles visible to anyone. But not all such profile information is public. As discussed above, the user has the option of making certain profile information private or only visible to users who have established a connection within the SNS.

Identification of other users. Normally SNSs prompt their new users to find other people they know who are already registered on the site. As noted above, the way connections are labeled varies depending on the site, but there are a number of terms which are very popular in SNSs such as the following: Friends, Contacts and Fans. Most of the connections (or relationships) are bidirectional and therefore need to be confirmed by both parties. Additionally it should be taken into account that the term "friend" in an SNS may lose some of its meaning offline, since a connection would not necessarily mean a friendship offline. Rather, this connection may arise for a number of other reasons (i.e. labor reasons, common interests, etc.).

Public display of connections between users, which is one of the most important components of SNSs. The Friends list contains links to the profile of each friend, who in turn can see the friends of their friends and surf (to some extent, depending on the SNS's and users' levels of privacy) the graph relationships. However, some MySpace users have hacked their profiles to hide their friends from other users.

Messages on profiles. Most SNSs allow users to leave messages on the profiles of their contacts. In addition to this form of public communication, they also tend to have a private messaging feature with a system similar to email.

In addition to the features mentioned above, the most widespread features available to users of SNSs are photo and video uploading and sharing capabilities, comments on other profiles, friends and private messages between users. Users of these sites can share a number of documents and communicate with each other. Not all SNSs began as such, and according to D. Boyd, some started as normal web sites providing certain information to the users who visited them. A social mass has gradually been gained around these websites demanding a number of features enabling users to interact with the site and each other. While SNS developers typically seek to make their sites as accessible and attractive to as many users as possible, in SNSs it is normal to find users divided by nationality, age, education or other factors that also sometimes lead to division offline.

An OSN's type of users is of great importance, since these users subsequently invite others to join the website. In addition to the findings of D. Boyd in her study, the following should be added: SNSs such as Tuenti can also be found, which rather than accessibility and registration made easy, seeks quite the opposite, trying to focus its social network on users ranging in age from16 to 30 years. This is achieved using an invitation system, by which to form part of the SNS you first need to be invited by one of the members who are already registered. It was previously pointed out that the identification of other users is usually bidirectional. However, there are cases such as Twitter where connections can be bidirectional or unidirectional and the nomenclature used in this case is follower. The fact that the users of Myspace hacked their profiles to prevent other users from seeing their friends leads to the question, do SNSs implement their privacy settings to enable their users to configure them as fully and freely as possible or, on the contrary, is their only aim to boost the graph of connections between users?

Finally, it should be pointed out that this section includes the main features of SNSs but does not encompass all features, some of which have not been mentioned, give the large number of SNSs currently available and their rapid rate of innovation and change.

2.4.2 Evolution

This section provides a general description of the history and evolution of SNSs, also based on the work of D. Boyd. According to the definition provided in the above sub-section the first SNS was SixDegrees.com which was launched in 1997 (it no longer exists). It allowed users to create profiles, list friends and surf these lists. These features (with some variations) previously existed in other systems. Profiles existed on most online dating sites and major Instant messaging clients such as ICQ supported lists of friends although characteristically other users could not see the friends that their friends had added. SixDegrees defined and promoted itself as a tool to help people connect with and send messages to others. While it had the ability to attract millions of users, it failed as a business model, and there are people who claim that its main problem was that SixDegrees was ahead of its time. Early users complained that there was little to do besides accepting friend requests and many of these users were not interested in meeting strangers. Finally given that it was not a viable business model at the time, Sixdegrees.com closed on 30 December 2000. When the site closed a door was left open to feedback from its users via email and referrals to other websites.

From 1997-2001 it was common for many web communities to begin to integrate tools for creating profiles and surfing between lists of friends. Sites emerged such as AsianAvenue, BlackPlanet and MiGente that allowed users to create personal, professional and dating profiles. On these sites the users could add friends without the need for approval by the other party. In the on-line press, users marked others as friends to follow what they published or to comment on the site. In 2001 the SNS Ryze.com was launched to help people leverage their business networks. The founder first introduced the site to his friends (not everyone, but rather those with a certain technological, entrepreneur and researcher profile). Friendster was launched in 2002 as a social complement to Ryze, and was designed to compete with Match.com (a dating website.) Unlike many dating sites where the focus was on meeting strangers, Friendster promoted the connection between friends of friends, based on the assumption that the friends of users' friends would make better partners than would strangers. As Friendster's popularity surged, the site encountered technical and social difficulties (D. Boyd 2006 "Friends, Friendsters, and MySpace Top 8: Writing community into being on social network sites."). Friendster's servers and databases were ill-equipped to handle its rapid growth, and the site faltered regularly. Socially, the website's popularity caused more people to become members on Friendster and older users were faced with the "problem" of having their bosses, coworkers, and relatives, etc. as friends.

The initial design of Friendster only permitted users to view the profiles of people who were four or less degrees away, i.e. friends-of-friends-of-friends-of-friends. In order to view additional profiles, users began looking for friends among strangers to expand their reach (collecting friends), an activity that was implicitly encouraged through one of the functions/features of the site called the "most popular". Finally it reached a point where users created fake profiles based on celebrities, concepts, ideologies and so on. Users and press called these profiles "Fakesters." These fake profiles were deleted by Friendster, and this signaled to some that the SNS did not share users' interests. Combined with this problem were technical difficulties and social collisions which caused some users to leave the site. But while its popularity faded in the USA, its popularity grew elsewhere such as on the Pacific islands. From 2003 onward, a large number of SNSs were launched. Most of these focused on the user profile, trying to replicate the success of Friendster. The social SNSs sought large numbers of users, whereas professional SNSs such as LinkedIn Xing sought business people. SNSs focused on hobbies and user passions such as Dogster, which helped strangers to meet others with similar interests. In addition, video and photo-based sites began implementing social network features. MySpace was begun in 2003 and quickly gained users. Much of its initial public was former users of Friendster, who had changed disenchanted for various reasons. While MySpace was not originally launched with bands in mind, their growth on MySpace was reinforced when the developers of MySpace contacted certain bands to see how they could help and better support them. The dynamic of relationships between bands and fans was mutually beneficial and led to the growth and expansion of MySpace. Noteworthy was the emergence of Facebook in 2004, which was first privately and then publicly available starting in 2006. Unlike other previous SNSs,

Facebook was designed for a particular group, i.e. college social networks and Tuenti was born with the same purpose (but in Spain) in January 2006. At present there is no doubt regarding the success of the SNS in terms of number of users and daily use by these users. Additionally, much of the research studies on OSNs are based on or take this SNS into account.

2.4.3 Implications of the Interactions

Christo Wilson (among others) highlights the implications of the interactions that occur between users in a SNS. This study focuses on the users of Facebook and how they interact through the events of this social network. In his study, C. Wilson stresses privacy and security, and in particular their improvement, as one of the fields in which most work has been undertaken in recent years. With respect to spam, internet searches and the defense against phishing attacks and data theft, he makes reference to the studies of Garris, Mislove and Yu, respectively (all in 2006). He points out that in each case, interactive relationships with friends are critical to the problems cited. But most SNSs assume that there is a single level of interpersonal association, which is friendship. and according to C. Wilson there is some research supporting the hypothesis that in certain cases the social links in OSNs connect users with no or a low level of mutual trust. This leads the author to the question: Are social links valid indicators of real user interaction? If not, then what can we use to form a more accurate model for evaluating the social connection of users in OSNs?

The three key contributions of this study are as follows:

1. A comprehensive study on the Facebook social network site. A detailed analysis of all data collected is presented with particular emphasis on user interactions showing that users tend to interact mostly with a small subset of friends, usually having practically no interactions with up to 50% of the people added to their profile as friends. On this basis, the authors conclude that social graphs based on relationships of friendship on a social network are not completely meaningful, and they suggest an alternative model which is another of their key contributions.
2. The authors propose the interaction graph for representing user relationships based on user interactions. This graph will contain all nodes (or users) of the graphs we have if taking into account Facebook friendships, but will have only a subset of links between nodes.
3. Finally, they use the graph proposed to evaluate social enhancement in applications. Based on the interaction graph, they simulate the impact on the Garriss (Reliable Email) and Yu (SybilGuard) studies of applying the graph they obtained and the graph of friendships on Facebook. The results they obtain demonstrate that the difference between the two graph models translate into significantly different performance results from the Garriss and Yu applications.

3. CONCLUSION

Collaborative systems are a very broad field of study and as can be seen, can encompass many different packets of knowledge. This study lays the first stone in the field of the state of the art. In the following chapters we delve deeper into case studies and especially issues relating to collaborative systems and online social networks. The conclusions contributed by our study are as follows:

- Collaborative systems are a set of applications that allow users to interact in a timely manner synchronously or asynchronously.
- The research field of collaborative systems is currently more centered on the usability

of systems and future studies should focus on this type of research to improve existing systems.

- Virtual reality and augmented reality is proposed as the immediate future of these systems.
- Social networks as an evolution of a part of collaborative systems are in full expansion phase so we have not yet seen its full potential.
- In the immediate future privacy systems will be the basic core in the development of social networks since their widespread use has given rise to serious problems in these areas.

REFERENCES

Andriessen, J. H. (2003). *Working with Groupware. Understanding and Evaluating Collaboration Technology*. London, New York: Springer.

Aoki, P. M., Honicky, R. J., Mainwaring, A., Myers, C., Paulos, E., Subramanian, S., & Woodruff, A. (2009). A vehicle for research: using street sweepers to explore the landscape of environmental community action. In *Proceedings of the 27th international Conference on Human Factors in Computing Systems (Boston, MA, USA, April 04 - 09, 2009). CHI '09*. (pp. 375-384). New York: ACM.

Baecker, R. (1995). A Historical and Intellectual Perspective. In Baecker, R. (Eds.), *Readings in Human–Computer Interaction: Toward the Year 2000* (pp. 35–47). San Francisco, CA: Morgan Kaufmann Publishers, Inc.

Bordeau, J., & Wasson, B. (1997). Orchestrating collaboration in collaborative telelearning. In du Boulay, B., & Mizoguchi, R. (Eds.), *Artificial Intelligence in Education* (pp. 565–567). IOS Press.

Boyd, D. (2007). The Significance of Social Software. In Burg, T. N., & Schmidt, J. (Eds.), *BlogTalks Reloaded: Social Software Research & Cases* (pp. 15–30). Norderstedt, Germany: Books on Demand.

Boyd, D., & Ellison, N. (2007). Social Network Sites: Definition, History, and Scholarship. *Journal of Computer-Mediated Communication, 13*(1). doi:10.1111/j.1083-6101.2007.00393.x

Brehmer, B. (1991). Distributed decision making: some notes on the literature. In Rasmussen, J., Brehmer, B., & Leplat, J. (Eds.), *Distributed decision making: cognitive models for cooperative work* (pp. 3–14). Chichester, England; New York: Wiley.

Buyya, R., Abramson, D., & Giddy, J. (2001). A Case for Economy Grid Architecture for Service Oriented Grid Computing. In *IPDPS '01 Proceedings of the 15th International Parallel & Distributed Processing Symposium*. Washington, DC: IEEE Computer Society.

Dillenbourg, P. M., Baker, A. B., & O'Malley, C. (1996). The Evolution of Research on Collaborative Learning. Learning in humans and machines. In Spada, E., & Reiman, P. (Eds.), *Towards an interdisciplinary learning science* (pp. 189–211). London: Pergamon.

Egido, C. (1988). Videoconferencing as a technology: A review of its failures. In L. Suchman (Ed.), *CSCW 88: Proceedings of the conference on computer-supported cooperative work, September 26-29, 1988, Portland, Oregon*. (pp. 13-24). New York: Association for Computing Machinery.

Engelbart, D. C. (1975). NLS teleconferencing features: The journal, and shared-screen telephoning. In *CompCon75 Digest, September 9-11, 1975* (pp. 173-176) Los Alamitos, CA: IEEE.

Engelbart, D. C., & English, W. K. (1968). A research center for augmenting human intellect. In *Proceedings of Fall Joint Computer Conference, San Francisco, USA, December 1968, vol. 33* (pp. 395-410) AFIPS conference proceedings.

Fish, R. S., Kraut, R. E., & Chafonte, B. L. (1990). The VideoWindow system in informal communications. In F. Halasz (Ed.), *CSCW'90: Proceedings of the conference on computer-supported cooperative work, October 7-10, 1990, Los Angeles, CA, USA* (pp. 1-11) New York: Association for Computing Machinery.

Goldberg, A. (1988). *A History of Personal Workstations*. New York: Addison-Wesley Publishing Company.

Greenhalgh, C. (1997). Creating large-scale collaborative virtual environments. In ter Hofte, G. H., & van der Lugt, H. J. (Eds.), *Advance proceedings of OOGP '97. The international workshop on object oriented groupware platforms, Lancaster, UK, 7 September 1997* (pp. 85–86). Enschede, Netherlands: Telematics Research Centre.

Greif, I. (1988). *Computer-Supported Cooperative Work: A Book of Readings*. San Mateo, CA: Morgan Kaufmann.

Grudin, J. (1994). CSCW: History and Focus. *IEEE Computer*, *27*(5), 19–26. doi:10.1109/2.291294

Harrison, C., & Hudson, S. E. (2008). Pseudo-3D Video Conferencing with a Generic Webcam. In *Proceedings of the 2008 Tenth IEEE international Symposium on Multimedia* (pp. 236-241). Washington, DC: IEEE Computer Society.

Hiltz, S. R., & Turoff, M. (1978). *The network nation: Human communication via computer*. London: Addison-Wesley.

Hofte, H. T. (1998). *Working Apart Together: Foundations for Component Groupware*. Enschede, The Netherlands: Telematica Instituut.

Horn, D. B., Finholt, T. A., Birnholtz, J. P., Motwani, D., & Jayaraman, S. (2004). *Six degrees of Jonathan Grudin: a social network analysis of the evolution and impact of CSCW research. ACM conference on computer supported cooperative work 2004* (pp. 582–591). Chicago: ACM Press.

Ishii, H., Kobayashi, M., & Grudin, J. (1992). Integration of inter-personal space and shared workspace: ClearBoard design and experiments. In J. Turner, & R.E. Kraut (Eds.), *CSCW'92: Proceedings of the conference on computer supported cooperative work, October 31 to November 4 1992, Toronto, Canada*. New York: ACM Press

Johansen, R. (1988). *Groupware: Computer support for business teams*. New York: The Free Press.

Johnson-Lenz, P., & Johnson-Lenz, T. (1981). Consider the groupware: Design and group process impacts on communication in the electronic medium. In Hiltz, S., & Kerr, E. (Eds.), *Studies of Computer-Mediated Communications Systems: A Synthesis of the Findings* (*Vol. 16*). Newark, NJ: New Jersey Institute of Technology.

Kawell, L. Jr, Beckhardt, S., Halvorsen, T., Ozzie, R., & Greif, I. (1992). Replicated document management in a group communication system. In Marca, D., & Bock, G. (Eds.), *Groupware: software for computer-supported cooperative work* (pp. 226–235). Los Alamitos, CA: IEEE Computer Society Press.

Larsen, M.Ch. (2007). 35 Perspectives on Online Social Networking. *Social Computing Magazine, 5th of July 2007*.

Luk, R., Ho, M., & Aoki, P. M. (2008, April). *Asynchronous remote medical consultation for Ghana*. Paper presented at CHI '08, Florence, Italy, April 05 - 10.

Myers, B. A. (1998, Mar.). A brief history of human-computer interaction technology. *Interaction*, *5*(2), 44–54. doi:10.1145/274430.274436

Newman, W. M. (1968). A System for Interactive Graphical Programming. In *Proceedings of AFIPS Spring Joint Computer Conference 28* (pp. 47–54). Washington: Thomson Book Company.

Nunamaker, J.F., Dennis, A.R., Valacich, J.S., Vogel D.R., & George, J.F. (1991). Electronic meeting systems to support group work. *Communications of the ACM, 34 (July 1991), 7*, 40-61.

Penichet, V. M. R. (2003). *Sistemas Groupware: Métodos y Herramientas. Estudio de Casos*. Albacete, Spain: UCLM.

Penichet, V. M. R., Lozano, M. D., Gallud, J. A., & Tesoriero, R. (2009, Dec.). User Interface Analysis for Groupware Applications in the TOUCHE Process Model. [ADES]. *International Journal of Advances in Engineering Software*, *40*(12), 1212–1222. doi:10.1016/j.advengsoft.2009.01.026

Penichet, V. M. R., Marin, I., Gallud, J. A., Lozano, M. D., & Tesoriero, R. (2007). A Classification Method for CSCW Systems. *Electronic Notes in Theoretical Computer Science*, *168*, 237–247. doi:10.1016/j.entcs.2006.12.007

Pinheiro da Silva, P. (2001). User Interface Declarative Models and Development Enviroments: A Survey. In *Proceedings of the 7th international conference on Interactive Systems Design, Specification, and Verification* (pp. 207-226). Berlin: Springer-Verlag.

Press, L. (1993). Before the Altair: The history of personal computing. *Communications of the ACM*, *36*(9), 27–33. doi:10.1145/162685.162697

Putnam, C., & Chong, L. (2008). Software and technologies designed for people with autism: what do users want? In *Assets '08. Proceedings of the 10th international ACM SIGACCESS conference on Computers and accessibility* (pp. 3-10). New York: ACM.

Raghavan, P. (2002, January). Social Networks: From the Web to the Enterprise. *IEEE Internet Computing*, *6*(1), 91–94. doi:10.1109/4236.989007

Root, R. W. (1988). Design of a multi-media vehicle for social browsing. In L. Suchman (Ed.), *CSCW 88: Proceedings of the conference on computer-supported cooperative work* (pp. 25-38). New York: Association for Computing Machinery.

Rudisill, M. (1996). *Human-Computer Interface Design: Success Stories, Emerging Methods, and Real-World Context*. San Francisco, CA: Morgan Kaufmann.

Salemi, J. (1994). Let's interface: Conferencing software. *PC Magazine*, *13*(11), 191–202.

Scheifler, R. W., & Gettys, J. (1986). The X window system. *ACM Transactions on Graphics*, *5*(2), 79–109. doi:10.1145/22949.24053

Sellen, A., Rogers, Y., Harper, R., & Rodden, T. (2009). Reflecting human values in the digital age. *Communications of the ACM*, *52*(3), 58–66. doi:10.1145/1467247.1467265

Smith, D. C., Irby, C., & Kimball, R. (1982). The Star User Interface: an Overview. In *Proceedings of the 1982 National Computer Conference* (pp. 515–528). AFIPS Press.

Stefik, M., Bobrow, D.G., Foster, G., Lanning, S., & Tatar, D. (1987) WYSIWIS revised: Early experiences with multiuser interfaces. *ACM transactions on office information systems, 5 (2)*, 147-167.

Sutherland, I. E. (1963) SketchPad: A Man-Machine Graphical Communication System. In *Proceedings of AFIPS Spring Joint Computer Conference 23* (pp. 329–346). AFIPS Press.

Szekely, P. (1996). Retrospective and Challenges for Model-Based Interface Development. In *Computer-Aided Design of User Interfaces* (pp. xxi–xliv). Namur, Belgium: Namur University Press.

Tesoriero, R., Tébar, R., Gallud, J. A., Penichet, V. M. R., & Lozano, M. (2008) Interactive EcoPanels: Paneles Ecológicos Interactivos basados en RFID. In *Proceedings of the IX Congreso Internacional de Interacción Persona-Ordenador* (pp. 155-165).

van der Aalst, W., & van Hee, K. (2004). *Workflow Management: Models, Methods, and Systems*. Cambridge, MA: MIT Press.

Wilson, C., Boe, B., Sala, A., Puttaswamy, K. P., & Zhao, B. Y. (2009). User interactions in social networks and their implications. In *Proceedings of the 4th ACM European Conference on Computer Systems (Nuremberg, Germany, April 01 - 03, 2009). EuroSys '09* (pp 205-218) New York: ACM.

Wilson, P. (1991). *Computer supported cooperative work: an introduction*. Oxford, England: Intellect.

Subsection

Metasearching/New Search Interfaces

Chapter 8
Adaptive Information Retrieval Based on Task Context

Bich-Liên Doan
Supélec, France

Jean-Paul Sansonnet
LIMSI-CNRS, France

ABSTRACT

This chapter discusses using context in Information Retrieval systems and Intelligent Assistant Agents in order to improve the performance of these systems. The notion of context is introduced and the state of the art in Contextual Information Retrieval is presented which illustrates various categories of contexts that can be taken into account when solving user queries. In this framework, the authors focus on the issue of task-based context which takes into account the current activity the user is involved in when he puts a query. Finally they introduce promising research directions that promote the use of Intelligent Assistant Agents capable of symbolic reasoning about users' tasks for supporting the query process.

INTRODUCTION

Since the 1950s, information retrieval has been a science dedicated to the storage, indexing and retrieval of information. Information retrieval systems aim to retrieve relevant documents to a user who expresses his need via a query. To date, their performances are mainly estimated with traditional precision and recall measures i.e. the Cranfield paradigm (Cleverdon C. W., 1960). With the growing of the Internet applications and services, this domain has become crucial, and search tools have to propose more and more intelligent interfaces together with efficient indexers.

Because of the heterogeneity of the platforms, tools and interfaces, with the increase of users' mobility and ubiquitous services, information is now accessed in various situations or contexts that are characterized by: available hardware and

DOI: 10.4018/978-1-61350-201-3.ch008

software tools; spatio-temporal position of the user; user's preferences and (in)capabilities, and user's activities etc. Not taking into account these new conditions lead to one-size-fit-all answers.

At the same time, users are reluctant to think deeper into formulating their queries (Jansen et al., 2000), they prefer very simplistic interfaces, such as Yahoo™ or Google™. Hence one cannot rely on the explicit cooperation of the user to elicit (with key-words or through a dedicated Graphical User Interface) the contextual parameters that would be useful in building more precise queries. This is the reason why current information retrieval research focuses on the elicitation of the various kinds of contexts in which the queries are put and try to develop more adaptive information retrieval systems that exploit contextual information.

Finding just-in-time information has raised new theories and new evaluations to manage the complexity of the situations and to anticipate or predict the needs of the users. In the domain of information retrieval, tremendous changes have to be done and it is now recognized that there is a paradigm shift from the Cranfield paradigm that was well adapted to general information retrieval systems, to a user-centered paradigm (Fisher et al., 2005).

Many definitions have been proposed to define the notion of context (Bazire and Brézillon, 2005). Among them, system configuration and user location are the most studied. User's preferences and capabilities are more related to the research area of adaptive personalized interfaces but they can be considered as part of the contextual information, especially when they interact with the system configuration and/or user location (in cases of user's disabilities, for example).

However one of the most promising features of contextual information is related to the current activity the user is involved in when he puts a query, namely the task at hand and more precisely the current stage within the current task. Knowing what the user is aiming at and knowing the current stage provides crucial cues to enrich information retrieval queries. The focus of our work is to present the latest works on using the context of a task in reformulating queries and to propose a framework for assisting the user that takes into account the profile of the user and the context of the current task (Asfari et al., 2009).

Task-based contextual information retrieval requires to be informed about the task and about its current status. While other contextual features can, not so easily, be extracted from various existing hardware and/or software devices (system configuration parameters, user physical location etc.), task-context data requires at least two extra resources: a symbolic model of the task at hand together with its current status; reasoning capacities upon the model in order to situate the query according to the model (Leray and Sansonnet, 2007). This work can be achieved by intelligent assistant agents that are endowed with two missions: first, perform rational symbolic reasoning over the task model and second provide conversational capabilities in order to dialogue with the user in a natural way when more help is required (Allen et al., 2001).

This chapter aims to:

- Present the background in the domains of contextual information retrieval. The survey will focus on the definition and the use of context in interactive, adaptive and personalized search;
- Discuss issues of handling interactivity and natural language in question answering, information retrieval and assistant agents. We present a task model and agent architecture as a solution to improve the performance of information retrieval systems;
- Provide some future directions and perspectives for integrating approaches coming from information retrieval and assistant agents.

BACKGROUND

Multiple Aspects of Context

Context is a complex notion, multidisciplinary and not yet consensual. (Bazire and Brézillon, 2005) gathered more than 150 definitions in areas such as decision aid, artificial intelligence, philosophy, computer science, psychology, linguistic and information retrieval. These definitions are dimensions oriented, i.e. they cover aspects related on perception, representation and use of context. In (Bazire and Brézillon, 2005) the context is analyzed according to different dimensions such as the nature, the structure, the behavior, the influence, the system, and the constraint. In the domain of computer science, historically, since 1994 (Schilit and Adams, 1994) the term "Context-Aware" has appeared to describe a computing model within which the users interact with computers static or mobile and systems context-aware that adapt to the location where they are used, to the objects and persons nearby and to the changing of these objects during time. The definition that we consider more general and more applied is (Dey and Abowd, 1999): "*Every information that can be used to characterize the situation of entities (either a person, a location or an object) that are considered as relevant to the interaction between the user and the application, including the user and the application themselves*". Other definitions (Brown et al, 1997), (Ryan et al, 1998), (Baldauf et al, 2007) use most often three entities as components of context: person, location and object together with the attributes describing these entities such as the identity, the location, the state of a task or activity, and time.

In the domain of information retrieval, (Wilson, 1981) analyzes the information seeking behavior and the user need according to his personal features (physiological, affective, cognitive), his social role (work, performance) and the environment (work, socio-cultural, politico-economics and physical). The user is at the center of the process of information retrieval. The domains of user modeling, human machine interaction, or cognition were separated from information retrieval. (Belkin, 1995), (Ingwersen, 1996), (Saracevic, 1997), (Saracevic, 1997) start integrating the cognitive models and interactions in information retrieval. (Saracevic, 1997) proposes a layered model which describes the dialog or interactions between different levels from the side of the user (cognitive, affective and situational) and from the side of the computer (material features of the computer, treatment and content). For (Belkin, 1995), during a search situation or information seeking, the user employs different strategies in order to solve an information need and to reach a target: "*Information seeking behaviors are characterized by going from one strategy to another within one single search session*". He proposes a schema to classify the strategies of search according to features such as the aim of the interaction (learning, selection), the considered resources, the method of interaction (searching for an item, reading) and the search mode (identifying by recognizing the searched item or specifying by similarity with other items). Context describes internal elements (for instance the mental state of the user) or external elements (for instance data of weather forecast). It can be either static (values linked to the parameters of context are stable, for instance the identity of a person) or dynamic (changeable values). The definitions given above allowed us to review the notion of context in different domains.

Beyond the numerous definitions of the notion of context, it comes out from this survey that context is taken into account within existing models, and that the parameters of context are not linked to the intrinsic properties of context but to its interpretation in a given situation. In the following, we are going to study different types of context which will serve us for representing their use in approaches of contextual information retrieval. (Göker and Myrhaug, 2002) recommends a model of stretchy context and offers five elements to characterize user context: the context of environment, personal context, context of task, social context and spatiotemporal context. (Ingwersen and Järvelin, 2005) defines six dimensions overlapped by context: the internal or external structure of the object (for instance the sentences which are part of a paragraph or the ownership of the documents which put them into contact with other documents such as hypertext links); interactions and activities which take place in the course of session; the social, systematic context, of task, emotional; spatiotemporal context i.e aspects such as the time and the geographical location; economic and technico-physical context; the context of review which consists of the past actions performed by the user during a session. To sum up, we shall retain the following elements to characterize the notion of context: context of the user, context of information, context of task or activity, context of the system, context of environment / physical appearance, the temporal context, and context of interactions.

Approaches in Contextual Information Retrieval

Contextual, interactive, adaptive and personalized information retrieval are interdependent. They respectively put forward aspects linked to context, to exchanges of information between the user and the system, the adaptation to the user in most cases (but also in resources, in system or in environment), and in profile or model of the user. Personalized information retrieval and adaptive information retrieval are particular cases of interactive information retrieval. Belkin (Belkin, 2006) explains that Personalized Information Retrieval is a subset of Adaptive Information Retrieval in the sense that the adaptive information retrieval can concern other parameters of adaptation than user, for instance adaptation to the system, to environment, while personalized information retrieval concerns the adaptation to the user. When only informational context is taken into account, information retrieval is not interactive. To illustrate informational context, let us cite works of (Skov et al, 2006) who are interested in multidimensional presentation and in poly-presentation of documents to improve information retrieval, or works of (Chibane and Doan, 2007) who are interested in the notion of 'neighborhood' of documents in order to propagate scores of relevance dynamically according to the terms of the query and the granularity of information. In exception of these examples, Contextual Information Retrieval concerns nearly only interactive information retrieval. The three types of research approaches of information were broadly carried out in workshops such as AIR, CIR, CIRSE and IRIX and at conferences such as IIiX. The growth of articles published in big conferences dedicated to information retrieval such as SIGIR since 2000, CIKM, ECIR, RIAO in 2010 whose topic was adaptation and fusion of heterogeneous documents, and at conferences on artificial intelligence such as FLAIR, UMAP or the workshop HCIR, manifests their multidisciplinary domains on the importance of this aspect of information retrieval, and, for these last ten years. For every type of approach, we shall analyze which dimensions of context are used and our study will throw into relief some models and applications.

Interactive Information Retrieval

Information retrieval has existed since 1950s and has been based on mathematical foundations which led to intensive and extensive proliferation on the automating of the processes of indexation and search. The evaluation of the systems of information retrieval in 1960s placed the emphasis on the importance of the performance of systems in terms of algorithms and measures of relevance, across the tests of Cranfield. This methodology remains predominant to the present time. The increase in the volume of information and the heterogeneity of information and available applications on the Internet brought about the necessity to develop tools to access information which explains the development of information retrieval. Besides, with the commercialization of search tools, the satisfaction of the users was prioritized and the interest in user models became the object of new research directions in information retrieval to such an extent that a paradigm shift in information retrieval begun recognition. Actually, classic information retrieval was criticized for not taking into account the cognitive and interactive aspects such as:

1. The evaluation of systems in 'batch mode' does neither allow an analysis of answers in real situation, nor an analysis of the interactions which can lead the user to specify or change his request;
2. The binary evaluation of precision and recall factors does not handle properly answers of type « don't know », that is to say the user does not know how to judge the relevance of the document turned out by the system.

However, the diversity of interaction modes due to the variety of interfaces and available Web tools calls to reconsider information retrieval according to the user model and information seeking behavior. The disciplines of user modeling, interaction between man and machine or cognition were separated from information retrieval. These were studied by (Belkin, 1995), (Ingwersen, 1996), (Saracevic, 1996), (Saracevic, 1997) who begun the integration of the cognitive models and interaction in information retrieval. (Saracevic, 1997) offers a stratified model which describes dialogue or interactions between different levels on the user's side (cognitive, emotional, and situational) and of the computer (material characteristics of the computer, treatment and contents). (Ingwersen and Järvelin, 1996) offers a cognitive model for information retrieval: interaction is modeled by a series of cognitive processes which implement the characteristics of the system (techniques of presentation of information, indexation and search), the situational characteristics of the user, and the functionalities of interface user or of the mediator between the user and the system. In this work, the user interacts not only with the system but also with the objects that he handles, the text, as well as the rules of indexation and the interface. Interactive information retrieval allows the user better control of the search process.

Following questions underline problems met in interactive information retrieval. Given that the information need is dynamic, that there are different interpretations of queries and of relevance, we ask if there is a means:

1. To reduce the changeability of queries;
2. To develop a system or an interface thus reducing uncertainty via refinement of interactive queries;
3. To define a task that fits into an interpretation, in case of numerous propositions of relevance, as quickly as possible;
4. To assess:
    a. how to stalk elements linked to the evolution of the needs which appears from interaction,
    b. how to be focused on terms linked to disambiguate requests,
    c. how to model the aspects of interaction.

Several distinct approaches have been proposed:

- An important preliminary task concerns the collection of the existing data of interactions. It is a question of acquiring the context of interactions or information retrieved from logs, http traffic, clicks and visited pages with time spent on surfing. This information is used to predict the type of user search and to re-rank results according to search type. When queries are repeated, the system deduces that the user likes to find the same results as before;

- From the observation that the longer the queries are, the more efficient the search systems are (Buckley et al., 1994), works of (White and Kelly, 1998), (Marsteller and Mizzy, 2003), (Kelly, 2007) were oriented towards the expansion of queries via the use of questionnaires to explain the need of information or via the use of thesaurus (Likke, 2004). Subjacent idea is the poly-representation defined by (Ingwersen, 2006) or to obtain several representations from the same information need, to determine in the course of interactions, the level of subject content knowledge by the user and what he wants to know about this subject;
- Within a single search session, the analysis of interactions shows that the user uses various behavioral according to distinct needs. The latest works and experimentation of (Nahl, 2008) concern detection and impact of affective and emotional context from the behavior of the user and of his interactions with the system.

Users interact with their environment in various ways and approaches to cope with their information needs. These approaches are derived from man/machine interaction, machine learning and artificial intelligence, in the form of personalized search agents or specialized search tools. Numerous tools were developed with these approaches, such as Meta Spider, CI Spider.

Adaptive Information Retrieval

(Belkin, 2000) places adaptive information retrieval within artificial intelligence, and particularly machine learning techniques. *An adaptive system improves its performances progressively as time goes by thanks to the 'feedback ' on its previous performances.* Feedback is given via questionnaires filled by the user or by machine learning techniques. One of the objectives of adaptive information retrieval is to develop techniques to predict which information the user will need to accomplish a task and to decide when and how to show him the right information. A better knowledge of the user allows adaptation of information retrieval process which suits his needs better. Subjacent hypothesis is that according to interactions with the system, the user discovers information which will allow him to refine his query. The user will provide information to the system which will be able to deduce on the users' needs thanks to the implicit relevance feedback. Ostensive techniques aiming at making explicit the needs and information seeking behaviors of the users have been studied in adaptive new video approach (Hopfgartner et al., 2008). Approaches used in adaptive research are questionnaires, expansion of query, the search of similar documents and collaborative systems. (Brusilovsky, 2001) evaluated the conception of adaptive interface users and adaptive hypermedia systems. (Lawless et al., 2010) proposes to combine the existing techniques of evaluation of adaptive hypermedia systems and of information retrieval within the same framework with the intention of evaluating a personalized information retrieval system.

Personalized Information Retrieval

Personalized information retrieval in most cases became famous in mobile applications, and in PIM (Personal Information Management). (Elsweiler and Ruthven, 2007) introduced Personal Information Management to organize heterogeneous information and to reuse them efficiently. His approach was based on the psychology of memory, on the behavior of the users giving indications to find partly forgotten information. Personalization is also exploited in the systems of recommendations or collaborative filtering.

The most part of works concerns the identification of an aspect of the common or past behavior, such as time spent on a page, the clicks, the informational objects either seen or used to be saved, and the use of this information as relevance feedback to change an initial query or rank results by taking into account this knowledge (Kelly and Teevan, 2003). However, this approach is restricted because personalization concerns the single aspect of a search situation and the prediction of the relevance of informational objects. But the effects of interactions on different types of traces affect their interpretation as indicators of relevance. Therefore the factors such as purposes, tasks and context have an effect on the interpretation of the traces of behaviors. The challenge of personalization is to consider dimensions according to which personalization must set up. It is then a question of identifying the values of each dimension in their interactions. It is finally necessary to develop techniques to take into account these values and to evaluate the results of the real experiments of personalization.

We focused our presentation on the context in information retrieval, in order to provide a state of the art of different models of context by carrying out the context of task more precisely. The most famous application in information retrieval is with no doubt the search tools that appeared with the beginning of the World Wide Web. Current search tools index documents that are harvested by robots and provide a user query interface to query the database.

INFORMATION RETRIEVAL BASED ON TASK CONTEXT

This section is the main focus of the chapter. We discuss issues, proposals and unsolved problems concerning models and systems that carry out the context, interactions as well as intelligent interfaces to assist the user in accomplishing his activities by a review of results on multimodalities, user context, natural language and our current work to model the tasks within the contextual information retrieval.

Issues, Controversies, Problems

Bringing Task Context to Information Retrieval

Bringing task context to information retrieval prompts new approaches in modeling and designing interactive systems and interfaces with both domains of artificial intelligence, cognitive and personalized information retrieval, adaptive Web, and user modeling. We open a discussion about the feasibility and relevance of the introduction of intelligent assistant agents (Maes, 1994) for improving user's queries. The presentation focuses on the complexity of conversational interactions using Embodied Conversational Agents (ECA), (Cassel et al., 2000) which integrate cognitive or emotional aspects and other levels of details in modeling interactions, in particular the multimodalities interactions to enhance the dialog between the machine and the user. That raises questions such as "*to what extend the model can help the user without being intrusive?*"

Current research in personalized information retrieval emphasizes the use of user profile, the navigation history, and some contextual information intended to improve the global quality of the search results. However the interest of the user changes over time, and he can perform several research activities over short periods with distinct purposes. The review of the data history or information profile does not necessarily bring to added values in these scenarios. The nature of the activity leading a user to start an information retrieval task has on the contrary an influence on the informational behavior of the persons. Research of (Luxenburger et al., 2008b) put in an obvious place the use of the activity knowledge of the user to improve the answers of the information retrieval system. For instance if they consider a search task of an item to be bought, the nature of the information retrieval changes according to the progress of the task: step of seller location, stage of prices comparison, etc.

A task in a functional perspective is a series of actions to be fulfilled to reach a particular purpose. In information retrieval, this mere notion of task has several definitions: goal to model, actions to be fulfilled... There is no acknowledged nomenclature or generic definition applicable to tasks. Instead we will find a multitude of works that emphasize one or several facets of the information retrieval tasks.

On the study of tasks as human information retrieval activities some research like (Freund et al., 2005) or (Elseweiler and Ruthven, 2007) focuses on the modeling and the characterization of the human situations of retrieval and discovery of information. Works of (Freund et al., 2005) focuses on information retrieval activities in the business world and put in an obvious place the relations between the exploited documents types and retrieval tasks. Works of (Elseweiler and Ruthven, 2007) are focused on retrieval task as part of the personal assistants and suggest a taxonomy for the message rediscovering activities of mail or Web pages, this for evaluation purposes.

The formal aspects of the task context are a fecund domain of research. This consists in defining a model capable of capturing the elements of the user activity, like purposes, intentions, procedures, having significant potentials to produce improved results. For example, (White and Kelly, 2006) defines tasks as being "the domain of interest" or searched items such as 'Travel', 'Shopping' or 'Article-Writing'. Nine labels are so specified and each task is attached to one of these cases: academic research, entertainment, actuality, weather forecast, personal communication, purchase/sale, education, pastime and topic of interest, trip, job/career. In a different way, (Luxenburger et al., 2008) use a statistical language model to specify the information retrieval tasks by focusing on the review of the user activities. A task describes the previous actions of the user to different levels of granularity. This work proposes an environment which dynamically fits the right level of granularity, to find the task which is the best adapted to the current activity of the user: assisting him to improve the results of a previous search or reformulating an ambiguous query. In (Asfari et al., 2009), the UML language is exploited to model the information retrieval tasks. The initial terms of the query as well as synonyms found in the WordNet lexical data base are used via the ODP ontology to extract the related concepts. These concepts are then compared with the nine task labels predefined by the classification of (White and Kelly, 2006), given above. A UML state diagram is associated to each task and allows the system to model the current state of the execution of the task by the user. States make it possible to define the ongoing stage linked to an information retrieval activity. By providing additional information, which is likely to improve the quality of answers, the task enables to enrich and complement the context of the search.

Next to these formal approaches for modeling contextual information retrieval tasks, there are also works directed to the detection or the study of the tasks themselves. For instance (Wu et al., 2007) work on the identification of the user search task within a perspective of information management, (Luxenburger et al., 2008b) develop a framework in order to correlate the informational needs of the users with the search tasks previously memorized. To end this section on the notion of task, it is necessary to note works of (Yuelin and Belkin, 2008), which is based on a classification and an exhaustive characterization of tasks in contextual information retrieval.

Queries put by users cannot be viewed as a complete specification of the information searched by the user. Certain terms can be absent or ambiguous. Indeed, users consider that the task, fulfilled by a user at the time of his query, provides supplementary information helpful to improve the answers of the search system. Several approaches are exploited to improve these results:

- Modification of the scoring function: it is a question of exploiting contextual information to re-rank the results of the search system of information and of presenting first the most appropriate results;
- Filtering the results: it is a question of complementing the initial query by restricting the possible answers of the system:
- Reformulation of the query: it is about a general implementation of the previous technology with rewriting of initial query. See (Vidal et al., 2006) for works on this domain.

Evaluation in Contextual Information Retrieval

Information retrieval is considered to be both a science and a domain of application, that is to say, when designing an information retrieval system, the definition of a protocol of evaluation and experimentations are necessary to validate a model or a theory. That's why evaluation is a primordial stage in information retrieval. Since the 1960s and until today, the tests of Cranfield have constituted the reference frame in which experimentations and validation are held. Tests concern collections of documents, queries and judgments of relevance provided by experts. They allow to compare the algorithms of relevance (rate of answers considered appropriate by the system in comparison with answers considered appropriate by the experts) generally thanks to the measurements of precision and recall. The model of Cranfield is of great interest to the information retrieval community because it defines a precise and efficient methodology to compare all systems on the same foundation. However this approach was criticized (Harter, 1996), because 1) it assumes that the user issues his query within a unique session, the system is therefore evaluated in batch mode, 2) it does not take into account the profile of the user, and 3) answers are binary (relevant/ non relevant) and concern only thematic relevance. The first attempts to adapt the model of Cranfield to the user profile consisted in incorporating the query information on his profile, for instance his level of expertise, or taking into account context by adding metadata to queries and to documents. It is the subject of "interactive track" and "hard track" in TREC conferences. But tracks did not show that the classical model can fit into interactions between the user and the system. Actually, the improvement of performance on the previous models and techniques is not significant (Spärk Jones, 2005) and this improvement is considered weak or even nonexistent compared with the judgement given by the users in interactive search mode (Turpin and Scholer, 2006). Measurements such as GRP (Generalized Recall and Precision) and CG (Accumulative Benefit) (Jarvelin and Kekalainen, 2002) allow to measure gradual precision and benefit in relevance held concurrently for the user according to the position of the document. More recently, the model of (Fuhr, 2009) could contribute to define a new methodology of test and to evaluate information retrieval systems. The difficulty in conceiving test collections taking into account both interactions and context is perceived according to the changeability of the users, the changeability of the user needs in an on-going situation and the taking into account of all the contextual factors. To be representative enough, all topics must be very broad; the corpus of documents and queries must take into account the identified changeability. The field therefore remains open to the discovery of new protocols and methodologies of evaluation, which it is the object of very recent workshops such as CIRSE (on 2009 and 2010) and future of information retrieval evaluation as part of SIGIR held in 2010. These controversies in evaluating the performance of the systems raise a shift paradigm between well-established standard collections (TREC or GOV) versus new collections of documents and queries together with situations reflecting real life conditions during the experimenting of an information retrieval task. That problem is not yet resolved.

Contributions from Help Systems Approaches

Assisting novice users of computer applications is a challenging task that has been addressed through different approaches since personal computers started to become available to a broader audience of non-expert users at the beginning of the 1980s. Indeed, despite the huge progress done in ergonomics, the variety and the complexity of applications (even when correctly designed, most current applications are very large and intricate) make it impossible for ordinary users, i.e. a non-expert person using a software application, not to face difficulties to find and follow the right procedures to reach their objectives (Sansonnet, 1999).

Therefore, the problem of assistance has long been addressed in various ways as the number of ordinary users was increasing. A mere transposition of a paper-based documentation into an electronic version has been shown to be actually less efficient (Capobianco, 2003), which has led to focus on the notion of *adaptation*, to bridge the semantic gap between novice users and expert developers. The need for adapting the help system according to the user's current task has progressively led to research on Contextual Help Systems (Carenini and Moore, 1993). In the same way, help systems can be adaptive depending on the profiles of the users: statically through the use of classes of users (Sumi and Mase, 2002) or dynamically with regular updates of a model of the current user (Jameson, 2001).

From a computational point of view, the main qualities of a help system are the precision and the completeness of its informational content. But as far as general public users are concerned, it has been shown that ease of use is by far the primary factor (otherwise the help system is merely left aside) since according to the 'Motivation paradox' (Carroll and Rosson, 1987) users prefer to ask from expert friends 'behind their shoulder' (Capobianco and Carbonell, 2001). In relation to this statement, recent studies have shown the positive impact of multimodality for help systems, and particularly the linguistic modality (Carbonell, 2003), i.e. natural language interaction, since it allows a clear separation between the user's task in the application and its interaction with the help system.

The typology of natural language interactions can vary according to the various kinds of interactional situations. Depending on the considered system, the design of efficient Natural Language Processing tools (NLP-tools) is more or less complex and their implementation involves more or less resources (manpower, time, financial cost). First considering the complexity of the interaction as a factor then the complexity of the processing of users' requests one can characterize three main categories of NLP-systems:

- Question/Answers systems;
- Chatbot systems;
- Dialogue-based systems.

The domain of Question and Answers (Q-A) (Voorhees and Harman, 2005), (Ligozat et al., 2006) can be viewed as close to information retrieval at the applicative level. However, those systems are distinct in nature due to the fact that linguistic analysis plays a major part in the requests synthesis process, which can be resolved afterwards through traditional information retrieval techniques. Q-A systems have in common with assistant agents the notion of isolated natural language request (meaning that no actual multi-turn dialogue is engaged between the user and the help system) and they can share the same kind of NLP-tools. The main difference is that Q-A requests are "informational request" (example from (Ligozat et al., 2006): Question: "*When was the Berlin wall demolished?*" Answer: "*in 1989*"), whereas an assistant agent must handle questions about the structure and the functioning of the current application (example from (Sansonnet et al., 2002) about controlling a Hanoi's game.

Question: "*Move the upper disk of the left stack to the right*", Answer: "*You can't put a disk on a smaller one!*"). Moreover at the methodological level, Q-A research is focused on nominal groups (the speech act part of users' utterances being restricted). On the contrary, assistant agents are concerned with few nominal references (they are restricted to the entities composing the assisted application) but with a large variety of speech acts, which are mainly supported by verbal groups (for more on speech acts, see (Searle, 1969)).

NLP-tools used in chatbots systems are often trivial, mainly based on keyword matching, though Wallace's Alice proposes a more sophisticated approach using rules and meta rules described in XML (AIML — Artificial Intelligence Markup Language (AIML url)). Hence, if they truly succeed in the chatting context, the semantic analysis of the utterances is insufficient to support questions about the structure and the functioning of an application. Moreover they lack the symbolic reasoning capabilities and the fine-grained semantics analysis capabilities required to support the function of assistance. This drawback has been analyzed by (Wollermann, 2005-2006) over four main chatbots (Alice, Ellaz, Elbot, and Hal): a collection of linguistic phenomena were evaluated qualitatively in the chatbot answers to users questions, first on semantics aspects (semantic relations, quantifiers, and anaphora) and secondly on pragmatics with some Grice's maxims (Grice, 1999). This study showed chatbots are failing in all these categories and that a deeper semantic/pragmatic analysis is required for finalized/task-oriented dialogue.

Dialogue-based systems have been studied as a major area of the NLP research for thirty years on; hence it is not possible here to review them, even briefly. Because they are typical of this research field, one cannot but mention the works of Allen et al. on the projects TRIPS and TRAINS (Allen et al., 1995), (Fergusson and Allen, 1998) or the works of Rich and Sidner on COLLAGEN (Rich and Sidner, 1998). Their current objective is to develop new *generic* frameworks that can be adapted easily and at low cost from a 'dialogized' application to a new one. This shows a posteriori the main issue encountered in the diffusion of such systems: while they are actually operational, it is at a cost too high to be integrated in the new Internet software technology, which is based on fast-developing and low-cost solutions.

Solutions and Recommendations

Virtual Characters in the Internet

One of the consequences of the need to provide a natural and intuitive assistance to people of the general public is the development of Embodied Conversational Agents (ECA), which are virtual characters able to interact with users through multimodal dialogues (Cassel et al., 2000). Studies on ECAs have shown that a human-like presence can have a positive impact on the global acceptance of the system thanks to increased agreeability and believability (this is the 'Persona effect', as described in (Lester et al., 1997)), which makes them a good support for the function of assistance, especially for novice users. As a consequence, they appear to be an ideal support for ordinary users' help systems of the future generation:

- Their reactivity is good since the agent can always be visible in a part of the screen, and it visually appears as independent from the application, preventing a cognitive mix between the help system and the application itself;
- They can work with (subsets of) natural language, so the user is not constrained in his vocabulary;
- They can provide information about the application, by browsing a symbolic model;

- They can have a representation of the dynamic state of the application, so they can provide diagnostics and planning;
- They can adapt the way they provide information depending on the user profile (by taking into account personal parameters and previous interactions) and through the use of multimodality (speech, gesture, facial expressions...);
- They can be proactive: if the agent is provided with a task model, it can anticipate user's needs.

When we consider the issue of helping general public novice users, the Internet provides a large domain of applications and services that could be improved by hosting assistant agents. Nowadays, many Web pages already display virtual agents. They serve two main purposes:

1. **Informational agents:** They give predefined static information about a website or about a specific product within a site. Users cannot interact with the agent which is just a 'speaker'. For example, Oddcast is a major provider of this technology on the Web for several general public corporations (Oddcast url).
2. **Chatbot agents:** They are long time successors of Eliza (Weizenbaum, 1966), which was originally designed as textual input/output interaction with a fake Rogerian therapist. Today, among outstanding Web-based chatbots we can mention Hal (Hal url), Jabberwacky (Jabberwacky url) or Alice (Alicebot url). They tend to incorporate speaking virtual characters in order to personify the chatbot. This kind of technology has been used in many corporate websites for the welcoming and the guidance of general public.

Handling Natural Language Assistance Requests

Despite the fact that ECAs have proved that a human-like presence can have a positive impact on the global acceptance of a system, the use of ECAs as a support for the function of assistance raises two main issues:

1. The first issue is that the level of efficiency required from ECA-based help system is more critical than in traditional help systems since, as explained in (Randall and Pedersen, 1998) (Cassel et al., 1999) with the example of the 'Clippy Effect' of Microsoft Office assistants, failures feel more jarring as the personification of the ECA makes it look stupid, and the perception shift is fast from the positive status of a friendly companion to the negative one of a useless gadget. Already, ECAs have been successfully used for training users to various tasks (Rickel and Johnson, 1999) but a lot of work remains to be done to attain a good efficiency, which we think requires a thorough analysis of the function of assistance through a study of actual novice users' requests, meaning that we need a corpus-based approach to their design.
2. The second issue is related to the decision to handle the natural language modality. One could argue that skilled users prefer interacting directly with graphical user interface elements rather than using natural language for the control of software applications. But on the other side, when assistance is required, novice users (and sometimes expert ones too) have been shown to spontaneously express their frustration in natural language in front of the machine (not unlike the 'thinking aloud effect' (Ummelen and Neutelings 2000)). Indeed, it seems that the natural language

modality surges when things tend to go wrong. This is the reason why we give it a first-class citizenship in the analysis of the function of assistance.

A first question that arises in developing conversational assistant agents is related to the precise nature of users' utterances. While we were studying the function of assistance in the context of the DAFT Project (Leray and Sansonnet, 2007) a primary requirement was then to collect data from ordinary people asking natural language requests when they were facing unfamiliar applications. This led to the collection of a corpus of 11000 requests. Figure 1 shows selected excerpts from this corpus, which reveals some of its characteristics (emphasized in bold):

- More than half of the user requests are not well-formed (expressions from the spoken language, spelling, syntactic or grammatical mistakes, acronyms from SMS and internet slang...) and some of those mistakes are not easy to detect and fix with classical NLP-tools;
- Requests are not stored as part of a dialogue, but as isolated sentences, since as mentioned by (Capobianco and Carbonell, 2002), in the domain of assistance, dialogical interactions are almost always limited to a single conversational turn and hence can be treated as isolated requests.

The collected corpus makes it possible to categorize the various activities the users are involved in when they put their questions to the agent (Bouchet and Sansonnet, 2007). The corpus can be divided into four sub corpora, each corresponding to a particular activity (the numbers given below as examples refer to sentences in Figure 1-left):

1. **Control activity:** corpus made of direct controls, to prompt the agent itself to interact directly with the application software in which it is embedded (sentences 1-4).

Figure 1. Left: Selected excerpts from the corpus (with spelling errors and idiosyncrasies emphasized in bold); Right: Distribution of four main activities in the corpus [From (Bouchet and Sansonnet 2007)]

1 **clicks** the quit button
2 **clickon** the back button
3 ok, come back to **th ehomepage**
4 give me a map of the website
5 what is this window for**,**
6 **WDYM** by GT ACA
7 do the "close" button and the "quit" button work exactly the same way?
8 I have a question to ask to one of the members, how can I contact him?
9 when is the next meeting?
10 where **can-we** find the conference schedule?
11 is there a shorten version of the help
12 I **cna't** see any **demso** page!!
13 the link seems to me to be broken
14 I was really surprised to see there's no global cancel function
15 it'd be better to be able to go directly at the beginning
16 **auf viedersen**
17 you good for nothing!
18 What kind of music do you like?
19 you're dressing the same way everyday?
20 works for me **:-)**

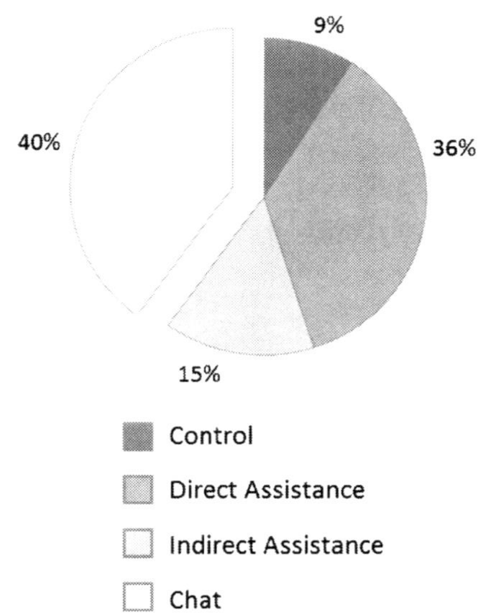

2. **Direct assistance activity:** corpus gathering help requests explicitly made by the user (sentences 5-11).
3. **Indirect assistance activity:** corpus made of user's judgments concerning the application that are actually implying the fact the user is in need of assistance; it certainly requires the system to use pragmatics to detect the implicit meaning (sentences 12-15).
4. **Chat activity:** corpus with all other activities which are not in direct relation with the application and often oriented towards the agent itself (sentences 16-20). It is noticeable that the chat activity amounts to 40% of the total users' utterances. Indeed, according to the Hofstadter's 'Eliza effect' (Chalmers et al., 1992), (Hughes, 2006), the personification of the assistant agent by a virtual character prompts the users to enter into affective chat activity.

In the following, we introduce on-going research works on a particular aspect of personalized information retrieval. In this approach, users' queries are processed with symbolic reasoning techniques that take into account the *current state* of the task at hand. We will explore two case-studies:

1. Reformulation of user's queries based on the current state of the task at hand;
2. Symbolic reasoning over the dynamic model of the task at hand in order to resolve runtime dependent queries.

Reformulation of Users' Queries Based on Current Task State

The State Reformulated Queries (SRQ) model introduced in (Asfari, 2009) is based on the reformulation of queries. In this model, the task at hand is deduced from the user query itself. A state model is responsible for the analysis of the current state within the user task. The personal assistant has knowledge about the user profile and has a predefined model of tasks. It will determine which task at hand the user is undertaking by interacting with the user and analyzing the terms of the queries or user's actions. For example, if one considers the activity of purchasing an item, the assistant will determine the states according to the following tasks by analyzing the user's queries:

- **T1:** You are in a Shopping Centre to find an item.
- **T1.1:** Point out what you search.
- **T1.1.1:** Where to find the item in relation to your current position?
- **T1.1.2:** What are items for sale?
- **T1.1.3:** Accomplish a valuable comparative.
- **T1.1.4:** Use your profile to choose the modalities of purchase.
- **T1.1.5:** Go back to T1.1.

Because the SRQ model is based on the notion of task state, the initial query can be reformulated according to the current state of a task (and also according to the user profile). Hence, depending on each state of the task, the results of a reformulated query can differ. The state of task and the user profile are modeled by predicates of form <attribute, value>. Some values of the predicates are added to the initial query and a reformulated query is generated. The task is modeled by an UML diagram. Every state Si of the diagram is linked to predicates of form <attribute, value>. In some cases, the values of the attributes can be synthetized with information found in the user profile.

Figure 2 describes the architecture of the SRQ system. The activity of the user is modeled by a UML state diagram. This diagram must contain at least one attribute of relevant state for the current task to be able to generate the State Reformulated Query.

Figure 2. General architecture of the SRQ system, from (Asfari, 2009)

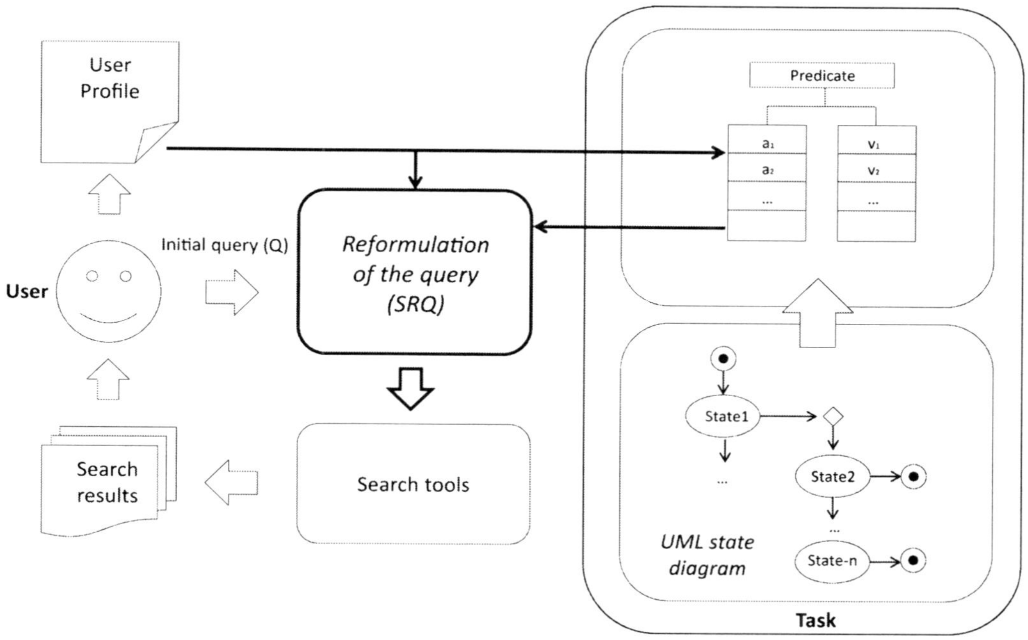

In this first part of the study of contextual information retrieval, we introduced different approaches using the dimensions of context in research process. We detailed the benefit of the context of tasks in information retrieval and more particularly in a model of reformulation of query which takes into account both the user profile and the state of the current task. In the second part, we are going to study the benefit of context the conversational assistant agents.

Using a Dynamic Task Model to Resolve Users' Queries

A typical architecture for a conversational assistant agent, as illustrated in Figure 3, is composed of two main software parts:

1. The application model: is the domain-specific part that contains a) the actual application code and b) the modeling files containing the description and useful information about the application (mainly XML-based files).
2. The assistant agent: is the generic part that contains domain independent tools: a) the NLP-tools translating the textual requests into a formal request form; b) the rule-based symbolic processing tools providing a library of standard reactions to formal requests while browsing the application model.

Figure 3 shows the typical processing path of a user's help request:

1. The users can put textual utterances into a so-called 'chat box' text field.
2. The textual input is transformed into a formal request by the toolkit NLP-tools. This part of the process is subject to a customization that is an adaptation to lexical content and the actual referential entities present in the assisted application.

Figure 3. A typical conversational assistant agent architecture

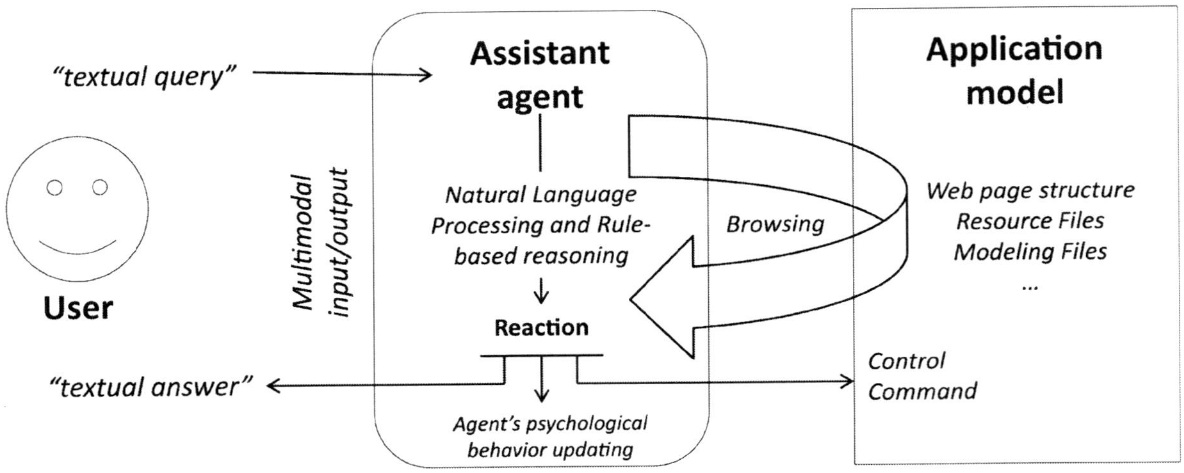

3. A request in formal form is then resolved by applying a list of symbolic rules that browse the application model to retrieve the relevant information so as to build a formal reaction;
4. A formal reaction is composed of three parts: the answer part of the reaction is sent to the user through multimodal devices; the control/command part of the reaction is applied to the runtime of the application; the dialogical part of the reaction updates the dialog session and the behavioral model of the virtual character (in case the assistant agent is given a personification).

Assistant agents can achieve symbolic reasoning over the description of the structure and the functioning of the applications they assist, also called the *assistance model* (in short model) of the application. The synthesis of application models, built for various purposes, is a research domain in its own, related to the community of Model Driven Architectures (MDA) in the framework of Model Driven Engineering (MDE) of the OMG (OMG, 2002), (Atkinson and Kuhne, 2003). Building models dedicated to the support of the function of assistance is part of this framework, though it is not much discussed to day (Leray and Sansonnet, 2006). Several formalisms can be used to support the modeling process: Logic-based using Prolog clauses; Concept networks; Description Logics etc. Recently, XML-based description, including RDF and OWL levels, are widely used.

In order to illustrate this process, Figure 4 describes a simple active component embedded in a Web page: a simple quiz where the user must click the correct operator to fulfill an equation. The symbolic representation in Figure 4-bottom is simplified in two ways: 1) we use an easier-to-read bracketed notation instead of XML tags; 2) it is abridged (e.g. not all elements are represented; elements are not completely described). Nonetheless, as such this form highlights the static structure and the dynamic functioning of the assisted component:

- The structure encompasses both the widgets hierarchy and the static information about the available actions;
- On the other hand, dynamic functioning requires registering in the model some information about the runtime that is the current execution state.

Figure 4. Top-left: A test Web-page including a simple active component; Top-right: Source code of the component embedded in the DHTML code of the Web page (in bold the Javascript code implementing buttons actions); Bottom: Abridged symbolic representation of the structure and the functioning of the component (in bold the modeling of the Javascript actions)

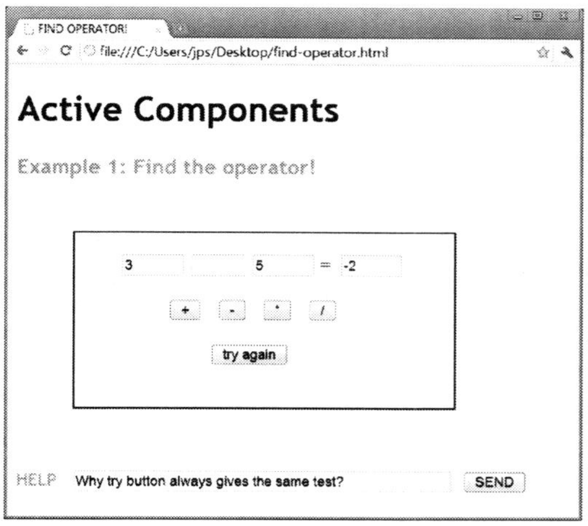


```
... html of top page
<div id="div1" class="divstyle" >
<input id="TF1" type="text" value="3" size="4" maxlength="3" />
<input id="TF2" type="text" value=" " size="3" maxlength="3" />
<input id="TF3" type="text" value="5" size="4" maxlength="3" /> =
<input id="TF4" type="text" value="-2" size="4" maxlength="3" />

<input id="B1" type="button" value=" + "
  onclick="TF2.value='+'; TF4.value=parseInt(TF1.value)+parseInt(TF3.value);" />
<input id="B2" type="button" value=" - "
  onclick="TF2.value='-'; TF4.value=TF1.value - TF3.value;" />
<input id="B3" type="button" value=" * "
  onclick="TF2.value='*'; TF4.value=TF1.value * TF3.value;" />
<input id="B4" type="button" value=" / "
  onclick="TF2.value='/'; TF4.value=TF1.value / TF3.value;" />

<input name="NEW" type="button" value=" try again "
  onclick="TF1.value=3;TF2.value=' ';TF3.value=5;TF4.value=-2;" />
</div>
... html of bottom page
```

```
PARTS[
 FIELD[
        ID[TF1],
        LABEL[None],
        VAL[3],
         LOCATION[{top, left}],
        USAGE["Contains the first operand."] ],
 ...
BUTTON[
        ID[TF2],
        LABEL["-"],
         LOCATION[{middle, left}],
         ACTIVATE[ SET[TF2.VAL, '-']; SET[TF4.VAL, GET|TF1.VAL] – GET[TF3.VAL]] ]
        USAGE["subtract field 1 from field 3 into field 4."] ],
 ....
 BUTTON[
        ID[NEW],
        LABEL["try again"],
         LOCATION[{bottom, middle}],
         ACTIVATE[[ SET[TF1.VAL, 3]; SET[TF2.VAL, " "]; SET[TF3.VAL, 5 ]; SET[TF3.VAL, -2 ] ],
         IDEMPOTENT[], // clicking this button several times does apparently nothing
        USAGE["Resets the quiz."] ],
... abridged
]
```

In the symbolic representation, each tag has a purpose in relation with the solving of user's help questions put into the chatbox at the bottom of the Web page:

- LABEL is used to detect direct references in users' questions. For example "*the + button*", "*try*"...

- LOCATION is used to detect indirect references in users' questions. For example "*the left one*"...
- IDEMPOTENT makes it possible to answer questions like: "*Why try button always gives the same test?*"
- ACTIVATE can be used in more complex reasoning. Etc.

Actually, the more the assistance model is filled with information about the application, the more the assistant agent is potentially able to build relevant answers for the user. However, such models are never complete that is they cannot contain all runtime information; hence many questions, like time situated question (e.g. questions about runtime's history), are difficult to resolve. Moreover, even if the relevant information is actually present in the model, the reasoning module is not always capable to access or exploit it, especially when the user's question is not cognitively aligned to the notions present in the application; again those questions are difficult for the agent to understand in the first place. All these considerations make the research area of task-based assistant agents a difficult and open issue.

FUTURE RESEARCH DIRECTIONS

In the previous section, we discussed the issue of improving the performance of information retrieval systems by introducing task context in information retrieval and intelligent assistants. We suggest virtual characters able to interact with users because they have a positive impact on the global acceptance of the system. The system is generally based on symbolic reasoning and requires natural language processing. On the other hand, we recommend on-going work on the context of task to model the interactions between the user and the system. In the domain of information retrieval, the system is generally based on statistical methods. Future research direction is to go further in integrating virtual assistants and a reasoning model to a context based information retrieval system. A unified framework combining symbolic and statistical models should provide a system capable of managing the interaction and adapting to the specific user needs.

Evaluation of contextual information retrieval systems is a very complex task because the evaluation has to reflect a real situation for a particular user and contextual data are rich and numerous. Therefore new protocols of evaluations and new measures of relevance have to be found to compare the context task based systems. Workshops such as (Doan et al., 2009) are organized to discuss them.

CONCLUSION

The Web has allowed access to information sources and systems which offer various interactive possibilities that have to adapt to the users. In this chapter, we explored the interest of introducing the context and particularly the task context in domains such as information retrieval and artificial intelligence. We showed that these two different domains can be complementary and they can benefit from each other because 1) information retrieval needs to establish a connection with both the laymen and expert users, this relation becomes socio-psychological and relies more and more on natural language processing 2) assistant agents initially perform both the on-going task and the task context, therefore they can provide tools to elicit the tasks context, within a process that performs in parallel with the search task. The future aim will be to unify both commercial and academic efforts in studying the user behavior and in designing interactive systems in order to bring about useful and usable systems that take into account the diversity of the population and the dynamic nature of the information. It will be a question of modeling interaction, personalization together with the context of the documents and to create new interfaces. For example, understanding a very complex user's information need and providing a very simple interface. The challenge is to provide others criteria of search without decreasing the performance of search tools.

REFERENCES

AIML. (n.d.). Retrieved from http://www.alicebot.org/aiml.html

Alicebot, by R. Wallace. (2011). Retrieved from http://alicebot.blogspot.com/

Allen, J. F. (1995). The TRAINS project: a case study in building a conversational planning agent. *Journal of Experimental & Theoretical Artificial Intelligence, 7*(1), 7–48. doi:10.1080/09528139508953799

Allen, J. F., Byron, D. K., Dzikovska, M., Ferguson, G., Galescu, L., & Stent, A. (2001). Toward Conversational Human-Computer Interaction. *AI Magazine, 22*(4), 27–37.

Arapakis, I., Jose, J. M., & Gray, P. D. (2008). Affective feedback: an investigation into the role of emotions in the information seeking process, *proceedings of the 31st annual international ACM SIGIR conference on Research and development in information retrieval.* Singapore.

Asfari, O., Doan, B.-L., Bourda, Y., & Sansonnet, J. P. (2009). Personalized Access to Information by Query Reformulation Based on the State of the Current Task and User Profile. *Third International Conference on Advances in Semantic Processing,* (113-116).

Atkinson, C., & Kuhne, T. (2003). Model-driven development: a metamodeling foundation. *IEEE Software,* 36–41. doi:10.1109/MS.2003.1231149

Baeza-Yates R.& Ribeiro-Neto B. (1999). *Modern Information Retrieval.* Addison-Wesley Longman. 1999.

Baldauf, M., Dustdar, S., & Rosenberg, F. (2007). A Survey on Context-aware Systems. *International Journal Ad Hoc and Ubiquitous Computing, 2*(4), 263–277. doi:10.1504/IJAHUC.2007.014070

Bazire, M., & Brézillon, P. (2005). Understanding Context Before Using It. *5th International and Interdisciplinary Conference, CONTEXT 2005,* Paris, France, (29-40).

Belew, R. K. (2000). *Finding Out About.* Cambridge, UK: Cambridge Univ. Press.

Belkin, N. J. (2006). Getting Personal: Personalization of Support for Interaction with Information. *Invited talk, Workshop AIR.*

Belkin, N. J. (2008). Some(what) grand challenges for information retrieval. *SIGIR Forum, 42*(1), 47–54. doi:10.1145/1394251.1394261

Belkin, N. J., Cool, C., Stein, A., & Thiel, U. (1995). Cases, scripts, and information- seeking strategies: On the design of interactive information retrieval systems. *Expert Systems with Applications, 9*(3), 379–396. doi:10.1016/0957-4174(95)00011-W

Bouchard, H., & Nie, J. Y. (2006). *Modèles de langue appliqués à la recherche d'information contextuelle », Actes de la Conférence en Recherche d'Information et Applications.* CORIA.

Bouchet, F., & Sansonnet, J. P. (2007) Caractérisation de Requêtes d'Assistance à partir de corpus. *Conférence MFI'07,* Paris.

Brezillon, P. (1999). Context in problem solving: a survey. *The Knowledge Engineering Review, 14*(1), 47–80. doi:10.1017/S0269888999141018

Brown, P. J., Bovey, J. D., & Chen, X. (1997). Context-aware applications: From the laboratory to the marketplace. *IEEE Personal Communications, 4*(5), 58–64. doi:10.1109/98.626984

Brown, P. J., & Jones, G. J. (2001). Context-aware Retrieval: Exploring a New Environment for Information Retrieval and Information Filtering. *Personal and Ubiquitous Computing, 5*(4), 253–263. doi:10.1007/s007790170004

Brusilovsky, P. (2001). Adaptive Hypermedia. *Journal of User Modeling and User-Adapted Interaction, Springer, 11*(1-2), 87–110. doi:10.1023/A:1011143116306

Buckley, C., Salton, G., & Allan, J. (1994). The effect of adding relevance information in a relevance feedback environment. *Proceedings of the 17th annual ACM international conference on research and development in information retrieval (SIGIR'94)*, Dublin, UK, (292–300).

Capobianco, A. (2003). Questioning the effectiveness of contextual online help: some alternative propositions. In M. Rauterberg, M. Menozzi, & J. Wesson, (eds), *Human-Computer Interaction INTERACT'03*, (65-72). New York: IOS Press

Capobianco, A., & Carbonell, N. (2001). Contextual online help: elicitation of human experts' strategies. *Proceedings of HCI'01*, New Orleans, (824-828).

Capobianco, A., & Carbonell, N. (2002). Contextual Online Help: a Contribution to the Implementation of Universal Access. In S. Keates, P.J. Clarkson & P. Robinson (eds.), *Universal Access and Assistive Technology*, (131-140). London: Springer.

Carbonell, N. (2003). Towards the design of usable multimodal interaction languages. *Universal Access in the Information Society, 2*(6), 143–159. doi:10.1007/s10209-003-0051-0

Carenini, G., & Moore, J. D. (1993). Generating explanations in context. *Proceedings of the ACM Conference on Intelligent User Interfaces*, Orlando (FL), (175-182). New York: ACM Press.

Carroll, J. M., & Rosson, M. B. (1987). The paradox of the active user. In Carroll, J. M. (Ed.), *Interfacing Thought: Cognitive Aspects of Human-Computer Interaction* (pp. 80–111). Cambridge, MA: MIT Press.

Cassell, J., Bickmore, T., & Billinghurst, M. (1999). *Embodiment in conversational interfaces: Rea.* CHI'99: Proceedings of the SIGCHI conf. on Human factors in comp. syst., (520-527). New York: ACM Press.

Cassell J., Sullivan J., Prevost S.& Churchill. (2000). *Embodied Conversational Agents.* Cambridge, MA: MIT Press.

Chalmers, D. J., French, R. M., & Hofstadter, D. R. (1992). High-level perception, representation, and analogy: A critique of artificial intelligence methodology. *Journal of Experimental & Theoretical Artificial Intelligence, 4*(3), 185–211. doi:10.1080/09528139208953747

Chibane, I., & Doan, B.-L. (2007). Impact of Contextual Information for Hypertext Documents Retrieval. *Workshop on Context-based Information Retrieval, CIR 07.*

Cleverdon, C. W. (1960). *Report on the first stage of an investigation into the comparative efficiency of indexing systems. Technical report.* Cranfield, UK: College of Aeronautics.

Cool, C., & Spink, A. (2002). Issues of context in information retrieval (IR): an introduction to the special issue. *Information Processing & Management, 38*(5), 605–611. doi:10.1016/S0306-4573(01)00054-1

Dey, A. K. (2001). Understanding and Using Context. *Personal and Ubiquitous Computing Journal, 5*(1), 4–7. doi:10.1007/s007790170019

Dey, A. K., & Abowd, G. F. (1999).Towards a better understanding of context and context-awareness. *Technical Report GITGVU-99-22, Georgia Institute of Technology, College of Computing.*

Doan, B.-L., Jose, J., Melucci, M., & Tamine-Lechani, L. (2010). *Workshop on Contextual Information Access, Seeking and Retrieval Evaluation*. ECIR 2010, Milton Keynes.

Elsweiler, D., & Ruthven, I. (2007). Towards Task-based Personal Information Management Evaluations. *Proceedings of the 30th annual international ACM SIGIR conference on Research and development in information retrieval*, (23-30).

Fergusson, G., & Allen, J. F. (1998). TRIPS: An Integrated Intelligent Problem-Solving Assistant, *Proceedings of the Fifteenth National Conference on AI (AAAI-98)*, Madison, WI, (26-30).

Freund, L., Toms, G., & Clarke, C. (2005). *Modeling Task-Genre Relationships for IR in the Workplace*. SIFIR.

Fuhr, N. (2009). Models for retrieval with probabilistic indexing. *Information Processing & Management*, *25*(1), 55–72. doi:10.1016/0306-4573(89)90091-5

Göker, A., & Myrhaug, H. I. (2002). User context and personalization. *Workshop proceedings for the* 6th *European Conference on Case Based Reasoning*.

Grice, P. (1999). Logic and Conversation. In Stainton, R. (Ed.), *Perspectives in the Philosophy of Language: A Concise Anthology*. Peterborough, ON: Broadview Press.

Hal. (2011). Zabaware. Retrieved from http://zabaware.com/

Harter, S. P. (1996). Variations in relevance assessments and the measurement of retrieval effectiveness. *Journal of the American Society for Information Science American Society for Information Science*, *47*(1), 37–49. doi:10.1002/(SICI)1097-4571(199601)47:1<37::AID-ASI4>3.0.CO;2-3

Hughes, L. (2006). *The Eliza Effect*. Conversational Agents and Cognition.

Ingwersen, P. (1996). Cognitive perspectives of information retrieval interaction: Elements of a cognitive IR theory. *The Journal of Documentation*, *52*(1), 3–50. doi:10.1108/eb026960

Ingwersen, P., & Belkin, N. (2004). Information retrieval in context. *IRiX workshop at SIGIR 2004*, Sheffield.

Ingwersen, P., & Järvelin, K. (2005). *The Turn: Integration of Information Seeking and Retrieval in Context*. Dordrecht, The Netherlands: Springer.

Jabberwacky. (2011). Retrieved from http://www.jabberwacky.com/

Jameson, A. (2003). Adaptive interfaces and agents, *The human-computer interaction handbook: fundamentals, evolving technologies and emerging applications*, Lawrence Erlbaum Associates, Inc., (305-330).

Jansen, B. J., Spink, A., & Saracevic, T. (2000). Real life, real users, and real needs: a study and analysis of user queries on the web. *Information Processing & Management*, *36*, 207–227. doi:10.1016/S0306-4573(99)00056-4

Jarvelin, K., & Kekalainen, J. (2002). Cumulative gain-based evaluation of IR techniques [ACM TOIS]. *ACM Transactions on Information Systems*, *20*(4), 422–446. doi:10.1145/582415.582418

Joachims, T., Granka, L. A., Pan, B., Hembrooke, H., Radlinski, F., & Gay, G. (2007). Evaluating the accuracy of implicit feedback from clicks and query reformulations in Web search. *ACM Transactions on Information Systems*, *25*(2). doi:10.1145/1229179.1229181

Jones, G. J. F., & Brown, P. J. (2004). The role of Context in Information Retrieval. *IRiX workshop at SIGIR 2004*, Sheffield.

Kelly, D., & Fu, X. (2007). Eliciting better information need descriptions from users of information search systems. *Information Processing & Management*, *43*(1), 30–46. doi:10.1016/j.ipm.2006.03.006

Kelly, D., & Teevan, J. (2003). Implicit feedback for inferring user preference: A bibliography. *SIGIR Forum*, *37*(2), 18–28. doi:10.1145/959258.959260

Kobayashi, M., & Takeda, K. (2000). Information retrieval on the web. *ACM Computing Surveys*, *32*(2), 144–173. doi:10.1145/358923.358934

Kobsa, A. (2001). Generic User Modeling Systems. *Journal of User Modeling and User-Adapted Interaction*, *11*(1-2), 49–63. doi:10.1023/A:1011187500863

Kofod-Petersen, A., & Cassens, J. (2006). *Using Activity Theory to Model Context Awareness: a Qualitative Case Study*. Berlin: American Association for Artificial Intelligence.

Lawless, S., O'Connor, A., & Mulwa, C. (2010). A proposal for the evaluation of adaptive personalized information retrieval, CIRSE 2010. *Proceedings of The 2nd International Workshop on Contextual Information Access, Seeking and Retrieval Evaluation*, Milton Keynes, UK.

Leray, D., & Sansonnet, J. P. (2006). Ordinary user oriented model construction for Assisting Conversational Agents, *International Workshop on Communication between Human and Artificial Agents, CHAA'06 at IEEE-WIC-ACM Conference on Intelligent Agent Technology*, Hong Kong.

Leray, D., & Sansonnet, J. P. (2007). Assisting Dialogical Agents Modeled from Novice User's Perceptions. *Proceedings of KES*, *07*, 1122–1129.

Lester, J. C., et al. (1997). The persona effect: affective impact of animated pedagogical agents, *Proceedings of the SIGCHI conference on Human factors in computing systems*, 359-366. Atlanta USA: ACM.

Ligozat, A. L., Grau, B., Robba, I., & Vilnat, A. (2006). L'extraction des réponses dans un système de question-réponse. *Conference TALN*, Leuven.

Likke, M. (2004). Task-based evaluation of associative thesaurus in real-life environment. *Proceedings of the ASIST 2004 Annual Meeting*, Providence, Rhode Island.

Luxenburger J., Elbassuoni S.& Weikum G. (2008). Task-aware Search Personalization. *SIGIR* 2008.

Luxenburger J., Elbassuoni S.& Weikum G. (2008b). Matching Task Profiles ans User Needs in Personalized Web Search. *CIKM* 2008.

Maes, P. (1994). Agents that reduce work and information overload. *Communications of the ACM*, *37*(7), 30–40. doi:10.1145/176789.176792

Mobasher, B. (2007). Data Mining for Web Personalization. *The Adaptive Web, Springer-Verlag* (90-135). Berlin Heidelberg, Muresan, G. (2006). An Integrated Approach to Interaction Modeling and Analysis for Exploratory Information Retrieval. *Workshop on Evaluating Exploratory Search Systems (EESS 2006) at SIGIR 2006*, Seattle, WA.

Nahl, D. (2007). Social-biological information technology: An integrated conceptual framework. *In JASIST -. Journal of the American Society for Information Science and Technology*, *58*(13), 2021–2046. doi:10.1002/asi.20690

Oddcast.(2011). Retrieved from http://www.oddcast.com/home/

OMG, Object Management Group. (2002). *Meta-Object Facility (MOF), version 1.4*. Retrieved from http://www.omg.org/technology/documents/formal/mof.htm.

Randall, N., & Pedersen, I. (1998). Who exactly is trying to help us? The ethos of help systems in popular computer applications. *Proceedings of the 16th annual international conference on Computer documentation, 63-69*. New York: ACM.

Rich, C., & Sidner, C. L. (1998). COLLAGEN: A Collaboration Manager for Software Interface Agents. *An International Journal: User Modeling and User-Adapted Interaction*, *8*(3/4), 315–350. doi:10.1023/A:1008204020038

Rickel, J., & Johnson, W. L. (1999). Animated agents for procedural training in virtual reality: perception, cognition and motor control. *Applied Artificial Intelligence*, *13*, 343–382. doi:10.1080/088395199117315

Ryan, N., Pascoe, J., & Morse, D. (1998). Enhanced reality fieldwork: the context-aware archaeological assistant. In Gaffney, V., van Leusen, M., & Exxon, S. (Eds.), *Computer Applications and Quantitative Methods in Archaeology, British Archaeological Reports*. Tempus Reparatum.

Sansonnet J. P., (1999) Description technique du projet InterViews. *Technical Report LIMSI (99-01)*.

Sansonnet, J. P., Sabouret, N., & Pitel, G. (2002). An Agent Design and Query Language dedicated to Natural Language Interaction. *First International Joint Conference on Autonomous Agents and Multi-Agent Systems, AAMAS'02*, Bologna.

Saracevic, T. (1996). Interactive models in information retrieval: A review and proposal. *Proceedings of the 59th Annual Meeting of the American Society for Information Science, 33,* (3-9).

Saracevic T. (1996b). Relevance reconsidered. *Proceedings of Colis 2*, Copenhagen, Denmark, (201-218).

Saracevic, T. (1997). The stratified model of information retrieval interaction: Extension and applications. *Proceedings of the American Society for Information Science*, *34*, 313–327.

Schilit, B. N., Adams, N. I., & Want, R. (n.d.). Context-Aware Computing Applications. *Proceedings of the Workshop on Mobile Computing Systems and Applications, IEEE Computer Society*, Santa Cruz, CA, (85-90).

Searle, J. R. (1969). *Speech Acts: An Essay in the Philosophy of Language*. Cambridge, UK: Cambridge University Press.

Skov, M., Larsen, B., & Ingwersen, P. (2006). Inter and intra-document contexts applied in polyrepresentation. *Proceedings of the 1st international Conference on information interaction in Context* (Copenhagen, Denmark, October 18 - 20, 2006). IIiX, vol. 176. (97-101). New York: ACM.

Spärck Jones, K. (2005). Meta-reflections on TREC. *TREC: Experiment and Evaluation in Information Retrieval,* (421-448). Cambridge, MA: MIT Press.

Sumi, Y., & Mase, K. (2002). Supporting the awareness of shared interests and experiences in communities. *International Journal of Human-Computer Studies*, *56*(1), 127–146. doi:10.1006/ijhc.2001.0518

Teixeira Lopes, C. (2009). Context Features and their use in Information Retrieval. *3rd Symposium on Future Directions in Information Access (FDIA'09)*.

Turpin, A., & Scholer, F. (2006). User performance versus precision measures for simple search tasks. *SIGIR 2006, Proceedings of the 29th Annual ACM SIGIR Conference on Research and Development in Information Retrieval,* (11-18). New York: ACM

Ummelen, N., & Neutelings, R. (2000). Measuring reading behavior in policy documents: a comparison of two instruments. *IEEE Transactions on Professional Communication*, *43*, 292–301. doi:10.1109/47.867945

Vidal, M. E., Raschid, L., Marquez, N., Cardenas, M., & Wu, Y. (2006). Query Rewriting in the Semantic Web. *Proceedings of the 22nd International Conference on Data Engineering Workshops, ICDEW'06*, Atlanta, USA.

Voorhees, E. M. (2002). Overview of the TREC 2002 Question Answering Track. *In Proceedings of the Eleventh Text REtrieval Conference (TREC)*, (115-123).

Voorhees, E. M., & Harman, D. K. (2005). *TREC: Experiment and evaluation in information retrieval*. Cambridge, MA: MIT Press.

Webb, G., Pazzani, M., & Billsus, D. (2001). Machine learning for user modeling. [Boston: Kluwer Academic Publishers.]. *User Modeling and User-Adapted Interaction, 11*, 19–29. doi:10.1023/A:1011117102175

Weizenbaum, J. (1966). ELIZA, a computer program for the study of natural language communication between man and machine. *Communications of the ACM, 9*(1). doi:10.1145/365153.365168

White, M. D. (1998). Questions in reference interviews. *The Journal of Documentation, 54*(4), 443–465. doi:10.1108/EUM0000000007177

White, R. W., & Kelly, D. (2006). A Study on the Effects of Personalization and Task Information on Implicit Feedback Performance. *Proceedings of the 15th ACM international conference on Information and Knowledge Management.*

Wilson, T. D. (1981). On user studies and information needs. *Journal of Librarianship, 37*(1), 3–15.

Wollermann, C. (2004). *Evaluierung der linguistischen Fähigkeiten von Chatbots. Magister report.* Rheinische-Friedrich-Wilhelms Universität Bonn.

Wollermann, C. (2006). *Proceedings of the Young Researchers' Roundtable on Spoken Dialogue Systems*. Pittsburgh, PA, (75-76).

Wu, I., Liu, D. R., & Chang, P. C. (2007). Toward incorporating a task-stage identification technique into the long-term document support process. *Information Processing & Management, 44*(5), 1649–1672. doi:10.1016/j.ipm.2007.11.005

Yuelin, L., & Belkin, N. J. (2008). *A faceted approach to conceptualizing tasks in information seeking, Information Processing and Management*. New York: Elsevier publisher.

KEY TERMS AND DEFINITIONS

Adaptive System: System capable of improving its performances progressively as time goes by thanks to feedback on its previous performances.

Assistant Agent: Agent dedicated to the Function of Assistance for applications and services to the general public.

Conversational Agent: Virtual characters able to interact with users through multimodal dialogues.

Context: Every information that can be used to characterize the situation of entities (either a person, a location or an object) that are considered as relevant to the interaction between the user and the application, including the user and the application themselves.

Natural Language Requests: Queries or user's need expressed in natural language.

Personalized Information Retrieval System: Information retrieval system that accommodate users' needs by taking into account the particular interests of individual users.

State Reformulated Query (SRQ): Reformulation of a query taking into account the context of the user's task (task at hand).

Task Context: Context of a task or an activity.

Chapter 9
Metadata for Information Retrieval in Archives

Vicent Giménez Chornet
Universitat Politècnica de València, Spain

ABSTRACT

The traditional system for searching for documents in archives is based on correct preparation of the description instruments: guides, inventories, catalogues and index cards. The emergence of three factors in the last few decades has made the system, used by archive institutions for centuries, no longer the most appropriate for information retrieval. These three factors are information and communication technologies, and electronic indexing, preferably using appropriate thesauri.

This chapter is an attempt to analyse which technological elements and which description and indexing elements directly impact information retrieval of documents. As a result of the analysis, some requirements are proposed that must be observed in archival information systems installed in organisations with the aim of optimising effective information retrieval.

INTRODUCTION

The features inherent in archival documentation, especially the high diversity of types and the absence of a title and intellectual author, which is not the same as the producer, has made its control more difficult, even using different description models. Therefore, this has slowed down implementation of a good system of information retrieval. Organisations have for centuries used archival staff for the control and search of documents that were more or less efficient for the amount of documentation managed. The current problem, since the 20th century, is the huge amount of documentation produced by public administrations, which has not corresponded with an increase in archival staff. The impossibility of cataloguing all the documents archived because of infrastructural deficiencies slows down the process of locating documents that any user might need at any given moment.

DOI: 10.4018/978-1-61350-201-3.ch009

Archivists are not uninvolved in research and in the search for solutions enabling more effective retrieval of documents produced by organisations. Often, the urgency to find documents is higher in administrative archives where, as a general rule, the main users are the document producers and they themselves require a rapid response in searching for documents in order to process or resolve current administrative situations. But a recent interest in locating documents has also arisen in historical archives, caused by the digitisation of the records. An essential requirement in this case is the document description and to be able to link digital images to a record of the document.

Due to the interest in information retrieval, researchers in archival centres and educational institutions have worked in a variety of environments to find effective solutions to the demands of today's society. These solutions have centred on the description, the incorporation of information and communication technologies and document management tools. The questions to be answered after some years of proposals are whether these are sufficient or should new requirements be put forward? And in the archives, has the problem of information retrieval been effectively resolved?

To analyze this issue we will see what proposals exist to describe metadata archival funds, following the implementation of international standards and the problems caused by inadequate description for a good retrieval. Finally, we will propose the basic requirements to be applied in the description in the various metadata standards for archival description, for the efficient retrieval of information.

METADATA PROPOSALS FOR INFORMATION RETRIEVAL

Seeing the effectiveness achieved by libraries in information retrieval, one of the solutions proposed in the sphere of archives is the normalisation of the description. In this sense, as far back as 1985, the AMC format was proposed, as a part of the MARC format, for describing hand-written documentation deposited in libraries (Sahli, N., 1985). In the 1990s, the archival community was developing its own standards for description and control of its assets (Jimerson, R.C., 2002). Thus EAD was born, based on XML tags (Pitti, Daniel V., 1997), and ISAD (G), created by the International Council of Archives, 2000). Their aim was to describe documents in an individual way and also to be able to describe series or other types of document groupings. Later, the EAC-CPF (Society of American Archivist, 2008) and the ISAAR (CPF) (International Council of Archives, 2004) were created to describe the producers of these documents: organisations, individuals or families.

The standardisation effort for archival descriptions was accompanied by technological advances. The improvements in communications implemented since the 1990s, fundamentally the Internet and Intranet, technological advances, computers with more storage capacity and processor speed and progress made in software are indispensable for and inseparable from archival description standards when implementing a system for document management.

The standards have been considered not as something new or "a revolutionary transformation of archival practice but just another step in the universal trend undertaken for over a century to convert this practice into a working method based on a terminology" (Esteban Navarro, M. A., Gay Molins, P., 1998). But the standards have brought something more that had not been considered in archival tradition; the description of the context, that is, of the producers of the documents: "archival descriptive traditions have placed greater emphasis on the context and function of records and collections, in keeping with the nature of archival materials, which are the product of organic activity rooted in the context of creation" (Freund, L., Butterworth, R., 2008). The elements of these standards serve as metadata labels, both for describing contemporary administrative archives and the documents of historical archives (Bekaert, J., et al., 2002).

There is also a contrary opinion in that the document description or the catalogue in archives is not the best tool for searching for documents. "It would not make sense to ask, in an archive, What is there on this subject? and What is there about this person? (as is unfortunately frequently asked by those who go to an archive without sufficient specific preparation)... By contrast, it is necessary to ask, Which was, at different times, the office responsible for handling the subject of interest? and What procedures did they use? that is, How was this office producing and organising its own documents? ... The inventory, then, is a compound instrument; the single means that enables making a search in an archive. A catalogue of documents would, by contrast, be totally useless, lacking sense among other considerations ... without addressing the fundamental archival aspect of the documents themselves, that is, their interdependence..." (Lodolini, E., 1993). Or that the "catalogue is the least useful of all the instruments of description from a practical and a service point of view because of the description needs and the lack of material means and human resources in the majority of archives" (Cruz Mundet, J. R.,1999). This opinion has motivated work to be centred on the inventories in many archives and that search for documents starts from investigation in inventoried documentary series. For this, the user must have good knowledge of the political-administrative system of the producing organisations, what were their functions or responsibilities in the given historical period.

The ISO 15489-1:2001 standard, the aim of which is the standardisation of the policies and procedures for document management in organisations so that the information they contain can be retrieved more efficiently and effectively, also fails to develop the issue of document description, ignoring the EAD, ISAD (G), EAC-CPF and ISAAR (CPF) standards. Its interest lies in the classification of the organisation's activities for establishing a link between the documents produced and the classification table developed; in this way, retrieval of documents relating to a specific function or activity of the organisation is facilitated. The use of controlled vocabularies is recommended as a support for classification tables and index creation.

Indexing of archived documents by the use of a thesaurus, specially developed for the particular assets, is another tool proposed as being beneficial for optimisation in information retrieval. For the indexing of French public archives, both historical and contemporary, the *Thésaurus W* was developed in XML/SKOS for subjects, and some lists for "Actions", "Document Type" and "Historical Context" (Archives de France, 2009). It is more common for indexing of archives to prepare thesauri for the control of the vocabulary related to the subjects, institutions, geographical sites and even a controlled language, generally lists, for names of people and families. The AIM25 database, accessible over the Web, which describes collections of manuscripts of different archives deposited in educational, cultural or company institutions, used the UK Archival Thesaurus and the UNESCO Thesaurus for the indexing of the descriptions (InforM25, 2002). In the Reino de Valencia Archive, we prepared three thesauri for indexing subjects, institutions and geographical sites (Giménez Chornet, V., 2007).

METADATA TO INFORMATION RETRIEVAL FROM ARCHIVES: PROBLEMS AND SOLUTIONS

Problems and Deficiencies in Archival Practice

The main problem of archives, which separates them hugely from libraries and documentation centres, is that the documentation unavoidably received is much greater than can be processed by the staff working there. In libraries, except those responsible for keeping specimens published in the nation, documents acquired are as a result of need and are viable according to the institution's budget. In archives, everything that is produced by the producing organisation is received, neither more nor less. The current situation of archives is that they have inherited consignments of documents over the years, in some cases more than a century's worth of documentation. The current prospect continues to be the same; consignments of many linear metres of documentation that cannot physically be processed by the inadequate numbers of archivists on the staff. If this problem is not addressed, it will be difficult to resolve the problem of information retrieval effectively. Is there any solution in the 21st century, with all the information and communication technologies at our disposal and with all the methodological progress achieved?

We have made progress in the standardisation of the description, even including multi-level description (from documents to document groupings), something which was unimaginable in archives a few years ago. The most positive aspect of standardisation is that, when creating specific fields, this enables description in networks of archives. For the first time we can make information interoperable in a network of archives because we have technologically ensured that these archives use the same description fields. This is the same as was achieved in libraries with the MARC and ISBD formats. However, archival practice is reducing this advantage. In many nations or nationalities, these international standards are being "adapted", preparing local standards in which new fields are being created, or existing fields are being given a different meaning or requirements to those in the international standard. This is going to cause a serious problem in the interoperability of the information in networks of archives and in the effectiveness of information retrieval. The DACS standard (Describing Archives: A Content Standard) approved by the Society of American Archivists has subdivided the ISAD (G) "Reference Code" into three fields, "Local identifier", "Repository identifier" and "Country identifier" (Society of American Archivists, 2004). This distorts the aim of ISAD (G), which is "to identify uniquely the unit of description and to provide a link to the description that represents it", making it more difficult to create networks of archives because some may have a single identifier for the unit of description in a single field and other may have three fields for the same purpose.

The "Title" field of ISAD (G) is one of the most important for correct identification of the archival unit being described and in the adaptation to some national standards but in description practice in some archives, criteria are being implemented that make information retrieval more difficult or impossible. The term "Title" has led many to confuse it with the term "title" in ISBD library standards. In archival documentation, titles do not exist. Antonia Heredia indicated very clearly that, "the documents of an archive or their groupings do not have a title, but a name, and this name is not arbitrary, as the title of a book can legitimately be arbitrary, but this name is a faithful representation of their origin, which is the identification mark of archival documents" (Heredia, A., 2000). The organisations producing documents do not give them a title, so, where does the confusion come from? Documentation, when it has passed to the archives or other centres where there are people responsible for its management, has been handled in some way by these people, who are not the producers but "archivists" who in carrying out their work have used various mechanisms for its speedy retrieval. These mechanisms include writing different phrases on the piece of documentation so that it can be quickly retrieved in a visible way. These phrases can range from a couple of words to entire paragraphs, or even the archive location number. It should be noted that this marking is different from that of the producer and that often many years have passed since when the document was produced. These phrases are neither more nor less than little descriptions made by the document management technicians of organisations' assets, whether this be the 13th or the 21st century. Often, this technical description made by the document manager has been confused with the intellectual title, such as in the case of printed works. Current archivists, in their description criteria, have no reason to make the same descriptions as their predecessors. A title only exists in the case of an intellectual work, where the author has assigned a title and where the original specimen is held in an archive. Copies (printed books) are held in libraries. But generally it is rare to find original intellectual works in archives (they can occur in archives of individuals or families, or in photographic archives, where the originals are preserved on celluloid or plates). For example, the adaptation of the ISAD (G) standard by Catalan archivists, the NODAC, in its rule 1.3.D12, accepts the formal title "*Llibre de privilegis, statuts e ordinacions de la ciutat de Leyda*", although this preserves medieval spellings of words such as *Leyda* that are not recognised in current spelling and accepts formal titles in Latin (rule 1.3.D10) although the database is not in Latin (Bernal, A.; Magrinyà, A.; Planes, R. (ed.), 2007). There are two problems with this that make information retrieval impossible: using archaic vocabulary that is no longer current and making a description in a language that is different from that of the database.

The access points in databases is another of the pillars for information retrieval. In libraries, the cataloguing rules regulate the access points in a bibliographic record. These are information units to facilitate search in a bibliographic collection, such as the main entry, the secondary positions or the subject headings, although now with practically automated bibliographic databases, access can be made from any information unit or fields, such as those of the MARC format. In archives, the same is not exactly the case. As regards the indexing of archival records through the ISAD (G) standard, nothing is regulated, but there are good archival practices being performed by outstanding archives. The only thing that has been regulated is the name of the producer of the documents. In the ISAD (G) standard, there is a field called "Name of producer" which is specified as "Record the name of the organization(s) or the individual(s) responsible for the creation, accumulation and maintenance of the records in the unit of description. The name should given in the standardized form as prescribed by international or national conventions in accordance with the principles of ISAAR (CPF)". Although it is clear that the ISAAR (CPF) standard describes the name of the producer, it has not been established exactly which fields of this standard are controlled by the field "Name of producer" of ISAD (G). The ISAAR (CPF) standard only regulates the producers of documents, which might be organisations, individuals or families (International Council of Archives, 2003). Another problem occurring in practice is related to the adaptation to the standard in some countries. For example in Spain, the Ministry of Culture has published a standard based on ISAAR (CPF) for describing access points on institutions, individuals, families, places and subjects in the system for archival description of state archives (Hernández, S., 2010). This incorporates criteria of bibliographic description into the standard and undermines the fundamental aim of the standard, which is to regulate the description of the producer; the place and a subject are not producers. Basically two aspects that are differentiated in archival information systems, the producers and the indexing, are being mixed in the access points.

Traditionally on paper index cards made in archives to be able to chronologically order them, the topical date was recorded in the following format: year, month, day and place (place where the document was signed). This enabled effective information retrieval by date in a manual paper-based environment. However, now in technological environments based on databases, these criteria for the topical date have changed. The ISAD (G) standard makes reference to a date field, where a date or various dates (for example the initial and the final date) can be recorded, and makes no reference for recording the place of the producer. This makes sense because the standard is very careful to require both the place of the producer and the name of the producer to be recorded in the "Name of producer" field. However, the possibility of using various dates for the same description has created the problem in the databases of deciding if one single field or two fields are to be created. This is very important because, depending on the characteristics and of the number of fields for the date, information retrieval may or may not be effective. And if a system of various networked archives is created, it is still more important to decide what characteristics and how many fields should be created to record dates. This is also a problem that is characteristic in archives because documents in libraries generally only have one date, that of the publication of the document. But in archives, it is common to have files that, as a set of documents, can be recorded in the database with the initial date of the file and the final date indicated on the document that concludes the file. Similarly, when series, fonds or collections are described, there is an initial date and a final date.

Information and Communication Technologies have allowed the creation of networks of archives, so that information produced by geographically separated archives can be shared. Some of these networks are available on the Internet (such as the Spanish PARES portal, http://pares.mcu.es/, or the London AIM25 portal http://www.aim25.ac.uk/). In order for information retrieval to be effective in these networks, two groups of problems must be resolved: the adoption of a standard and its implementation criteria, and the adoption of a single documentary language for indexing. The adoption of a standard is rarely problematic, mainly because there are not many standards for archival description. What causes the most conflicts are the distinct criteria for the adaptation of the standard such as allowing the description in different languages in the same database; applying description levels differently depending on the archive (there are archives that call installation units, such as bundles of papers or record books, "compound documentary unit" and others have created a new level for installation units); naming the description levels differently in each archive or creating different description levels; that in the same database, in some archives the topical date is put into the date field and in others only the date without the place; that in some archives the "Attributed title" or phrase that appears on the cover of the file or the book is put in the "Title" field, whereas other archives describe the archival unit with the current criteria and language in the "Title" field.

Indexing of archives is not regulated by the ISAD (G) or EAD standards. Current practice is that each network of archives, or single archives, decide whether to index or not to index the descriptions in their databases. The majority of large archives or networks of archives have decided to index the descriptions, creating a field in the database for the indexes, or various fields if they decided to classify the indexing (generally by subjects, geographical names, institutions or names of people). The problem arises when the option has been taken to use natural and unconstrained language in indexing and archivists use whatever term that occurs to them at the time of indexing the documents. This results in the use of different terms for the same descriptor that in principle pursue the same aim (for examples the terms "slave", "slaves", "Slave", "Slaves"). The result is gaps in information retrieval. Also, when each archive uses an indexing language in a network of archives, retrieval is incomplete because in the network of archives there will be records indexed with synonymous terms, and the result is gaps in retrieval. The absence of a unified policy of criteria in the construction of the documentary language and in indexing limits the effectiveness of an archival database.

Basic Requirements for Information Retrieval

One of the basic problems in information retrieval in archives is caused because there are insufficient describe all the documentation that is added to the assets or, in the case of electronic administration, to the electronic repositories. The ISO 15489 standard recommends that when documentation is added to a document management system, it must be described, classified and indexed. But it remains to be resolved at which moment the documentation is considered to be added to the system and who should be responsible for describing, classifying and indexing it in this system. What the evidence demonstrates is that the archivists cannot do everything due to lack of staff and infrastructure. In the era of the Information and Communication Technologies and with the methodological development in document management achieved, the movement of enormous volumes of documentation from office archives to the assets without control of the description should not continue to be made. In this sense, the first requirement is to resolve the information architecture in a system or network of archives and who has responsibility for the elements of this architecture.

Requirement 1: *A single database on a server computer must have client/user computers in each office that allows the description of the document using the ISAD (G) or EAD standard when the administrative staff produce it. A "Reference Code" is captured that the archivist will have previously established in a classification system. The indexing will also be performed by the administrative staff.*

Requirement 2: *The information architecture of the system must allow the metadata related to the incorporation of the document to be always associated with it throughout its life cycle, from the office archive, through the intermediate archives, to the historical archive. The physical transfer of the documentation is accompanied by the transfer to the corresponding level in the database classification table.*

When an archive creates a database to manage its documentary assets, the criteria, standards and fields of this database can be different from international standards and yet information retrieval may function correctly to satisfy the needs of the organisation. But if the archive wants to be prepared for information exchange and to create networks of archives, it must apply an international standard, either ISAD (G) or EAD, for the description of the archival units and ISAAR (CPF) or EAC-CPF for the description of the producers. If this requirement is not met, neither the database fields nor their objectives will coincide, making interoperability non-viable and therefore reducing the effectiveness of information retrieval.

Requirement 3: *Scrupulously apply the international standards for archival description, fundamentally in the creation of the database fields.*

The absence of international standards for indexing of records made with ISAD (G) or EAD have caused each archive or network of archives to opt for some criteria. Rejecting indexing with natural language, which is the most unreliable for information retrieval, the database must control four blocks of vocabulary. To resolve errors of the disconnection between the vocabulary or thesaurus and the ISAD (G) or EAD record card, the tool for constructing the thesaurus, must be integrated into the database, so that a change in vocabulary may allow correction of the indexing in all the records made.

Requirement 4: *Tool for construction and control of the indexing vocabulary (thesaurus) integrated into the database.*

Requirement 5: *Construction of four control blocks of the vocabulary, preferably thesaurus,* *for subjects, organisations, geographical sites and people's names.*

For information retrieval to operate correctly in databases, all those criteria for adaptation of the ISAD (G) standard, such as those considering it legitimate to populate Attributed titles with archaic texts and even dead languages or languages different from the language adopted for the description, must be rejected. The professionalism of the people who make the descriptions overrides the description criteria of past periods. In general, a single criterion is pursued in archival descriptions to optimise information retrieval.

Requirement 6: *Use of a single language in the database (there may be parallel database for other languages) and scrupulous application of spelling rules and the use of proper names (geographical names, people's names, etc.).*

Requirement 7: *Description made by current professionals and rejection of adopting attributed titles.*

Currently, with the automation of archives, all the fields of the database can be recoverable. There is only one field that, due to its application criteria, interconnects the two standards, ISAD (G) and ISAAR (CPF): the field "Name of producer". This field must be specified according to the ISAAR (CPF) standard, but the three fields of this standard may be captured to correctly identify the essential elements of the producer's identification. Similarly, the producers' description database must be connected to the archival units' description database. This will allow interrogating the database on how many documents a specific organisation has produced.

Requirement 8: *The "Name of producer" field of the ISAD (G) standard must capture the data of the fields "Authorised form of name", "Dates of existence" and "Places" of the ISAAR (CPF) standard.*

Requirement 9: *The producers' description database must be related to the archival units' description database.*

CONCLUSION

In order to become more efficient in information retrieval or search for documents in archives, it is not enough to apply the international standards for archival description or Information and Communication Technologies, as is already common practice in many archives. There still remain many aspects of the problems of retrieval to be resolved, even for documentation generated in organisations in this 21st century. The reason for this is that the problems also lie in the criteria for application of the standards and in the information architecture derived from the technologies. After the identification of the most common problems, we have proposed some requirements that would particularly resolve information retrieval in networks of archives.

REFERENCES

Archives de France. (2009). *Thésaurus pour la description et l'indexation des archives locales anciennes, modernes et contemporaines*.Retrieved from http://www.archivesdefrance.culture.gouv.fr/gerer/classement/normes-outils/thesaurus/

Bekaert, J., Ville, D. V. D., Rogge, B., Strauven, I., Kooning, E. D., & Walle, R. V. d. (2002). Metadata-based access to multimedia architectural and historical archive collections: a review. *Aslib Proceedings*, *54*(6), 362–371. doi:10.1108/00012530210452564

Bernal, A., Magrinyà, A., & Planes, R. (2007). *Norma de Descripción Archivística de Cataluña (NODAC), (Arxivística i gestió documental. Eines; 1)*. Barcelona, Generalitat de Cataluña, from http://www20.gencat.cat/docs/CulturaDepartament/Cultura/Temes/Arxius/Norma%20de%20Descripcio%20Arxivistica%20de%20Catalunya/arxius/NodCast.pdf

Cruz Mundet, J. R. (1999). *Manual de archivística*. Madrid: Fundación Germán Sánchez Ruipérez.

Esteban Navarro, M. A., & Gay Molins, P. (1998). *La normalización de la descripción y la recuperación de información en los archivos: vino viejo en odres nuevos. Boletín de la ANABAD, (48)*. Madrid: ANABAD.

Freund, L., & Butterworth, R. (2008). Tagging for Use: an analysis of use-centred resource description. *ACM International Conference Proceeding Series* (348), 6-12. London.

Giménez Chornet, V., Escrig Giménez, M., Villalmanzo Cameno, J., & Viciano Navarro, P. (2007). *Tesauros del Archivo del Reino de Valencia = Tesaurus de l'Arxiu del Regne de València*. Valencia: Conselleria de Cultura i Esport.

Heredia, A. (2000). *La norma ISAD (G) "Análisis Crítico". Norma Internacional para la descripción archivística*. México, INFOLAC. Retrieved from http://infolac.ucol.mx/documentos/isad.pdf

Hernández, S. (2010). *Norma para la elaboración de puntos de acceso normalizados de instituciones, personas, familias, lugares y materias en el sistema de descripción archivística de los archivos estatales*. Madrid: Ministerio de Cultura, from http://www.mcu.es/archivos/docs/Novedades/Norma_puntos_acceso2010.pdf

InforM25. (2002). *AIM25, Archives in London and the M25 area*. Retrieved from http://www.aim25.ac.uk/index.stm

International Council of Archives. (2000). *ISAD (G): General International Standard Archival Description, Second edition*. Ottawa: ICA. Retrieved from http://www.ica.org/en/node/30000

International Council of Archives. (2003). *ISAAR (CPF), International Standard Archival Authority Record for Corporate Bodies, Persons and Families. Second Edition*. Paris: ICA. Retrieved from http://www.ica.org/sites/default/files/ISAAR2EN.pdf

International Council of Archives. (2004). *ISAAR (CPF): International Standard Archival Authority Record for Corporate Bodies, Persons, and Families, Second edition*. Paris, CIA. Retrieved from http://www.ica.org/en/node/30230

ISO 15489-1:2001. *Information and documentation-Records management - Part 1: General*. Geneva: ISO

Jimerson, R. C. (2002). Archival description and finding aids. *OCLC Systems & Services*, *18*(3), 125–129. doi:10.1108/10650750210439331

Lodolini, E. (1993). *Archivística. Principios y problemas*. Madrid: ANABAD.

Pitti, D. V. (1997). Encoded Archival Description: The Development of an Encoding Standard for Archival Finding Aids. *The American Archivist*, (60): 268–283.

Sahli, N. (1985). *MARC For Archives and Manuscripts: The AMC Format*. Chicago: The Society of American Archivists Society of American Archivist (2008). *EAC-CPF, Encoded Archival Contex. Corporate Bodies, Persons, and Families*. Retrieved from http://eac.staatsbibliothek-berlin.de/

Society of American Archivists. (2004). *Describing Archives: A Content Standard. Appendix C. Table C5: DACS to EAD and MARC*. Chicago, SAA.Retrieved from http://www.archivists.org/publications/DACS_TableC5_Erratum.pdf

ADDITIONAL READING

Dryden, J. E. (Ed.). (2007). *Respect for authority: authority control, context control, and archival description*. Binghamton, NY: Haworth Information Press.

Procter, M., & Cook, M. (2000). *Manual of archival description*. Aldershot; Burlington (Vt.): Gower.

Stockting, B., & Queyroux, F. (Eds.). (2005). *Encoding across frontiers: proceedings of the European Conference on Encoded Archival Description and Context (EAD and EAC), Paris, France, 7-8 October, 2004*. New York: Haworth Information Press

Subsection
Automatic References

Chapter 10
Management Systems of User Interfaces Functionalities in Latin: American Web OPACs

Elsa Barber
Universidad de Buenos Aires, Argentina

Silvia Pisano
Universidad de Buenos Aires, Argentina

Sandra Romagnoli
Universidad de Buenos Aires, Argentina

Verónica Parsiale
Universidad de Buenos Aires, Argentina

Gabriela de Pedro
Universidad de Buenos Aires, Argentina

Carolina Gregui
Universidad de Buenos Aires, Argentina

Nancy Blanco
Universidad de Buenos Aires, Argentina

ABSTRACT

Taking into account the fundamental role of online public access catalogs in the dissemination of scientific and technical information, it was considered relevant to look into the situation of user interfaces of OPACs Web of university, special, public and national libraries in Latin America. A quantitative methodology has been adopted and a checklist of system functions (Hildreth, 1982) updated was used as data collection tool. A sample of 846 OPACs was obtained from predefined search queries and classified according to type of software, type of library and country. A subset of 374 units was selected of those whose system presented a frequency of appearance ≥ 10. The percentage of presence of functionalities in each area was calculated and functionalities were compared according to type of software by test of independence. It was then possible to typify the interfaces of the analyzed OPACs according to the selected types of software and in relation to their category.

DOI: 10.4018/978-1-61350-201-3.ch010

INTRODUCTION

Library automation in Latin America first started in the 80's in midst of an extremely complex context. The political, social and economic conditions prevailing in the region impacted the area of education and culture where the absence of planning and investment affected automation processes from the very beginning. Thus, early Systems were implemented in a context of serious restrictions in terms of infrastructure and equipment, as well as, in terms of software programs used.

Already at earlier stages, when the traditional library model prevailed in the countries of Central and South America, most of these institutions had limited resources available to show their collections in catalogues and to provide visibility to the services they offered. The erratic information policies always coincided with budgetary difficulties and prevented them from having a balanced and rational development to support the changes evolved in the transition process toward an automated library, first, and later toward a hybrid or digital library.

In the face of this situation, and given the importance of these institutions as organizations capable of contributing to the encouragement of technical and scientific development, as well as to the improvement of the quality of life of citizens, the decision was made between 1995 and 2003, to look into the status of automation processes in the different types of libraries in Argentina. This lead to a real diagnosis of public and private university libraries of the entire country and of public libraries of the City of Buenos Aires and its surrounding areas.

Certain difficulties were identified in the libraries that were studied hindering the progress of automation processes. Included among others were: the absence of standards implemented to have distributed exchange and processing of information (client-server architecture, open Operating Systems, MARC format, Internet access, Z39.50 protocol, etc), the selection of database managers to the detriment of library management integrated systems, the absence of information quality control systems, the limited use of information and communication technologies applied to the provision of services (Barber et al., 1999; Barber, Tripaldi & Pisano, 2003; Barber et al., 2006).

These issues triggered a series of questions which lead to the analysis of OPACs interfaces available in the Web environment of Mercosur libraries. The research team focusing on issues related to the use of new information technology found that most of on-line catalogues that are available to the public in Mercosur member and associate countries only provided minimum services and were at a very early stage of development (Barber et al., 2007).

Given the fact that the real situation in Latin America was unknown and because the preliminary observation survey had shown that the interface capabilities implemented up to that point were limited, the team concluded that a survey was necessary to look into the situation of Web OPAC user interfaces of all university, specialized, public and national libraries in the region. The criteria followed was that different types of software packages impacted the presence/absence of interface functionalities, and that there were differences among Web based OPACs implemented by information units, depending on the type of software selected by the countries of the region. This chapter shows the results of the survey completed for comparison purposes of this assumption.

The team concluded that it was necessary to know the characteristics of the Web OPACs implemented in the study's target region with the purpose of showing the available possibilities to the involved information units to undertake projects that would better position them for the emerging context lead by the Web 2.0. The assumption used was that the findings resulting from this effort would be the starting point in association with the studies conducted on the use of catalogs guiding the actions aimed at establishing collaborative information systems using their Web OPACs.

BACKGROUND

New Information and Communication Technologies have produced qualitative changes in the way knowledge is built and managed. Information habits within different practice landscapes and communities have been modified. Both in the professional / work environment as well as in the academic / scientific / technical context, collaborative / participative / recommender information systems have gained an increasingly significant presence and have become a choice that is apparently expanding to grow into a trend in the short and long term.

Lloyd (2010) states that in the communications space, people develop their identities and build relationships based on shared practices and on ways of doing and saying things. These are inter-subjectively created spaces resulting from human interaction, within which information has been created, gathered and eventually consolidated into knowledge. Consequently, its social, historic, political and economic laws are established to become the fundamentals of the inter-subjective space.

Information needs to be situated in a context for it to make sense and for it to be used in a significant manner by people. From the viewpoint of this approach, information is not static nor is it objectively available, it is the outcome of a negotiated construe between individuals interacting with devices, texts, symbols, actions and in conjunction with other individuals in the context. The transformation of data into information is an active process under the influence of the situated experiences of individuals (Lloyd, 2010).

This dynamics produces knowledge which, in this manner, is only defined in the context of specific practices and emerges from the combination of a regime of competencies and meaningful experiences. It is through the situated dialogic relationships that the information is turned into knowledge (Wenger, 1998). It is formed by a combination of scientific postulates, expertise and underlying unconscious, selective or cultural assumptions (Talja, 1997). Lave and Wenger (1991) define practice communities as a set of relationships extending over time among people, activities and the world. They also include tangential and overlapping relationships with other practice communities. They constitute an intrinsic condition for the existence of knowledge and provide the interpretation support that is necessary for the inherited transmitted legacy to be meaningful.

In the view of these authors, participation in the cultural practice within which any knowledge exists, is an epistemology principle of learning. The social structure of a given practice, its relationships of power and its legitimating conditions define learning possibilities. They indicate that a person's learning intentions are involved in the process of becoming a participating being complete in the socio-cultural practice of the community he/she wishes to join. Consequently, the meaning of his/her learning is configured through the same process and is conceived as "situated learning".

In the framework of these theories, Web 2.0 as a concept first appeared in 2004 to name a new generation of Web options seeking to meet the needs of various communities of users by providing interactive and collaborative services such as social networks, blogs, wikis and folksonomies facilitating the exchange of information. These options, contrast with earlier Web sites because they act as meeting points. Ribes (2007), refers to the evolution undergone by the Web service: a first level including static web sites in HTML (Web 1.0); a second level (Web 1.5), characterized by the creation of dynamic documents; a new stage in the Web, involving deeper and more complex changes, known as Web 2.0, which in the view of this author includes Internet tools and services supported by a database with functionalities allowing users to modify its contents (adding, changing, deleting information, associating metadata to existing information), to make changes to material formats, or both at the same time.

In turn, Ben Shneiderman (2008), one of the most important experts in the development of relations between computers and people, proposed that the scientific method accommodate the new networked world reality. Shneiderman (2008) named this new method Science 2.0 combining conventional scientific research, based on hypothesis rigorously contrasted in the lab, with social science research methods. This is with the purpose of having a better understanding and making better use of social networks that have made the society of information possible. Though Science 1.0 continues to be essential, according to Shneiderman (2008), Science 2.0 will modify priorities and will affect education, financing and the evaluation of research results.

One of the multiple applications included by Codina (n.d.) in his conceptual map about Web services using the Science 2.0 model is the academic search engine application. This map lists various search engines targeting the scientific community. There are general use search engines, covering all fields of knowledge, such as *Scirus* (http://www.scirus.com), a comprehensive tool which, with over 450 million indexed scientific items, with capabilities to search not only in scientific journals but also in home pages of scientists, courses, pre-prints, patents, institutional repositories and information in Web Sites. There is a free wiki service managed by SciTopics where the scientific community can gather, communicate and update scientific knowledge, and can also interact with other researchers to receive suggestions and exchange views.

On the other hand, *Scholar o Google Scholar* (http://scholar.google.com) is designed to search for specialized bibliography in a simple manner. It provides access to studies reviewed by experts, to doctoral theses, books, abstracts and articles from sources such as academic publishers, professional associations, pre-prints depositories, universities and other academic organizations. Results are order based on relevance. Its ranking technology takes the full text of every article into account, as well as, the author, where it was published and citation frequency in other specialized sources.

WorldCat (http://www.worldcat.org/default.jsp) is the catalogue of a world network devoted to providing Web based access to the resources of numberless participating libraries. It is managed by OCLC Online Computer Library Center. It allows users to obtain information in different media types: books, scores, movies, video recordings, DVDs, CDs, diskettes, CD-ROMs, audio books. It retrieves citations from articles with links to the full text, digital versions of rare books, photographs with a historic value. It provides services to various communities in a large number of countries, and that is the reason for providing services in multiple languages. The site allows users to create lists of elements to share or of elements which wish to be followed, and bibliographies can also be built.

YoVisto (http://www.yovisto.com) is a Web 2.0 platform to watch, search and discuss academic videos. In addition to operating as a search engine for videos, it also allows users to search in these resources, since it has a mechanism which creates a full text index of these resources. Users may add key words or tagging to any position within the video (collaborative tagging). Users are also allowed to write or edit wiki pages to enrich the index contents. The service was first founded by Friedrich Schiller University, Jena, Germany, in cooperation with the Swiss Federal Institute of Technology, Zurich, and has developed the Open Code Multimedia Portal System REPLAY, to automatically and interactively produce, support, index, archive and distribute audiovisual recordings. REPLAY is the core software for the Opencast community, the only network of international institutions focusing on multimedia services in higher education.

Q Sensei (http://www.qsensei.com) has over 7 million citations available from scientific documents. The service compiles books, research articles, blogs, news and wikis. Retrieved items are displayed using a structure of classes and attributes. The site's search engine facilitates browsing within a data source and finding cross-references among individual records. It applies innovative search technologies to various pools of heterogeneous data. The site provides intuitive access, supports multi-dimensional searches, offers suggestions to receive feedback about them, and provides clear and concise descriptions about the current status of knowledge about a specific search issue. The site accepts user interaction that can therefore improve the item available data about and enrich the information.

Shared knowledge construction includes tools that are even less conventional *Lumifi (*http://www.lumifi.com*),* for example, has been designed to assist experts and their peers to organize their research projects in a collaborative manner. The site proposes research projects to be organized thinking of it as if it were an electronic personal booth which can be accessed by the research team. Based on this metaphor, after establishing an account, the site suggests that "notebooks" should be opened, which may contain the files uploaded from the computer or items retrieved from the Web. It provides a notes search service and a Web search service where relevance is based on the information of interest included in each account and uses algorithms for content analysis purposes.

Using different applications (Gmail for enterprises, Google Calendar, Google Docs, Google Groups, Google Sites, and Google Videos) *Google Docs (*http://docs.google.com*)* through *Google Apps* offers integrated services to produce, display, share and retrieve contents. The site adjusts it offering to the needs of different practice communities. There is an education edition available (with versions for universities, high schools and elementary schools) providing a free set of customizable tools, with no publicity that allows faculty, administrative staff and students to work together and improve the learning process; it also promotes an edition for enterprises or administrative organizations.

In this context, the conversion of public access online catalogues into collaborative information systems is a still-to-be-undertaken challenge. As instruments per excellence to retrieve the bibliographic universe managed by libraries, they have suffered the impact that they themselves have experienced as institutions providers of information services. The strong competition originated by the efforts described in earlier paragraphs for bibliographic catalogues has at first, meant a threat and it later became an opportunity for them to evolve in the direction envisioned by researchers decades ago. WorldCat as a design, allows us to verify the viability of the stances that claim for a protagonist role for library catalogues.

ONLINE PUBLIC ACCESS CATALOGS

Limitations of the User Interface

In the early stages, first and second generation on-line catalogues offered menu-driven user interfaces or command-driven user interfaces. Because of the limitations that both approaches had, an evolution process was initiated toward a more interactive system which led to the advancement toward the following generation of OPACs (Clifford, 1987). Williams, Kinnucan, Smith, Lannom and Cho (1986), based on this analyzed associative interfaces, Williams, Sawyer and Hutchinson (1995), in addition, referred to the Graphical User Interface (GUI); Yee and Layne (1998) referred to the Form fill-in, to client-server interfaces and to Web-based interfaces. Dowling (1997), warned about the "technology immaturity" shown by many OPACs, though recommended their implementation on the Web anyway.

The Statement of International Cataloguing Principles (2009) discussed traditional functions attributed to catalogues and new functions were assigned to them: locate, identify, select, obtain, and browse. Beheshti (2003) and Byrum (2005), among others, indicated that OPACs based on Web interfaces were still non-integrated information access systems. The designs intending to overcome these restrictions had the characteristics of a portal (Arant & Payne, 2001; Beheshti, 2003; Dorner & Curtis, 2003; Library of Congress Portals Applications Issues Group, 2005), with a "Common user interface" (Boss, 2005).

In contrast, Amazon, eBay, Netflix, MySpace, Facebook, Wikipedia, flickr, YouTube, Yahoo! Answers, even with different functions and goals, were founded on the creation of knowledge through communications and shared actions among people participating of different practice communities through collaborative user interfaces. Precisely, the huge potential emerging from their interaction, the responses they can provide thanks to crossed fertilization are the most important attribute of the new model (Udell, 2004; Bénaben, Touzi, Rajsiri & Pingaud, 2006; Blake & Pratt, 2006a, 2006b; Topcu, Mustacoglu, Fox & Cami, 2007; Javanmardi & Videira Lopes; 2007).

The socio-technical systems referenced by Shneiderman (2008) that are necessary to solve interdisciplinary problems that will concern humankind over the next few years help to bring people and technology together; facilitate the collection and monitoring of data in real communications and exchange scenarios. These systems require that the performance of new critical variables, of the reliability, empathy, responsibilities and privacy be predicted. Integrated Library Management Systems and Data Bases management systems used to manage current information systems in libraries shall have to mutate to ensure that they play a dialogic role from which to be in a position to discuss with new players, co-protagonists of the Science 2.0 staging.

Along this path, the decision will have to be made as to whether it is better to design new academic search engines; or, whether integrated or separate general search engines are the best option, given the fact that there are many factors impacting the performance of these information retrieval and search tools. On the other hand, these qualities are not necessarily mutually exclusive; Scirus, Google Scholar and WorldCat bring both attributes together. Actually, these search engines increasingly offer the alternative to redirect the search toward the general Web using the most popularly known search engines.

In favor of the integrated approach, note should be taken about the fact that it prevents users from having to run duplicate searches and the opportunity for interdisciplinary and accidental findings is increased. The separate engine approach, instead, favors the use of specific terminology tools and since it is openly oriented to the academic and professional audience, it offers more sophisticated services to narrow searches down. An intermediate possibility could be the use of a common interface with a multiple variety of options to narrow searches down, a versatile engine and the use/development of metadata to improve relevance despite the size of the data base.

Situation of OPACs Web in Latin-American Libraries

A quantitative methodology was adopted to analyze the development status of user interfaces in Latin American Web OPACs. The decision was made to apply the updated Hildreth (1982) criteria (Appendix), which, using 38 close-ending questions, allowed the team to study the functionalities of four areas: Area I, operations control; Area II, search formulation control and access points; Area III, output control; Area IV; user assistance: information and instruction.

As this project does not intend to evaluate systems used o consider adequate guidelines for their design, the list provided by Cherry and Cox (1996) or the guidelines for OPACs display design developed by Yee (1998) under IFLA requirement have not been used. The criteria developed by Dorner and Curtis (2003) to compare and evaluate library portals has not been used either as it has been developed to examine different objects of study which are still absent in most libraries in countries belonging to Latin-America.

Despite the fact that the adopted grid had been built to study on-site on-line catalogues, it included the indispensable functionalities that needed to be present to have a successful implementation of 2.0 services typical of collaborative systems; and in addition, it had been used in other descriptive and comparative studies (Zumer & Zeng, 1994; Badu & O'Brien, 2000; Ramesh Babu & Tamizhchelvan, 2003; Játiva Miralles, 2004). In each area the following functionalities were taken into account:

- **Area I, Operational control,** default function, select function, select file, default values, dialogue levels, edit input, combine commands, refine search statement
- **Area II, Search formulation control,** derived search keys, access to authority catalog, free text search on selected fields, free text search in entire record, restrict search results, boolean search, boolean search on selected fields, boolean search in entire record, relational operators, truncation, proximity operators.
- **Area II, Access points,** author, title and subject search.
- **Area III, Output control,** select a format for display, select records, select results order, print results online, save and/or mail results.
- **Area IV, User assistance: information and instruction,** list of files, list of access points, list of commands, index terms, search history, item location, item availability, system messages, procedural prompts, help messages, online tutorials.

The study sample was formed by 846 OPACs, which had been selected using predetermined syntaxes searches, classified by type of software, type of library and by country. A subset was selected formed by 374 units in which the selected system reported appearance frequency, in the total sample, ≤ than 10 including Integrated Library Systems – ILS – internationally marketed (Aleph, Unicorn, Dynix), others regionally marketed systems (Pergamum, Janium, Alejandría, Ms Info, SIABUC, GLIFOS) or using Database Management System – DBMS – (Winisis). An estimate was made of the average presence of functionalities in every area according to adopted software and to type of software; these variables were compared using an independence test. This allowed the team to characterize the interfaces of the surveyed OPACs according to each one of the specific software packages considered and relative to the software category which they were included in, and the team was also able to determine if there were any significant differences between the presence/absence of functionalities associated to them.

From all the different types of libraries included in the study, university libraries (64.7%) and specialized libraries (31.0%) stood out as the predominant libraries relative to national (1.9%) and public libraries (2.4%). In turn, most of the countries in the region were characterized by contributing with a very low percentage of Web OPACs, and Argentina, Brazil and Mexico were the only countries reporting a presence higher than 10% in that subset (Argentina, 14.2%; Brazil, 15.5%; Paraguay, 0.3%; Uruguay, 1.6%; Bolivia, 0.8%; Chile, 7.5%; Colombia, 7.0%; Ecuador, 1.3%; Peru, 3.2%; Venezuela, 5.9%; Barbados, 0.5%; Costa Rica, 2.9%; Cuba, 1.1%; El Salvador, 0.5%; Guatemala, 3.2%; French Guyana, 1.3%; Jamaica, 0.5%; Mexico, 27.3%; Nicaragua, 1.9%; Panama, 0.8%; Puerto Rico, 2.1%; Surinam, 0.3%; Trinidad y Tobago, 0.3%).

In regards the systems in place, international software packages amounted to a 37.2% presence, using 3 ILS (Aleph, 99 units, 26.5%; Unicorn, 22 units, 5.9% and Dynix, 18 units, 4.8%). Regionally marketed software packages with ILS too, accounted for a 29.5% share of the subset breakdown. In this case, note was taken of the fact that there were several projects in place with a more limited area of impact and a lower percentage presence. The following systems were considered: Pergamum, 31 units, 8.3%; Janium, 10 units, 2.7%; Alejandría, 10 units, 2.7%; Ms Info, 12 units, 3.2%; SIABUC, 31 units, 8.3% and GLIFOS, 16 units, 4.3%. Finally, in the Isis family, the Winisis system was include, with a high usage rate in the studied area (125 units, 33.4%), despite the fact that it is a DBMS.

A total score was estimated for the functionalities present in each area and for each one of the selected software systems with the purpose of estimating the average of functionalities configured by the information units, in the Web OPACs' user interfaces (Figure 1). This contributed in addition, to the collection of evidence to corroborate that library decisions were a factor influencing the presence/absence of services.

In Area I, Operational Control, the study found that out of the 8 functionalities included; only one software system, Unicorn, had an average presence above 50% (4.1). The study showed that the average of all the remaining software systems reported lower average numbers, in a range between 3.6 and 3.0. However, subgroups were found formed by Aleph, Janium and Alejandria that were closer to Unicorn; Winisis and GLIFOS, with a somewhat wider gap and Pergamum, Dynix, Ms Info and SIABUC at the lowest functionality levels.

In Area II, Search Formulation Control, 11 functionalities were taken into consideration by the study and 3 for Access Points. Again, the highest average was found in Unicorn (8.0), though, in general, it appeared to be low relative to the total number of functionalities included in the area. On the other hand, listed close to Unicorn were Aleph and Ms Info; at the intermediate level, ranging between 7.4 / 6.8, were Winisis, Janium, Alejandría, SIABUC and GLIFOS; and the lowest averages, below 6 were found for Pergamum and Dynix.

Area III is a an essential area to verify OPACs' interface suitability levels relative to the users' tasks to be performed. In Area III, Output Control, the study surveyed 5 functionalities. The area revealed an uneven performance among the software packages included in the study. Despite the fact that Unicorn again stood out with a 3.4 average, followed at a significant distance by Alejandría (2.8) and Ms Info (2.6), the percentage of functionality presence appeared to be significantly lower than in software packages with a higher performance in other areas. In connection to this, what was

Figure 1. Functionalities average for each software package on a per-area basis

Software	Operational Control	Search Formularion Control / Access points	Output Control	User Assistance	Total score
Aleph	3.5	7.4	2.3	4.5	17.7
Unicorn	4.1	8.0	3.4	5.3	20.7
Winisis	3.3	6.8	2.2	3.8	16.1
Pergamum	3.0	5.9	1.6	3.2	13.7
Janium	3.6	6.9	2.4	3.8	16.7
Dynix	3.0	5.7	1.6	2.9	13.2
Alejandria	3.5	7.0	2.8	4.8	18.1
Ms Info	3.0	7.8	2.6	4.6	17.9
SIABUC	3.1	6.7	2.4	4.7	16.9
GLIFOS	3.4	7.2	2.1	4.8	17.4

particularly striking was that Aleph. Winisis, Janium, SIABUC and GLIFOS again ranked close to each other. And Pergamum and Dynix reported an average below 2 functionalities again.

Last, in Area IV, User Assistance, where 11 functionalities were surveyed by the study, Unicorn was the only software reporting an average above 5. Aleph, Alejandría, Ms Info, SIABUC and GLIFOS were positioned close to Unicorn (Aleph, 4.5; Alejandría, 4.8). Both Winisis and Janium performed at a similar level (3.8). Whereas Pergamum and Dynix shared the lowest average performance.

Despite the differences found by the survey, results demonstrated that the sample was homogeneous (Figure 2); disparities among areas between the various software packages compared in the study were not big enough to be significant. Total figures did not counter the trend that had already been found in each area because no relevant variations were found among each other.

Instead, when surveying the link between functionalities in each area and the type of software (International, Regional, and Isis) the figures found were highly significant ($p < 0,0001$) in 31 of the 38 functionalities (Figure 3). 3 applications showed a weaker link and only 4 showed no differences that could lead the study to corroborate that performance was associated to that.

However, despite the fact that a strong link had been found between the presence/absence of functionalities and the type of software implemented, criteria used among information units to configure the selected systems were so different that they became a factor that impacted interface elements. This situation was reflected in the maximum and minimum presence values reported for the different software packages in the areas considered by the study (Figure 4).

Though all areas revealed inexistent or insignificant values for certain OPACs, in those areas controlling general operations aspects and results output aspects, several software packages actually reached the maximum presence values for the area in accordance with the functionalities surveyed by the study (8 for Area I; 5 for Area

Figure 2. Functionalities average for each software package on a per-area basis

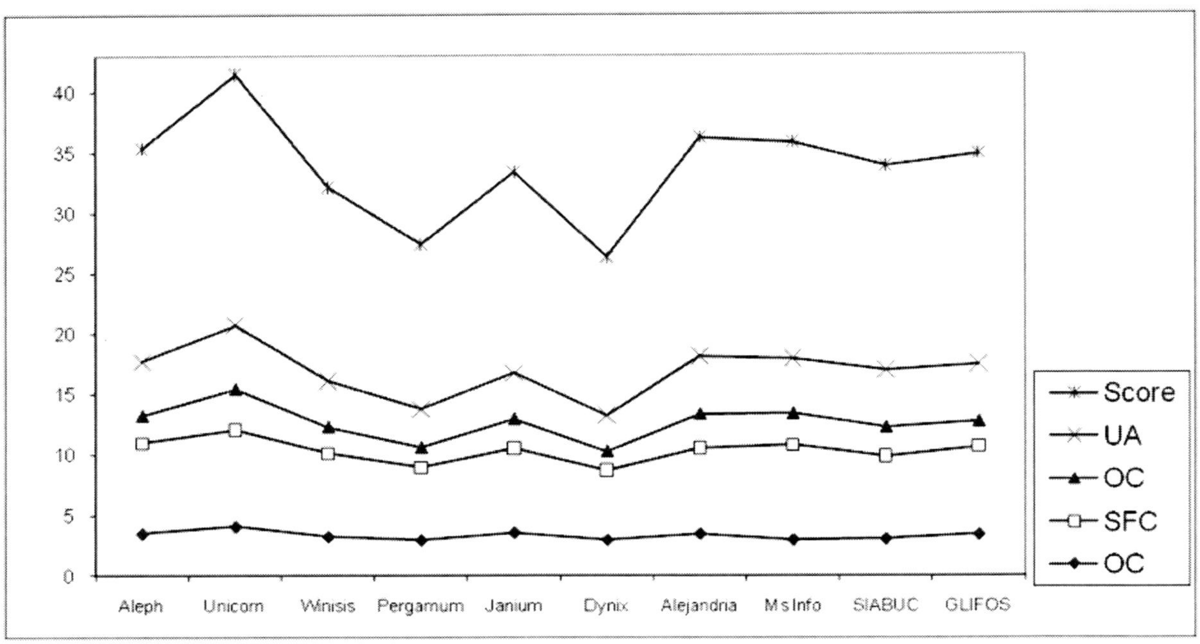

Figure 3. Functionalities vs. type of software

Functionalities	Type of software			
	I	R	Is	*P*
Area I – Operational control				
Default function	33.3	28.0	38.7	0. 001
Select function	47.6	32.0	20.4	0.0001
Select file	39.9	29.7	30.4	NS: 0.088
Default values	66.4	5.5	28.2	0.0001
Dialogue levels	50.0	28.6	21.4	0.0001
Edit imput	59.1	16.4	24.5	0.0001
Combine commands	65.4	15.1	19.5	0.0001
Refine search statement	75.0	7.1	17.9	0.0001
Area II – Search formulation control				
Derived search keys	41.7	0.0	58.3	NS: 0.049[1]
Access to authority catalog	44.0	50.0	6.0	0.0001
Free text search on selected fields	42.1	32.1	25.8	0.0001
Free text search in entire record	41.8	27.7	30.5	0.0001
Restrict search results	64.4	18.5	17.1	0.0001
Boolean search	42.1	25.0	32.9	0.0001
Boolean search on selected fields	45.1	25.3	29.6	0.0001
Boolean search in entire record	47.7	22.4	29.9	0.0001
Relational operators	67.7	18.5	13.8	0.0001
Truncation	54.6	18.5	26.9	0.0001
Proximity operators	78.2	9.9	11.9	0.0001
Author	39.3	30.2	30.5	0.0001
Title	39.4	30.3	30.3	0.0001
Subject	40.4	29.9	29.7	0.0001
Area III – Output control				
Select a format for display	50.6	30.0	19.4	0.0001
Select records	44.0	33.2	22.8	0.0001
Select results order	66.1	23.3	10.6	0.0001
Print results online	44.0	27.7	28.3	0.020
Save and/or mail results	70.0	16.7	13.3	0.0001
Area IV – User assistance				
List of files	35.9	32.6	31.5	NS: 0.404
List of access points	48.0	27.2	24.7	0.0001
List of commands	65.6	25.8	8.6	0.0001
Index terms	51.6	20.4	28.0	0.0001
Search history	87.9	4.5	7.6	0.0001
Item location	39.2	30.4	30.4	0.0001
Iten availability	54.4	36.3	9.3	0.0001
System messages	45.8	29.8	24.4	0.0001
Procedural prompts	47.7	22.9	29.4	0.023
Help messages	56.2	23.7	20.1	0.0001
Online tutorials	37.5	31.3	31.3	NS: 0.979

[1] 3 boxes (50. 0%) have an expected frequency below 5. The minimum expected frequency is 3. 53.

I = International R = Regional Is = Isis NS = Non Significative

Figure 4. Minimum/maximum values for each area vs. software

Software	Operacional Control		Search formulation control / Access points		Output control		User Assistance	
	Minimum	Maximum	Minimum	Maximum	Minimum	Maximum	Minimum	Maximum
Aleph	1	8	1	14	0	5	0	10
Unicorn	1	8	1	13	1	5	1	10
Winis is	0	8	1	13	0	5	0	10
Pergamum	1	7	1	10	0	5	0	7
Janium	1	8	4	10	0	5	1	8
Dynix	1	6	1	13	0	5	0	8
Alejandria	1	7	1	13	1	5	1	9
Ms Info	1	6	5	12	0	5	2	8
SIABUC	1	7	1	12	0	5	1	8
GLIFOS	1	7	4	11	0	5	1	9

III). In contrast, in Area II, and barely in one case out of the 99 cases in which it had been accounted for, only Aleph exhibited a possible maximum value (14 functionalities). In Area IV none of the software packages included the 11 selected functionalities. Based on these data, the study inferred that in many cases, libraries had not enabled all the functionalities that the systems were in a position to offer.

FUTURE RESEARCH DIRECTION

The picture described so far, in the context of current world trends, highlights the need to expand knowledge about the use of ICTs across Latin American information units to participate in the collaborative construction of reality. A study of the processes used by libraries in this region to implement Web 2.0 projects and to move toward the 2.0 libraries and OPAC will contribute to the construction of a foundation of knowledge helping to guide and strengthen all developments implemented in this direction. Research projects about these issues applied to Latin America are nearly inexistent, and this area is almost unexplored despite the potential offered by technology advances to describe and explain the prevailing situation related to this issue.

There are many aspects to be surveyed and therefore many open questions around them, the following among others: Which are the libraries that implement Web 2.0 projects? What are the peculiarities identified in each country around this issue? How are the organization and the recovery of bibliographic resources managed in libraries optimized and modified? What services are provided in the Web 2.0 environment based on the design of collaborative information systems? Which are the technologies used? What qualitative changes are brought about in terms of opportunities for users to perform their tasks? Which are the collaboration modes that arise? How high is the participation rate of users in them? What impact do they have on the different practice communities? How does this encourage change in the way domains as sensitive as science, education, healthcare, government, business and entertainment are created and carried out?

Using these questions as a basis, the study team plans to research user interfaces of Latin American OPACs with the purpose of identifying the presence of Web 2.0 functionalities in them. This research should shed light on the course followed by libraries in the region regarding the implementation of collaborative information systems. In the compilation of data, consideration will be given to the list of desirable functionalities in 2.0 OPACs put together by Margaix-Arnal (2007), which are available in information architecture, in interoperability and content syndication, in social information, in social interaction among users, in librarians' functions and that are displayed in the search interface, in the formats of results and of a bibliographic registry. Findings of this research work will reveal the ability the surveyed libraries have to support and supplement the development of Science 2.0 and of the methodologies it feeds from with other tools.

CONCLUSION

The importance of the challenges they will have to face becomes evident when observing the current situation of Latin American Web OPACs, which has been verified in this research, as it has been possible to prove that:

- Even when some inconsistencies in the implemented functionalities were found in every analyzed software, the sample proved to be homogeneous; instead, the most significant differences were observed when comparing international to regional software and DBMS;
- These differences were evident even when libraries showed a clear tendency to under-utilize systems capabilities;
- Therefore, those information units that chose an ILS to manage their information resources and services offered their patrons a greater number of options for search, retrieval and use of information;
- Despite this, less than 50% of the studied functionalities were implemented in each area;
- There are strong contrasts among the different types of software in relation to their functionalities, like Default values, Combine commands, Refine search statement, Restrict search results, Relational operators, Proximity operators, Select results order, Save and/or mail results, List of commands, Search history, that are very important in order to customize and refine the search or to use results. This limits the possibility of synergy and fertilization between concepts during the process of information retrieval and remains far from the spirit of collaborative systems that promote these aspects.

Due to the above, the analyzed Web OPACs are now limited tools to create collaborative scientific knowledge. However, through the identification and description of the information resources that are representative of the knowledge production of the region, library catalogs happen to be a potentially natural vehicle to reach this purpose.

A key aspect that is necessary for them to become the foundation for the collaborative construction of new knowledge is the libraries′ decision to adopt systems and technologies that allow to diversify and increase the number of functionalities in their interfaces. For all these reasons the information units of the region should encourage changes regarding the use of TICs in order to incorporate all the advantages they offer in their catalogs to foster collaborative knowledge creation.

REFERENCES

Arant, W., & Payne, L. (2001). The common user interface in academic libraries: Myth or reality? *Library Hi Tech*, *19*(1), 63–73. doi:10.1108/07378830110384601

Badu, B. R., & O'Brien, A. (2000). Web OPAC interfaces: An overview. *The Electronic Library*, *18*(5), 316–327. doi:10.1108/02640470010354572

Beheshti, J. (2003). The future of OPAC interfaces. In *ALA / CLA Annual Conference. Optimal Design Considerations for Web OPAC Interfaces: A program sponsored by LITA: June 22, 2003, Toronto*. Retrieved June 13, 2005, from http://www.calstatela.edu/library/ALA/ala-claOPAC.htm

Bénaben, F., Touzi, J., Rajsiri, V., & Pingaud, H. (2006). Collaborative Information System Design. In *11th International Conference of the Association Information and Management (AIM)*,Luxembourg, June 8th to 9th (pp. 281-296). Retrieved May 14, 2009, from http://subs.emis.de/LNI/Proceedings/ Proceedings92/gi-proc-092-018.pdf

Blake, C., & Pratt, W. (2006a, November). Collaborative information synthesis I: A model of information behaviors of scientists in medicine and public health. *Journal of the American Society for Information Science and Technology*, *57*(13), 1740–1749. doi:10.1002/asi.20487

Blake, C., & Pratt, W. (2006b, December). Collaborative Information Synthesis II: Recommendations for Information Systems to Support Synthesis Activities. *Journal of the American Society for Information Science and Technology*, *57*(14), 1888–1895. doi:10.1002/asi.20486

Boss, R. W. (2005, March). *Library portals*. Retrieved from American Library Association Website: http://www.ala.org/ala/pla/plapubs/technotes /librarywebportals.htm

Byrum, J. D. (2005). Online catalogs and library portals in today's information environment. *Journal of Library Administration*, *43*(1/2), 135–154. doi:10.1300/J111v43n01_09

Cherry, J. M., & Cox, J. P. (1996). *World Wide Web displays of bibliographic records: An evaluation*. Retrieved June 15, 2005, from http://www.fis.utoronto.ca/research/programs/ displays/caispck1.htm

Clifford, A. L. (1987). The use of heuristics in user interfaces for online information retrieval systems. In *ASIS '87: Proceedings of the 50th ASIS Annual Meeting, 24*, 148-152.

Codina, L. (n.d.). *Ciencia 2.0*. Retrieved March 01, 2009, from http://www.mindomo.com/view.htm?m =d4d1f77be0d04af0804c719038144de8

Dorner, D. G., & Curtis, A. M. (2003, June). *A comparative review of common user interface software products for libraries*. Retrieved June 15, 2005, from http://www.museglobal.com/PDF/Review-Common%20Search%20Interfaces.pdf

Dowling, T. (1997). The World Wide Web meets the OPAC. *From Catalog to Gateway: Briefings from the CFFC*. Published as a supplement to the *ALCTS Newsletter, 8*(2), A-D.

Játiva Miralles, M. V. (2004). Indicadores de calidad aplicables al análisis, evaluación y comparación de opacs. *El Profesional de la Información*, *13*(1), 28–46. doi:10.1076/epri.13.1.28.29023

Javanmardi, S., & Videira Lopes, C. (2007). *Modeling Trust in Collaborative Information Systems*. Retrieved May 14, 2009, from http://www.ics.uci.edu/~lopes/documents/collaboratecom %20 07/CollabComCameraReadyOCT09.

Lave, J., & Wenger, E. (1991). *Situated learning: Legitimate peripheral participation*. New York: Cambridge University Press.

Library of Congress Portals Applications Issues Group. (2005, December 14). *Portals Applications Issues Group*. Retrieved from Library of Congress Website: http://www.loc.gov/ catdir/lcpaig/

Lloyd, A. (2010). *Information literacy landscapes: Information literacy in education, workplace and everyday contexts*. Oxford: Chandos Publishing.

Margaix-Arnal, D. (2007). El OPAC 2.0: Las tecnologías de la Web 2.0 aplicadas a los catálogos bibliográficos. In *Actas del VI Workshop CALSI*. Retrieved May 25, 2009, from http://www.calsi. org/2007/wp-content/uploads/2007/11/didac_margaix.pdf

Ramesh Babu, B., & Tamizhchelvan, M. (2003). An investigation into the features of OPACs in Tamil Nadu (India). *Library Review*, *52*(5-6), 257–267. doi:10.1108/00242530310482033

Ribes, X. (2007). La Web 2.0: El valor de los metadatos y de la inteligencia colectiva. *Telos: Cuadernos de Comunicación e Innovación, 73*. Retrieved from http://www.telos.es/articuloperspectiva.asp ?idarticulo= 2&rev=73

Shneiderman, B. (2008, March 7). Science 2.0. *Science, 319*, 1349–1350. doi:10.1126/science.1153539

Statement of International Cataloguing Principles. (2009). Retrieved from IFLA Website: http://www.ifla.org/files/cataloguing/icp/icp_2009-en.pdf

Talja, S. (1997). Constituting 'information' and 'user' as research objects: A theory of knowledge formations as an alternative to the information man - theory. In P. Vakkari, R. Savolainen, & B. Dervin (Eds.), *Information seeking in context: Proceedings of a meeting in Finland 14-16 August 1996* (pp. 67-80). London: Taylor Graham.

Topcu, A. E., Mustacoglu, A. F., Fox, G., & Cami, A. (2007). Integration of Collaborative Information Systems in Web 2.0. In *Third International Conference on Semantics, Knowledge and Grid (SKG 2007)* (pp. 523-526). Xian, Shan Xi, China: IEEE Computer Society. doi: ieeecomputersociety.org/10.1109/SKG.2007.137

Udell, J. (2004). *Collaborative knowledge gardening*. Retrieved May 14, 2009, from http://www.infoworld. com/article/04/08/20/34OPstrategic_1.html

Wenger, E. (1998). *Communities of practice: Learning, meaning and identity*. Cambridge: Cambridge University Press.

Williams, B. K., Sawyer, S. C., & Hutchinson, S. E. (1995). *Using information technology: A practical introduction to computers and communications*. Chicago: Irwin.

Williams, M. E., Kinnucan, M., Smith, L. C., Lannom, L., & Cho, D. (1986). Comparative analysis of online retrieval interfaces. In *ASIS '86: Proceedings of the 49th ASIS Annual Meeting, 23*, 365-370.

Yee, M. M. (1998, November). *Guidelines for OPAC displays* (prepared for the IFLA Task Force on Guidelines for OPAC Displays by Martha M. Yee). Retrieved May 18, 2005, from http://www.ifla.org/ifla/VII/s13/guide/ opac-d.pdf

Yee, M. M., & Layne, S. S. (1998). *Improving online public access catalog*. Chicago: American Library Association.

Zumer, M., & Zeng, L. (1994). Comparison and evaluation of OPAC end-user interfaces. *Cataloging & Classification Quarterly, 19*(2), 67–98. doi:10.1300/J104v19n02_05

ADDITIONAL READING

Chen, A. Y., & McLeod, D. (2006). *Collaborative Filtering for Information Recommendation Systems*. Retrieved from the University of Southern California Website: http://sir-lab.usc.edu/publications/121new.pdf

Fox, G. C., Pierce, M. E., Mustacoglu, A. F., & Topcu, A. E. (2007). Web 2.0 for E-Science Environments. In *Third International Conference on Semantics, Knowledge and Grid (SKG 2007)* (pp.1-6). doi: ieeecomputersociety.org/10.1109/SKG.2007.142

Golovchinsky, G., Pickens, J., & Back, M. (2008). *A Taxonomy of Collaboration in Online Information Seeking*. Paper presented at the 1st International Workshop on Collaborative Information Retrieval. JCDL 2008. Retrieved June 18, 2010, from http://arxiv.org/ftp/arxiv/papers/0908/0908.0704.pdf

Lanping, F., Lijun, Z., & Jiguo, Z. (2007). A Model of Reliability Evaluation for Multi-User Collaborative Building Ontology. In *Third International Conference on Semantics, Knowledge and Grid (SKG 2007)* (pp. 326-329). doi: ieeecomputersociety.org/ 10.1109/SKG.2007.53

Liu, K., Sun, L., Dix, A., & Narasipuram, M. (2001). Norm-based agency for designing collaborative information systems. *Information Systems Journal*, *11*, 229–247. doi:10.1046/j.1365-2575.2001.00102.x

Maini, S., Rosen, J., Pierce, M. E., & Fox, G. C. (2009). *AVATS: Audio-video and textual synchronization. In International Symposium on Collaborative Technologies and Systems* (pp.455-464). doi: ieeecomputersociety.org/10.1109/CTS.2009.5067514

Méndez Núñez, S., De Andrés Suárez, J., Labra Gayo, J. E., & Ordóñez de Pablos, P. (2008). A Semantic Based Collaborative System for the Interoperability of XBRL Accounting Information. In Emerging Technologies and Information Systems for the Knowledge Society. *Lecture Notes in Computer Science, 5288,* 593-599. doi: 10.1007/978-3-540-87781-3_64

Paul, S. A., & Morris, M. R. (2009). CoSense: Enhancing sensemaking for collaborative web search. In *Conference on Human Factors in Computing Systems Proceedings of the 27th international conference on Human factors in computing systems* (pp. 1771-1780). New York: ACM.

Schulte, J., Hampel, T., Bopp, T., & Hinn, R. (2007). Wasabi Framework An Open Service Infrastructure for Collaborative Work. In *Third International Conference on Semantics, Knowledge and Grid (SKG 2007)* (pp. 242-247). doi: ieeecomputersociety.org/10.1109 /SKG.2007.155

Shah, C. (2009). *Toward Collaborative Information Seeking (CIS)*. Paper presented at the 1st International Workshop on Collaborative Information Retrieval JCDL 2008. Retrieved June 18, 2010, from http://workshops.fxpal.com/jcdl2008/submissions/tmpE1.pdf

Snowden, D. (1999). Liberating knowledge. In Reeves, J. (Ed.), *Liberating Knowledge* (pp. 6–19). London: Caspian.

Talja, S. (2002). Information sharing in academic communities: Types and levels of collaboration in information seeking and use. *The New Review of Information Behaviour Research: Studies of Information Seeking in Context (Proceedings of ISIC 2002), 3*, 143-160.

Talja, S., Keso, H., & Pietiläinen, T. (1999). The production of 'context' in information seeking research: A metatheoretical view. *Information Processing & Management*, *35*(6), 751–763. doi:10.1016/S0306-4573(99)00024-2

Von Krogh, G., Ichijo, K., & Nonaka, I. (2000). *Enabling knowledge creation*. Oxford: Oxford University Press. doi:10.1093/acprof:oso/9780195126167.001.0001

KEY TERMS AND DEFINITIONS

Collaboration: A process through which different persons or communities can go beyond their own individual expertise and vision by constructively exploring diverging aspects of a problem and searching for common solutions.

Collaborative Community Networks: Online networks that form discussion communities and work towards a common purpose, share curriculum materials, ideas and professional development or other learning resources.

Folksonomy: System of classification derived from collaboratively creating and managing tags to annotate and categorize content.

Online Public Access Catalog: A database composed of bibliographic records describing bibliographic resources owned by a library or library system accessible to the users.

OPAC Web: Online public access catalog that uses a graphical user interface (GUI) accessible via the World Wide Web.

Open Collaborative Systems: Systems that enable people to connect and collaborate through computer-mediated communication. Simple editing interfaces encourage users to create and maintain repositories of shared content.

User Interface: Point or process that joins two components of a data processing system, for example, the screen display that functions as intermediary between a software program and its human users.

Web 2.0: Web applications that facilitate interactive information sharing, interoperability, user-centered design, and collaboration on the World Wide Web.

APPENDIX

CHECKLIST OF THE INTERFACE FUNCIONALITIES OF OPACs WEB

Name of the institution:
URL:
Type of library:
Type of software:
System:
Record number in the directory:
Record number in the SPSS database:

Funcionalities (available to the user)	YES	NO
Area I. Operational Control		
1. Default function		
2. Select function		
3. Select file		
4. Default values		
5. Dialogue levels		
6. Edit input		
7. Combine commands		
8. Refine search statement		
Area II. Search Formulation Control		
9. Derived search keys		
10. Access to authority catalog		
11. Free text search on selected fields		
12. Free text search in entire record		
13. Restrict search results		
14. Boolean search		
15. Boolean search on selected fields		
16. Boolean search in entire record		
17. Relational operators		
18. Truncation		
19. Proximity operators		
Area II. Access Points		
20. Author search		
21. Title search		
22. Subject search		

continued on following page

Appendix continued

Funcionalities (available to the user)	YES	NO
Area III. Output Control		
23. Select a format for display		
24. Select records		
25. Select results order		
26. Print results online		
27. Save and/or mail results		
Area IV. User Assistance: Information and instruction		
28. List of files		
29. List of access points		
30. List of commands		
31. Index terms		
32. Search history		
33. Item location		
34. Item availability		
35. System messages		
36. Procedural prompts		
37. Help messages		
38. Online tutorials		

Subsection

Open Source Software to Collaborative Information Services

Chapter 11
Academic Libraries as Complex Systems

Álvaro Quijano-Solís
El Colegio de México, Mexico

Guadalupe Vega-Díaz
El Colegio de México, Mexico

ABSTRACT

The purpose of this chapter is to describe how the concepts and principles from the Systems Approach may be helpful in understanding and modeling the collaborative group cognitive processes in information handling in an academic library. In order to address complexity and dynamics, this chapter analyzes several theoretical positions, which together may help us to shape the academic library from a comprehensive and systemic point of view (such as Systems Approach, Communities of Practice, Activity Theory and the Viable System Model). This chapter suggests focalizing on the activity (performed by a community) as the basic unit of analysis in studying the complexity of academic libraries. This activity is what allows the transmission of tacit and explicit knowledge and the skills from an expert to a novice. Other elements in the activity are objectives, rules and regulations, and importantly the learning processes that occur dialectically between subjects and community. A model such as Beer's in the way the authors presented it in this chapter fits well to decompose reality and synthesize it to analyze the proposed complexity. This may allow facing organizational problems by focusing in the way people act to transform the inputs into products and add value to them by teaching and learning.

I. INTRODUCTION

Academic libraries are information systems that may be perceived as an uncomplicated organism, a simple organization, whose productive processes are linear events that end after a product is elaborated or a service is delivered, with no further complications during that time. This perception is promoted by the fact that libraries are embedded in a larger organization (college, university or research center), so we might assume that environment is a placid one (cfr. Emery and

DOI: 10.4018/978-1-61350-201-3.ch011

Trist, 1965), meaning that adaptation processes in academic libraries are quick and smooth.

However a detailed analysis of academic library allows us to see that they are dynamic and complex organizations which are in constant evolution. So, the environment of an academic library is close to what Emery and Trist (1965) call turbulent field, with dynamic properties that move constantly the library's "ground". For example, some operations that are perceived as simple, such as locating information, requesting books on loan, going to the reference desk, etc., involve a wide range of activities developed by working groups that share a common purpose, working tools and follow a set of rules and principles.

As it may be seen there is a need to rethink academic libraries as complex systems with a huge amount of components and relations between them, all this in a turbulent environment. The purpose of this paper is to describe how the concepts and principles from Systems Approach may be helpful in understanding and modeling the collaborative group cognitive processes in information handling in an academic library.

In attempting such an explanation of an academic library, we stick to Morin's thoughts in the sense that "…we must question the adequacy of all explanations based on simplification of principles. Complexity is not a surface noise of the real, but is the very principle of the real…Uncertainty, indeterminism, randomness and contradictions occur, not as residues to be eliminated by explanation, but as non-eliminatable ingredients of our perception/cognition of the real." (Morin, 1992, cited by Leleur, 2008, p. 73).

In order to address complexity and dynamics, this chapter analyzes several theoretical positions, which together may help us to shape the academic library from a comprehensive and systemic point of view. This chapter is divided into eight sections, this Introduction being section one.

The first theoretical approach is the System Approach itself, from which we introduced the recognition of environment and context as elements of the metasystem that drive the analysis of the role and functions of the academic library (section II). In section III we present the general characteristics of a system and the importance of academic libraries being observed as organization whose components are interrelated among them by human processes such as collaboration (developed in section IV).

The next theoretical position, refers to communities of practice (CoP) (section V), These communities are not hierarchically structured nor established, thus allowing individuals to organize them independently, in a spontaneous way in order to meet the demands coming from the information systems environments (cfr. Wilson, 2008; Davenport and Hall, 2002).

CoP promote situated learning and the application of knowledge in solving problems and hence allow to establish collaborative partnerships among subjects who develop an activity in an academic library. From the CoP we may observe that the ways of using the tools and applying the rules in the work place, go from one generation to the other through processes of experience in daily practice in solving problems. For instance, in the case of the rules and principles used in cataloguing it could be argued that these have historically been agreed from the knowledge and experiences that have aroused when developing cataloguing items.

To identify the components that enable the transmission of experience and knowledge in a community of practice, in Section VI we outline Theory of Activity (TA) that we suggest focalizing on the activity (performed by a community) as the basic unit of analysis in studying the complexity of academic libraries. This activity is what allows the transmission of tacit and explicit knowledge and the skills from an expert to a novice. Other elements in the activity are objectives, rules and regulations, and importantly the learning processes that occur dialectically between subjects and community.

After analyzing these two first theoretical positions, in section VII we present the comprehensive view of the academic library as a collaborative system, where it becomes evident the importance of the CoP for the processes of adaptation to change brought by changes in the environment. In this section we explain the possible relationships among CoP´s and the possibility that they relate to each other creating complex systems of activity in the academic library.

In section VIII we present the third theoretical position based on the *Viable System Model* (VSM) of Stafford Beer, which is used to differentiate primary activities (production) carried out by the CoP's and other intellectual activities for planning, managing and evaluating a system such as an academic library.

II. ENVIRONMENT IN ACADEMIC LIBRARY

A conventional definition of an academic library is that such a library is a part of a larger organization (a higher education institution) which the library has to provide with information resources and services for students and faculty members while satisfies information needs for research of faculty members as well. So, an academic library selects, catalogs and classifies bibliographic materials in order to provide them to its users in any format those materials are available (Hoare, 1997).

Academic libraries have experienced important changes within the last years. Most of them have been conciliated by the continuous change in science, technology, and economic, social and political conditions. All the organizations, seen as systems with a constant exchange within their environment, perceive this transformation from a larger presence of competitors, a constant technological innovation, the need of access to new markets, the development and commercialization of new products, and the demand to maintain financial sustainability. All of the above demand a larger acclimatization need to the conditions of such environment in order to guarantee survival and success.

Attention areas in academic libraries can be pointed out as being the ones that affect its future directly:

- Tools to improve processes.
- Technology innovation and supply.
- Changes in publishing market.
- Deeper study of its community of users.
- Impact of changes in education: new models and methods.
- Knowledge management.
- Connectivity to the worldwide web of information.
- Access to and integration into new communities

Besides these attention areas, libraries are urged to revaluate and adjust their missions, functions and services as part of a reinvention which allows them to face a world where other information providers contend for users. All of these imply a change in ways of working, processes, routines, and more importantly, organizational culture.

The "academic market" requires more competitive libraries that can foresee possible demands of users and therefore, to be more proactive in their services offers. In contrast with the passive image of a library, this presumes a major agility for the organizational development of libraries, which allows them to effectively manage information and to deliver it in due time to the user. Hence, there is a need for a larger innovation capacity in organizational culture and the use of technological infrastructure.

Being inserted in an environment growingly dominated by Internet and electronic resources, university libraries, seeing as social organizations, need to understand that their environment is mainly a communication environment where all organizations and businesses are being reinvented based on Internet, its potentials and deficiencies.

Internet opens great opportunities and also sets challenges in the creation and development of learning communities that do not constrain, as mentioned before, to university library as the only information provider.

In parallel, there is a need to provide value added services in order to face the accelerated growth of Internet and the growing wireless environment. Internet allows larger access to information, but it does not guarantee a better quality of it. As a matter of fact, although the amount of digital information available is larger every time, our expectations of assimilating and "digesting" it with reasonable effort and time have also grown. Facing such facts, users demand for a greater organization and control of information and at the same time, they demand simplicity and easiness (usability) in the access to information services, including libraries.

To sum up, there is a complex environment in the information world that determines means and contents for libraries, specially the academic ones, as they are subject to additional pressures from an educational model that tends to center itself more into learning and less into teaching.

Specially, the most recent technological innovations used in academic libraries tend to emphasize qualitative improvement in order to give effective services, instead of just increasing the amount offered.

In short, libraries are urged to review and adjust their missions, functions and services as part of a reinvention which allows them to face a world where other information providers contend for users (Google, for instance, is more used that libraries catalogues for browsing information in Internet). All of these imply a change in the ways of focusing work, processes, routines, and more importantly, the organizational culture.

Such a review should be considered in the light of a demand for enhanced competences and skills for creativity and innovation in the handling of information and creation of new knowledge, at the organizational level, as well as in the group and the individual levels. In discussing cyberculture, for instance, García argues that it is based on a distributed intelligence process, generating at the same time cognitive processes which tend to keep structural equilibrium in the individual (2000). This makes libraries and librarians to play a new role in their institutions in order to push a vital, dynamic and creative process. Introduction of new technologies for information management has created an unbalanced condition in libraries and therefore, creates opportunities for organizational transformation.

III. SYSTEMS: CONCEPT AND CHARACTERISTICS

Bunge (2008) considers that one of the most promising approximations to approach any theoretical and practical problem is the systemic approach linked to the scientific method. The first one helps setting out problems and the second one helps solving them. In his conception, "a system is a complex object that has global properties and it behaves as a whole, due to the fact that its components are held together" (p. 9). The characteristics of a system are:

"Its composition or set of its parts; its environment or set of surrounding objects with which it is related to, and [third] its structure or set of links among the components, and among them and those components in the environment that affect the system or are affected by it" (p.11).

He states that these three components are enough to characterize a static system (conceptual or semiotic), while in other dynamic systems it is necessary a fourth characteristic, considered as the peculiar mechanism that keeps or transforms the system (p.11). As of the previous, we can infer that the characterization of a static system does not respond to time, while the one from a dynamic depends on it to understand transformation processes such as fermentation, learning and information flows.

For Bunge, the systemic approach to society is an alternative to globalism (holism) and to individualism (atomism). According to this, for individualism the main view is the one of the subject and his actions, while for globalism the view is set on the society and its structure. Bunge suggests that for a systems approach, the main focus is the individual and his actions in the society.

IV. COLLABORATION AND THE SYSTEMS APPROACH

The notion of collaboration is a wide concept that can be applied to different aspects, for example to businesses and to learning, among others; it can also have different levels, such as collaboration among subjects, departments, organizations and even, nations, and in every case the collaboration comprises different actions, conditions and limits of itself.

The term collaboration has also been linked to the one of cooperation, and in many cases they have been used as synonyms or as if they were concepts depending on one another. For this chapter, we have taken up again the concept of collaboration, which refers to the recurring process happening among two or more people or organizations that make their knowledge, experiences and resources of any kind available to the collaborators so as to achieve a common good or goal (cfr. Oxford English Dictionary).

From our point of view, collaboration supposes joint development and agreement on the common goals and objectives, it comprises sharing the responsibility and joint work to achieve them while making use of collaborators' knowledge and skills. As collaboration means shared responsibilities, it requires building up consensus and therefore, it should not be hierarchically imposed. Collaboration is time consuming due to the fact that while an activity is being developed, learning processes on the roles and responsibilities of each collaborator are carried out, and setting out objectives and decision making activities are performed in a group process (Bruner, 1991).

Throughout history, work organization has been observed in different ways, from taylorism to the socio technical approaches from the *Tavistock Institute in London*. The concept of collaborative work is more recent and it has been linked to the information systems development so as to support the implementation of this kind of working system as well to the need to share information, to develop collaborative responsibilities, to empower workers and to improve work quality. This has led to the design of diverse information flow models, which have derived in new shapes of organizational designs. From this tendency, we propose that the work analysis developed in an academic library be carried out from the systemic approach linked to the community of practice concept (CoP) and to the activity theory (AT). We believe this path allows us to better explain the complexity of the academic library. In the following sections we will analyze in detail the concept of communities of practice (CoP) and the theoretical perspective (AT) from which we have approached them.

V. COMMUNITIES OF PRACTICE

The community of practice (CoP) term was coined by Lave and Wenger (1991), from the studies on "situated learning". This type of learning was conceptualized by Lave (1988) as that one that allows to link real experiences coming from activities happening in different contexts of daily life to learning. Lave's findings were extended to explain how interactions among different group members allow knowledge transference among "expert" subjects and novice subjects, who are involved in the problem solution or in carrying out a task (we will further explain this relation in Section VI on Activity Theory).

In "situated learning" (Lave and Wenger, 1991), learning is recognized as social by nature and it is centered in how apprentices or novices are inserted within a community of practice, going from an authorized peripheral participation to a complete and very close participation to the experts, who move in the center of the community, helping or supervising new participants. In this study, Lave and Wenger (1991) consider that aulic spaces decontextualize knowledge and take historicity away, in spite of the school being itself in a specific context within a historic framework.

As far as Wenger is concerned, in 1998 he conceptualized the CoP as a space for learning, negotiation, meaning and identity, where subjects participating mutually grant each other a sense of belonging to the community and a "legitimate" participation, which can be central or peripheral (Wenger, 1998/2001). In the CoP, members interact and generate norms and relationships; besides creating and sharing common resources, routines and artifacts. This whole exchange allows social building of knowledge, assuming each individual is a historic subject and it is better understood from a systemic approach with well defined components, interrelations and environment.

In fact, among the main characteristics of the CoP, the following are highlighted: a) The coexistence of harmony and conflict relationships, b) The interest from its members to carry out joint activities, c) Adequate and agile flows of information and of diffusion of innovation, d) The existence of an adequate environment that allows problems discussion without more ado, e) The existence of an unwritten code for common elements among all its members, f) The conscience on the capacities and knowledge of all members forming the community, g) The communication among its members, which is given through common jargon and specific terms; and h) Sharing a common discourse on the world vision (Wenger 1998/2001).

One of the basic concepts of the CoP is the distributed cognition, with which it is recognized that in a community there are actors who cover different roles and have different levels of knowledge and expertise so as to carry out an activity in a systemic way. For Dalkir (2005), the roles covered are:

- **Experienced members.** Considered as experts and reliable sources of knowledge. They are familiarized with the professional and community matters. They represent the historic memory of the CoP and they can be consulted by other members.
- **Leaders.** They direct and give all their support for its correct operation.
- **Regular members.** They carry regular contributions out within the CoP and they interact with other members under sustained basis.
- **Beginning members.** New members who fend for themselves until they have completed the learning process of the community and its members. It is on these members where legitimate peripheral participation is centered.
- **Visitors.** People interested in the activities carried out by the community of practice.

For Loyarte and Rivera (2007), there are critical aspects that affect the CoP, among the ones highlighted: a) The type of knowledge desired to be shared; b) The degree of connection and identity existing among the members of the community; and c) The integration in exchange of knowledge and work. For these authors an important aspect is the utility of Wenger's theory to evaluate the integration of the CoP within the organizations, which is essentially based on four aspects: meaning (learning as an experience), practice (learning the know-how), community (belonging) and identity.

More recently, Niemeyer (2004, 2006) consider the CoP concept has evolved toward learning communities centered in practice. Specifically, Niemeyer (2006) analyzes the concept of this type of communities so as to present an insertion proposal of higher education students into the labor market. The idea is that students can learn in a better way when they are actively involved in the solution of real problems related to the activities in a community they will eventually belong to, a concept which is central to activity theory as we may see at section VI. From our point of view, these activities are the ones that allow the exchange of meaning and give a sense of identity to the group. This exchange of meanings requires for the subject to integrate his capacities, knowledge and attitudes so as to participate, share information; and therefore, to help bring the community together.

In organizations, the CoP represents a complementary structure of informal and integrating character, whose goal is to improve daily tasks in an organization. Among them, learning finds an indissoluble link to practice and socialization of knowledge and experience. The relationships established within the community take hierarchy among members forming it; these relationships are dynamic in relation to the evolution of peripheral participants to experts, and the multiple symmetric and asymmetric interactions among the different actors.

The CoP concept in libraries and information systems has already been discussed by other authors. One of the first studies is the one from Yates and Orlikowski (1992), who applied it to analyzing the use of literary genres among subjects from different communities. Gracy (2001) applied the CoP concept in order to analyze the work of archivists as "communities of individuals who generate, gather and preserve documentary evidence" (p. 212). The study is based on the analysis of processes and practices of subjects who build, produce, keep and use the documents in the contexts where activities occur. Also, it includes an analysis of apprentices' perceptions on the experts who organize and preserve the documents.

Davenport and Hall (2002) carried out a meta-analysis for the *Annual Review of Information Science and Technology*. In his study, they cited Jubert's (1999, p.166) definition of a CoP as a "flexible group of professionals, informally bound by common interests, who interact through interdependent tasks guided by a common purpose thereby embodying a store of common knowledge" (p.171). In their analysis, Davenport and Hall points out that in a CoP it is possible to explore the social and physical context in which artifacts are used to understand the internal roles carried out by objects. The authors identified three types of studies of the CoP in information science. The first one is found to be related to situated learning, the second one to distributed cognition and the third one refers to the studies on the speech analysis. Davenport and Hall includes an analysis of communities of practice in the library work, in the framework of access to information and knowledge as part of the rewards for belonging to a community, including the status and reputation. Lastly, Davenport and Hall analyses the bibliometric studies and the citation analysis as part of the evidences that account for belonging to a scientific community, although their points out that more than directing them to individual retrieval of documents, these studies refer to the relationships among members of the same community who cite and are cited in it.

Finally, another study in which the CoP are included is the one from Triggs and John (2004), which is based upon the analysis of a community of lawyers, where three levels of interconnected communities are identified, the micro, meso and macro communities. The dialogues established among researchers and apprentices using information technologies are analyzed.

VI. THE CoP AND THE ACTIVITY THEORY

From our perspective, academic libraries could be approached as complex systems whose achievements and services would be based in the activities developed in the communities of practice (CoP). This approach allows us to highlight in the analysis we will make that, more than a production system, the library is a human communication system where individuals interact and negotiate so as to carry out their activities, in a recurring process that generates learning from real context situations.

In order to complete the analysis of the activities carried out in the CoP of the academic library, it is necessary that these activities are seen as something more than mere lineal processes of transformation. In order to look deeply into the analysis, we have picked up on the "activity theory" (AT), which provides us with the framework to see the activity as a system. In this sense, the activity goes from being the act undertaken by a subject, to solving a problem or reaching a purpose, starting from certain needs and making use of its potentials. This subject reaches his objective in collaboration with his community and utilizing tools or instruments (facilitators).

From the AT, we can observe in a holistic manner the elements that give shape to the activity: the subject, the object and the mediation. Daniels proposes three moments in the evolution of the AT (2001/2003). At first, he finds Vigotsky's proposal (1978), which formulates the mediation concept and it relates it to the psychological tools and the learning object. In a second moment, Leontiev (1977/1993) identifies that mediation is formed by three elements that are interrelated: the activity, the actions and the operations (see Figure 1).

In the model from Figure 1, there exist three hierarchical levels of mediation. The first one is from the activity related to the motives and goals established by subjects in order to know a determined object. The actions are linked to the subject's knowledge and abilities to know such an object. Lastly, the operations are associated to specific conditions where the activity is carried out, as well as the routines and standardization involved (Barab, Evans and Baek, 2004). The activity occurs in the group environment, while the actions and operations occur in the individual one.

In a third moment, the AT is enriched with the contributions from Engeström, who contextualizes the activity and integrates it to the community concept (see Figure 2).

In his proposal, Engeström (1987) affirms that human activities are carried out in two levels. The first one retakes the proposal from Vigotsky (1978) and the second one integrates the rules, the community and the work division. Engeström highlights the role of dialectic contradictions such as structural tensions, whose solution is the catalyst for change. In his proposal, Engeström specifies the importance of the communities in the learning

Figure 1. Mediation Process (adapted from Leontiev, 1977/1993)

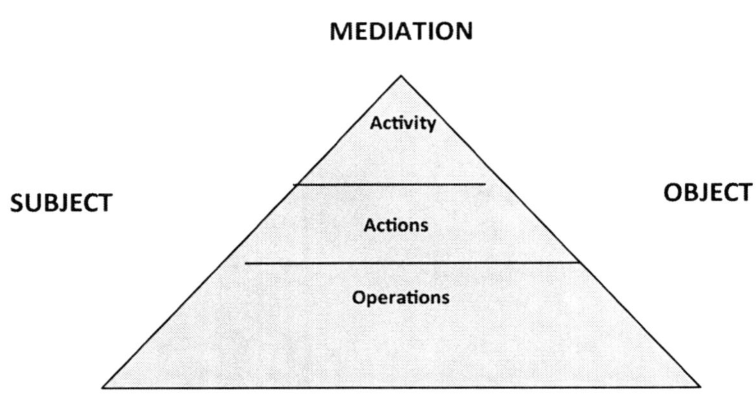

Figure 2. Human System of Activity (adapted from Engeström, 1987)

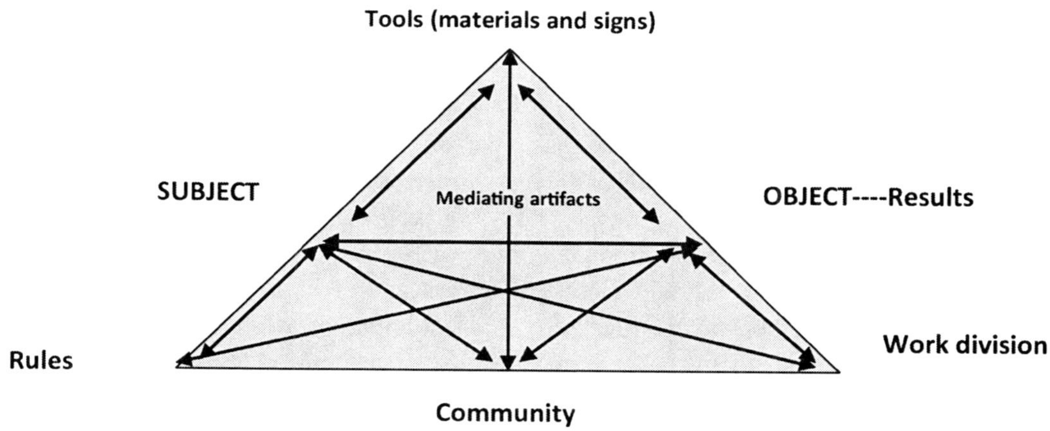

processes and he picks them up on as part of the process to get to know and apply this knowledge.

Daniels (2001/2003) points out that artifacts have historicity and orientation, and that mediation is based upon the notion of dialectic processes where qualitative changes are carried out permanently, which makes transformation and evolution of knowledge possible at generational level.

In Information Science, the AT has been used to understand information behavior from its social meaning in the framework of communities of practice and of learning (Wilson 2000, 2008). Wilson (2008) reviewed the applications from the AT in the literature from that discipline, making emphasis on the research agenda of information literacy. Wilson also identified the works from Hjørland (1997), who applied the AT in the classification processes that a catalogers group carried out.

For Wilson (2008), the understanding of the AT in Information Science is observed in four dimensions: practical, cognitive, educational and organizational. In all of them, it is emphasized that the core activity is the bibliographic, as it comprises a systemic integration of the data produced in different supports, and it is in many senses, a complex social phenomenon that has multiple individual and social representations (library catalogues, encyclopedias, bibliographic research, etc.). In that sense, bibliography means internal and external actions, and it has influence from specific interests and goals, besides responding to specific historic and socio-cultural contexts.

In our analysis, we talk about AT from an organizational perspective. Furthermore we take up on the activity as the unit of analysis for the organizational behavior of an academic library and we integrate the concepts of systems approach, collaboration and communities of practice.

VII. THE ACADEMIC LIBRARIES AS A COLLABORATIVE SYSTEM

From a systems approach academic libraries, as social organizations, are composed of actors who interpret each other as members of this organization and such mutual acknowledgement allows the organization to function as a macro level system, with auto-organization properties, as an autopoietic social system (Maturana and Varela, 1980; Luhmann, 1996; Scott, 2002).

In our perspective a major systemic property in academic libraries is the adaptation to disturbances introduced by changes in the environment, which fertilizes the ground for planning processes that give shape to the organization in order to intervene it through micro-processes that allow change. That property requires differentiated micro-processes of intervention to keep the library dialectical equilibrium. Interventions are performed on those subsystems that should facilitate changes that allow the system to maintain itself in spite of environment disturbances.

To face the dynamics of turbulent environments subsystems within the library should analyze and organize micro-processes to adjust to those turbulences. From this analysis subsystems may become associated with other subsystems or members of them to create the emergent properties that are necessary. One of these properties is the collaborative learning which should be based on reflection and action, even if the group of strategies and policies that guide the change are often given from the highest levels of the organization.

As in any other social organization, this collaborative learning in academic libraries assumes there is a "trust" in library's ventures. Both, authorities and librarians are supposed to hold principles and practices based upon an institutional positive *ethos* that allows people to learn and communicate by reflecting those principles and practices on their own actions and establishing peer-to-peer networks of trusted colleagues (Scott; 2007, 16-18). Hence, such an *ethos* is the base of CoP, as they were conceived by Wenger. Moreover any kind of collaboration within the CoP takes place on this base.

From our perspective, the CoP turns out to be a natural way to carry out group work, promoting collaboration in the social environment. We consider that in the CoP it is possible to call enthusiasm from collaborators, who see in it an opportunity to share daily experiences of learning and teaching in the development of a task and therefore an opportunity to learn and improve everybody's practices.

In fact, working coordinately does not necessarily implies that subjects share responsibility, a common perspective and joint work so as to reach a goal by making use of knowledge and capacities from everyone. For instance, in an academic library many of the activities carried out require the professional participation from librarians, who work coordinately so as to reach an objective (for example, to answer a question, a reference librarian uses a bibliographic catalogue in whose maintenance there is participation from catalogers, classifiers, data center personnel and assistants). Nevertheless, the notion of implicit participation in the previous example does not necessarily mean collaboration, understood as it was mentioned in section IV of this text.

Taking up on the previous example, in reference work the answer to a user could mean a consultation to other colleagues who have solved similar problems or to the FAQ's archive (Frequently Asked Questions). In libraries, the FAQ's archive is compiled by reference librarian through the years on questions that were posed to them by the users. This archive is a good example of a cultural artifact in Activity Theory, since it is used to mediate the reference activities. That is, it represents the historical development of knowledge in the form of reference questions that have been answered during the years, in such a kind of "tradition" that goes from experts to newcomers being either users or librarians.

Along Wilson's suggestion, the most relevant mediating artifact in academic libraries is the bibliographic catalogue. In this artifact, built collectively and throughout time, bibliographic entries are being integrated, which respond to historic moments of an institution, for example the bibliographic entries from collections of a study program or from research that were relevant at a certain time.

The abilities and knowledge from people who collaborate in the creation of a catalogue are also reflected in the bibliographic records; although, they respond to certain standardization, they also reflect the experiences and knowledge of each one of the cataloguers who contribute to its creation. Each one of these actors is a historic being, in the sense that their personal history is due to unrepeatable sociocultural environments. This history is conditioned by competences that every cataloguer puts into play at the time of elaborating this collective work along with the use of other tools that also have historicity, such as subject headings, the classification system and the cataloguing norms and rules. These tools are part of the language that keeps cohesion and standards in the community that catalogues bibliographic items.

This community is linked in turn to other communities that coexist developing other activities that contribute to achieving the library's goals. Desirably, the link established among such communities should be of a collaborative nature. Taking up again our example, a researcher could suggest to the reference librarian new uses in relation to a subject heading or to indicate him which ones are not longer used. The reference librarian in turn, could build along with the cataloguer the pertinent subject heading that reflects this new subject. So, collaboration would imply that whoever provides service and whoever catalogues assume themselves as part of the community where the activity is no longer about answering questions or cataloguing, but creating a common language with the users. In such a sense, actors coexist in a simultaneous manner in different communities, without a formal redefinition of functions or an official designation mediating.

From these previous lines, we can highlight the importance of the activity as an analysis unit. In our example work analysis, the ways to mediate it, the learning generated and the relationships among experts and beginners are better understood if we analyze the group of actions and operations that give shape to the activity of organizing the information.

In summary, in order to structure and consider a situation within the academic library as an information system, we would have the possibility to analyze each activity in more specific units of actions and operations, which can be seen as activities in themselves. Each activity, as a system of actions and operations, is linked to a greater system in which other activities are taking place and establishing multiple and numberless relations among them. These relations are dynamic since they are continuously linking dispersion to articulate actions and operations in order to carry on the activity. This complexity of the total system requires a good capacity of abstraction to approach the subsystems of actions and operations at every level of the system of activities. In that sense, the location of a problem would be determining the abstraction level needed to analyze the components of the specific activities system where the problem is located. To illustrate the previous, we present and comment on the following sequence of Figures (3 to 5).

In Figure 3, we take up again the concept of activity system proposed by Engeström in order to illustrate the analysis unit related to the mentioned example about the CoP that produce the library catalogue. The arrows indicate the relationships established among the different components of the activity system. When linking an activity system to another, these relationships are multiplied (see Figure 4).

In Figure 4 it is illustrated, as an example, some relationships that could be established among the activity systems, which can give an idea of the complexity of the academic library seen as a system. The hexagon, where activities 1 to 4 are linked, tries to illustrate that the activity systems have relationships among them and that these relationships can be established between the rules of a system with the ones from another, between the community that participates in a system with the one that participates in another, and even more between the artifacts used in one or another system. Besides the coexistence of multiple activities systems, it is observed that the CoP have the characteristic to organize and disorganize themselves in relation to temporality and recurrence of an activity system.

Figure 3. Tools for descriptive cataloguing (Adapted from the Activity Human System, Engeström, 1987)

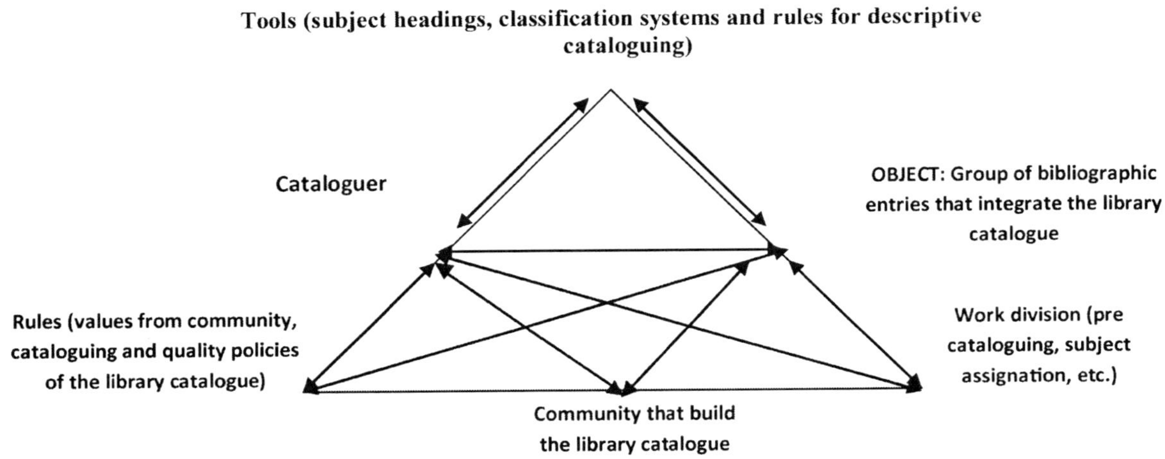

Figure 4. Conglomeration of activity systems

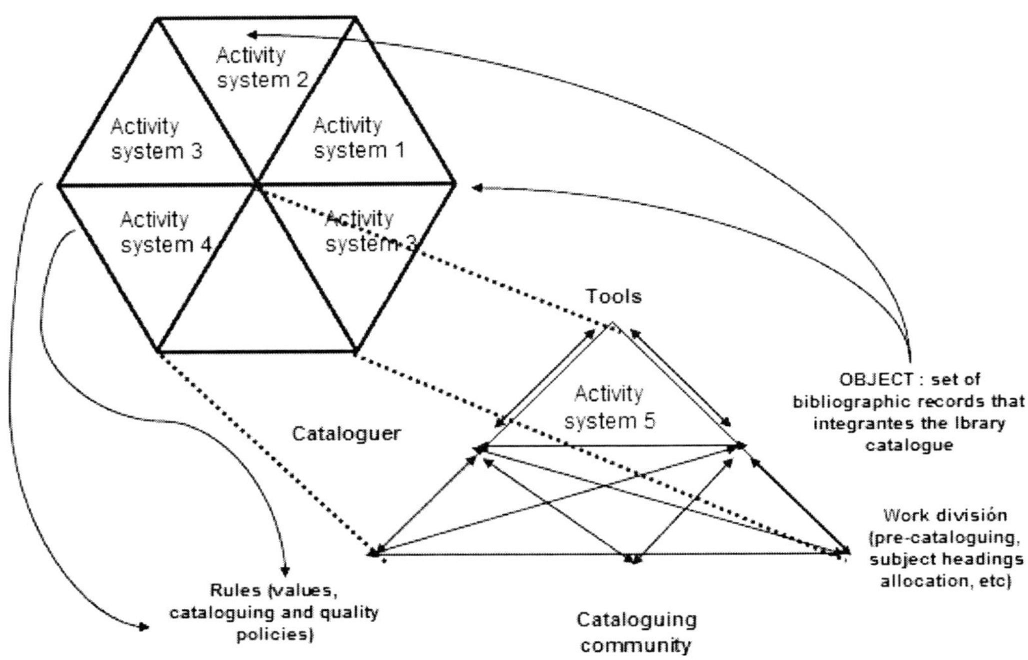

Figure 5. The library as a conglomeration of conglomerations of activity systems

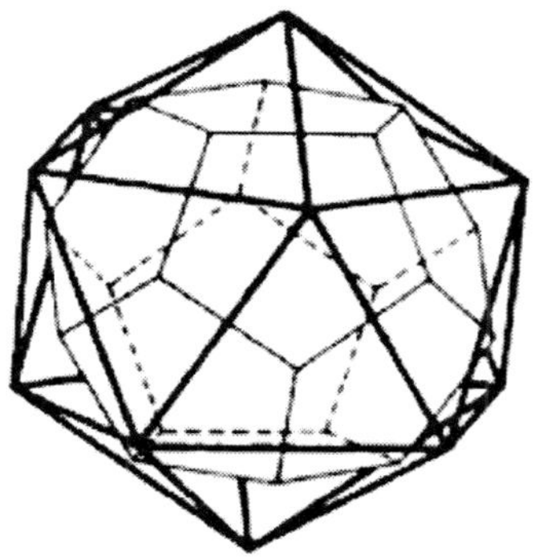

A comprehensive and total vision of a library as a complex system integrated by activity systems could be seen in Figure 5.

In Figure 5 relationships between the academic librarian system and its environment would need to be added as well as those relations with the institution the library belongs to, besides relations with other library systems. In the real life of organizations, the relationships among activity systems do not necessarily have the symmetry the figures suggest.

In the previous paragraphs, we have reflected the daily practice of libraries, which have pieces of information as an input that would be processed, adding value to them with the intention of optimizing the time the user dedicates to search and retrieve documents for supporting his activities of learning, teaching and research; that is why we have considered as our base the analysis of processes related with organization of information and with reference services. Both processes constitute the center of the primary activity system in the library.

Taking the two processes that we have mentioned as a primary activity system that we will call "production subsystem", in the coming section we will make an initial approximation to the complexity of the academic library, by following a "soft" version of the Beer's Viable System Model (1984) as developed by Fitch (2007). Complexity will be drawn along the lines of Fitch's model identifying in general the other subsystems that integrate it. In this approximation, we take on again the figure of the CoP as those other subsystems, which besides carrying out processes, they adapt to change and generate learning and new ways of work. In order to understand the previous, we will assume the vision of the activity as the generator of permanent learning situations.

VIII. ACADEMIC LIBRARY AS A COMPLEX SYSTEM[1]

Practice here is assumed to be approached from Activity Theory prospective; i. e. focused on the "contextualized activity of the system as a whole" (Barab, Evans & Baek, 2004, p. 200) to understand how individual actually perceive their workplace activities, in order to perform them. This approach becomes crucial for organizational learning and collaborative work since analysis is done through models where learning is supposed to occur when activities cannot be reduced to preexisting operations, and a need pops up to invent a new set of operations. As Mwanza and Engeström (2003, p. 2) pointed out: "...learning is driven by genuine developmental needs in human practices and institutions, manifested in disturbances, breakdowns, problems, and episodes of questioning the existing practice...[it] proceeds through complex cycles of learning actions in which new objects and motives are created and implemented, opening up wider possibilities for participants involved in that activity".

As we mentioned above, to draw our conceptual model we have used some of the lines suggested by Fitch (2007) to understand Beer's VSM, and our own experience. Beer's VSM assumes an abstraction exercise consisting in constructing subsystems of virtual activities that are performed to guarantee not only the survival of the organization but its autonomy or viability to operate in a turbulent environment. So those subsystems are a product of a reflexive view of the set of activities that are performed "in the ground" by the CoP, the primary activities that conform the production subsystem, the organization's *leit motif*. In other words, those subsystems that are composed by virtual activities are the product of a system's view on itself, i.e. those activities conduct the production subsystem through the turbulent environment.

In that sense, we claim that an academic library is integrated by the following subsystems:

1. **Primary activities (production).** In this subsystem we find those processes that are carried out daily in academic libraries, such as document selection, analysis, identification and codification of metadata[2] (semantic and syntactical). The aim is to produce that selected bibliography that the library offers (technology mediated) to its community as the collective and authorized knowledge on specific issues. Here we include all those activity systems that were drawn in Figures 3 to 5.
2. **Coordination.** This subsystem is the one that glues subsystem 1 together. It designs policies and procedures that make the system operate. The subsystem distributes tasks and responsibilities, provides leadership, and supplies services and resources to the system.
3. **Management.** This subsystem establishes how it is done what the system does, in the direction provided by subsystem 4. It includes quality assurance and human resources.
4. **Strategies and planning.** This subsystem defines the mission, vision, goals for short, medium and long ranges, as well as strategic programs. It sets out why it is done what the system does.
5. **Evaluation and feedback.** This subsystem is the one that maintains the relationship with the environment and along with system 4 ensures that the whole system continues doing what it does or what it has to do.
6. **Learning and Innovation.** It is responsible for increasing the intelligence of the organization.

Figure 6 presents a preliminary view of interactions among those subsystems .

A turbulent environment for academic libraries is mostly characterized by a continuous process of change and hence adaptation of information technologies, along with an expanding market of information products, repackaging of existing ones, information brokers offering full text databases that keep very tiny differences among them, confuse licensing for access, and the like. Figure 6 above tries to emphasize that users are not just another stakeholder to the system; they are the real "owners" of the whole thing in a way that even slight perceptions on failures detected by users of the system should become a warning for those librarians in the production subsystem.

Therefore the evaluation subsystems acts as a filter for the library's main product: its catalogue, which offers that set of selected information representations that are the key to validated information on every knowledge subject. These representations are the product of a highly cognitive work of the library's communities of practice in the "activity system triangle", as it may be observed at the bottom of the Figure 6.

The learning and innovation system is the key factor to the system. It embraces at every moment those cognitive outputs that come from the work that groups perform daily to represent knowledge. It is in this work that cognitive sharing occurs among members of those communities and it is that cognition process the one that this system is monitoring constantly for the knowledge to become explicit.

As we have tried to show, the apparent simplicity of an academic library as a system which acquires organizes and borrows books and other materials, is instead a collaborative complex entity based on a structured production subsystem, namely cataloguing processes and reference services, with a teleological principle: serving the

Figure 6. Academic library system

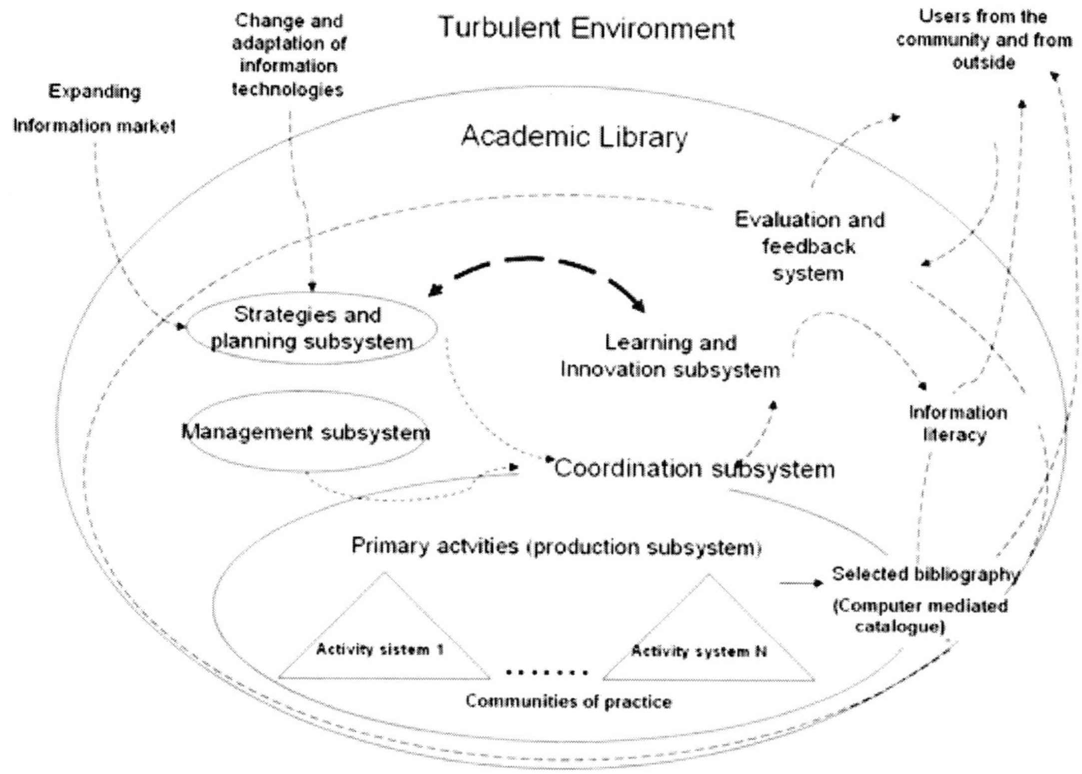

user. In order to do so, academic libraries have embedded subsystems for coordinating, managing, planning, evaluating and improving learning and innovation. In such a sense, an academic library is an organization which may be seen as a viable system along Beer's model. Central to this viewpoint is the concept of a set of persons working together as a community of practice to carry on specific activities.

CONCLUSION

Libraries may be approached as complex systems by using some of the properties of communities of practice and by using the elements of activity theory. A model such as Beer´s in the way we presented it in this paper fits well to decompose reality and synthesize it to analyze the proposed complexity. This may allow facing organizational problems by focusing in the way people act to transform the inputs into products and add value to them by teaching and learning.

In using approaches such as CoP and AT, we attempt to incorporate new elements to the traditional study of libraries as service institutions, focusing on those relations that are established among individuals that have to collaborate to realize activities that are at the core of the production system in a library.

After setting the production subsystem we proceeded to explain those subsystems that may give autonomy to the organization in order to build a viable system capable of adaptations and self organizing its communities in a continuous fashion. One of key features of the VSM is to realize that learning and innovation as a subsystem that allows the academic library to face a turbulent environment as Emery and Trist point out reliance on research and development increase the organization's capacity to cope with competitive challenge which comes from a permanent change gradient in the environmental field.

Approaches to study libraries as complex systems, as the one we proposed here, may be useful to increase success in implementation of new technologies. In fact, innovation in information technologies do not just comprise the process of technology changes in use, but also a change in work conditions of those who make use of such technology (in our case, members of de CoP). Success in library implementation process of such technologies is expected to be increased if it is approached with than intention to model the cognitive dimensions of activities that carried out in the CoP. The main feature of our approach is to take the activity as an analysis unit to display the characteristics of this activity in the nucleus of a community of practice, and from there to better understand the role of the subjects that use information technology as a tool that mediates the transformation activity, for instance of data into information that goes to the catalogue.

REFERENCES

Barab, S., Evans, M., & Baek, E. (2004). Activity theory as a lens for characterizing the participatory unit. Ed. D. Jonassen, *Handbook of research on educational communications and technology* (pp. 99-214). 2ed. Mahwah, NJ: Lawrence Erlbaum.

Beer, S. (1984). The Viable System Model: its provenance, development, methodology and pathology. *The Journal of the Operational Research Society*, *35*(1), 7–25.

Bruner, Ch. (1991). *Thinking collaboratively: ten questions and answers*. Washington, DC: Education and Human Services Consortium.

Bunge, M. (2008). *Filosofía y sociedad*. México, D.F.: Siglo XXI, 189 p

Dalkir, K. (2005). *Knowledge management in theory and practice*. Burlington, M.A.: Elsevier Butterworth Heinemann.

Daniels, H. (2001/2003). *Vygotsky y la pedagogía*. D.F., México: Paidós. (Original work published 2001)

Davenport, E., & Hall, H. (2002). Organizational knowledge and communities of practice. *Annual Review of Information Science & Technology*, *36*, 171–227.

Emery, F., & Trist, E. (1965). The causal texture of organizational environments. *Human Relations*, *18*, 21–32. doi:10.1177/001872676501800103

Engeström, Y. (1987). *Learning by expanding: An activity-theoretical approach to developmental research*. Helsinki: Orienta-Konsultit.

Fitch, D. (2007). A cybernetic evaluation of organizational information systems (pp. 61-74). Eds. Williams & I. Imam. In *Systems concepts in evaluation: an expert anthology*. Point Reyes, Calif.: EdgePress of Inverness American Evaluation Association.

García, R. (2000). *Conocimiento en construcción: de las formulaciones de Jean Piaget a la teoría de sistemas complejos*. Barcelona: Gedisa.

Gracy, K. F. (2001). Documentar comunidades: el caso de la etnografía archivística. Editores Anne Gilliland & Sue McKemmish. In *Nuevos métodos de investigación en archivística*, (pp. 211-244). Madrid, España: 3000 Informática.

Hjørland, B. (1997). *Information seeking and subject representation. An activity-theoretical approach to information science*. Westport, CT; London: Greenwood Press.

Hoare, P. (1997). *Academic Libraries in International Encyclopedia of Information and Library Science*. John Feather & Paul Sturges (eds). New York: Routledge. pp. 2.

Jubert, A. (1999). Developing an infraestructure for communities of practice. In B. McKenna (Ed.). In *Proceedings of the 19th International Online Meeting* (pp. 165-168). Hinkesey Hill, U.K.: Learned Information.

Lave, J. (1988). *Cognition in practice: mind, mathematics, and culture in everyday life*. New York: Cambridge University. doi:10.1017/CBO9780511609268

Lave, J., & Wenger, E. (1991). *Situation learning: legitimate peripheral participation*. Cambridge, UK: Cambridge University Press.

Leleur, S. (2008). Systems science and complexity: some proposals for future development. *Journal of Systems Research and Behavioral Science, 25*(1), 67–79. doi:10.1002/sres.860

Leontiev, A. N. (1977/1993). *Actividad, conciencia y personalidad*. D.F., México: Asbe. (Original work published 1977)

Loyarte, E., & Rivera, O. (2007). Communities of practice: a model for their cultivation. *Journal of Knowledge Management, 11*(3), 67–77. doi:10.1108/13673270710752117

Luhmann, N. (1996). *Introducción a la teoría de sistemas*. México: Universidad Iberoamericana.

Maturana, H., & Varela, F. (1980). *Autopoiesis and Cognition: the Realization of the Living (Boston Studies in the Philosophy of Science, 42)*. Netherlands: D. Reidel Publishing.

Morin, E. (1992). The concept of system and the paradigm of complexity. In Maruyama, M. (Ed.), *Context and complexity: cultivating contextual understanding* (pp. 125–142). Berlin: Springer Verlag. doi:10.1016/1061-7361(92)90024-8

Mwanza, D., & Engeström, Y. (2003) Pedagogical adeptness in the design of e-learning environments: experiences from the Lab@Future Project. Editor E. Rossett. In *Proceedings of E-learn 2003 International Conference on E-learning in Corporate*. Retrieved from: http://www.edu.helsinki.fi/activity/pages/files/research/lab/Daisy-YrjoElearn03.pdf in 31/05/08]

Niemeyer, B. (2004). Situated learning for social and vocational integration in Germany. Editors B. Evans & Niemeyer, B. In *Reconnection: Countering social Exclusion Through Situated Learning*. Dordrecht, NL, pp. 47-62.

Niemeyer, B. (2006). El aprendizaje situado una forma de escapar del enfoque de déficit. *Revista de Educación, 341*, 99–121.

Quijano, A., & Vega, M. G. (2008) Academic Libraries as a Complex Systems: A First Approach. In: *8th International Conference of Sociocybernetics: Complex Social Systems, Interdisciplinarity and World Futures*. Ciudad de México, México

Scott, B. (2002). A design for the recursive contruction of learning communities. *International Review of Sociology, 12*(2), 257–268. doi:10.1080/0390670022000012486

Scott, B. (2007). Facilitating organizational change: some sociocybernetic principles. *Journal of Organizational Transformation and Social Change, 4*(1), 13–23. doi:10.1386/jots.4.1.13_1

Scott, W. R. (1992). *Organizations: Rational, natural and open systems* (3rd ed.). Englewood Cliffs, N.J.: Prentice Hall.

Simpson, A. & Weiner [Ed.], (1989). *Oxford English Dictionary*, 2a ed. Oxford, UK: Oxford University Press

Triggs, P., & John, P. (2004). From to transformation: information and Communications technology, professional development and the formation of communities of practice. *Journal of Computer Assisted Learning, 20*, 426–439. doi:10.1111/j.1365-2729.2004.00101.x

Vygotsky, L. S. (1978). *Mind in society: The development of higher psychological processes*. Cambridge, MA: Harvard University Press.

Wenger, E. (1998/2001). *Communities of practice: learning, meaning, and identity*. Cambridge: Cambridge University Press. (Original work published 1998)

Wenger, E., & Snyder, W. (2000). Communities of practice: the organizational frontier. *Harvard Business Review*, 139–145.

Wilson, T. D. (2000). Human information behavior. *Informing Science*, *3*(3), 49–55.

Wilson, T. D. (2008). Activity theory and information seeking. *Annual Review of Information Science & Technology*, *42*, 119–161. doi:10.1002/aris.2008.1440420111

Yates, J., & Orlikowski, W. (1992). Genres of organizational communication: a structuration approach to studying communication and media. *Academy of Management Review*, *17*(2), 299–326.

ENDNOTES

1 This section is taken out of a previous presentation in 8th International Conference of Sociocybernetics. Complex Social Systems, Interdisciplinarity and World Futures. Ciudad de México, México, 24-28 June, 2008.

2 Data on data. For a library, metadata include description of the content, the author, the publication date and the physical location of those bibliographical materials that constitute the data themselves, the items shelved.

Chapter 12
Cultural Management 2.0

Margarita Cabrera Méndez
Universitat Politècnica de València, Spain

ABSTRACT

The Internet has become the essential media for daily work of cultural management professionals. Its richness of contents and the fast evolution of technologies do even exceed the capacity of adaptation and decision of the professionals due to the wide range of possibilities that the Internet offers. It is in this new context where technologies and cultures get mixed up as cultural institutions cannot play the same roles as they did in the analogic world. Not only the classical functions of conservation, research, commission or exhibition have to be valued, but also in the role of broadcasting, doors to communication 2.0 should be opened, getting into the social networks, not only sharing but also listening what the users have to say.

This new step has to be managed by institutions that are able to understand and add the new philosophy 2.0 in their corporative and communication culture. It is not longer one-way communication as the role of the users is essential. The author will analyse the strategies and models of some institutions that have incorporated digital practices and culture in their organizations and communication and therefore, the way they connect with their different audiences (Creators/artists, users and other organizations.) have changed.

1. INTRODUCTION

It is obvious that we have entered into a new Internet stage, in which not only it is necessary to have a web site with information about the institution, the author, the works, related events and basically all the information that a leaflet may have, but also in the new Internet generation, what it is called 2.0, the user is the king. The information that the institution has to communicate is important but it is more important the opinion of the users, of the experts in that field, of creators or artists and even the opinion of similar institutions or researchers.

DOI: 10.4018/978-1-61350-201-3.ch012

A specialist in virtual communities said that his most relevant tests workshop is the reaction of his clients on social networks as they are who will help us to improve.

The term "Web 2.0" was coined in January 1999 by Darcy DiNucci, a consultant on information architecture. In her article, "Fragmented Future", DiNucci writes:

"The Web we know now, which loads into a browser window in essentially static screenfuls, is only an embryo of the Web to come. The first glimmerings of Web 2.0 are beginning to appear, and we are just starting to see how that embryo might develop. The Web will be understood not as screenfuls of text and graphics but as a transport mechanism, the ether through which interactivity happens. It will [...] appear on your computer screen, [...] on your TV set [...] your car dashboard [...] your cell phone [...] hand-held game machines [...] maybe even your microwave oven."

Angelina Russo writes in her blog: Social Media and Cultural Communication: "The underlying principle are that cultural and commercial organisations are now no longer just using the same tools (marketing, exhibition, events) etc. they're occupying the same spaces (Facebook, YouTube) etc."

It is a plural communication that felicitates a communication space in which all the actors participate. It is also timeless and without a particular physical space. We can take part in it from any place of the world, comment on the artwork of the day of the New York Metropolitan Museum, we can also have a debate with the last photographer that is exposing in a Brasilian gallery or give ideas for the new book of a prestigious French writer.

The doors are open to everyone, the Digital Culture 2.0 allows listening, sharing and extending the influence level. This can be done through a blog and its comments, through a social network or through videos or photos shared by the visitors or exhibitors, or through comments on an Internet forum.

New Technologies and their influence in our social evolution has exceed the concept of "publishing space" or window, showing more and more linked and relational strategies, which are reflected in the Web 2.0 and in the current and discussed data web site or Semantic Web 3.0. There is a need of information that releases these new tools and provides knowledge that can be applied to the current reality. This chapter tries to give an answer to this need offering a prospect of the current situation with brief comments of future for cultural managers.

1.1 Objectives

The main objective of this chapter is to describe the condition of the general art about the cultural management 2.0 analysing where we came from and where we lend to. To do so, we will carry out an analysis of the most relevant cultural institutions dealing nowadays with social network communications and the observed trends.

Likewise, this chapter aims to summarise the best practices or advice for cultural managers and their communication on the Internet through new tools.

2. CULTURE 2.0: COLLECTIVE CULTURE

Cultural management refers to an advanced version of broadcasting and communication of cultural management in what is called Web 2.0. This is only a new generation of web sites based on communities of users and a special range of services. These services are the sale of products, clubs, forums, encyclopedia, common topics, etc. and they can be defined according to some formats, such as social networks, blogs, wikis, the syndication or folksonomies. This is a term linked to other contexts that take it as their own and therefore produces "Type 2.0" developments. The most relevant point is that they encourage collaboration and exchange of information between users. As Angela McFarlene pointed out "Information and communication technologies have to be seen as a group of skills and competences, a group of tools to do what we always do but in an easier way, better and more economical and with a revolutionary impact." The big change is not technological but change of attitude.

According to Jubany, " *The Web 2.0 allows to use any type of digital tools in an intuitive and participative way. Tools and environments such as social networks help personal communication, information exchange and generation of knowledge.*" (Jubany, 2009).

As the core of its functionality, communication is focused in the users, achieving a more participative activity, more proactive, getting further away than the never called Web 1.0, in which the user was only a mere spectator. Users can participate without having computer skills, as everything is simpler for them. This degree of influence converts users into an essential phenomenon of research and also into an application pattern. In this sense, the user is a figure that generates management models that could help to improve the competences of the cultural management, particularly from the social insertion point of view and communication in general.

Therefore, in the Web 2.0, collective intelligence, the sum of the opinions and the actions of all the users that make up the society have to be pointed out. As Óscar Martínez and David Casacuberta mentioned in an article about this topic:

The most clear and rellevant knowledge is what we could call "wisdom of crowds." The idea that there is more intelligence in a group that in the most intelligent members of the group is the most powerful feature of the Web 2.0 and it is also the most important feature for cultural management. Deep down, their idea of the wisdom of crowds is an attempt of transferring some of the mechanisms of the traditional culture to the digital world. After all, how do we understand culture but as the wisdom of crowds codified through other slower processes? Do not Google and the word of mouth share a series of social features? No doubt that culture and the word of mouth are more reliable than a web search engine or a blog, as the Web 2.0 still needs many refinement levels to be exactly the same as the analogue crowds. (Martínez 2007).

In the international context, we can talk about an incipient presence of the cultural world into social networks. In fact, there are already many museums, foundations or libraries that have a page on Facebook, comment their events and activities on Twitter or they have their own channel on YouTube. We say incipient because, although some of them are getting into social networking in a very professional way, most of them do not find the way of getting into social networks or if they do it, they do it in a very tepid way, as they create a page and only get into it from time to time. It has also to be pointed out that, in general, for the time being, they transfer press releases or information generated for other media as a post or tweet on social networks. Therefore, they are not making profit and getting into the new communication scheme but they are communicating in a new media with others' tools.

On a personal level, there are also many artists that are making profit of this media to reach the audience better and know their opinions and interests. How could we imagine direct contact with our favourite writer, singer or artist? If he wants we can daily follow his opinions, sketches, and steps. Some of them even publish each trip they do, any conference they make or any new idea for the new book they are writing. Although not many have entered into this world, as cultural managers, we should know which ones of the artists we work with do this in order to coordinate with them communication strategies on the new Web 2.0.

Gradually, cultural entities accept the importance of their presence on social networks of general type. As Javier Celaya estates: *"35% of the museums in Spain have already their own profile on Facebook, although we can advance that there are other profiles on Facebook created by users, which have been created because users have empathy, interest or like this or that centre."*

This brings us to the above mentioned issue: it does not matter if we want to or not as people will talk about us and our work. Therefore, it will be better if this is coordinated and managed by our centre or entity. The cultural management involves a wide range of people that are interested in participating.

There is no space or time for the new communication of culture. We live in a global world where everything can be shared. No matter where or at what time we look it up. As an example of this, there is an initiative of some public transport entities that start sharing culture with their users through their mobiles or via Wi Fi. Today, we can travel in the underground and download a chapter of a book with our iphone, or check the information about the cultural activities in our city, share the comments about these cultural activities or applying for more information about them in real time. And all of this can be done with our mobile in the meantime we do a journey in the underground, which is managed by the corresponding transport company.

What is true is that many cultural institutions (Art galleries, publishing companies, foundations, etc.) have recently entered into the World 2.0 creating pages or profiles on different social networks (Facebook, Tuenti, Xing, Flickr or Twitter, among others.) However, we do not have so clear if they have previously thought about the communication objectives they wish to achieve with their presence on these platforms.

Most of the cultural entities start to join social networks as they got into Internet: they have to be there because the rest are there, without understanding the rules of the game, without responding the users or without knowing how to manage communication in this new media. Many cultural entities are reluctant to get involved with this and they do not want to hear about joining a social network. However, in our opinion, this is only a matter of time and development of cultural managers. We would like to remember that only two decades ago most of them stated that they would never use mobile phones. Today, they may have the same model.

It is a fact that that the society is changing its habits with regard to culture. For instance, they are changing the preliminary steps of a visit to a museum, to an exhibition or when choosing a book. With the arrival of 2.0 applications and the massive use of them, there are changes in the way that we plan a visit a cultural entity. We take care of comments of friends or people we know about what they have seen, we take into consideration and get guided by the information that is shared on social networks. Every day we are more and more interconnected, which allows us to participate with impressions and experiences in an agile and immediate way with other people.

In order to have an idea of the importance that social networking is reaching in museums, we will focus on their number of followers or people who like the official page of several of the most important museums of the world. The British Museum has approx. 50,000 friends on Facebook, El Prado National Museum has 60,000, the Solomon R. Guggenheim Museum has 137,000, the Musée du Louvre has 141,000, The New York Metropolitan Museum of Art has 287,000 and the MoMa, the Museum of Modern Art has 527,000. The same happens with libraries: the British Library has 20,000 followers, the New York Public Library has 25,000 and the Spanish National Library has 71,000.

If we focus in another social network we will see that the same happens, for instance, in the case of MoMa in Twitter, it has 300,000 followers, or the Getty Museum in Los Angeles has 111,000. The same happens in several social networks. However, there are not many museums which manage this communication strategy correctly and only a few have been doing it for a long time.

As cultural users we can follow close up, only with some clicks, the activity carried out by these entities. In their Pages, they advertise their next exhibitions, weekend events, courses for children, and sometimes, as the Metropolitan in New York, they show us the artwork of the day, offering the users the possibility to know the treasures of the museum with detailed information about the artwork of the day. Users can comment it, share it and enjoy it, each one from one part of the world. They also open discussions or galleries to share photographs and experiences. The virality that has the fact that any follower can make a comment about an exhibition or work of art is unbelievable. This makes the number of followers to increase day by day.

3. RECOMMENDATIONS FROM REPEATED OBSERVATION OF USE OF SOCIAL NETWORKS IN CULTURAL MANAGEMENT

As we were talking before, it is essential to understand from the beginning that users are the centre of communication on social networks; the user is "the king". It should be a real and transparent communication. It is based on people and not on trademarks or institutions.

The 2.0 communication about cultural topics exists: museums, books, cinema, exhibitions, concerts... There is no way to control people talking about this. However, what we can control from our cultural entity is focusing on and providing another communication channel with users interested in our field of action. This will provide us with a large window to share experiences, interests and events and all of them are related to what we are managing. For sure, if we decide to bet on this way of communicating, we should have clear some basis on which we have to build our information system and play with the rules of the game of the new media.

We have to choose cautiously the person or people to represent the entity on social networks. This person has to be a good communicator and has to be related to the digital culture. Therefore, this person or people will have to join skills related with communication and technology and will also need to have a wide cultural knowledge. This person or people should also pay attention to all the changes, because innovation on the Internet goes very fast and trends change in a short period of time. We have to know where our audience is in order to reach it through its media and language.

Some minimum guidelines for the cultural management 2.0 are detailed below:

3.1. Establishing Objectives and E-Strategy

We can point out that it does not make sense to get into the social networking world as cultural managers if we have not established some objectives and strategies to carry this out. We should know them at the institutional level or we can also establish them ourselves by informing the board of directors to covert this into a common and shared tactic for all the organization, as we have to involve all the members in some way or another. It should be integrated in the corporative culture of the institution.

The objectives can go from interaction with the potential clients (users, visitors ... who, in short, are our target), to ensuring and consolidating trade contacts or creating a data base of interested people ... In any case, we have to understand that this will provide us with a real contact with our audience and will also allow us to share a value-added content.

3.2. Opportunities and Tools Knowing the Audience

Depending on the goals we want to achieve, we should use different tools. We need to be clear about the media in which we will work. To do this, it is necessary do a research about our audience, what they do, what are their information needs, the advertising campaigns that have been carried out by our alleged competence (or institutions of our range), the communication niches we should cover and, in short, search opportunities or generate a need even if it does not exist, as sooner or later we will be searched.

Knowing the habits and needs of the audience will allow us to give continuity to the presence in social media integral management. We can have feedback from them and therefore we can know what they expect of this communication.

To do this, we have to choose the tools to participate. We recommend analysing which are the most influential tools in the market we want to focus. This will vary depending on the group of age, country or intellectual level. Therefore, prior to choosing a tool we need to know the audience we want reach.

3.3 Getting Users

In the social dimension of social networking, the user is in the centre and generates contents and excels in participation and information exchange. This exercise of sharing and adding information is motivated by common interests, which generates different communities. They may be related to hobbies, business, kinship…

In the case of cultural entities, their users, also known as audience or community, are made up, in the first place, by their members or, at least, we think it should be like this. That is, all the staff should know the project or the new communication system, add themselves as users and, secondly, they should spread it between their friends, as far as possible, and participate. With this first step only, we are opening the possibility of an internal communication of the entity. Therefore, any event, news or topic related to the entity will be immediately known through this new media, offering the whole team the possibility of participating and expressing their opinion.

In order to make the social network larger, it has to be advertised. This can be done with a link on a web site or with the typical text of "Follow us in …" with leaflets, posters, ads or any other material related to the entity.

Once we have informed our team and suggested them to send it to their contacts, we should keep it alive for other users interested in our entity or in the activities carried out to join our entity. To do this, it is advisable to visit other similar or related entities (Tourist, official, discussion …), social networks, forums, blogs, etc., as well as participate by expressing your opinion about the topic that is being discussed, for the users of similar networks to know that we exist and join our network.

3.4 Immediacy

In social networking, conversation with users and followers is one of the most relevant topics. It is essential that the manager of the entity in charge of its maintenance answers the comments of users fast. This means that the manager has to read the comments daily and he has not only to start a comment, but also to answer the topics that are being discussed. It is important to listen and talk, raise an issue for discussion and leave the users to discuss themselves.

3.5 Freedom and Transparency

Participants have to be free, be able to express their opinions without restrictions, but always within the limits of good manners. There are several opinions about deleting comments. In our opinion, rude comments have to be deleted. The rest, although they are negative or critical with the entity have to be responded and our opinion or version about the entity has to be given. In this way, all the audience will be able to know what happened with a possible mistake or misunderstanding. We can consider it as constructive criticism, it is like a R&D laboratory where experts express their opinions about our work and we can make profit of them to improve.

3.6 Close and Accessible

It is important to show the human side of the entity, that the person who answers is a close and accessible person. It has to be a cordial person, who always answers to any doubt, thanks for the participation and supports the conversation. This will make our users to be more comfortable and participate. We do not have to understand this media as an institutional and formal communication; it has to be understood as communication in equal terms.

In some cases, it is even advisable that the manager of a social site has a personal profile apart from the institutional website, so that when the manager answers, he or she is a person with names and surname, who is liable for that business profile. This favours proximity.

3.7 Encouraging the Conversation

Burning topics can be brought up for discussion, making open questions for the users to answer them, generating expectations about something or making comments about an inauguration that took place the previous day, even with details such as if the speakers were close and friendly or if it was a dinner afterwards with the artists, can be techniques to encourage the conversation. In the same way, we can also encourage the users to share pictures, videos or experiences.

3.8 Being Constant

There is no need to overwhelm the users with information every hour. However, it is not convenient not to add any information for a month. Therefore, it would be advisable to find the balance between overwhelming and leaving aside our followers. One or two comments a day may be enough and if there is any outstanding event or activity, we can inform with more detail.

3.9 Searching Information on the Internet

An article of a digital magazine or a comment on a blog may be of the interest of our followers. There is no harm in knowing what it is said about us on the Internet and sharing it.

3.10 Languages

When we focus on an international audience, it is convenient not to forget it at any time. We can add comments in a profile in several languages. (We recommend not having more than two.) We can translate our comments and allow our followers to use the language they prefer. There is also the option of publishing only in English or creating a profile in each language. This last option is harder to maintain and users loose the comments of other users in another language.

4. CONCLUSION

We are in the age of the universalization of culture. Everything or almost everything is available in digital libraries, video libraries, data bases, art galleries, etc. and all of them with cheap and easy access. The Web 2.0 favours the approach of culture to all the users. It is fresher and more natural than the cultural management we had with the Web 1.0, in which each entity had a web site with static contents and the audience could get information about it. However, they could not participate. At the most, the audience was informed with news or an updated agenda about what's new and activities.

The XX century critics, who stated what was good or not are now devalued. Today, new channels with thousand of "opiners" and critics carry out this function. Therefore, we can say that social networking applied to the cultural management provides the digital tools for a lot of people to talk to a lot of people and generates collective contents. This is what we have called collective intelligence or, in our particular case, we could call it collective culture. We have put aside the model of publishing a book by one person for a lot of people, the individual criticism… to reach an explosion of comments where everything makes its influence in the online reputation. This may benefit us.

The possibility of collective sharing allows creating information. Due to the contribution of many users, a large repository of information about culture is created, which would be very difficult to achieve without social networking. Not only generating information contributes to this repository of information but also the immediacy and the spontaneity when sharing information is involved in this new media

The Web 2.0 is also a much more suitable system to the new status of the cultural object and its broadcasting. The big difficulty that cultural managers based in Web 2.0 have to face is participation. Unfortunately, if participation is not enough, the elements that have been collectively generated would be imperceptible and even ignored. Apart from online and offline broadcasting, it is compulsory to have a 2.0 communication strategy. This new way to face the audience that has to be agile, sincere, direct and transparent and the cultural manager has to be attentive and proactive at any time.

Cultural entities have to be professional when answering their followers through an official profile. This profile has to be suitable for any event, exhibition, activity, inauguration, etc. in order to be able to interact with all their audience in a simple and natural way.

REFERENCES

Celaya, J. (2008) *La empresa en la Web 2.0*. Barcelona, Spain: Ediciones Gestión 2000.

Celaya, J. (2009) Study *La visibilidad de los museos en la Web 2.0*. Retrieved September 2, 2010, from http://www.dosdoce.com/articulo/estudios/3071/la-visibilidad-de-los-museos-en-la-web-2-0

Charlene, L. Bernoff, J. (2008) *Groundswell, winning in a world transformed by social technologies*. United States of America: Forrester Research.

Courtney, N. (2007). *Library 2.0 and beyond: innovative technologies and tomorrow's user*. Libraries Unlimited.

Dinucci, D. (1999). Fragmented future. *Print*, *53*(4), 32.

Fotis, L. Georgios, S. Dimitrios, K. (2010) *Handbook of Research on Technologies and Cultural Heritage: Applications and Environments*. IGI Global snippet

Grossman, Lev. (2006) *Person of the Year: You*. December 25. Time.com

Jubany, J. (2009). Guía práctica para participar activamente en una red social y educativa digital. *Revista Didáctica, Innovación y Multimedia, 5, 13*. Retrieved September 10, 2010, from http://www.pangea.org/dim/revistaDIM13/Articulos/jordijubany.doc

Kelly, L. (2009). *The Impact of Social Media on Museum Practice*. In the Exhibitionist Fall 2009. Presented at the National Palace of Tapei. Retrieved September 10, 2010, from http://www.archimuse.com/mw2008/papers/kelly_l/kelly_l.html

Margolis, J. (2009). *Culture and Cultural Entities - Toward a New Unity of Science*. New York: Springer; 2nd ed. edition.

Martínez, O. Casabuerta, D. (2009). Gestión cultural y TICs. Una perspectiva desde la web 2.0." *Cibersociedad*. 2007. Retrieved August 28, 2010 from http://www.redinterlocal.org/Gestion-cultural-y-TICs-Una

Mcfarlane, A. (2001). *El aprendizaje y las tecnologías de la Información*. Madrid, Spain: Aula XXI Santillana.

Nafría. I. (2007) *Web 2.0*. Barcelona, Spain: Ediciones Gestión 2000.

O'reilly, T. Battelle, J. (2004) *Opening Welcome: State of the Internet Industry*. San Francisco, California

Russo, A. Kelly, L. Chan, S. (2010) *Social Media and Cultural Communication* Retrieved September 9, 2010 http://nlablog.wordpress.com

Simon, N. (2010) *The participatory museum*. Santa Cruz, Calif.: Museum 2.0.

Van der veer, E. (2008) *Facebook: the missing manual*. Sebastopol: Pogue Press/O'Reilly.

Chapter 13
Coagmento:
A Case Study in Designing a User-Centric Collaborative Information Seeking System

Chirag Shah
Rutgers, The State University of New Jersey, USA

ABSTRACT

The author describes Coagmento, a system that provides integrated tools and workflow for doing collaborative information seeking in online environment. Coagmento's inception followed a need to provide essential tools to collaborators without them having to learn an entirely new system or work in an unfamiliar environment. Here they describe how the author designed, developed, and deployed Coagmento. The design of this system was facilitated using several pilot runs and cognitive walkthroughs. A fully functional version of Coagmento was then developed and evaluated using laboratory study, and its design optimized using participatory design sessions. Finally, the author describes how they made the enhanced version of Coagmento available to wider group of users, along with issues and challenges faced. They summarize lessons learned and provide a guideline for designing and developing such collaborative information seeking systems.

INTRODUCTION

It is widely acknowledged that many complex problems can be solved by people working in collaboration (e.g. Denning, 2007; Denning and Yaholkovsky, 2008). The same has been argued for information seeking tasks. For instance, Twidale and Nichols (1996) argued that introducing support for collaboration into information retrieval systems would help users to learn and use the systems more effectively. Levy and Marshall (1994, p.163) noted "...support for communication and collaboration is as important for information-seeing activities, and ... indeed, support for the former is needed to support the latter." Morris

DOI: 10.4018/978-1-61350-201-3.ch013

(2008) also found that people working in information intensive projects often desire to collaborate.

Despite the importance of collaborating in information seeking projects, there is a lack of specialized tools that support collaborative information seeking (CIS). Systems such as Ariadne (Twidale et al., 1997) and SearchTogether (Morris and Horvitz, 2007) provide specialized solutions to particular domains, viz., reference desk and web searching respectively, but we have yet to see a wider and more ubiquitous spread of such tools in CIS activities.

In this chapter we describe our efforts over two years duration to design, develop, and deploy a CIS System using good design practices from literature, understandings gained by interviewing and studying users, and a drive to provide specialized solutions within a user's existing and familiar environment. The evolution of this system, called Coagmento,[1] is presented in the remainder of this chapter with logical sections on design, development, and deployment, along with relevant studies. The chapter concludes with a summary of lessons learned and directions for the future work.

DESIGN

To provide an effective solution for CIS, we spent significant efforts on the design phase. This section provides details about how we derived design specifications for Coagmento, built a preliminary interface, tested it with pilot runs, obtained feedback using cognitive walkthroughs, and enhanced the design specifications using participatory design sessions.

Personal Interviews

As Grudin (1994, p.93) pointed out, *"many expensive failures in developing and marketing software that is designed to support groups are not due to technical problems; they result from not understanding the unique demands this class of software imposes on developers and users."* Such views are reaffirmed by recent works such as (Shah, 2009). Keeping this in mind, we interviewed a number of people who work and/or teach in information intensive domains, asking questions about their past and present collaborative projects. The details of this study are reported in (Shah, 2010a). Here we will report only those findings that are relevant to the system design.

We discovered that email and face-to-face meetings are some of the most popular methods of collaboration. These methods represent two extremes of the classical model of collaborative methods (Rodden, 1991; Twidale and Nichols, 1996), where email fits on the remote and asynchronous end, and meetings fit on the co-located and synchronous end. However, due to the changing structure of work environments and habits (people working on multiple projects with different sets of collaborators, across multiple sessions, and with multiple devices), the need to fill in the gap between these extremes is more apparent than ever.

While most of the respondents wished for better tools for collaboration, they agreed they would have a hard time departing from familiar tools, such as email and IM, even though these tools were not explicitly designed to support collaboration. Even if people know about tools such as del.icio.us, they still send website links to each other over email. System designers and developers face a grave implication due to this fact; they need to provide seamless integration of tools that support collaboration within a user's existing working environment rather than making him choose between his tried-and-tested method and a new tool. This finding reflects the views of Grudin (1994), where he suggested extending an existing single-user system, with which a user is already familiar, with groupware features to minimize the cognitive load and maximize the adoption rate. As one of the respondent admitted in our interviews, "We focus on results, and not how to do it."

Preliminary Design of Coagmento

In order to come up with initial design specifications for Coagmento, two works are particularly helpful: one based on a general notion of collaboration, and the other more specific to designing a collaborative system. Surowiecki (2004) lists four conditions for a successful collaboration: (1) diversity of opinion, (2) independence, (3) decentralization, and (4) aggregation. Morris and Horvitz (2007) presented the SearchTogether system based on supporting (1) awareness, (2) division of labor, and (3) persistence for collaboration. Based on these works and the responses from the personal interviews, the following set of guidelines for designing a user-centered CIS system are inferred.

1. The system should provide an effective way for users to communicate with each other.
2. The system should allow (and encourage) each user to make individual contributions to the collaboration.
3. The system should coordinate user actions, information requests, and responses to support an active and interactive collaboration. This collaboration could be synchronous or asynchronous, and co-located or remote.
4. Users need to agree to and follow a set of rules to carry out a productive collaboration. For instance, if they have a disagreement on the relevancy of an information object, they should discuss and negotiate; they should arrive at a mutually agreeable solution rather than continuing to dispute it. The system needs to support discussion and negotiation processes among the users.
5. The system should provide a mechanism to let the users not only explore their individual differences, but also negotiate roles and responsibilities. There may be a situation in which one user leads the group and others follow (cooperate), but the real strength of collaboration lies in having the authority vested in the collective.

Using the above guidelines, a prototype system called Coagmento was developed that allows two people to work together for seeking information. Collaborators can work synchronously or asynchronously, and they may be co-located or remotely connected. This version of Coagmento was designed to work with a specific collection rather than the open web. The main screen of Coagmento is shown in Figure 1. Let us now see how the above listed characteristics are realized in Coagmento.

- Coagmento includes a search interface, chat, and document space (the same space where the results are displayed in the figure), as well as various marking facilities (discussed later) - all in one place.
- All of these tools are presented on a single interface and readily accessible. There is no need to switch to different windows or tabs as in SearchTogether.
- Coagmento displays the partnership information and provides visual feedback based on one's partner's as well as one's own actions. For instance, if a document is already viewed by either of the persons in a pair, it will be highlighted anywhere it appears in a rank-list for both of them.
- Coagmento keeps a log of all the queries used during a search session.[2] The list of these queries is presented on the interface. Unlike SearchTogether, clicking on a query executes fresh results, and not its history.
- The users of Coagmento can save any document that they find useful or flag it to be discussed with their partners (Figure 2). Once again, these two lists are readily available on the interface and clicking on the name of a document there brings up that document to view.

Figure 1. Coagmento v1: design version

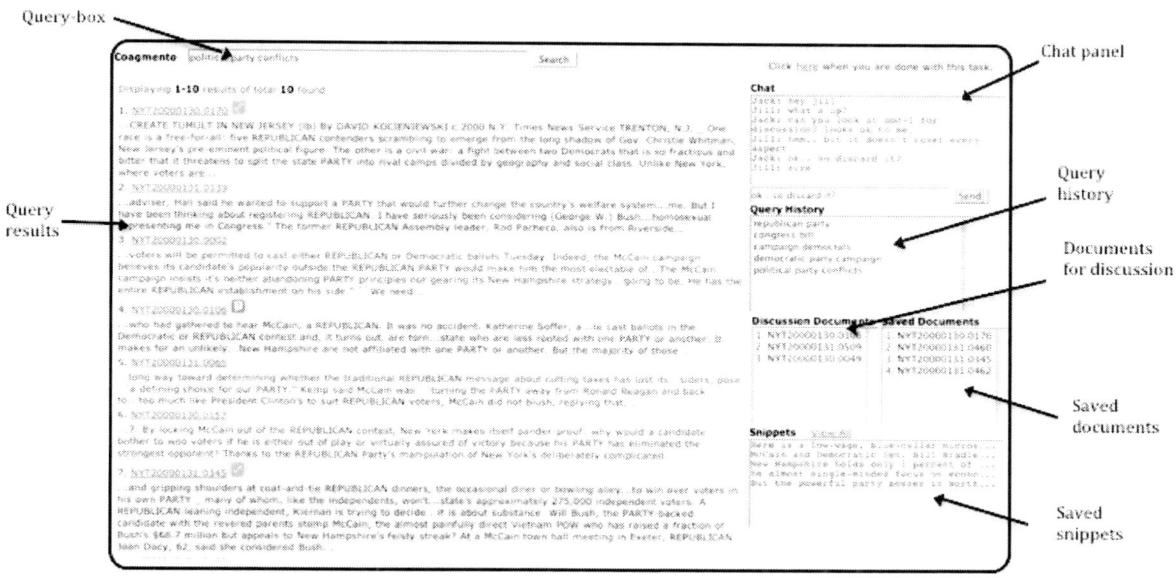

- If a user is working alone, he may not see much use in writing notes about everything that is saved as he may have an intuitive understanding about the relevance of those results. While working with a partner, on the other hand, the user may need to convey *what* and *why* aspects about the usefulness of a document. Coagmento allows a user to add notes to any document (Figure 2). Morris and Horvitz (2007) found such a feature useful, but they also realized that they needed a way for users to simply highlight and save portions of pages. Coagmento provides a way to 'snip' a passage while viewing a document that the user found useful (Figure 2). This is done by highlighting any text on any displayed page and clicking on the 'Snip' button on the toolbar.
- Coagmento saves the state information. This means a user can leave a session and when he comes back, he will find the session as it was, with some possible updates in case his partner kept working while he was gone. This allows the users to collaborate in either synchronous or asynchronous mode. There is an indication on the interface to let a user know if his partner is online or not.

Based on the description above, it should be clear that in principle, Coagmento builds on the framework of other tools such as SearchTogether, and extends them in certain ways. One aspect of SearchTogether that Coagmento does not implement fully is the division of labor. There are three ways in which this feature is realized in SearchTogether: (1) chat, (2) recommendations, and (3) split search. Coagmento has a chat feature, which can be used to talk about the distribution of the work. As far as the recommendations feature is concerned, the authors of SearchTogether found it underutilized. They concluded that rather than providing a "recommend" option, providing a "share this" option would allow a better way of sending pages back and forth. Coagmento does this through its "discuss this document" feature. For the SearchTogether system, it was found that

Figure 2. Toolbar provided on top of the document being viewed with Coagmento

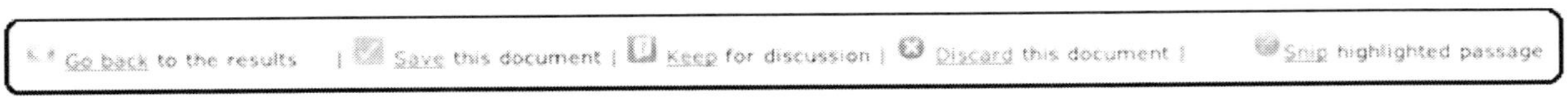

the automatic division of labor features such as split search were not heavily used. The usefulness of such features needs further investigation.

Cognitive Walkthroughs

To obtain feedback on various functions that Coagmento offered, we provided cognitive walkthroughs to 11 different participants from age 25 to 58 and with diverse backgrounds. These participants were graduate students and faculty members in the fields of information science, library science, social science, and journalism. In general, the participants were mature researchers and/or academicians in their respective fields. A majority of these participants also taught various courses relating to information and library science, and media and journalism. They, therefore, could talk not only from their personal experiences, but also from those of their students. Further details of this study can be found in (Shah, 2009). The findings from this study can be summarized as follows.

- Ability to effectively collect and share information is highly desired from a CIS system. People typically do this using traditional tried-and-tested tools such as email and IM, without realizing that there could be more effective ways of doing it in collaborative projects. Coagmento allows the users to easily collect and share snippets of information, which most participants reported to be a unique feature. However, one may not want to use a CIS system such as Coagmento just because it has a couple of unique features. As noted before, we need to understand the larger context and environment in which people collaborate for information seeking projects.
- It was a pleasant discovery that the participants saw Coagmento's use even in non-collaborative projects. Such appropriation is important to have for a successful groupware system, as Grudin (1994) noted.
- The participants asked to see more information on the interface, including time stamps. This was important feedback, yet at the same time created a design challenge. How much information is enough and how much is too much? Should we show day, date, as well as time in hour, minutes, and seconds? We need to develop systems that allow the users to choose this. Having a configurable interface can let the users work through its features without getting overwhelmed.

Based on the lessons learned from the demonstrative walkthroughs, Coagmento was enhanced primarily to support a real life testing of the system. The TREC ciQA (Complex Interactive QA) 2007 data-set was used as the collection for this version of Coagmento. This data-set had nearly one million documents from various news sources. The collection was indexed using the Lemur Toolkit,[3] and a modified Indri[4] search service served the requests in the background. The following subsection describes a few pilot runs done with this system.

Pilot Runs

To test the effectiveness of Coagmento in terms of providing appropriate functionalities for people working together while seeking information, three pilot runs were conducted during three different undergraduate classes at UNC Chapel Hill. Together, these three pilot runs had 36 participants, paired randomly in 18 groups.

At the start of a run, usernames and passwords were handed out in a random order to the participants. That way, they were not able to pick their partners, although they might already know each other. At first, a brief overview of Coagmento was presented. Then they were allowed to login to the system. Following is the outline of the entire experiment.

1. Each participant was given a drill task: "You are reporters at New York Times. You are working on a story that could show a possible link between President Bush and Bono, the U2 Rock Star. In order to do this, you are first investigating what common interests they both have. May be they are involved in the same project or cause, or they like the same baseball team! It's your job to find out as many such common interests as you can. Find relevant documents and collect the snippets that have the related information on this topic." When the users first login, they were presented with this drill task. They were also given a printed copy of this task, so that they could refer to it during the task.
2. Once they read the task description on the screen, they could start the task and were taken to the main interface screen of Coagmento.
3. The participants were allowed to try this interface out with the given drill task for about 5 minutes. One of the first things they did during this time was introducing themselves to their partners and finding out who their partners were. They were encouraged to use every feature of the interface.
4. They were asked to click 'Done' and the system took them out of that task.
5. The users were now presented with a new task: "You are detectives, specializing in antiquities and historical documents thefts. Your current assignment is to find the evidence for transport of stolen antiquities from Egypt to other countries. Since such evidence often appears when such antiquities are returned to Egypt from other countries, you should search and file news about these goods being returned. Find relevant documents and collect the snippets that have the related information on this topic." This was the real task and once again they were given a written copy of the task.
6. They were asked to take about 10 minutes to do this task, and allowed about 12 minutes before asking them to declare this task 'Done'.
7. The participants filled in the end of task questionnaire and the exit questionnaire.

At the end of this exercise an open discussion about this experience and the system was conducted. From log mining and discussions with the participants, it became clear that the participants rarely looked at a document already viewed by their teammates. Given the nature of the system, the participants had to start with a query to get a list of documents to look at. At the level of query formulation, the participants in the same team may use the same or similar queries, but once they get a list of results, they would avoid looking at each other's documents. This has two implications. First, if a task is time-bound, exploratory, and easily dividable, the participants may try not to do overlapping work. They may work individually trying to get as much information as possible, and then combine with their collaborators' individual information to create the group's product. Second, in order to easily know what has already been done by one's self and/or others in the group the interface needs to provide ready support. This reaffirms the value of awareness in collaborative projects.

Participatory Design Phase I

To further obtain and revise our design specifications, we organized participatory design sessions in a graduate HCI seminar class at UNC Chapel Hill during Fall 2008 semester. There were about a dozen graduate students who participated over four sessions, separated by 3-5 weeks. These sessions focused on discussing certain theoretical ideas of collaboration, and coming up with design specifications for an ideal CIS system.

Some of the early discussions during these sessions were focused on definitions of collaboration, describing past experiences with collaborative projects, and identifying difficulties in such situations. Later the discussions were targeted to come up with design specifications for an ideal CIS system.

The participants mentioned several situations in which they were required to or wanted to do collaboration. Given that the participants were graduate students, a common situation was collaborating with co-authors on an article.

One of the issues that the participants reported during such collaborations is coordination. Often, the work is divided among the collaborators in the beginning of the project and a good amount of coordination is required to make sure that everyone is following a common timeline, and that their individual contributions come together in a meaningful product. For instance, in the case of co-authoring an article, the authors have to do their parts, exchange them with each other by a set deadline, and then arrange them to create the final write-up.

Most participants reported using general tools such as email, and specialized tools such as Google Docs for collecting and sharing information with their collaborators. Some of the participants had used RefWorks for collaborative writing projects. While Google Docs was a common choice for writing-related projects, the participants identified several issues with it. They include not being able to attach files, not having search queries captured, and not having time stamp information stored with different actions.

Overall, these participatory design sessions helped us reaffirm some of the issues that were discovered during the literature review and previous design studies, and helped in obtaining a variety of ideas from the participants through highly interactive group discussions.

Two major issues were identified during these sessions for designing a CIS system: (1) the role of awareness, and (2) support for a common workspace. The following suggestions were received for presenting *awareness* on the interface.

1. A tree or a map to see what path other collaborators took.
2. Personal histories for each of the persons in the group using a zoomable timeline or flowchart.
3. Provide history with different layers like Photoshop. One can then select the layer that he wants to look or work with, but finally they all come together to produce a finished picture.
4. Create switchable overlays of the interface, so one could switch between overlays depending on the requirement at the moment.
5. Provide a histogram of activities.
6. Have multiple tabs on the interface, like a modern browser, allowing one to have multiple views of the same project open and switch between them as needed.
7. Provide feed updates like Twitter.

The following suggestions were given with respect to the *workspace* that the participants would like to see in a CIS system.

1. Ability to choose one's role (e.g., supervisor, reader, information gatherer) and contribute through the workspace based on that role.
2. Sticky notes to remind one's self or give to other collaborators.
3. Use different attributes for/with different objects on the workspace to communicate effectively with each other. Such attributes include color, icons, size, location, gradients, avatars, and sounds.

A fair amount of discussion was also devoted to the issue of searching in groups. The participants concurred that how one searches in collaboration depends on where the search falls in the whole continuum of creativity, and creativity is an individual thing. Given that, a system that lets multiple people search together and share their results, should allow the participants to express their individual creativity and then bridge multiple inputs to create a collaborative product.

Based on these discussions and findings, we enhanced Coagmento, specifically paying attention to awareness and common workspace functions. While other suggestions and realizations from this study were also valuable, we decided to keep them for the future work. This allowed us to develop a complete CIS system that we could test in laboratory. The next section provides details of the development phase.

DEVELOPMENT

Based on the findings and experiences with previous studies involving Coagmento, it was once again redesigned. The version of Coagmento used in each of the design studies described so far was website based, which means, that all the participants of a collaborative project had access to the various services such as searching, saving and sharing the results, and chat through a single website. An advantage of this approach is that it gives good control to the researcher over what the users do on this website. However, the biggest disadvantage is that the user is not able use the web as he wishes. Besides, the user may not always want to search. This realization led to redesigning Coagmento with a very different approach, while still offering the same functionalities as before.

The new Coagmento was developed with a client-server architecture, where the client is implemented as a Firefox plug-in that helps multiple people working in collaboration to communicate, and search, share and organize information. The server component stores and provides all the objects and actions collected from the client. Due to this decoupling, Coagmento provides a flexible architecture that allows its users to be co-located or remote, working synchronously or asynchronously, and use different platforms. This version of Coagmento used several of the suggestions and lessons derived from the design studies, while leaving out others due to the limited scope of this work. In particular, Coagmento was redesigned considering the aspects of awareness, communication, and ease of use of sharing while online information seeking.

A screenshot of this new Coagmento is given in Figure 3. As we can see, it includes a toolbar and a sidebar. The toolbar has several buttons that helps one collect information and be aware of the progress in a given collaboration. The toolbar has three major parts:

1. **Buttons for collecting information and making annotations.** These buttons help one save or remove a webpage, make annotations on a webpage, and highlight and collect text snippets. The windows that pop-up while collecting a snippet and making an annotation from/on a webpage are shown in Figure 4 and 5.
2. **Page-specific statistics.** The middle portion of the toolbar shows various statistics, such as the number of views, annotations, and snippets, for the displayed page. A user can click on a given statistic and obtain more

Figure 3. Coagmento v2: development version

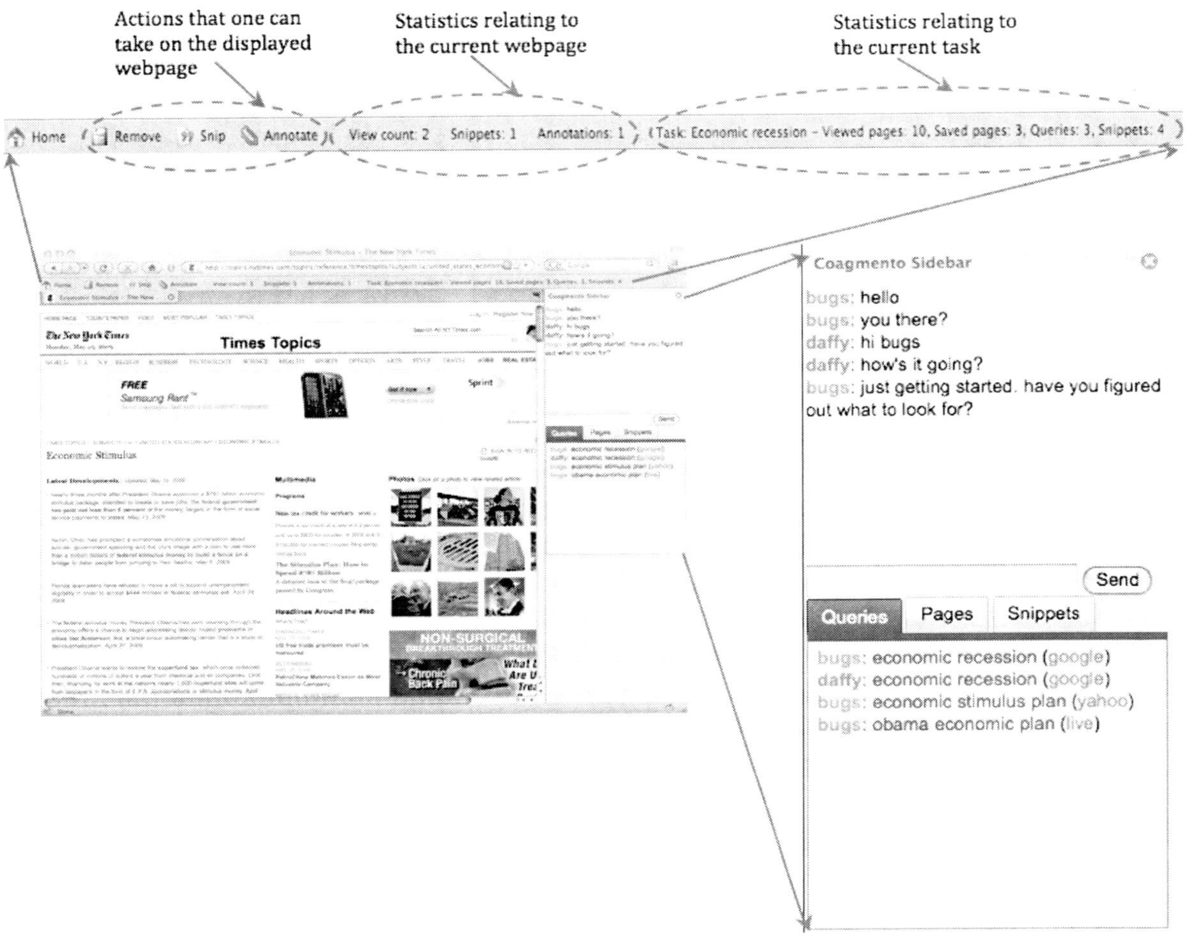

information. For instance, clicking on the number of snippets will bring up a window that shows all the snippets collected by the collaborators from the displayed page.

3. **Project-specific statistics.** The last portion of the toolbar displays task/project name and various statistics, including number of pages visited and saved, about the current project. Clicking on that portion brings up the workspace where one can view all the collected objects (pages and snippets) brought in by the collaborators for that project.

The sidebar features a chat window, under which there are three tabs with the history of search engine queries, saved pages and snippets. With each of these objects, the user who created or collected that object is shown. Anyone in the group can access an object by clicking on it. For instance, one can click on a query issued by anyone in the group to re-run that query and bring up the results in the main browser window.

Laboratory Study

To test various awareness and other functions of Coagmento, we conducted a laboratory study in-

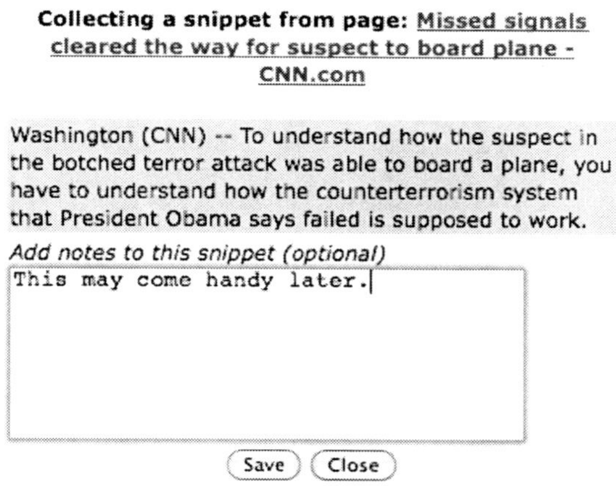

Figure 4. Snippets window

volving 84 participants in 42 pairs recruited from UNC Chapel Hill. These participants were asked to come to the lab for two different sessions, which were one to two weeks apart. The participants were able to choose the day and time convenient to them using the online recruiting system. Since the participants had to sign up in pairs, both the participants in a given pair already knew each other. In addition to this, it was required that the participants in a given pair should have done some collaborative work with each other before; thus, making sure they not only know each other, but also are comfortable working with each other on a collaborative project. The approval of a pair's participation in this study was based on these criteria. Participants were compensated $25 each for their participation in two sessions.

During the first session the participants were shown a video tutorial demonstrating the use of Coagmento and the process of collecting relevant information (snippets of text). After the tutorial, the participants were placed in different rooms so that they could not talk to each other directly or see what the other person was doing (Figure 6). Both the participants used typical mid-end PC workstations, running Windows XP, with Ethernet connectivity and 19" monitors.

The participants were given two exploratory search tasks, one on economic recession and the other on social networking. They started with the first task, and were asked to switch to the second task after about 20 minutes.

For the second session, the participants were given a refresher of the system and shown how to compile their final report by grouping their collected snippets into different categories for a given task. The categories were presented in the task statement and corresponded to different aspects of the work task. The participants were then asked to take their places in the room other than the one they had used the last time, to take care of any bias the participants may have for the machine or the room they used. They resumed their first task that they had started in the previous session. About 15 minutes later, they were asked to switch to the second task from the first session.

The participants were asked to rate (scale 1 to 7) several factors about the system at the end of each session as shown in the following questionnaire. The questionnaire was derived from the original Computer System Usability Questionnaire (Lewis, 1995)[5] removing those statements that were not relevant for this study.

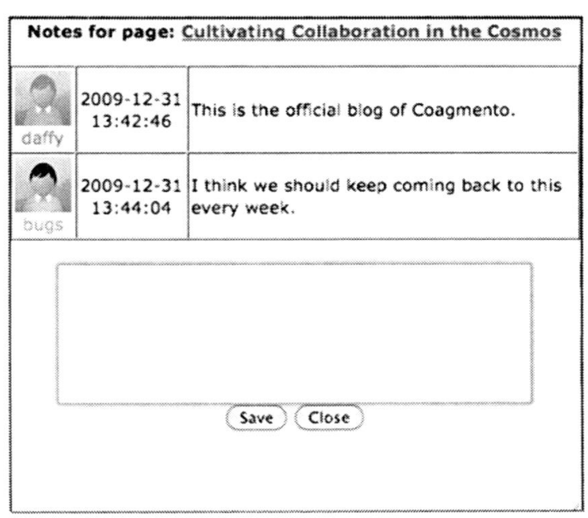

Figure 5. Annotations window

Figure 6. Participants during a study session

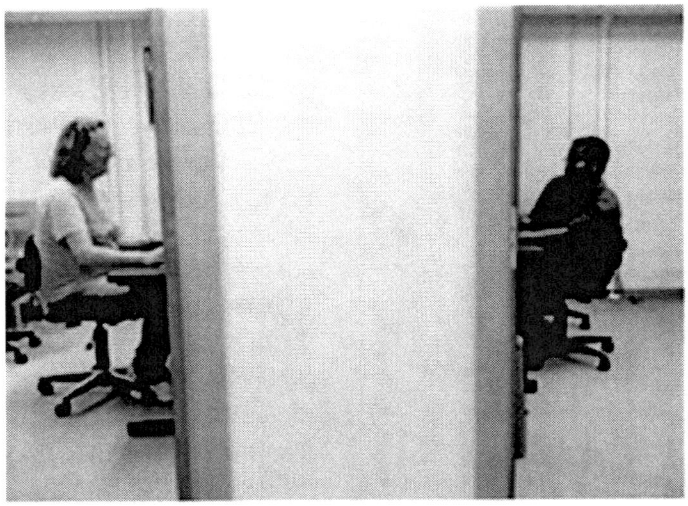

Q1. Overall, I am satisfied with how easy it is to use this system.
Q2. I can effectively complete my work using this system.
Q3. I am able to efficiently complete my work using this system.
Q4. I feel comfortable using this system.
Q5. It was easy to learn to use this system.
Q6. I believe I became productive quickly using this system.
Q7. It is easy to find the information I need.
Q8. The information provided for the system is easy to understand.
Q9. The organization of information on the system screens (toolbar, sidebar) is clear.
Q10. The interface of this system is pleasant.
Q11. I like using the interface of this system.
Q12. This system has all the functions and capabilities I expect it to have.
Q13. Overall, I am satisfied with this system.

The responses on this questionnaire are summarized in Figure 7. As we can see, the participants rated each of the statements quite high, indicating good ease of use and satisfaction with the system. In addition to these responses, we let the participants make free-form suggestions about improving Coagmento. Two of the most common features we received the requests for were: having ability to make notes for a project, and receiving notifications of their collaborators' actions in real-time.

Figure 7. Summary of responses by 84 participants on ease of use and satisfaction questionnaire for the lab study

Question	Mean	s.d.
Q1	5.45	1.781
Q2	5.47	1.801
Q3	5.48	1.844
Q4	5.58	1.830
Q5	5.89	1.859
Q6	5.51	1.798
Q7	5.63	1.846
Q8	5.76	1.772
Q9	5.60	1.890
Q10	5.21	1.834
Q11	5.20	1.802
Q12	4.70	1.866
Q13	5.35	1.768

We redesigned Coagmento based on these findings, which is presented in the following subsection.

Enhanced Coagmento

A re-conceptualized and re-implemented Coagmento is shown in Figure 8. This version of Coagmento has two core components: a plug-in for Firefox browser, and a web-based collaborative space, called *CSpace*. The plug-in includes a toolbar and a sidebar. Following is a brief description of how different components of Coagmento support collaborative information seeking, synthesis, and sense-making.

Using Coagmento, one could now do the following activities related to information seeking effectively: collect, share, and recommend webpages using the toolbar, refind and reuse information using the sidebar, and add value (tags, notes, etc.) to found information. Coagmento supports information synthesis by the way of providing a workspace in *CSpace*, where an individual or group could organize the collected information and compile a report. Coagmento also includes support for alerts or notifications, ability to make recommendations to an individual or the whole group, and a function to monitor and relate information as the group works through their information seeking process. Such support could help one in their sense-making processes. In addition, Coagmento provides integrated support for communication, note-taking, and collecting text snippets or other objects from webpages.

Figure 8. Coagmento v3: deployment

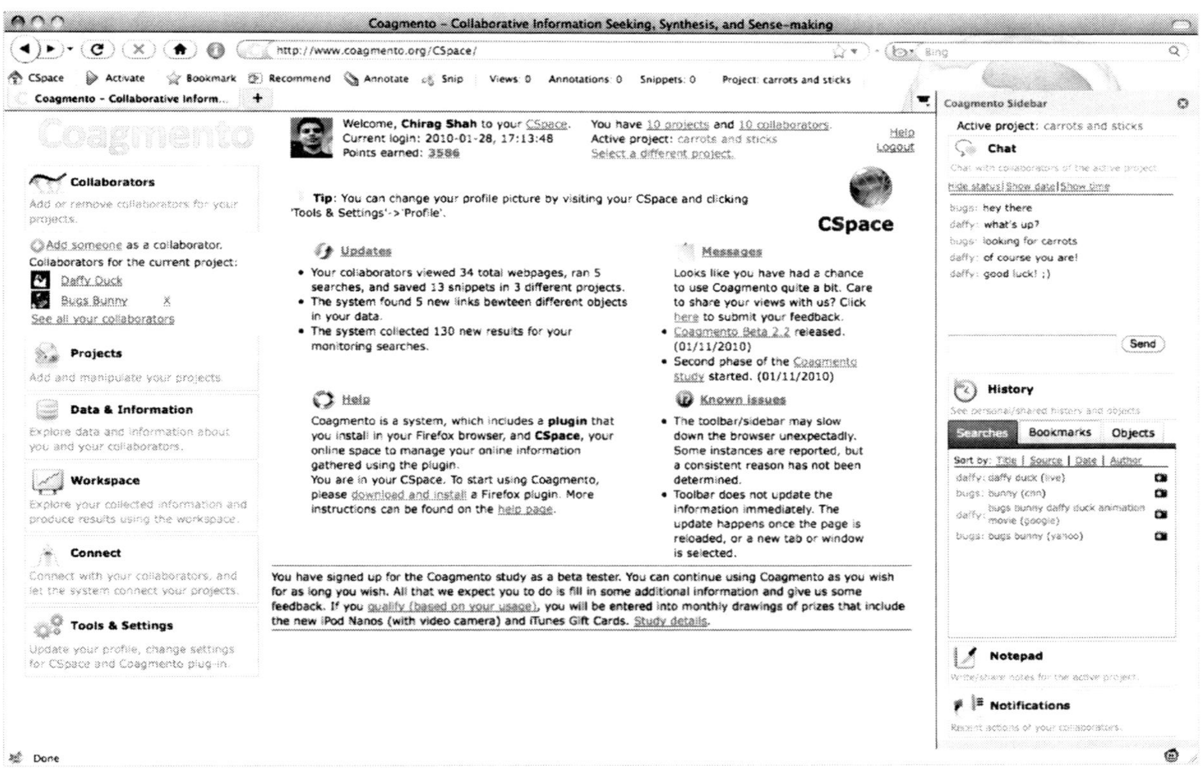

DEPLOYMENT

In this section we will discuss how we deployed Coagmento as a freely available system for anyone to try, and an online field study conducted with it. We will wrap up our discussion by presenting another phase of participatory design sessions, informing us about the next iteration of the design phase.

Field Study

Using several email lists, we announced the availability of Coagmento (Shah, 2010b). Nearly 100 individuals joined Coagmento as users. We also encouraged these users to sign up as participants for our online field study, and provide us periodic feedback. 24 users agreed to be such participants, but not all of them provided the requested feedback. A summary of the responses on the same questionnaire with 13 statements presented before is provided in Figure 9.

Here we can see that the ratings are not as high as those obtained during the laboratory study, even though the new version of Coagmento includes several enhancements. A part of this disparity can be attributed to the fact that for a lab study, the subjects had to appear in person, and they may have felt more sympathetic to the project while providing their feedback. It is still encouraging to learn that people find this system easy to learn (Q4), even when we could not directly teach them its operation.

Figure 9. Summary of responses by 19 participants on ease of use and satisfaction questionnaire for the field study

Question	Mean	s.d.
Q1	4.00	1.371
Q2	4.55	1.810
Q3	3.80	1.567
Q4	5.44	1.688
Q5	3.83	1.823
Q6	3.88	1.536
Q7	4.05	1.248
Q8	4.71	1.382
Q9	4.16	1.465
Q10	4.77	1.563
Q11	3.15	1.625
Q12	3.76	1.300
Q13	3.82	1.467

Participatory Design Phase II

In order to revise our design specifications, we conducted another phase of participatory design sessions during the Fall 2009 semester for the same graduate level HCI seminar, now with a different set of nearly 15 students. This time, we not only discussed general issues relating to CIS system design and implementation, but also specific aspects of Coagmento as available at the time.

We let the participants try the enhanced Coagmento (v3) and provide us feedback. Similar to the previous studies, we asked the participants to rate various aspects of the system for its ease of use and satisfaction. Once again, not everyone that tried the system responded. A summary of the responses that we received is given in Figure 10.

As we can see, once again, the participants found it relatively easy to learn the system (Q4), and reported reasonably high ratings for other aspects of the system as well. In the free-form field asking them about two aspects that they liked about Coagmento, a majority of the participants identified the ability to save (bookmark) any webpage and collect snippets from anywhere as the biggest positive points. One of the participants suggested incorporating a citation builder like Zotero[6] with snippets collection. In general, the participants appreciated having ready access to their history (saved pages, snippets, and queries).

The participants, however, expected several other features not offered by the version of Coagmento they tried. This came up in Q12 (Figure 10) as well as in the responses to an open-ended

Figure 10. Summary of responses by 8 participants on ease of use and satisfaction questionnaire for the participatory design phase II study

Question	Mean	s.d.
Q1	4.75	1.16
Q2	4.38	1.50
Q3	4.50	0.92
Q4	6.00	0.53
Q5	4.13	0.99
Q6	4.50	1.30
Q7	3.88	0.99
Q8	4.50	0.75
Q9	3.63	0.91
Q10	4.50	2.13
Q11	5.00	1.60
Q12	4.25	0.46
Q13	5.50	0.75

question asking them to list a couple of aspects of Coagmento that they did not like. One of the common feature requests that Coagmento did not have was the ability to save snippets from PDF files. This was identified as a highly valuable function in academia, since many scholarly articles appear in PDF format. Another requested feature was the way to organize collected snippets and notes.

In the discussion session followed by online feedback, the following additional issues came up.

- The participants reported experiencing an additional overhead for using Coagmento. They found the installation and learning to use Coagmento to be easy, but incorporating it in existing practices a bit hard. Due to the overhead involved with different actions, starting with login to selecting a project, and finally revisiting the collected information, the participants found themselves not utilizing Coagmento much.
- As a feature, Coagmento allows one to explicitly turn on and off its ability to record one's browsing. While this feature was provided as a way to facilitate privacy, it ended up being an obstacle sometimes as the participants forgot to turn it on. The participants were divided on the issue of making the recording on or off by default.
- Another issue the participants reported facing was of remembering to label a new project. Some of the participants also indicated that it was difficult for them to remember the actual name they gave to a project several days back. In other words, project management was below par and unclear.

Overall, the participatory design sessions provided a platform to engage in interactive discussions with several experienced participants, identify some of the key issues in designing a CIS system, and obtain feedback on an enhanced version of Coagmento.

CONCLUSION AND FUTURE WORK

We presented a description of a new CIS system, Coagmento, from its design to deployment over a period of two years. There are several realizations we had during the course of designing, developing, and deploying this system. Some of the relevant lessons learned are listed below. These may help researcher and developers working in this field for developing and evaluating their own systems, as well as investigating various issues relating to CIS.

- It does not take long for people to learn such a new kind of collaborative interface. They may still not see the usefulness of all its features, but they can certainly start using them in a matter of a few minutes.
- There are certain tools that an average user is very familiar with and he expects certain kind of behavior from such a tool. In Coagmento, these were search results and

chat box. For search results, people tend to compare with their familiar search services, such as Google. They want their results fast, and a lot in number, even if they never go past the first page. Similarly, almost everyone has used some kind of IM and they expect the chat panel to behave just like their favorite IM program.

- It is hard to make people collaborate in an unrealistic situation. Most of these users did not see the value in collaborating for such a common task as searching. The cognitive load for using the tools and/or collaborating was probably more than the potential return. However, it is quite possible that the same set of users would be more willing to use these tools the next time as they may have become more comfortable with them.
- People appreciate and desire unique features, such as collecting and sharing snippets of information effectively. However, such features themselves may not be compelling enough to adopt the whole system. One needs to understand these features in a larger context and provide proper support for that context as well. In the case of snippets, it was discovered that, while effectively collecting snippets is a desired feature, the users want to be able to use those snippets in some way. This may involve organizing the snippets and using them to synthesize a report. Thus, without the support for this larger context of being able to utilize the snippets, allowing the users to simply collect the snippets may not be a strong reason for system adoption.
- Shared awareness and workspace were found to be some of the most desired features a CIS system should provide.
- Using a new CIS system is not simply about adopting a new tool, but it is about getting used to a new way of thinking about exploratory and collaborative work practices. Managing a multi-session collaborative project that already has enough complexity could become even more difficult and confusing while using a completely new interface, as reported by our participatory design participants. It is valuable to provide appropriate support for control, communication, and awareness; but, if it is done without understanding existing practices and cognitive load required to adopt the system, we may end up hurting its usage and adoption.

We are continuing to monitor and analyze the usage of Coagmento v3. This version is available as a free and open-source system from http://www.coagmento.org/, allowing many to not only use it for personal and collaborative information seeking projects, but also experiment with various aspects of CIS system designs and functions.

Currently we are re-implementing several parts of Coagmento to create a highly modular and flexible framework that can be easily extended and integrated into exiting personal, social, and collaborative work environments. For instance, we are in the process of implementing a plug-in for Facebook that will allow the users to connect to potential collaborators through their social network, thus, leveraging social ties for collaborative projects.

ACKNOWLEDGMENT

A part of the work reported here is supported by NSF grant # IIS 0812363, and a part supported by the Yahoo! Campus Innovation Award.

REFERENCES

Denning, P. J. (2007). Mastering the mess. *Communications of the ACM, 50*(4), 21–25. doi:10.1145/1232743.1232763

Denning, P. J., & Yaholkovsky, P. (2008). Getting to "We.". *Communications of the ACM, 51*(4), 19–24. doi:10.1145/1330311.1330316

Grudin, J. (1994). Groupware and social dynamics: eight challenges for developers. *Communications of the ACM, 37*(1), 92–105. doi:10.1145/175222.175230

Levy, D. M., & Marshall, C. C. (1994). What color was George Washington's white horse? A look at assumptions underlying digital libraries. In *Proceedings of Digital Libraries* (pp. 163-169).

Lewis, J. R. (1995). IBM Computer Usability Satisfaction Questionnaires: Psychometric Evaluation and Instructions for Use. *International Journal of Human-Computer Interaction, 7*(1), 57–58. doi:10.1080/10447319509526110

Morris, M. R. (2008). A Survey of Collaborative Web Search Practices. In *Proceedings of ACM SIGCHI Conference on Human Factors in Computing Systems* (pp. 1657-1660). Florence, Italy.

Morris, M. R., & Horvitz, E. (2007). SearchTogether: An Interface for Collaborative Web Search. In *ACM Symposium on User Interface Software and Technology (UIST)* (pp. 3-12). Newport, RI.

Rodden, T. (1991). A Survey of CSCW Systems. *Interacting with Computers, 3*(3), 319–353. doi:10.1016/0953-5438(91)90020-3

Shah, C. (2009). Lessons and Challenges for Collaborative Information Seeking (CIS) Systems Developers. In *GROUP 2009 Workshop on Collaborative Information Behavior*. Sanibel Island, Florida.

Shah, C. (2010a). *Proceedings of Collaborative Information Retrieval workshop at CSCW 2010*. Savannah, GA: Working in Collaboration - What, Why, and How.

Shah, C. (2010b). (an integrated demo). In *Proceedings of Computer Supported Cooperative Work (CSCW)*. Savannah, GA: Coagmento – A Collaborative Information Seeking, Synthesis and Sense-Making Framework.

Surowiecki, J. (2004). *Wisdom of Crowds: Why the Many Are Smarter Than the Few and How Collective Wisdom Shapes Business, Economies, Societies and Nations*. New York: Doubleday Publishing.

Twidale, M. B., & Nichols, D. M. (1996). Collaborative browsing and visualisation of the search process. In *Proceedings of Aslib* (Vol. 48, pp. 177-182). Retrieved from http://www.comp.lancs.ac.uk/computing/research/cseg/projects/ariadne/docs/elvira96.html.

Twidale, M. B., Nichols, D. M., & Paice, C. D. (1997). Browsing is a Collaborative Process. *Information Processing & Management, 33*(6), 761–783. doi:10.1016/S0306-4573(97)00040-X

ENDNOTES

1. In Latin, Coagmento means working or joining together.
2. The session can span several sittings or usage of the system throughout the project.
3. http://www.lemurproject.org/
4. http://www.lemurproject.org/indri/
5. Also available from http://oldwww.acm.org/perlman/question.cgi?form=CSUQ.
6. http://www.zotero.org/

Compilation of References

AIML. (n.d.). Retrieved from http://www.alicebot.org/aiml.html

Albers, M. J. (2008). Human-information interaction. In C. J. Costa, A. Protopsaltis, M. Aparicio, & H. O'Neill (Eds.), *Proceedings of the 26th Annual ACM International Conference on Design of Communication* (pp. 117-124). New York, NY: Association for Computing Machinery.

ALFIN/EEES. (2005). *Habilidades e competencias de gestión da información para aprender a aprender en el marco del espacio europeo de enseñanza superior*. Espanha: Universidade de Granada. Retrieved October 15, 2009, from: www.um.es/dp-lengua-espa/.../habilidades-competencias.pdf.

Alicebot, by R. Wallace. (2011). Retrieved from http://alicebot.blogspot.com/

Allen, J. F. (1995). The TRAINS project: a case study in building a conversational planning agent. *Journal of Experimental & Theoretical Artificial Intelligence*, *7*(1), 7–48. doi:10.1080/09528139508953799

Allen, J. F., Byron, D. K., Dzikovska, M., Ferguson, G., Galescu, L., & Stent, A. (2001). Toward Conversational Human-Computer Interaction. *AI Magazine*, *22*(4), 27–37.

American Library Association. (1989, January). *Report of the presidential Committee on information literacy: final report.* Retrieved October 3, 2009, from: http://www.ala.org/ala/mgrps//divs/acrl/publications/whitepapersreports.cfm

Arant, W., & Payne, L. (2001). The common user interface in academic libraries: Myth or reality? *Library Hi Tech*, *19*(1), 63–73. doi:10.1108/07378830110384601

Arapakis, I., Jose, J. M., & Gray, P. D. (2008). Affective feedback: an investigation into the role of emotions in the information seeking process, *proceedings of the 31st annual international ACM SIGIR conference on Research and development in information retrieval*. Singapore.

Archives de France. (2009). *Thésaurus pour la description et l'indexation des archives locales anciennes, modernes et contemporaines*.Retrieved from http://www.archives-defrance.culture.gouv.fr/gerer/classement/normes-outils/thesaurus/

Arntz, H. (1983). *Information und Hominisation: Grenzlinie der Entwicklung. Vorstudie zu einer Paläologie der Information*. The Hague: FID 627.

Asfari, O., Doan, B.-L., Bourda, Y., & Sansonnet, J. P. (2009). Personalized Access to Information by Query Reformulation Based on the State of the Current Task and User Profile. *Third International Conference on Advances in Semantic Processing*, (113-116).

Atkinson, C., & Kuhne, T. (2003). Model-driven development: a metamodeling foundation. *IEEE Software*, 36–41. doi:10.1109/MS.2003.1231149

Badu, B. R., & O'Brien, A. (2000). Web OPAC interfaces: An overview. *The Electronic Library*, *18*(5), 316–327. doi:10.1108/02640470010354572

Baeza-Yates R.& Ribeiro-Neto B. (1999). *Modern Information Retrieval.* Addison-Wesley Longman. 1999.

Bakhtin, M. (1981). *Marxismo e filosofia da linguagem*. (6Th Ed.). Translated by Michel Lahud e Yara F. Vieira (da edição de Paris: Les Éditions de Minuit, 1977), São Paulo: Hucitec.

Baldauf, M., Dustdar, S., & Rosenberg, F. (2007). A Survey on Context-aware Systems. *International Journal Ad Hoc and Ubiquitous Computing*, *2*(4), 263–277. doi:10.1504/IJAHUC.2007.014070

Barab, S., Evans, M., & Baek, E. (2004). Activity theory as a lens for characterizing the participatory unit. Ed. D. Jonassen, *Handbook of research on educational communications and technology* (pp. 99-214). 2ed. Mahwah, NJ: Lawrence Erlbaum.

Bar-Hillel, Y., & Carnap, R. (1953). Semantic information. *British Journal of Science*, *4*, 147–157. doi:10.1093/bjps/IV.14.147

Barki, H., & Hartwick, J. (2001). Interpersonal conflict and its management in information system development. *Management Information Systems Quarterly*, *25*(2), 195–228. doi:10.2307/3250929

Barthes, R. (1992). *Elementos de semiologia*. Translated by de Izidoro Bilkstein (do original Élements de Sémiologie, Paris: Seuil, 1964). São Paulo: Editora Cultrix.

Barwise, J., & Perry, J. (1983). *Situations and Attitudes*. Cambridge, MA: MIT Press.

Barwise, J., & Seligman, J. (1997). *Information Flows: The Logic of Distributed Systems*. Cambridge, RU: Cambridge University Press.

Bateson, G. (1972). *Steps to an ecology of mind*. New York: Ballantine Books.

Bazire, M., & Brézillon, P. (2005). Understanding Context Before Using It. *5th International and Interdisciplinary Conference, CONTEXT 2005*, Paris, France, (29-40).

Beer, S. (1984). The Viable System Model: its provenance, development, methodology and pathology. *The Journal of the Operational Research Society*, *35*(1), 7–25.

Beghtol, C. (1986, June). Bibliographic classification theory and text linguistics: aboutness analysis, intertextuality and the cognitive act classifying documents. *The Journal of Documentation*, *42*(2), 84–113. doi:10.1108/eb026788

Beghtol, C. (2003). Classification for information retrieval and classification for knowledge discovery: Relationships between "professional" and "naïve" classification. *Knowledge Organization*, *30*(2), 64–73.

Beheshti, J. (2003). The future of OPAC interfaces. In *ALA / CLA Annual Conference. Optimal Design Considerations for Web OPAC Interfaces: A program sponsored by LITA: June 22, 2003, Toronto*. Retrieved June 13, 2005, from http://www.calstatela.edu/library/ALA/ala-claOPAC.htm

Bekaert, J., Ville, D. V. D., Rogge, B., Strauven, I., Koning, E. D., & Walle, R. V. d. (2002). Metadata-based access to multimedia architectural and historical archive collections: a review. *Aslib Proceedings*, *54*(6), 362–371. doi:10.1108/00012530210452564

Bekenstein, J. D. (2003). Information in the Holographic Universe. *Scientific American Magazine*, *289*(2), 58–65. doi:10.1038/scientificamerican0803-58

Belew, R. K. (2000). *Finding Out About*. Cambridge, UK: Cambridge Univ. Press.

Belkin, N. J. (2008). Some(what) grand challenges for information retrieval. *SIGIR Forum*, *42*(1), 47–54. doi:10.1145/1394251.1394261

Belkin, N. J., Cool, C., Stein, A., & Thiel, U. (1995). Cases, scripts, and information- seeking strategies: On the design of interactive information retrieval systems. *Expert Systems with Applications*, *9*(3), 379–396. doi:10.1016/0957-4174(95)00011-W

Belkin, N. J. (2006). Getting Personal: Personalization of Support for Interaction with Information. *Invited talk, Workshop AIR*.

Bénaben, F., Touzi, J., Rajsiri, V., & Pingaud, H. (2006). Collaborative Information System Design. In *11th International Conference of the Association Information and Management (AIM)*, Luxembourg, June 8th to 9th (pp. 281-296). Retrieved May 14, 2009, from http://subs.emis.de/LNI/Proceedings/Proceedings92/gi-proc-092-018.pdf

Benito Ruiz, E. (2009). Infoxication 2.0. In Thomas, M. (Ed.), *Handbook of Research on Web 2.0 and Second Language Learning*. London: Information Science Reference. doi:10.4018/978-1-60566-190-2.ch004

Bergstrom, R. M. (1988). Man as an Information Processor. In P. Hämäläinen, B. Koskkiala, & A.J. Repo (Eds.), *44th FID Conference and Congress records book* (pp. 7-9). Helsinki: FID.

Bernal, A., Magrinyà, A., & Planes, R. (2007). *Norma de Descripción Archivística de Cataluña (NODAC), (Arxivística i gestió documental. Eines; 1)*. Barcelona, Generalitat de Cataluña, from http://www20.gencat.cat/docs/CulturaDepartament/Cultura/Temes/Arxius/Norma%20de%20Descripcio%20Arxivistica%20de%20Catalunya/arxius/NodCast.pdf

Bhattacherjee, A. (2001). Understanding information systems continuance: An expectation-confirmation model. *Management Information Systems Quarterly*, *25*(3), 351–370. doi:10.2307/3250921

BITrum. (n.d.). Retrieved from http://sites.google.com/site/proyectobitrum/

Blake, C., & Pratt, W. (2006a, November). Collaborative information synthesis I: A model of information behaviors of scientists in medicine and public health. *Journal of the American Society for Information Science and Technology*, *57*(13), 1740–1749. doi:10.1002/asi.20487

Blake, C., & Pratt, W. (2006b, December). Collaborative Information Synthesis II: Recommendations for Information Systems to Support Synthesis Activities. *Journal of the American Society for Information Science and Technology*, *57*(14), 1888–1895.doi:10.1002/asi.20486

Bloom, B. S. (1979). *Taxionomia de Objetivos Educacionais, domínio cognitivo 1*. (7Th Ed.). Translated by Flávia Maria Sant'Anna, Porto Alegre: Editora Globo.

Bloom, B. S., & Krathwohl, D. R, Masia, Bertran B. (1974). *Taxionomia de Objetivos Educacionais, domínio afetivo 2*. Translated by Jurema Alcides Cunha. 3ª impressão. Porto Alegre: Editora Globo.

Bondarenko, D. M. (2007). Approaching "complexity" in anthropology and complexity studies: The principles of sociopolitical organization and the prospects for bridging the interdisciplinary gap. *E:CO, 9(3)*, 62-74. Retrieved January 22, 2011, from http://emergentpublications.com/eco/ECO_papers/Issue_9_3_6_PH.pdf

Boss, R. W. (2005, March). *Library portals*. Retrieved from American Library Association Website: http://www.ala.org/ala/pla/plapubs/technotes/librarywebportals.htm

Boterf, G. L. (2003). *Desenvolvendo a competência dos profissionais*. Porto Alegre: Artmed.

Bouchard, H., & Nie, J. Y. (2006). *Modèles de langue appliqués à la recherche d'information contextuelle », Actes de la Conférence en Recherche d'Information et Applications*. CORIA.

Bouchet, F., & Sansonnet, J. P. (2007) Caractérisation de Requêtes d'Assistance à partir de corpus. *Conférence MFI'07*, Paris.

Bourdieu, P. (1982). *Ce que parler veut dire*. Paris: Fayard.

Bradley, G. (2006). *Social and community informatics: Humans on the Net*. New York, NY: Taylor & Francis.

Branski, R. M. (2004, January/June). Recuperação de informações na Web. *Perspectiva Ciência Informação*, *9*(1), 70–87.

Brezillon, P. (1999). Context in problem solving: a survey. *The Knowledge Engineering Review*, *14*(1), 47–80. doi:10.1017/S0269888999141018

Brier, S. (2008). *Cybersemiotics: why information is not enough*. Toronto: University of Toronto Press.

Brier, S. (1996). Cybersemiotics. A New Interdisciplinary Development Applied to the Problems of Knowledge Organization and Document Retrieval in Information Science. *The Journal of Documentation*, *52*(3), 296–344. doi:10.1108/eb026970

Brillouin, L. (1962). *Science and information theory*. New York: Academic Press.

Brookes, Bertram C. (1980, October). The forms of information science: part 1. Philosophical aspets. *Journal of Information Science*, 2, (3/3), 125-133.

Brown, P. J., Bovey, J. D., & Chen, X. (1997). Context-aware applications: From the laboratory to the marketplace. *IEEE Personal Communications*, *4*(5), 58–64. doi:10.1109/98.626984

Brown, P. J., & Jones, G. J. (2001). Context-aware Retrieval: Exploring a New Environment for Information Retrieval and Information Filtering. *Personal and Ubiquitous Computing*, *5*(4), 253–263. doi:10.1007/s007790170004

Bruner, J. (1990). *Acts of meaning*. Cambridge, Massachusetts: Harvard University Press.

Bruner, Ch. (1991). *Thinking collaboratively: ten questions and answers*. Washington, DC: Education and Human Services Consortium.

Bruni, L. E. (2008). Hierarchical Categorical Perception in Sensing and Cognitive Processes. *Biosemiotics*, *1*(1), 113–130. doi:10.1007/s12304-008-9001-9

Brusilovsky, P. (2001). Adaptive Hypermedia. *Journal of User Modeling and User-Adapted Interaction, Springer*, *11*(1-2), 87–110. doi:10.1023/A:1011143116306

Buckland, M. (1991). Information as thing. *Journal of the American Society for Information Science American Society for Information Science*, *42*(5), 351–360. doi:10.1002/(SICI)1097-4571(199106)42:5<351::AID-ASI5>3.0.CO;2-3

Buckland, M. (1991). Information as Thing. *Journal of the American Society for Information Science American Society for Information Science*, *42*(5), 351–360. doi:10.1002/(SICI)1097-4571(199106)42:5<351::AID-ASI5>3.0.CO;2-3

Buckley, C., Salton, G., & Allan, J. (1994). The effect of adding relevance information in a relevance feedback environment. *Proceedings of the 17th annual ACM international conference on research and development in information retrieval (SIGIR'94)*, Dublin, UK, (292–300).

Bullock, A., & Trombley, S. (1999). *The Fontana Dictionary of Modern Thought* (pp. 669–737). London: Harper-Collins.

Bunge, M. (2008). *Filosofía y sociedad*. México, D.F.: Siglo XXI, 189 p

Burgin, M. (2003). Information Theory: a Multifaceted Model of Information. *Enthropy*, *5*, 146–160. doi:10.3390/e5020146

Burgin, M. (2010). *Theory of Information: Fundamentality, Diversity and Unification*. Singapore: World Scientific Publishing.

Byrum, J. D. (2005). Online catalogs and library portals in today's information environment. *Journal of Library Administration*, *43*(1/2), 135–154. doi:10.1300/J111v43n01_09

Calude C.S. and M.A. Stay (2005). From Heisenberg to Gödel via Chaitin. *Int. J. Th. Phys.*, *44*(7). 2005. pp. 1053-1065.

Capobianco, A. (2003). Questioning the effectiveness of contextual online help: some alternative propositions. In M. Rauterberg, M. Menozzi, & J. Wesson, (eds), *Human-Computer Interaction INTERACT'03*, (65-72). New York: IOS Press

Capobianco, A., & Carbonell, N. (2001). Contextual online help: elicitation of human experts' strategies. *Proceedings of HCI'01*, New Orleans, (824-828).

Capobianco, A., & Carbonell, N. (2002). Contextual Online Help: a Contribution to the Implementation of Universal Access. In S. Keates, P.J. Clarkson & P. Robinson (eds.), *Universal Access and Assistive Technology*, (131-140). London: Springer.

Capurro, R., & Hjørland, B. (2003). The concept of information. *Annual Review of Information Science & Technology*, *37*, 313–411.

Capurro, R. (1978). *Information. Ein Beitrag zur etymologischen und ideengeschichtlichen Begründung des Informationsbegriffs* [Information: A contribution to the foundation of the concept of information based on its etymology and in the history of ideas]. Munich, Germany: Saur. [Also online. Retrieved September 3, 2010, from http://www.capurro.de/info.html]

Capurro, R., & Hjørland, B. (2003). The Concept of Information. [Draft version available online. Retrieved September 3, 2010, from http://www.capurro.de/infoconcept.html]. *Annual Review of Information Science & Technology*, *37*(8), 343–411.

Capurro, R. (1989). *Hermeneutik der Fachinformation*. Freiburg: Alber.

Capurro, R. (2000) *Einführung In Den Informationsbegriff. I Kapitel: Der Informationsbegriff in den Informationswirtschaft*. Retrieved July 5, 2011, from http://www.capurro.de/infovorl-kap1.htm

Capurro, R. (2000). *Einführung In Den Informationsbegriff. II Kapitel: Der Informationsbegriff in der Informationswissenschaft*. Retrieved July 5, 2011, from http://www.capurro.de/infovorl-kap2.htm

Capurro, R. (2000): *Einführung In Den Informationsbegriff. IV Kapitel: Zur Geschichte des Informationsbegriffe*. Retrieved July 5, 2011, from http://www.capurro.de/infovorl-kap4.htm

Capurro, R. (2007). Epistemologia y ciencia de la información. *Enl@ace: Revista Venezolana de Información, Tecnología y Conocimiento, 4(1)*, pp. 11-29. Retrieved December 29, 2010, from http://www.capurro.de/enancib.htm

Capurro, R. (2009). Past, present, and future of the concept of information. *TripleC: Cognition, Communication, Co-operation, 17*(2).

Carbonell, N. (2003). Towards the design of usable multimodal interaction languages. *Universal Access in the Information Society*, *2*(6), 143–159. doi:10.1007/s10209-003-0051-0

Carenini, G., & Moore, J. D. (1993). Generating explanations in context. *Proceedings of the ACM Conference on Intelligent User Interfaces*, Orlando (FL), (175-182). New York: ACM Press.

Carroll, J. M., & Rosson, M. B. (1987). The paradox of the active user. In Carroll, J. M. (Ed.), *Interfacing Thought: Cognitive Aspects of Human-Computer Interaction* (pp. 80–111). Cambridge, MA: MIT Press.

Cassell J., Sullivan J., Prevost S.& Churchill. (2000). *Embodied Conversational Agents*. Cambridge, MA: MIT Press.

Cassell, J., Bickmore, T., & Billinghurst, M. (1999). *Embodiment in conversational interfaces: Rea*. CHI'99: Proceedings of the SIGCHI conf. on Human factors in comp. syst., (520-527). New York: ACM Press.

Castells, M. (1996). *The rise of the network society*. Malden, Mass.: Blackwell Publishers.

Castells, M. (1997). *The power of identity*. Malden, Mass.: Blackwell.

Castells, M. (1998). *End of millennium*. Malden, MA: Blackwell Publishers.

Cejpek, J. (1995). Aportaciones checas a la ciencia de la información. *AABADOM*, *2*(April-June), 4–7.

Cejpek, J. (1998). *Informace, komunikace a mysleni: Uvod do informacni vedy*. Prague: Karolinum.

Celaya, J. (2008) *La empresa en la Web 2.0*. Barcelona, Spain: Ediciones Gestión 2000.

Celaya, J. (2009) Study *La visibilidad de los museos en la Web 2.0*. Retrieved September 2, 2010, from http://www.dosdoce.com/articulo/estudios/3071/la-visibilidad-de-los-museos-en-la-web-2-0

Chaitin, G. J. (1966). On the length of programs for computing finite binary sequences. *Journal of the Association for Computing Machinery*, *13*, 547–569.

Chaitin, G. J. (1982b). Gödel's theorem and information. *International Journal of Theoretical Physics*, *22*, 941–954. doi:10.1007/BF02084159

Chaitin, G. J. (1982a). Algorithmic Information Theory. In *Encyclopedia of Statistical Sciences*, 1, 38-41. New York: Wiley.

Chalmers, D. J., French, R. M., & Hofstadter, D. R. (1992). High-level perception, representation, and analogy: A critique of artificial intelligence methodology. *Journal of Experimental & Theoretical Artificial Intelligence*, *4*(3), 185–211. doi:10.1080/09528139208953747

Charlene, L. Bernoff, J. (2008) *Groundswell, winning in a world transformed by social technologies*. United States of America: Forrester Research.

Checkland, P. (1981). *Systems thinking, systems practice*. Chichester: Wiley.

Checkland, P., & Holwell, S. (1998). *Information, systems and information systems: making sense of the field*. Chichester: John Wiley & Sons.

Chen, A. P., & Chen, M. Y. (2005). A unifying ontology modeling for knowledge management. *Lecture Notes in Computer Science*, *3681*, 318–324. doi:10.1007/11552413_46

Cherry, J. M., & Cox, J. P. (1996). *World Wide Web displays of bibliographic records: An evaluation*. Retrieved June 15, 2005, from http://www.fis.utoronto.ca/research/programs/ displays/caispck1.htm

Chibane, I., & Doan, B.-L. (2007). Impact of Contextual Information for Hypertext Documents Retrieval. *Workshop on Context-based Information Retrieval, CIR 07*.

Choo, C. W. (2006). *A organização do conhecimento: como as organizações usam a informação para criar significado, construir conhecimento e tomar decisões* (2nd ed.). São Paulo: Editora do Senac.

Chowdhury, G. (1999). *Introduction to modern information retrieval*. London: Library Association Publishing.

Cleverdon, C. W. (1960). *Report on the first stage of an investigation into the comparative efficiency of indexing systems. Technical report*. Cranfield, UK: College of Aeronautics.

Clifford, A. L. (1987). The use of heuristics in user interfaces for online information retrieval systems. In *ASIS '87: Proceedings of the 50th ASIS Annual Meeting, 24*, 148-152.

Cobos, R., Alamán, X., & Esquivel, J.A. (2001). Know-Cat: Catalizador de conocimiento. KnowCat: Knowledge Catalyser. *RedIRIS, Boletín de la red nacional de I+D. Nº 58-59 (December 2001 - January 2002)*, 7-10.

Codina, L. (n.d.). *Ciencia 2.0*. Retrieved March 01, 2009, from http://www.mindomo.com/view.htm?m=d4d1f77be0d04af0804c719038144de8

Collier, J. (2011). Kinds of Information is Scientific Use. [in press.]. *Triple, C*, 9.

Comte, A. (1844). *Discours sur l'Esprit positif.* [transl.: *A general view of positivism.* London, 1856. Retrieved September 3, 2010, from Google Books: http://books.google.com]

Cool, C., & Spink, A. (2002). Issues of context in information retrieval (IR): an introduction to the special issue. *Information Processing & Management, 38*(5), 605–611. doi:10.1016/S0306-4573(01)00054-1

Cork, R. D., Detmer, W. M., & Friedman, C. P. (1998). Development and initial validation of an instrument to measure physicians' use of, knowledge about, and attitudes toward computers. *Journal of the American Medical Informatics Association, 5*(2), 164–176. doi:10.1136/jamia.1998.0050164

Courtney, N. (2007). *Library 2.0 and beyond: innovative technologies and tomorrow's user*. Libraries Unlimited.

Covey, S. R. (1989). *The seven habits of highly effective people: restoring the character ethic*. New York: Simon and Schuster.

Cruz Mundet, J. R. (1999). *Manual de archivística*. Madrid: Fundación Germán Sánchez Ruipérez.

Currás, E. (1981). ¿Estaremos en la Época del Informacionismo? *Rev. Univ. Complutense, 2*, 186–188.

Currás, E. (1983). Ciertos Principios Científico-Filosóficos de las Ciencias de la Documentación. *Rev. Univ. Complutense, 1*(4), 83–88.

Currás, E. (1998). *La información en sus nuevos aspectos*. Madrid: Paraninfo.

Currás Puente, E. (2008). Ciencia de la información bajo postulados sistémicos y sistemáticos. Caracas: Edición personal.

Currás, E. (1984). Moral and Social Implications of the New Technologies in Information Science. In Van Der Laan, A., & Winters, A. (Eds.), *The Use of Information in a Changing World* (pp. 417–432). Amsterdam: FID Publications.

Currás, E. (1985) La Información como Cuarto Elemento Vital y su Influencia en la Cultura de los Pueblos. *Toletum. Año LXIX, 2ª época, 20*, 27-46.

Currás, E. (1988). *Aktuell Probleme der Information. Inst. für Informationswissenschaft, Erfindungwesen und Patentrechts. Technische Universität, Ilmenau.* Typed text.

Currás, E. (1990). *El Dato Informativo en la Industria Alimentaria*. Paper presented at Congreso Internacional de Tecnología y Desarrollo Alimentario, Murcia, Spain.

Currás, E. (1993). The influence of System Science on the concept of Information. *ICS Innovazione, Comunicazione, Sviluppo, anno V, 3*, 5-6.

Currás, E. (2008). Interacción Dialéctica en la Ciencia. In E. Currás (Ed.), *Ciencia de la información bajo postulados sistémicos y sistemáticos* (pp. 37-50). Madrid: edición personal.

Dalkir, K. (2005). *Knowledge management in theory and practice*. Burlington, M.A.: Elsevier Butterworth Heinemann.

Daniels, H. (2001/2003). *Vygotsky y la pedagogía*. D.F., México: Paidós. (Original work published 2001)

Davenport, E., & Hall, H. (2002). Organizational knowledge and communities of practice. *Annual Review of Information Science & Technology*, *36*, 171–227.

Denning, P. J. (2007). Mastering the mess. *Communications of the ACM*, *50*(4), 21–25. doi:10.1145/1232743.1232763

Denning, P. J., & Yaholkovsky, P. (2008). Getting to "We.". *Communications of the ACM*, *51*(4), 19–24. doi:10.1145/1330311.1330316

Dervin, B. (2003). *Sense-making methodology reader: selected writings of Brenda Dervin Cresskill*. NJ: Harupton Press.

Dervin, B. NILAN, M. (1986). Information needs and uses. *Annual Review of Information Science and Technology*, *21*, (pp. 03-33). NY: Knowledge industry publications

Descartes, R. (1649). *A discourse of a method for the well guiding of reason, and the discovery of truth in the sciences*. London: Thomas Newcombe. [Also online. Retrieved September 3, 2010, from Guttemberg Project: http://www.gutenberg.org/files/25830]

Dey, A. K. (2001). Understanding and Using Context. *Personal and Ubiquitous Computing Journal*, *5*(1), 4–7. doi:10.1007/s007790170019

Dey, A. K., & Abowd, G. F. (1999).Towards a better understanding of context and context-awareness. *Technical Report GITGVU-99-22, Georgia Institute of Technology, College of Computing*.

Díaz Nafría, J. M. (2010a). What is information? A multidimensional concern. *TripleC*, *8*(1), 77–108.

Díaz Nafría, J. M., & Pérez-Montoro, M. (2011a). Is information a sufficient basis for cognition? (Part 1: Critique on Dretske's vision). [in press.]. *Triple*, *C*, 9.

Díaz Nafría, J. M., & Pérez-Montoro, M. (2011b). Is information a sufficient basis for cognition? (Part 2: physical foundations). [in press.]. *Triple*, *C*, 9.

Díaz Nafría, J. M., & Salto Alemany, F. (2011). Towards a transdisciplinary frame: Bridging domains, a multidimentsional approach to information. [in press.]. *Triple*, *C*, 9.

Díaz Nafria, J. M. (in press). What Is Information? An Enquiry Beyond Information Science From A Systemic Point Of View. In Currás, E., & Lloret, N. (Eds.), *Systems Science And Collaborative Information Systems: Theories, Practices And New Research*. Hershey: IGI Global.

Díaz Nafría, J. M. (2003). *Contribución en métodos inversos para la caracterización de sistemas radiantes* ("Contributions in inverse methods for the characterization of radiant systems" in Spanish). Madrid: Universidad Politécnica de Madrid. Retrieved May 2010 from Novatores: http://www.novatores.org/html/es/eprint/show.html?ePrintId=119

Díaz Nafría, J. M. (2008). The interminacy of observation. In Díaz & Salto (eds.) *¿Qué es información?* (What is information? Proceedings of the I International Meeting of Experts in Information theories. An interdisciplinar approach). León: Universidad de León, pp. 489-502. Retrieved September, 2010 from http://wp.me/pzKNC-58

Díaz Nafría, J. M. (2010b). Holographic principle. In Díaz, Salto and Pérez-Montoro (eds.) *Glossarium BITri: Glossary of concepts, metaphors, theories and problems regarding information*. León: Universidad de León. Retrieved September, 2010 from http://glossarium.bitrum.unileon.es

Díaz Nafría, J. M., & Aguado, J. M. (2010). Cybernetics. In Díaz, Salto, & Pérez-Montoro (Eds.). *Glossarium BITri, op. cit.*

Díaz Nafría, J. M., & Capurro, R. (2010). Hermeneitics. In Díaz, Salto, & Pérez-Montoro (Eds.). *Glossarium BITri, op. cit.*

Díaz Villa, Mario. (2002). *Flexibilidad y educación superior en Colômbia*. Bogotá: Série Calidad de la Educación, n. 02. ICFES-MEN.

Diemer, A. (1975). Information Science: a new science. *Problems of Information Science*, 192-203.

Dinucci, D. (1999). Fragmented future. *Print*, *53*(4), 32.

Doan, B.-L., Jose, J., Melucci, M., & Tamine-Lechani, L. (2010). *Workshop on Contextual Information Access, Seeking and Retrieval Evaluation*. ECIR 2010, Milton Keynes.

Dodig-Crnkovic, G., & Stuart, S. (2010). *Computation, Information, Cognition – The Nexus and The Liminal*. Cambridge, UK: Cambridge Scholars Publishing.

Dorner, D. G., & Curtis, A. M. (2003, June). *A comparative review of common user interface software products for libraries*. Retrieved June 15, 2005, from http://www.museglobal.com/PDF/Review-Common%20Search%20Interfaces.pdf

Dowling, T. (1997). The World Wide Web meets the OPAC. *From Catalog to Gateway: Briefings from the CFFC*. Published as a supplement to the *ALCTS Newsletter, 8*(2), A-D.

Dretske, F. I. (1981). *Knowledge and the flow of information*. Cambridge, MA: MIT Press.

Dretske, F. (1987). *Conocimiento e información*. Barcelona: Salvat.

Duarte, Newton. (1993). *A Individualidade para SI: contribuição a uma teoria histórico-social da formação do indivíduo*. Campinas, S.P: Editora Autores Associados.

Duhem, P. (1962). *The aim ans structure of physical theory*. New York: Atheneum.

Ellis, D. (1989). Behavioural approach to information retrieval system design. *The Journal of Documentation, 45*(3), 171–212. doi:10.1108/eb026843

Ellis, David; Haugan, M. (1997). Modelling the information-seeking patterns of engineers and research scientists in an industrial environment. *The Journal of Documentation, 53*(4), 384–403. doi:10.1108/EUM0000000007204

Elsweiler, D., & Ruthven, I. (2007). Towards Task-based Personal Information Management Evaluations. *Proceedings of the 30th annual international ACM SIGIR conference on Research and development in information retrieval*, (23-30).

Elzaburu, F., & Martintegui, J. (1987). *De la incertidumbre a la esperanza*. Madrid: AINPA.

Emery, F., & Trist, E. (1965). The causal texture of organizational environments. *Human Relations, 18*, 21–32. doi:10.1177/001872676501800103

Engeström, Y. (1987). *Learning by expanding: An activity-theoretical approach to developmental research*. Helsinki: Orienta-Konsultit.

Esteban Navarro, M. A., & Gay Molins, P. (1998). *La normalización de la descripción y la recuperación de información en los archivos: vino viejo en odres nuevos. Boletín de la ANABAD, (48)*. Madrid: ANABAD.

Fávero, M. H. (2005). *Psicologia e Conhecimento. Subsídios para a análise do ensinar e aprender*. Brasília: EDUnB.

Fávero, M. H. Os fundamentos teóricos e metodológicos da Psicologia do Conhecimento. In M. H. Fávero & C. Cunha (Coord.) (2008). *Psicologia do Conhecimento. O diálogo entre as ciências e a cidadania.* Brasília: UNESCO.

Fenzl, N., & Hofkirchner, W. (1997). Information Processing in Evolutionary Systems. An Outline Conceptual Framework for a Unified Information Theory. In Schweitzer, F. (Ed.), *Self-Organization of Complex Structures: From Individual to Collective Dynamics* (pp. 59–70). London: Gordon and Breach.

Fergusson, G., & Allen, J. F. (1998). TRIPS: An Integrated Intelligent Problem-Solving Assistant, *Proceedings of the Fifteenth National Conference on AI (AAAI-98)*, Madison, WI, (26-30).

Fernández Molina, J. C. (1994). Enfoque objetivo y subjetivo del concepto de información. *Revista Espanola la de Documentacion Cientifica, 17*(3), 320–331.

Ferreira, S. M. S. P. (1997). *Estudo de necessidades de informação: dos paradigmas tradicionais à abordagem Sense-Making*. Porto Alegre: ABEBD.

Feuerstein, R. (1980). *Instrumental enrichment: an intervention program for cognitive modifiability*. Baltimore: University Park Press.

Fidel, R. (2006). An ecological approach to the design of information systems. *Bulletin of the American Society for Information Science and Technology, 33*(1), 6–8. doi:10.1002/bult.2006.1720330103

Fitch, D. (2007). A cybernetic evaluation of organizational information systems (pp. 61-74). Eds. Williams & I. Imam. In *Systems concepts in evaluation: an expert anthology*. Point Reyes, Calif.: EdgePress of Inverness American Evaluation Association.

Floridi, L. (2004). Outline of a theory of strongly semantic information. *Minds and Machines*, *14*(2), 197–221. doi:10.1023/B:MIND.0000021684.50925.c9

Floridi, L. (2005b). Is Semantic Information Meaningful Data? *Philosophy and Phenomenological Research*, *70*(2), 351–370. doi:10.1111/j.1933-1592.2005.tb00531.x

Floridi, L. (2005d). Consciousness, Agents and the Knowledge Game. *Minds and Machines*, *15*(3-4), 415–444. doi:10.1007/s11023-005-9005-z

Floridi, L. (2005a). Information. In Mitcham, C. (Ed.), *Encyclopedia of Science, Technology and Ethics*. New York: Macmillan.

Floridi, L. (2005c). Semantic Conceptions of Information. In E. N. Zahlta (Ed.) *Stanford Encyclopedia of Philisophy*. Stanford: The Metaphysics Research Lab. Retrieved September 3, 2010, from http://plato.stanford.edu/entries/information-semantic/

Flückiger, F. (2005). Mathematical Foundation of Information Theory. A Set Theoretical Approach. In Michel Petitjean (ed.) *Proceedings of FIS2005, The Third Conference on the Foundations of Information Science*.

Fotis, L. Georgios, S. Dimitrios, K. (2010) *Handbook of Research on Technologies and Cultural Heritage: Applications and Environments*. IGI Global snippet

Foundations of Information Science. (n.d.). Retrieved from http://fis.icts.sbg.ac.at/

Freire, P. (1979). *Educação e mudança*. Rio de Janeiro: Paz & Terra.

Freire, P. (1980). *Conscientização*. São Paulo: Moraes.

Freire, P. (1985). *Educación y concientización*. Salamanca: Sigüeme.

Freire, P. (2002). *Pedagogia do oprimido* (32nd ed.). Rio de Janeiro: Paz & Terra.

Freund, L., Toms, G., & Clarke, C. (2005). *Modeling Task-Genre Relationships for IR in the Workplace*. SIFIR.

Freund, L., & Butterworth, R. (2008). Tagging for Use: an analysis of use-centred resource description. *ACM International Conference Proceeding Series* (348), 6-12. London.

Froehlich, T. (1988). Relevance and the relevance of social epistemology. In P. Hämäläinen, B. Koskkiala, & A.J. Repo (Eds.), *44th FID Conference and Congress records book* (pp. 9-19). Helsinki: FID.

Fuhr, N. (2009). Models for retrieval with probabilistic indexing. *Information Processing & Management*, *25*(1), 55–72. doi:10.1016/0306-4573(89)90091-5

Fujita, M. S. L. (1999, January/June). A leitura do indexador: estudo de observação. *Perspectiva em Ciência da Informação*, *4*(1), 101–116.

Fujita, M. S. L. (2006). Abordagem cognitiva e sócio-cognitiva da leitura documentária na formação inicial do indexador: análise da perspectiva individual em contexto sociocultural. In UNESP (Ed), *ENANCIB, 7, Encontro Nacional de Pesquisa em Ciência da Informação,* Anais. Marília, SP: UNESP.

Gal-Or, E., & Ghose, A. (2004). The economic consequences of sharing security information. In Camp, L. J., & Lewis, S. (Eds.), *Economics of Information Security* (pp. 95–104). New York, NY: Springer. doi:10.1007/1-4020-8090-5_8

García, R. (2000). *Conocimiento en construcción: de las formulaciones de Jean Piaget a la teoría de sistemas complejos*. Barcelona: Gedisa.

García Gutiérrez, A. (1990). *La estructura lingüística de la documentación*. Murcia: Universidad de Murcia.

García Marco, F. J. (1998). El concepto de información: una aproximación interdisciplinar: I: Hacia una definición objetiva. *Revista General de Información y Documentación*, *8*(1), 303–326.

García Marco, F. J. (2010). Las instituciones de la memoria ante el cambio digital: una propuesta sobre la articulación interdisciplinar de las ciencias de la documentación. *Pliegos de Yuste: revista de cultura y pensamiento europeos* (11).

García Marco, F. J. (2011). La pirámide de la información revisitada: enriqueciendo el modelo desde la ciencia cognitiva. *El profesional de la información, 20*(1).

Giménez Chornet, V., Escrig Giménez, M., Villalmanzo Cameno, J., & Viciano Navarro, P. (2007). *Tesauros del Archivo del Reino de Valencia = Tesaurus de l'Arxiu del Regne de València*. Valencia: Conselleria de Cultura i Esport.

Gitt, W. (1996). Information, Science and Biology. *Technical Journal*, *10*(2), 181–187.

Glaser, B. G., & Strauss, A. (1967). *Discovery of Grounded Theory: Strategies for qualitative research*. Mill Valley, CA: Sociology Press.

Gödel, K. (1931). Über formal unentscheidbare Sätze der Principia Mathematica und verwandter Systeme. *Monatshefte für Mathematik und Physik*, *38*, 173–198. doi:10.1007/BF01700692

Göker, A., & Myrhaug, H. I. (2002). User context and personalization. *Workshop proceedings for the* 6th *European Conference on Case Based Reasoning*.

Goldman, L. (1973). *Lukács et Heidegger* (p. 39). Paris: Denoël/Gonthier.

Gracy, K. F. (2001). Documentar comunidades: el caso de la etnografía archivística. Editores Anne Gilliland & Sue McKemmish. In *Nuevos métodos de investigación en archivística*, (pp. 211-244). Madrid, España: 3000 Informática.

Grice, P. (1999). Logic and Conversation. In Stainton, R. (Ed.), *Perspectives in the Philosophy of Language: A Concise Anthology*. Peterborough, ON: Broadview Press.

Griffiths, J. R. (2007). User satisfaction as a measure of system performance. *Journal of Librarianship and Information Science*, *39*(3), 142–152. doi:10.1177/0961000607080417

Grossman, Lev. (2006) *Person of the Year: You*. December 25. Time.com

Grudin, J. (1994). Groupware and social dynamics: eight challenges for developers. *Communications of the ACM*, *37*(1), 92–105. doi:10.1145/175222.175230

Günther, G. (1963). *Das Bewußtsein der Maschinen. Eine Metaphysik der Kybernetik. Krefeld/Baden-Baden*. Germany: Agis Verlag.

Hal. (2011). Zabaware. Retrieved from http://zabaware.com/

Hall, A. D., & Fagen, R. E. (1956). Definition of a system. In Society for the Advancement of General Systems Theory, Society for General Systems Research & et al. (Eds.), *General systems: yearbook of the Society for the Advancement of General Systems Theory*, 1, 18. Ann Arbor, MI: The Society.

Harter, S. P. (1996). Variations in relevance assessments and the measurement of retrieval effectiveness. *Journal of the American Society for Information Science American Society for Information Science*, *47*(1), 37–49. doi:10.1002/(SICI)1097-4571(199601)47:1<37::AID-ASI4>3.0.CO;2-3

Heisenberg, W. (1930). *Die physikalische Prizipien der Quantentheorie*. Leipzig: Hirzel.

Hemingway, C. J. (1998). Toward a socio-cognitive theory of information systems: An analysis of key philosophical and conceptual issues. In T. J. Larsen, L. Levine, & J. I. DeGross (Eds.), *Information systems: Current issues and future changes, Proceedings of the International Federation for Information Processing, 10-13 December 1998, Helsinki, Finland* (pp. 275-286). Helsinki, Finland: Kluwer.

Henrichs, N. (2001). *Einführung in die Informationswissenschaft. Gegenstand, Erkenntnisinteresse Und Zielsetzung Der Informationswissenschaft*. Düsseldorf: Universität Düsseldorf.

Henrichs, N. (1994). Informationswissenschaft als angewandte Antropologie: Der Düsseldorfer Ansetz. In Saur, K. G. (Ed.), *Bucher für die Wissenschaft* (pp. 445–461). Munchen: Festschrift für Günter Gattermann.

Henrichs, N. (1997). Informationswissenschaft. Grundlage des praktischen Information und Dokumentation. *4 Aufl. Munchen*, 945-957.

Heredia, A. (2000). *La norma ISAD (G) "Análisis Crítico". Norma Internacional para la descripción archivística*. México, INFOLAC. Retrieved from http://infolac.ucol.mx/documentos/isad.pdf

Hernández, S. (2010). *Norma para la elaboración de puntos de acceso normalizados de instituciones, personas, familias, lugares y materias en el sistema de descripción archivística de los archivos estatales*. Madrid: Ministerio de Cultura, from http://www.mcu.es/archivos/docs/Novedades/Norma_puntos_acceso2010.pdf

Herrschaft, L. (2000). II Kapitel: Der Informationsbegriff in der Informationswissenschaft. In R. Capurro (Ed.), *Einführung In Den Informationsbegriff*. Retrieved July 5, 2011, from http://www.capurro.de/infovorl-kap2.htm

Hjørland, B. (1995). Toward a new horizon in information science: domain analysis. *Journal of the American Society for Information Science American Society for Information Science*, *46*(6), 400–425. doi:10.1002/(SICI)1097-4571(199507)46:6<400::AID-ASI2>3.0.CO;2-Y

Hjørland, B. (1998). Theory and metatheory of information science: a new interpretation. *The Journal of Documentation*, *54*, 606–621. doi:10.1108/EUM0000000007183

Hjørland, B. (2003). Fundaments of knowledge organization. *Knowledge Organization*, *30*(2), 87–111.

Hjørland, B. (2002). Domain analysis in information science: Eleven approaches – traditional as well as innovative. *The Journal of Documentation*, *58*(4), 422–462. doi:10.1108/00220410210431136

Hjørland, B. (2007). Information: Objective or subjective/situational? *Journal of the American Society for Information Science and Technology*, *58*(10), 1448–1456. doi:10.1002/asi.20620

Hjørland, B. (1997). *Information seeking and subject representation. An activity-theoretical approach to information science*. Westport, CT; London: Greenwood Press.

Hoare, P. (1997). *Academic Libraries in International Encyclopedia of Information and Library Science*. John Feather & Paul Sturges (eds). New York: Routledge. pp. 2.

Hofkirchner, W. (2009). How to achieve a unified theory of information. *TripleC*, *7*(2), 357–368.

Hofkirchner, W. (1999a). Towards a Unified Theory of Information. The Merging of Second-Order Cybernetics and Semiotics into a Single and Comprehensive Information Science. In: *15e Congrès International de Cybernétique, Namur 1998*, Namur, pp. 175-180.

Hughes, L. (2006). *The Eliza Effect*. Conversational Agents and Cognition.

Huygens, C. (1690). *Traite de la Lumiere*. Leyenden. Translated to English by Thompson, S.P., London, 1912. Retrieved July, 2010 from Project Gutemberg: http://www.gutenberg.org/etext/14725

InforM25. (2002). *AIM25, Archives in London and the M25 area*. Retrieved from http://www.aim25.ac.uk/index.stm

Ingwersen, P. (1995). Information and Information Science. *Enciclopedia of Library and Information Science*, *56*(Suppl.), 137–174.

Ingwersen, P. (1982, September). Search procedures in the library: analyzed from the cognitive point of view. *The Journal of Documentation*, *38*(3), 165–191. doi:10.1108/eb026727

Ingwersen, P. (1996, March). Cognitive Perspective of Informaction Retrieval Interaction: elements of a Cognitive IR Theory. *The Journal of Documentation*, *42*(1), 3–50. doi:10.1108/eb026960

Ingwersen, P., & Järvelin, K. (2005). *The Turn: Integration of Information Seeking and Retrieval in Context*. Dordrecht, The Netherlands: Springer.

Ingwersen, P. (2002). *Information retrieval interaction*. London: Taylor Graham. 246 p. ISBN: 0-947568-54-9. PDF Version. Retrieved December 13, 2005, from: www.db.dk/pi/iri

Ingwersen, P., & Belkin, N. (2004). Information retrieval in context. *IRiX workshop at SIGIR 2004,* Sheffield.

Ingwersen, P., & Borlund, P. (1996) Information transfer viewed as interactive cognitive processes. In P. Ingwersen, P., & N. Pors, N. (Ed.), *Information Science: Integration in Perspective. Proceedings of the 2nd. International Conference on Conceptions of Library and Information Science (CoLIS 2), Oct. 13-16, 1996*. Copenhagen: The Royal School of Librarianship.

Instituto Paulo Montengro (IPM). (2007). *Indicador de Alfabetismo Funcional (INAF); relatório*. São Paulo: IPM.

International Council of Archives. (2000). *ISAD (G): General International Standard Archival Description, Second edition*. Ottawa: ICA. Retrieved from http://www.ica.org/en/node/30000

International Council of Archives. (2003). *ISAAR (CPF), International Standard Archival Authority Record for Corporate Bodies, Persons and Families. Second Edition.* Paris: ICA. Retrieved from http://www.ica.org/sites/default/files/ISAAR2EN.pdf

ISO 15489-1:2001. *Information and documentation-Records management - Part 1: General.* Geneva: ISO

Israel, D., & Perry, J. (1990a). What is information? In Hanson, P. (Ed.), *Information, language and cognition* (pp. 1–19). Vancouver, Canada: University of British Columbia Press.

Jabberwacky. (2011). Retrieved from http://www.jabberwacky.com/

Jameson, A. (2003). Adaptive interfaces and agents, *The human-computer interaction handbook: fundamentals, evolving technologies and emerging applications*, Lawrence Erlbaum Associates, Inc., (305-330).

Janich, P. (1998). Informationsbegriff und methodisch-kulturalistische Philosophie. *Ethik und Sozialwissenschaften, 2*, 169–182.

Jank, D. (2010b). Toward a unifying ontology for human-information interaction. *Canadian Journal of Information and Library Science, 34*(4), 403–432.

Jank, D. (2010a). Collaborative systems and groupware. In Bates, M. J. (Ed.), *Encyclopedia of Library and Information Sciences* (3rd ed., pp. 1088–1096). New York, NY: Taylor & Francis.

Jansen, B. J., Spink, A., & Saracevic, T. (2000). Real life, real users, and real needs: a study and analysis of user queries on the web. *Information Processing & Management, 36*, 207–227. doi:10.1016/S0306-4573(99)00056-4

Jarvelin, K., & Kekalainen, J. (2002). Cumulative gain-based evaluation of IR techniques [ACM TOIS]. *ACM Transactions on Information Systems, 20*(4), 422–446. doi:10.1145/582415.582418

Játiva Miralles, M. V. (2004). Indicadores de calidad aplicables al análisis, evaluación y comparación de opacs. *El Profesional de la Información, 13*(1), 28–46. doi:10.1076/epri.13.1.28.29023

Javanmardi, S., & Videira Lopes, C. (2007). *Modeling Trust in Collaborative Information Systems.* Retrieved May 14, 2009, from http://www.ics.uci.edu/~lopes/documents/collaboratecom %2007/CollabComCameraReadyOCT09.

Jimerson, R. C. (2002). Archival description and finding aids. *OCLC Systems & Services, 18*(3), 125–129. doi:10.1108/10650750210439331

Joachims, T., Granka, L. A., Pan, B., Hembrooke, H., Radlinski, F., & Gay, G. (2007). Evaluating the accuracy of implicit feedback from clicks and query reformulations in Web search. *ACM Transactions on Information Systems, 25*(2). doi:10.1145/1229179.1229181

Jones, G. J. F., & Brown, P. J. (2004). The role of Context in Information Retrieval. *IRiX workshop at SIGIR 2004*, Sheffield.

Jubany, J. (2009). Guía práctica para participar activamente en una red social y educativa digital. *Revista Didáctica, Innovación y Multimedia, 5, 13.* Retrieved September 10, 2010, from http://www.pangea.org/dim/revistaDIM13/Articulos/jordijubany.doc

Jubert, A. (1999). Developing an infraestructure for communities of practice. In B. McKenna (Ed.). In *Proceedings of the 19th International Online Meeting* (pp. 165-168). Hinkesey Hill, U.K.: Learned Information.

Karpatschof, B. (2007). *Human activity. Contributions to the anthropological sciences from a perspective of activity theory.* Lund, Sweden: InformationR.net. Retrieved in 12/11/09 from http://informationr.net/ir/12-3/Karpatschof/Karp00.html

Katuščák, D., & Matthaeidesová, M., & Nováková, M. (1998). Informačná výchova. Terminologický a Výkladový slovník. Odbor knižničná a informačná veda. *Slovenské pedagogické nakladatelstvo. 1. vyd.*, 375 s.

Kaula, P. N. (2002). Reflections on the Organisation and Working of the National Library and the Efforts at the Establishment of the National Central Library. *Herald of Library Science, 41*(1-2), 37–47.

Kelly, D., & Fu, X. (2007). Eliciting better information need descriptions from users of information search systems. *Information Processing & Management, 43*(1), 30–46. doi:10.1016/j.ipm.2006.03.006

Kelly, D., & Teevan, J. (2003). Implicit feedback for inferring user preference: A bibliography. *SIGIR Forum*, *37*(2), 18–28. doi:10.1145/959258.959260

Kelly, L. (2009). *The Impact of Social Media on Museum Practice*. In the Exhibitionist Fall 2009. Presented at the National Palace of Tapei. Retrieved September 10, 2010, from http://www.archimuse.com/mw2008/papers/kelly_l/kelly_l.html

Kelton, K., Fleischmann, K. R., & Wallace, W. A. (2008). Trust in digital information. *Journal of the American Society for Information Science and Technology*, *59*(3), 363–374. doi:10.1002/asi.20722

King, A. (1989). The Great Transition. *Int. Forum Inf. Docum*, *14*(2), 3–8.

Kobayashi, M., & Takeda, K. (2000). Information retrieval on the web. *ACM Computing Surveys*, *32*(2), 144–173. doi:10.1145/358923.358934

Kobsa, A. (2001). Generic User Modeling Systems. [New York: Springer]. *Journal of User Modeling and User-Adapted Interaction*, *11*(1-2), 49–63. doi:10.1023/A:1011187500863

Kofod-Petersen, A., & Cassens, J. (2006). *Using Activity Theory to Model Context Awareness: a Qualitative Case Study*. Berlin: American Association for Artificial Intelligence.

Kolmogorov, A. N. (1965). Three approaches to the quantitative definition of 'information'. *Problems of Information Transmission*, *1*(1), 3–11.

Kornwachs, K. (1996). Pragmatic information and System surface. In Kornwachs, K., & Jacoby, K. (Eds.), *Information. New questions to a multidisciplinary concept* (pp. 103–118). Berlin: Akademie Verlag.

Krumholz, W. (2004). Grenzen der physiologischen Informationsverarbeitúng des Menschen. *Information Wissenchaft und Praxis*, *55*(5), 283–287.

Kuhlthau, C. C. (1991). Inside the search process: information searching from the user's perspective. *Journal of the American Society for Information Science American Society for Information Science*, *42*(5). doi:10.1002/(SICI)1097-4571(199106)42:5<361::AID-ASI6>3.0.CO;2-#

Kuhlthau, C. C. (1993). A principle of uncertainty for information seeking. *The Journal of Documentation*, *49*(4), 339–355. doi:10.1108/eb026918

Kuhlthau, C. C. (1993). *Seeking Meaning: process approach to Library and information services*. Norwood: Ablex Publishing.

Kuhlthau, C. C. (1996). *The Concept of a zone of intervention for identifying the role of intermediaries in the information search process*. New Brunswick, NJ: Rutgers University. Retrieved March 30, 2010, from: http://mail.asis.org/annual-96/electronic proceedings/kuhlthau.html.

Kuhn, T. S. (1962). *The Structure of Scientific Revolutions*. Chicago: University of Chicago Press.

Lakatos, I. (1978). *The methodology of scientific research*. Cambridge: Cambridge University Press.

Lancaster, F. W. (2004). *Indexação e resumos: teoria e prática* (2nd ed.). Brasília: Briquet de Lemos Livros.

Lancaster, F. W., & Warner, A. J. (1993). *Information Retrieval Today*. Information Resources Press.

Laudan, L. (1977). *Progress and its problems*. Berkley: University of California Press.

Lave, J., & Wenger, E. (1991). *Situated learning: Legitimate peripheral participation*. New York: Cambridge University Press.

Lave, J. (1988). *Cognition in practice: mind, mathematics, and culture in everyday life*. New York: Cambridge University. doi:10.1017/CBO9780511609268

Lave, J., & Wenger, E. (1991). *Situation learning: legitimate peripheral participation*. Cambridge, UK: Cambridge University Press.

Lawless, S., O'Connor, A., & Mulwa, C. (2010). A proposal for the evaluation of adaptive personalized information retrieval, CIRSE 2010. *Proceedings of The 2nd International Workshop on Contextual Information Access, Seeking and Retrieval Evaluation*, Milton Keynes, UK.

Leibniz, W. (orig. 1714, trans. 2007). *Monadology*. Trans. J. Bennett. Retrieved September 6, 2010 from http://www.earlymoderntexts.com/pdf/leibmon.pdf

Leleur, S. (2008). Systems science and complexity: some proposals for future development. *Journal of Systems Research and Behavioral Science*, *25*(1), 67–79. doi:10.1002/sres.860

Lemmermann, E. (1913). In Pascher, A. (Ed.), *Eugleninae* (pp. 115–174). Jena: G. Fischer.

Leontiev, A. N. (1977/1993). *Actividad, conciencia y personalidad.* D.F., México: Asbe. (Original work published 1977)

Leray, D., & Sansonnet, J. P. (2007). Assisting Dialogical Agents Modeled from Novice User's Perceptions. *Proceedings of KES*, *07*, 1122–1129.

Leray, D., & Sansonnet, J. P. (2006). Ordinary user oriented model construction for Assisting Conversational Agents, *International Workshop on Communication between Human and Artificial Agents, CHAA'06 at IEEE-WIC-ACM Conference on Intelligent Agent Technology*, Hong Kong.

Lester, J. C., et al. (1997). The persona effect: affective impact of animated pedagogical agents, *Proceedings of the SIGCHI conference on Human factors in computing systems*, 359-366. Atlanta USA: ACM.

Leupolt, M. (1978). Some considerations on the nature of information. *Int. Forum Inform. Docum*, *3*(3), 29–34.

Leupolt, M. (1981). Information Science. Its Object and Termonology. *Int. Forum Inform. Docum*, *6*(2), 19–21.

Levy, D. M., & Marshall, C. C. (1994). What color was George Washington's white horse? A look at assumptions underlying digital libraries. In *Proceedings of Digital Libraries* (pp. 163-169).

Lewis, J. R. (1995). IBM Computer Usability Satisfaction Questionnaires: Psychometric Evaluation and Instructions for Use. *International Journal of Human-Computer Interaction*, *7*(1), 57–58. doi:10.1080/10447319509526110

Liang, T. P., Lai, H. J., & Ku, Y. C. (2007). Personalized content recommendation and user satisfaction: Theoretical synthesis and empirical findings. *Journal of Management Information Systems*, *23*(3), 45–70. doi:10.2753/MIS0742-1222230303

Library of Congress Portals Applications Issues Group. (2005, December 14). *Portals Applications Issues Group.* Retrieved from Library of Congress Website: http://www.loc.gov/ catdir/lcpaig/

Ligozat, A. L., Grau, B., Robba, I., & Vilnat, A. (2006). L'extraction des réponses dans un système de question-réponse. *Conference TALN*, Leuven.

Likke, M. (2004). Task-based evaluation of associative thesaurus in real-life environment. *Proceedings of the ASIST 2004 Annual Meeting*, Providence, Rhode Island.

Lloyd, A. (2010). *Information literacy landscapes: Information literacy in education, workplace and everyday contexts*. Oxford: Chandos Publishing.

Lodolini, E. (1993). *Archivística. Principios y problemas*. Madrid: ANABAD.

Lopes, I. L. (1985, January/June)... *Ciência da Informação*, *14*(1), 55–60.

Lotman, Y. M. (1998). The semiotics of culture and the concept of a text. *Social Psychology*, *26*(3), 52–58.

Loyarte, E., & Rivera, O. (2007). Communities of practice: a model for their cultivation. *Journal of Knowledge Management*, *11*(3), 67–77. doi:10.1108/13673270710752117

Lucrecio. (2003). *La naturaleza*. Madrid: Editorial Gredos.

Luhmann, N. (1987). *Soziale Systeme*. Frankfurt am Main: Suhrkamp.

Luhmann, N. (1996). *Introducción a la teoría de sistemas*. México: Universidad Iberoamericana.

Luxenburger J., Elbassuoni S.& Weikum G. (2008).Task-aware Search Personalization. *SIGIR* 2008.

Luxenburger J., Elbassuoni S.& Weikum G. (2008b). Matching Task Profiles ans User Needs in Personalized Web Search. *CIKM* 2008.

Lyre, H. (1998). *Quantentheorie der Information. Zur Naturphilosophie der Theorie der Ur-Alternativen und einer abstrakten Theorie der Information. Viena*. Springer.

Lyre, H. (2002). *Informationstheorie. Eine philosophisch-naturwissenschftliche Einführung* [Theory of information. A philosophical and scientific introduction]. Munich, W.: Fink Verlag.

Maes, P. (1994). Agents that reduce work and information overload. *Communications of the ACM*, *37*(7), 30–40. doi:10.1145/176789.176792

Mähler, G. (1996). Quantum Information. In Kornwachs, K., & Jacoby, K. (Eds.), *Information. New questions to a multidisciplinary concept* (pp. 103–118). Berlin: Akademie Verlag.

Manzelli, P. (1991). *Nueva Química para la Vida. Speech made at ATENEO in Madrid.* Typed text.

Margaix-Arnal, D. (2007). El OPAC 2.0: Las tecnologías de la Web 2.0 aplicadas a los catálogos bibliográficos. In *Actas del VI Workshop CALSI.* Retrieved May 25, 2009, from http://www.calsi. org/2007/wp-content/uploads/2007/11/didac_margaix.pdf

Margolis, J. (2009). *Culture and Cultural Entities - Toward a New Unity of Science.* New York: Springer; 2nd ed. edition.

Martínez Comeche, J. A. (1995). *Teoría de la información documental y de las instituciones documentales.* Madrid, Spain: Sintesis.

Martínez, O. Casabuerta, D. (2009). Gestión cultural y TICs. Una perspectiva desde la web 2.0." *Cibersociedad.* 2007. Retrieved August 28, 2010 from http://www.red-interlocal.org/Gestion-cultural-y-TICs-Una

Matsuno, K. (1998). Dynamics of time and information in a dynamic time. *Bio Systems, 46,* 57–71. doi:10.1016/S0303-2647(97)00081-6

Maturana, H., & Varela, F. (1980). *Autopoiesis and Cognition: the Realization of the Living (Boston Studies in the Philosophy of Science, 42).* Netherlands: D. Reidel Publishing.

McCrank, L. (2001). *Historical Information Science: An Emerging Undiscipline. Medford.* New Jersey: Information Today, Inc.

Mcfarlane, A. (2001). *El aprendizaje y las tecnologías de la Información.* Madrid, Spain: Aula XXI Santillana.

McHale, J. (1981). *El entorno cambiante de la información.* Madrid: Técnos.

McKnight, D. H., & Chervany, N. L. (2002). What trust means in e-commerce customer relationships: An interdisciplinary conceptual typology. *International Journal of Electronic Commerce, 6*(2), 35–59.

Mead, G. (1992). *Mind, Self, and Society* (Morris, C. W., Ed.). Chicago: University, Chicago Press.

Mikhailov, A. I. (1982). Science As A System Of Cyclic Process of Generation, Processing, Accumulation and Transfer of Scientific Information. *Theoretical Problems of Informatics: Place of Information in the Global Problems of the World, FID 659.*

Miller, R. H., & Sim, I. (2004). Physicians' use of electronic medical records: Barriers and solutions. *Health Affairs, 23*(2), 116–126. doi:10.1377/hlthaff.23.2.116

Mobasher, B. (2007). Data Mining for Web Personalization. *The Adaptive Web, Springer-Verlag* (90-135). Berlin Heidelberg, Muresan, G. (2006). An Integrated Approach to Interaction Modeling and Analysis for Exploratory Information Retrieval. *Workshop on Evaluating Exploratory Search Systems (EESS 2006) at SIGIR 2006,* Seattle, WA.

Moehr, J. R. (2002). Evaluation: Salvation or nemesis of medical informatics? *Computers in Biology and Medicine, 32*(3), 113–125. doi:10.1016/S0010-4825(02)00009-4

Moreiro González, J. A. (2005). *Conceptos introductorios al estudio de la información documental.* Salvador, Bahía: EDUFBA.

Morin, E. (1986). *La Connaissance de la connaissance* (*Vol. 3*). Paris: Le Seuil.

Morin, E. (1995). *A educação e a complexidade do ser e do saber.* Petrópolis, Rio de Janeiro: Vozes.

Morin, E. (1996). A noção de sujeito. In *Schnitman, Dora Fried (Org.). Novos paradigmas, cultura e subjetividade.* Porto Alegre: Artes Médicas.

Morin, E. (2000). *Os sete saberes necessários à educação do futuro. Translated by Catarina Eleonora F. da Silva e Jeanne Sawaya. São Paulo: Cortez.* Brasilia: Unesco.

Morin, E. (2005). *O Método 3: Conhecimento do Conhecimento* (3rd ed.). Porto Alegre: Sulina.

Morin, E. (1992). The concept of system and the paradigm of complexity. In Maruyama, M. (Ed.), *Context and complexity: cultivating contextual understanding* (pp. 125–142). Berlin: Springer Verlag. doi:10.1016/1061-7361(92)90024-8

Morin, E. (1998). *Ciência com consciência.* (2nd ed.) Translated by Maria D. Alexandre e Maria Alice Sampaio Dória. Rio de Janeiro: Bertrand.

Morris, C. W. (1938). *Foundations of the theory of signs.* Chicago: International Encyclopaedia of Unified Science.

Morris, M. R. (2008). A Survey of Collaborative Web Search Practices. In *Proceedings of ACM SIGCHI Conference on Human Factors in Computing Systems* (pp. 1657-1660). Florence, Italy.

Morris, M. R., & Horvitz, E. (2007). SearchTogether: An Interface for Collaborative Web Search. In *ACM Symposium on User Interface Software and Technology (UIST)* (pp. 3-12). Newport, RI.

Moscovici, S. (1988). Notes towards a description of Social Representations. *European Journal of Social Psychology, 18*, 211–250. doi:10.1002/ejsp.2420180303

Mwanza, D., & Engeström, Y. (2003) Pedagogical adeptness in the design of e-learning environments: experiences from the Lab@Future Project. Editor E. Rossett. In *Proceedings of E-learn 2003 International Conference on E-learning in Corporate*. Retrieved from: http://www.edu.helsinki.fi/activity/pages/files/research/lab/Daisy-YrjoElearn03.pdf in 31/05/08]

Nafría. I. (2007) *Web 2.0.* Barcelona, Spain: Ediciones Gestión 2000.

Nahl, D. (2007). Social-biological information technology: An integrated conceptual framework. *In JASIST -. Journal of the American Society for Information Science and Technology, 58*(13), 2021–2046. doi:10.1002/asi.20690

Nicholas, D., Huntington, P., Williams, P., & Dobrowolski, T. (2004). Re-appraising information seeking behaviour in a digital environment: Bouncers, checkers, returnees and the like. *The Journal of Documentation, 60*(1), 24–43. doi:10.1108/00220410410516635

Nicolaou, A. I., & McKnight, D. H. (2006). Perceived information quality in data exchanges: Effects on risk, trust, and intention to use. *Information Systems Research, 17*(4), 332–351. doi:10.1287/isre.1060.0103

Niemeyer, B. (2006). El aprendizaje situado una forma de escapar del enfoque de déficit. *Revista de Educación, 341*, 99–121.

Niemeyer, B. (2004). Situated learning for social and vocational integration in Germany. Editors B. Evans & Niemeyer, B. In *Reconnection: Countering social Exclusion Through Situated Learning*. Dordrecht, NL, pp. 47-62.

Novellino, Maria Salet Ferreira. (1996, july/december) *Instrumentos e metodologias de representação da informação, 1*(2), 37-45.

Oddcast.(2011). Retrieved from http://www.oddcast.com/home/

Oeser, E. (1976). *Wissenschaft und Information.* Vienna, Austria: Oldenbourg.

OMG, Object Management Group. (2002). *Meta-Object Facility (MOF), version 1.4.* Retrieved from http://www.omg.org/technology/documents/formal/mof.htm.

O'reilly, T. Battelle, J. (2004) *Opening Welcome: State of the Internet Industry.* San Francisco, California

Ortega y Gasset, J. (1932). *The revolt of the masses.* New York: Norton.

Pantic, M., & Rothkrantz, L. J. M. (2003). Toward an affect-sensitive multimodal human-computer interaction. *Proceedings of the IEEE, 91*(9), 1370–1390. doi:10.1109/JPROC.2003.817122

PEET. (2010). The Euglenoid Project (web). Partnership for Enhancing Expertise in Taxonomy-National Science Foundation. Retrieved September, 2010 from http://euglena.msu.edu

Pérez-Montoro, M. (2007). *The Phenomenon of Information. A Conceptual Approach to Information Flow.* Lanham, Maryland: Scarecrow Press.

Pérez-Montoro Guitiérrez, M. (2003). *The phenomenon of information.* Lanham, MD: Scarecrow Press.

Perrenoud, P. (2000). *Dez novas competências para ensinar* (Ramos, P. C., Trans.). Porto Alegre: Artes Médicas Sul.

Piaget, J. (1977). *A tomada de consciência.* São Paulo: Edições Melhoramentos/Editora de São Paulo.

Piaget, J. (1971). *A epistemologia genética.* Petrópolis: Vozes.

Pinto Molina, M., García Marco, F. J., & Agustín Lacruz, M. C. (2002). *Indización y resumen de documentos digitales y multimedia: técnicas y procedimientos*. Gijón: Trea.

Pinto Molina, M. (1994, June). Intedisciplinary approaches to the concept and practice of written text documentary content text. *The Journal of Documentation*, *50*(2), 111–133. doi:10.1108/eb026927

Pitti, D. V. (1997). Encoded Archival Description: The Development of an Encoding Standard for Archival Finding Aids. *The American Archivist*, (60): 268–283.

Popper, K. R. (1972). *Objective knowledge; an evolutionary approach*. Oxford: Clarendon Press.

Popper, K. R. (1978). Three worlds. *The Tanner Lectures on Human Values*, *80*, 141–167.

Quijano, A., & Vega, M. G. (2008) Academic Libraries as a Complex Systems: A First Approach. In: *8th International Conference of Sociocybernetics: Complex Social Systems, Interdisciplinarity and World Futures*. Ciudad de México, México

Quine, W. O. (1953). Two dogmas of empiricism. In *From a logical point of view*. Cambridge: Harvard University Press.

Ramesh Babu, B., & Tamizhchelvan, M. (2003). An investigation into the features of OPACs in Tamil Nadu (India). *Library Review*, *52*(5-6), 257–267. doi:10.1108/00242530310482033

Randall, N., & Pedersen, I. (1998). Who exactly is trying to help us? The ethos of help systems in popular computer applications. *Proceedings of the 16th annual international conference on Computer documentation, 63-69*. New York: ACM.

Ribes, X. (2007). La Web 2.0: El valor de los metadatos y de la inteligencia colectiva. *Telos: Cuadernos de Comunicación e Innovación, 73*. Retrieved from http://www.telos.es/articuloperspectiva.asp ?idarticulo= 2&rev=73

Rich, C., & Sidner, C. L. (1998). COLLAGEN: A Collaboration Manager for Software Interface Agents. *An International Journal: User Modeling and User-Adapted Interaction*, *8*(3/4), 315–350. doi:10.1023/A:1008204020038

Rickel, J., & Johnson, W. L. (1999). Animated agents for procedural training in virtual reality: perception, cognition and motor control. *Applied Artificial Intelligence*, *13*, 343–382. doi:10.1080/088395199117315

Robles-De-La-Torre, G., & Hayward, V. (2001). Force Can Overcome Object Geometry In the perception of Shape Through Active Touch. *Nature*, *412*(6845), 445–448. doi:10.1038/35086588

Robles-De-La-Torre G. (2006). The Importance of the Sense of Touch in Virtual and Real Environments. *IEEE Multimedia 13(3)*, Special issue on Haptic User Interfaces for Multimedia Systems: 24–30.

Rock, I. (1984). *Perception*. New York: Scientific American Library.

Rodden, T. (1991). A Survey of CSCW Systems. *Interacting with Computers*, *3*(3), 319–353. doi:10.1016/0953-5438(91)90020-3

Rorty, R. (1982). *Consequences of Pragmatism*. Minneapolis: University of Minnesota Press.

Rosnay, J. d. (1975). *Le macroscope: vers une vision globale*. Paris: Éditions du Seuil.

Russo, A. Kelly, L. Chan, S. (2010) *Social Media and Cultural Communication* Retrieved September 9, 2010 http://nlablog.wordpress.com

Ryan, N., Pascoe, J., & Morse, D. (1998). Enhanced reality fieldwork: the context-aware archaeological assistant. In Gaffney, V., van Leusen, M., & Exxon, S. (Eds.), *Computer Applications and Quantitative Methods in Archaeology, British Archaeological Reports*. Tempus Reparatum.

Sagredo Fernández, F., & Izquierdo Arroyo, J. M. (1983). *Concepción lógico-lingüística de la documentación*. Madrid: Universidad Complutense de Madrid, Departamento de Documentación.

Sahli, N. (1985). *MARC For Archives and Manuscripts: The AMC Format*. Chicago: The Society of American Archivists Society of American Archivist (2008). *EAC-CPF, Encoded Archival Contex. Corporate Bodies, Persons, and Families*. Retrieved from http://eac.staatsbibliothek-berlin.de/

Salzer, M. S., & Burks, V. (2003). A mediational study of computer attitudes, experience, and training interests among people with severe mental illness. *Computers in Human Behavior*, *19*(5), 511–521. doi:10.1016/S0747-5632(03)00020-7

Sansonnet J. P., (1999) Description technique du projet InterViews. *Technical Report LIMSI (99-01)*.

Sansonnet, J. P., Sabouret, N., & Pitel, G. (2002). An Agent Design and Query Language dedicated to Natural Language Interaction. *First International Joint Conference on Autonomous Agents and Multi-Agent Systems, AAMAS'02*, Bologna.

Santosa, P. I., Wei, K. K., & Chan, H. C. (2005). User involvement and user satisfaction with information-seeking activity. *European Journal of Information Systems*, *14*(4), 361–370. doi:10.1057/palgrave.ejis.3000545

Saracevic, T. (1996, January/February). Ciência da Informação: origem, evolução e relações. *Perspectivas em Ciência da Informação*, *1*(1), 41–62.

Saracevic, T. (1997). The stratified model of information retrieval interaction: Extension and applications. *Proceedings of the American Society for Information Science*, *34*, 313–327.

Saracevic T. (1996b). Relevance reconsidered. *Proceedings of Colis 2*, Copenhagen, Denmark, (201-218).

Saracevic, T. (1996). Interactive models in information retrieval: A review and proposal. *Proceedings of the 59th Annual Meeting of the American Society for Information Science, 33*, (3-9).

Schelkunoff, S. A. (1936). Some equivalence theorems of electromagnetics and their application to radiation problems. *The Bell System Technical Journal*, *15*, 92–112.

Schilit, B. N., Adams, N. I., & Want, R. (n.d.). Context-Aware Computing Applications. *Proceedings of the Workshop on Mobile Computing Systems and Applications, IEEE Computer Society*, Santa Cruz, CA, (85-90).

Schmidt, A. (2000). Implicit human-computer interaction through context. *Personal and Ubiquitous Computing*, *4*(2-3), 191–199. doi:10.1007/BF01324126

Scott, B. (2002). A design for the recursive contruction of learning communities. *International Review of Sociology*, *12*(2), 257–268. doi:10.1080/0390670022000012486

Scott, B. (2007). Facilitating organizational change: some sociocybernetic principles. *Journal of Organizational Transformation and Social Change*, *4*(1), 13–23. doi:10.1386/jots.4.1.13_1

Scott, W. R. (1992). *Organizations: Rational, natural and open systems* (3rd ed.). Englewood Cliffs, N.J.: Prentice Hall.

Searle, J. R. (1969). *Speech Acts: An Essay in the Philosophy of Language*. Cambridge, UK: Cambridge University Press.

Ségal, J., & Danchin, A. (2003). *Le zéro et le un: histoire de la notion scientifique d'information au 20e siècle*. Paris: Syllepse.

Sellars, W. (1962). Philosophy and the scientific image of man. In Colodny, R. (Ed.), *Frontiers of Science and Philosophy* (pp. 35–78). Pittsburgh: University of Pittsburgh Press. [Also online. Retrieved September 3, 2010, http://www.ditext.com/sellars/psim.html]

Shah, C. (2010a). *Proceedings of Collaborative Information Retrieval workshop at CSCW 2010*. Savannah, GA: Working in Collaboration - What, Why, and How.

Shah, C. (2010b). (an integrated demo). In *Proceedings of Computer Supported Cooperative Work (CSCW)*. Savannah, GA: Coagmento – A Collaborative Information Seeking, Synthesis and Sense-Making Framework.

Shah, C. (2009). Lessons and Challenges for Collaborative Information Seeking (CIS) Systems Developers. In *GROUP 2009 Workshop on Collaborative Information Behavior*. Sanibel Island, Florida.

Shannon, C. E. (1993). *Collected Papers*. New York: IEEE Press.

Shannon, C. E., & Weaver, W. (1949). *The Mathematical Theory of Communication*. Urbana: The University of Illinois Press.

Shannon, C. E. (1949). Communication in the presence of noise. *Proc. IRE, 37(1)*, 10-21.

Shneiderman, B. (2008, March 7). Science 2.0. *Science*, *319*, 1349–1350. doi:10.1126/science.1153539

Silveira Zaragoça, F. J. (1980). Consideraçoes generais sobre a Problematica en Informaçao. *Revista Espanola la de Documentacion Cientifica*, *3*(2), 159–168.

Simon, N. (2010) *The participatory museum*. Santa Cruz, Calif.: Museum 2.0.

Simpson, A. & Weiner [Ed.], (1989). *Oxford English Dictionary*, 2a ed. Oxford, UK: Oxford University Press

Skov, M., Larsen, B., & Ingwersen, P. (2006). Inter and intra-document contexts applied in polyrepresentation. *Proceedings of the 1st international Conference on information interaction in Context* (Copenhagen, Denmark, October 18 - 20, 2006). IIiX, vol. 176. (97-101). New York: ACM.

Snow, P. C. (1998). *The Two Cultures. A Second Look.* Cambridge: Cambridge University Press.

Society of American Archivists. (2004). *Describing Archives: A Content Standard. Appendix C. Table C5: DACS to EAD and MARC.* Chicago, SAA.Retrieved from http://www.archivists.org/publications/DACS_TableC5_Erratum.pdf

Solomonoff, R. J. (1964). A formal theory of inductive inference. *Inf. Control, (7)*, 1-22 (I part), 224-254 (II part).

Souza, Ana Maria Martins de; Despresbiteris, Lea; Machado, Osny Telles Marcondes. (2004). *A mediação como princípio educacional* – bases teóricas de Reuven Feuerstein. São Paulo: Editora do Senac.

Spärck Jones, K. (2005). Meta-reflections on TREC. *TREC: Experiment and Evaluation in Information Retrieval,* (421-448). Cambridge, MA: MIT Press.

Statement of International Cataloguing Principles. (2009). Retrieved from IFLA Website: http://www.ifla.org/files/cataloguing/icp/icp_2009-en.pdf

Sternberg, R. J. (2000). *Psicologia cognitiva*. Porto Alegre: Artes Médicas.

Stone, D. L., & Stone, D. (2005). *User interface design and evaluation*. San Francisco, CA: Morgan Kaufmann.

Stonier, T. (1991). Towards a new theory of information. *Journal of Information Science*, *17*, 257–263. doi:10.1177/016555159101700501

Stonier, T. (1999). The Emerging Global Brain. In Hofkirchner, W. (Ed.). *The quest for a unified theory of information. Proceedings of the Second International Conference on the Foundations of Information Science.* Amsterdam: Gordon and Breach. pp. 561-578.

Sugimoto, C. R., Pratt, J. A., & Hauser, K. (2008). Using field cocitation analysis to assess reciprocal and shared impact of LIS/MIS fields. *Journal of the American Society for Information Science and Technology*, *59*(9), 1441–1453. doi:10.1002/asi.20863

Sumi, Y., & Mase, K. (2002). Supporting the awareness of shared interests and experiences in communities. *International Journal of Human-Computer Studies*, *56*(1), 127–146. doi:10.1006/ijhc.2001.0518

Surowiecki, J. (2004). *Wisdom of Crowds: Why the Many Are Smarter Than the Few and How Collective Wisdom Shapes Business, Economies, Societies and Nations*. New York: Doubleday Publishing.

Susskind, Leonard (1997). Black holes and the information paradox. *Scientific American*, Special Issue "The edge of physics", April 1997, 52-57.

Talja, S. (1997). Constituting 'information' and 'user' as research objects: A theory of knowledge formations as an alternative to the information man - theory. In P. Vakkari, R. Savolainen, & B. Dervin (Eds.), *Information seeking in context: Proceedings of a meeting in Finland 14-16 August 1996* (pp. 67-80). London: Taylor Graham.

Teixeira Lopes, C. (2009). Context Features and their use in Information Retrieval. *3rd Symposium on Future Directions in Information Access (FDIA'09).*

Teixeira, G. (2008). *Significado de competência. Ensino e aprendizagem. Ser professor universitário.* Retrieved September 28, 2009, from: http://www.serprofessoruniversitario.pro.br/ler.php?modulo=12&texto=728

Terenziani, P. (2002). Toward a unifying ontology dealing with both user-defined periodicity and temporal constraints about repeated events. *Computational Intelligence*, *18*(3), 336–385. doi:10.1111/1467-8640.00194

Tillett, B. (1991). A taxonomy of bibliographic relationships. *Library Resources & Technical Services, 35*(2), 150–158.

Topcu, A. E., Mustacoglu, A. F., Fox, G., & Cami, A. (2007). Integration of Collaborative Information Systems in Web 2.0. In *Third International Conference on Semantics, Knowledge and Grid (SKG 2007)* (pp. 523-526). Xian, Shan Xi, China: IEEE Computer Society. doi: ieeecomputersociety.org/10.1109/SKG.2007.137

Treisman, A. (1996). The binding problem. *Current Opinion in Neurobiology, 6*(2), 171–178. doi:10.1016/S0959-4388(96)80070-5

Triggs, P., & John, P. (2004). From to transformation: information and Communications technology, professional development and the formation of communities of practice. *Journal of Computer Assisted Learning, 20*, 426–439. doi:10.1111/j.1365-2729.2004.00101.x

Turpin, A., & Scholer, F. (2006). User performance versus precision measures for simple search tasks. *SIGIR 2006, Proceedings of the 29th Annual ACM SIGIR Conference on Research and Development in Information Retrieval*, (11-18). New York: ACM

Twidale, M. B., Nichols, D. M., & Paice, C. D. (1997). Browsing is a Collaborative Process. *Information Processing & Management, 33*(6), 761–783. doi:10.1016/S0306-4573(97)00040-X

Twidale, M. B., & Nichols, D. M. (1996). Collaborative browsing and visualisation of the search process. In *Proceedings of Aslib* (Vol. 48, pp. 177-182). Retrieved from http://www.comp.lancs.ac.uk/computing/research/cseg/projects/ariadne/docs/elvira96.html.

Udell, J. (2004). *Collaborative knowledge gardening.* Retrieved May 14, 2009, from http://www.infoworld.com/article/04/08/20/34OPstrategic_1.html

Ummelen, N., & Neutelings, R. (2000). Measuring reading behavior in policy documents: a comparison of two instruments. *IEEE Transactions on Professional Communication, 43*, 292–301. doi:10.1109/47.867945

UNESCO – CIRET. (1998, April). Que Universidade para o Amanhã? Em busca de uma evolução transdisciplinar da Universidade. *Congresso Internacional de Locarno*. Retrieved August 15, 2010, from: http://perso.club-internet.fr/nicol/ciret/.

UNESCO. (1998, October 5-9). Declaración Mundial sobre la Educación Superior en el siglo XXI: Visión y Acción. *Conferencia Mundial sobre la Educación Superior*. Paris. Dervin, B. (1983). An overview of sense-making research: concepts, methods and results to date. In *International Communications Association Annual Meeting*. Dallas, Texas.

Urdaneta, I. P. (1992). *Gestión de la Inteligência. Aprendizaje Tecnológico y Modernización del Trabajo Informacional. Retos y oportunidades*. Caracas, Venezuela: Instituto de Estúdios del Conocimento de la UniversidadSimon Bolívar /Consejo Nacional de Investigaciones Científicas Y Tecnológicas.

van Benthem, J. (2003). Logic and the Dynamics of Information. *Minds and Machines, 13*(4), 503–519. doi:10.1023/A:1026296600182

van Benthem, J. (2008). Tell It Like It Is: Information Flow in Logic. [Humanities and Social Science Edition]. *Journal of Peking University, 1*, 80–90.

Van der veer, E. (2008) *Facebook: the missing manual.* Sebastopol: Pogue Press/O'Reilly.

Vedral, V. (2006). *Introduction to quantum information.* Oxford, UK: Oxford University Press. doi:10.1093/acprof:oso/9780199215706.001.0001

Vidal, M. E., Raschid, L., Marquez, N., Cardenas, M., & Wu, Y. (2006). Query Rewriting in the Semantic Web. *Proceedings of the 22nd International Conference on Data Engineering Workshops, ICDEW'06*, Atlanta, USA.

von Foerster, H. (1981). *Observing systems*. Seaside, CA: Intersystems Publications.

Von Neumann, J. (1932). *Mathematische Grundlagen der Quantenmechanik*. Berlin: Springer.

von Weizsäcker, C. F. (1974). *Die Einheit der Natur*. Munich: Deutscher Taschenbuch Verlag.

von Weizsäcker, C. F. (1985). *Aufbau der Physik*. Munich: Hanser.

Voorhees, E. M., & Harman, D. K. (2005). *TREC: Experiment and evaluation in information retrieval*. Cambridge, MA: MIT Press.

Voorhees, E. M. (2002). Overview of the TREC 2002 Question Answering Track. *In Proceedings of the Eleventh Text REtrieval Conference (TREC)*, (115-123).

Vygotsky, L. S. (1991). *A formação social da mente*. São Paulo: Martins Fontes.

Vygotsky, L. S. (1978). *Mind in society: The development of higher psychological processes*. Cambridge, MA: Harvard University Press.

Vygotsky, LS. (1979). *Consciousness as a Problem in the Psychology of Behavior Soviet Psychology*, Summer 1979/vol. XVII, no. 4, p. 35.

Wagner, G. D., & Flannery, D. D. (2004). A quantitative study of factors affecting learner acceptance of a computer-based training support tool. *Journal of European Industrial Training*, *28*(5), 383–399. doi:10.1108/03090590410533071

Wallon, H. (1963). "Psychologie et matérialisme dialectique" *Enfance, Numero special*. In *Henri Wallon, buts et méthodes de la psychologie* (pp. 31–34). Janvrier-avril.

Wang, F. Y., Carley, K. M., Zeng, D., & Mao, W. (2007). Social computing: From social informatics to social intelligence. *Intelligent Systems, IEEE*, *22*(2), 79–83. doi:10.1109/MIS.2007.41

Webb, G., Pazzani, M., & Billsus, D. (2001). Machine learning for user modeling. [Boston: Kluwer Academic Publishers.]. *User Modeling and User-Adapted Interaction*, *11*, 19–29. doi:10.1023/A:1011117102175

Weizenbaum, J. (1966). ELIZA, a computer program for the study of natural language communication between man and machine. *Communications of the ACM*, *9*(1). doi:10.1145/365153.365168

Weng, S. S., Tsai, H. J., & Liu, S. C. (2006). Ontology construction for information classification. *Expert Systems with Applications*, *31*(1), 1–12. doi:10.1016/j.eswa.2005.09.007

Wenger, E. (1998/2001). *Communities of practice: learning, meaning, and identity*. Cambridge: Cambridge University Press. (Original work published 1998)

Wenger, E., & Snyder, W. (2000). Communities of practice: the organizational frontier. *Harvard Business Review*, 139–145.

Wersig, G. (1971). *Information-Kommunication-Dokumentation*. München; Berlin.

White, H. D. (2003). Author cocitation analysis and *Pearson's r. Journal of the American Society for Information Science and Technology*, *54*(13), 1250–1259. doi:10.1002/asi.10325

White, H. D., & McCain, K. W. (1998). Visualizing a discipline: An author co-citation analysis of information science, 1972-1995. *Journal of the American Society for Information Science American Society for Information Science*, *49*(4), 327–355.

White, M. D. (1998). Questions in reference interviews. *The Journal of Documentation*, *54*(4), 443–465. doi:10.1108/EUM0000000007177

White, R. W., & Kelly, D. (2006). A Study on the Effects of Personalization and Task Information on Implicit Feedback Performance. *Proceedings of the 15th ACM international conference on Information and Knowledge Management*.

Wiener, N. (1948). *Cybernetics: Or Control and Communication in the Animal and the Machine*. Cambridge, MA: MIT Press.

Williams, B. K., Sawyer, S. C., & Hutchinson, S. E. (1995). *Using information technology: A practical introduction to computers and communications*. Chicago: Irwin.

Williams, M. E., Kinnucan, M., Smith, L. C., Lannom, L., & Cho, D. (1986). Comparative analysis of online retrieval interfaces. In *ASIS '86: Proceedings of the 49th ASIS Annual Meeting, 23*, 365-370.

Wilson, D., & Sperber, D. (1993). Linguistic form and relevance. *Lingua*, *90*, 1–25. doi:10.1016/0024-3841(93)90058-5

Wilson, T. D. (1999). Models in information behaviour research. *The Journal of Documentation*, *55*(3), 249–270. doi:10.1108/EUM0000000007145

Wilson, T. D. (1981). On user studies and information needs. *Journal of Librarianship*, *37*(1), 3–15.

Wilson, T. D. (2000). Human information behavior. *Informing Science*, *3*(3), 49–55.

Wilson, T. D. (2008). Activity theory and information seeking. *Annual Review of Information Science & Technology*, *42*, 119–161. doi:10.1002/aris.2008.1440420111

Wilson, T. D. (1981). *On user studies and information needs. Journal of Documentation, 37*, (1), 03–15. Retrieved April 23, 2007, from: http://informationr.net/ir/9-1/paper164.html

Wilson, T. D. (1996). *Information behaviour, an interdisciplinary perspective*. Retrieved April 23, 2007, from: http://informationr.net/tdw/publ/infbehav/

Wollermann, C. (2004). *Evaluierung der linguistischen Fähigkeiten von Chatbots. Magister report*. Rheinische-Friedrich-Wilhelms Universität Bonn.

Wollermann, C. (2006). *Proceedings of the Young Researchers' Roundtable on Spoken Dialogue Systems*. Pittsburgh, PA, (75-76).

Wu, I., Liu, D. R., & Chang, P. C. (2007). Toward incorporating a task-stage identification technique into the long-term document support process. *Information Processing & Management*, *44*(5), 1649–1672. doi:10.1016/j.ipm.2007.11.005

Yates, J., & Orlikowski, W. (1992). Genres of organizational communication: a structuration approach to studying communication and media. *Academy of Management Review*, *17*(2), 299–326.

Yee, M. M., & Layne, S. S. (1998). *Improving online public access catalog*. Chicago: American Library Association.

Yee, M. M. (1998, November). *Guidelines for OPAC displays* (prepared for the IFLA Task Force on Guidelines for OPAC Displays by Martha M. Yee). Retrieved May 18, 2005, from http://www.ifla.org/ifla/VII/s13/guide/opac-d.pdf

Yuelin, L., & Belkin, N. J. (2008). *A faceted approach to conceptualizing tasks in information seeking, Information Processing and Management*. New York: Elsevier publisher.

Zadeh, L. A. (1986). Test-Score Semantics and a Basis for a Computational Approach to the Representation of Meaning. *Literary and Linguistic Computing*, *1*(1), 24–35. doi:10.1093/llc/1.1.24

Zubiri, X. (1999). *Sentient Intelligence. Tr. by Thomas B. Fowler*. Washington: Xavier Zubiri Foundation of North America.

Zumer, M., & Zeng, L. (1994). Comparison and evaluation of OPAC end-user interfaces. *Cataloging & Classification Quarterly*, *19*(2), 67–98. doi:10.1300/J104v19n02_05

Zviran, M., Glezer, C., & Avni, I. (2006). User satisfaction from commercial web sites: The effect of design and use. *Information & Management*, *43*(2), 157–178. doi:10.1016/j.im.2005.04.002

About the Contributors

Emilia Currás is a researcher and teacher, Ph D in Chemistry, University Professor for Information Sience (LIS); Introducer of LIS studies in Spain and some Iberoamerican countries; Founder of SEDIC (Spanish Society for Inf. Science); Fellow of Inst for Inf. Scientists; IBI (UK) Distinguished Woman; Decorated by the Colombian Republic Government whit Pergamino and Cruz de Caballero; has been paid tribute in Spain and a book has been dedicated to her "A life: Profession and Passion". She is Academician: Royal Doctor's Academy, Madrid; Royal Academy of Fine Arts and Historical Sciences, Toledo and Academy of Fine Arts Brasilia; Woman of Year 2004 (USA); Isko-Spain Honorary President. Has received several gold, silver Medals and Emblems from Asian, Middle East, European and Iberoamerican LIS Institutions; Distinguished member of Official Chemical Spanish Association and Doctor and Teacher Spanish Association; Founder member of several Spanish LIS Societies; Invited from Asian, American, European and Middle East government to delivery lectures and conferences. She has held several executive positions at national and international Universities and Institutions. She belongs to several national and international Editorial Board, such as Journal for Information Science; Vice-president of ATENEO (Cultural Spanish Society) -Section for Science and Technology-. As consequence of her research has formulated a New Epistemological Theory: *Informationism* and an *Integral Vertical of Science* and also has developed new educational and professional teaching methods. Introductory in Spain of the *General Theory of Systems* and *Systematics* applied to LIS. Emilia Currás is a member of Club of Rome-Spanish Chapter and Foundation Pro Academia Española, among other religious and cultural Associations.

Nuria Lloret Romero, PhD, is a researcher and university professor for Information Services Planning and Evaluation of Quality in Information Services. Current director of the Department of Audiovisual Communication, History of Art and Information Science (DCADHA) in the Universitat Politècnica de València, she was deputy director of the *Instituto Tecnológico del Plástico* (AIMPLAS) from 1990 to 1999. She is also director of the CALSI Master's Programme in the Universitat Politècnica de València, as well as director of the CALSI Research Group, where she has focused her research on collaborative systems. She is co-founder and CEO of MASmedios SL, and has also worked as an expert for project evaluation within EU's Programme for Information Society IST. Among other positions held, she is founder member and former president of AVEI (Valencian Association for Information Specialists), former president of FESABID (Spanish Federation of Associations of Information Specialists), former president of IFLA's Latin American Caucus, member of EBLIDA's (European Bureau of Information Systems) Executive Committee, member of the National Committee for Certification of Information Professionals and Vice-president of AECTA (Association of Innovative Companies from the Valencian Community).

* * *

Marilene Lobo Abreu Barbosa holds a degree in Library Science by Universidade Federal da Bahia (1966) and licensed Vernacular Literature in the Universidade Católica de Salvador (1972), Diplôme d'Etudes en Approfondies Information Scientifique et Technique, Université Aix-Marseille III (2000), Masters Information Science by Universidade Federal da Bahia (2005). Specialization in Archival (1990) and Competitive Intelligence, by Universidade Federal da Bahia (1999). Professor at the Instituto de Ciência da Informação, Universidade Federal da Bahia; Member of the Research Group on Information Sciences: Cognition, Representation and Knowledge Construction Research Group and the Knowledge and Practices in Information Management and Knowledge (GEINFO), conducting studies, research and publications focusing on issues of information management and systems and information services, organizational intelligence, professional competence, training, and cognitive theories of learning and its interface with the studies and practices in information services.

Elsa Barber is Subdirector of the National Library of Argentina ("Biblioteca Nacional de la República Argentina"). Director of the Department of Library and Information Science, Faculty of Philosophy, University of Buenos Aires 1994 – 2002 and 2005 - March 2009. "Licenciada en Bibliotecología y Documentación" (Graduate in Library Science). Master in Digital Documentation. She is Professor of the Department, having a tenure in the information organization area. She is head of UBACYT F 036 research project "Online Public Access Catalogues (OPACs) in Latin American countries" and participates in other research projects in foreign universities. She is a class I researcher in the Incentive Program of the National Ministry of Education, Science and Technology. She has taken part in juries of Doctoral thesis, of selection processes ("Concursos de Antecedentes y Oposición"), been an external evaluator in the selection process of research grants, and evaluator of UBACYT and other universities research projects.

Nancy Blanco is "Bibliotecaria en Bibliotecología y Documentación" (Graduate in Library Science). She is Professor in the information organization area of the Library and Information Science School, at the University of Buenos Aires; researcher of UBACYT F036 research project "Online Public Access Catalogues (OPACs) in Latin American countries". She has given training courses for librarians in Argentina. She is also co-author of articles in specialized journals and of contributions to congresses on Library and Information Science.

Vicent Giménez Chornet has spent most of his professional life in the field of archives, although he is currently a lecturer at the Universitat Politècnica de València in Information and Documentation. He is a member of Comité 50 for Documentation of AENOR (Spanish Association for Standardisation and Certification), President of the Colegio Oficial de Bibliotecarios y Documentalistas (Official College of Librarians and Documentation Specialists) of the Valencia Region (Spain) and a member of FESABID (Spanish Federation of Archival, Library, Documentation and Museology Societies).

Bich-Liên Doan received her PhD in Computer Science in 2000. Since 2001, she has been a teacher and researcher in Computer Science at Supélec, in Gif sur Yvette, France. Since 2008; she is Deputy Dean of Research and Industrial Partnerships at Supélec. Her main interest domain is information retrieval, particularly the structural and link analysis. Her current research is related to contextual and more particularly personalized information retrieval. She co-organized in 2005 and 2007 the context-based information retrieval workshop hold in conjunction with the international "Context" conference. She co-organized in 2008, 2009 and 2010 the Contextual Information Access, Seeking and Retrieval Evaluation (CIRSE) Workshop in conjunction with the European Conference on Information Retrieval (ECIR).

Carolina Gregui is "Licenciada en Bibliotecología y Documentación" (Graduate in Library Science). She is professor in the Information organization area of the Library and Information Science School, at the University of Buenos Aires; researcher of UBACyT F036 research project "Online Public Access Catalogues (OPACs) in Latin American countries". She has taken part of congresses on Library and Information Science in Argentina, Brazil, Chile, Uruguay, Colombia, Dominican Republic, Costa Rica, Mexico and France. She is also co-author of several articles in national and international journals.

David Jank has more than 25 years experience in information services, holding a variety of positions in libraries and technology consulting firms. He has also been prominent in many business services segments of the IT industry. He holds a BA from Northeastern University, an MLS degree from Simmons College, an MS in psychology from the City University of New York, and a Ph.D. in information studies from Long Island University. Dr. Jank has worked in various public, academic and special libraries, and has served as a library automation consultant and systems integrator throughout North America and Europe. His published research focuses on knowledge organization and human-information interaction. Dr. Jank also has many years experience as a professor of library and information science, is a former member of the national advisory council of the Special Libraries Association, and is active in both the American and Canadian Societies for Information Science.

Francisco Javier García Marco achieved his PhD in Philosophy and Arts in 1994 and is Professor of Information and Library Science at the University of Zaragoza from 1996. He has been director of the Department of Library and Information Science and organized the LIS postgraduate programme of the University of Zaragoza. He is the chair of Ibersid, an international conference in information and documentation Systems (1996-), the director of the journal "Scire" and a committee member of several Spanish and Brazilian journals. He has researched and published extensively on the theory of information, knowledge organization and digital change.

Margarita Cabrera Méndez Professor at the Universitat Politècnica de València, Spain. PhD in Audiovisual Communication, with the research "Analysis for the Development of a Project for Applying New Information Technologies to the Marketing and Promotion of Tourism". She has been working as a full-time professor in the subject of Audiovisual Communication since 2003, teaching both: under and post-graduate students. Margarita is currently developing her research in social media, the communication through social networks, and specifically about the communication by cultural entities using web 2.0. Actually she is the director of the social media Workshop: Comunica 2.0: www.comunica2gandia.com.

José María Díaz Nafría, born in 1970 in Salamanca (Spain), is currently visiting professor in the field of logics and philosophy of science at the University of León (Spain), as well as in the field of philosophy of information at the Faculty of interdisciplinary studies of the Munich University of Applied Sciences (Germany). He studied engineering sciences and philosophy at the University of Basque Country and Universidad Nacional de Educación a Distancia respectively, and is Doctor by the Technical University of Madrid. He has been research fellow at the Vienna University of Technology and at the Technical

University of Madrid; associated professor at the Universidad Alfonso X el Sabio, Madrid, and invited lecturer at several universities in Germany and Austria. He has organized several international research activities in the field of interdisciplinary information studies. Since 2008, he coordinates the international research group BITrum, devoted to the interdisciplinary study of information, http://en.bitrum.unileon.es.

Verónica Parsiale is "Licenciada en Bibliotecología y Documentación" (Graduate in Library Science), Master in Library and Information Science, and earned a Certificate of Endorsement in Organization and Management of Digital Information. She is Officer of Information, Documents and Communication Management in the International Labour Office in Buenos Aires; and researcher of UBACYT F036 research project "Online Public Access Catalogues (OPACs) in Latin American countries".

Gabriela de Pedro is "Licenciada en Bibliotecología y Documentación" (Graduate in Library Science). She is Professor in the information organization area of the Library and Information Science School, at the University of Buenos Aires; and researcher of UBACYT F036 research project "Online Public Access Catalogues (OPACs) in Latin American countries". She has given training courses for librarians in Argentina. She has taken part of congresses on Library and Information Science in Argentina, Chile, Uruguay. She works in National Institute for Agricultural Technology's "Biblioteca y Archivo Documental" in Buenos Aires.

Silvia Pisano is "Licenciada en Bibliotecología y Documentación" (Graduate in Library Science), Master in Digital Documentation. She is Professor in the information organization area of the Library and Information Science School, at the University of Buenos Aires; researcher of UBACYT F036 research project "Online Public Access Catalogues (OPACs) in Latin American countries". She has given training courses for librarians in Argentina. She has taken part of congresses on Library and Information Science in Argentina, Brazil, Chile, Uruguay, Colombia, Dominican Republic, Costa Rica, Mexico, United States, Spain and France. She is also co-author of books and articles in national and international journals.

Alvaro Quijano-Solis is a research fellow of the Mexican Resarch System (SNI). He holds a Ph D. in Engineering and a M. S. L. S. and a M. S. O. R. both from Case Western Reserve University (Cleveland, OH). He has been visiting professor in every Mexican library school and in Argentina, Colombia and Spain. A former Library Director at El Colegio de México, he is now a Professor at the Graduate Program in Library Science. He teaches courses in Methodology as wella as in Systems Approach for solving problems. His interests are on human processes related with information technology acceptance in information and library organizations and on the systemic construction of solutions to solve organizational problems in libraries and information systems.

Sandra Romagnoli is graduate in Library Science. She is a Professor in the information organization area of the Library and Information Science School at the University of Buenos Aires. She is a researcher in the UBACYT F036 research project about "Online Public Access Catalogues (OPACs) in Latin American countries". She has participated in congresses on Library and Information Science in Argentina, Brazil, Chile, Uruguay, Colombia, Dominican Republic, Costa Rica, Mexico, United States, Spain and France and she is also a co-author of articles in national and international journals.

Jean-Paul Sansonnet received a PhD degree in Computer Science in 1977 and a full Doctorate of State in 1982 from the University of Toulouse for his research on early Lisp-Machines In 1988 he was applied CNRS Research Director at the CNRS-LRI Laboratory in Paris and worked on massively Distributed Artificial Intelligence architectures (MEGA project) and languages. Since 2000, he is Senior Research Director at CNRS-LIMSI where he heads the Architecture and Model for Interaction (AMI) research group at CNRS-LIMSI in Paris. His current research is related to the problematic of the Dialogical Agents which is dedicated to the study of communicative interaction, with strong semantic and linguistic components, between human and/or software agents in mediated information systems. He is the co-animator of the French working group on the Animated Conversational Agents (GT ACA) created in 2003.

Chirag Shah is an assistant professor in School of Communication & Information (SC&I) at Rutgers University. He received his PhD from School of Information & Library Science (SILS) at UNC Chapel Hill, under the guidance of Dr. Gary Marchionini. His research interests include various aspects of interactive information retrieval/seeking, especially in the context of online social networks and collaborations, contextual information mining, and applications of social media services for exploring critical socio-political issues. He is also interested in various theoretical and practical aspects of information as a thing, and online information propagation. He leads a research group on Information Seeking at Rutgers University, and has published numerous articles related to social and collaborative information seeking. For his recent work on this topic, he has been recognized by Yahoo! with the Yahoo! Campus Innovation Award.

Aida Varela Varela received her Bachelor of Letters by the Universidade Federal da Bahia (1967); Pedagogy by the Faculdade de Educação da Bahia – FEBA (1981); degree in Social Work by the Universidade Católica do Salvador UCSal (1982); Specialization: Adult Education (900h) by the University of British Columbia UBC (1985), Continuing Education and Distance Learning (600h), Universidade de Brasília – UnB (2000), Instrumental Enrichment Program (IEP), levels I and II, LPAD Course, Level I and Trainer (600h), by the International Center for the Enhancement of Learning Potential-ICELP/Jerusalem Israel (2000), Masters in Information Science by the Universidade de Brasília (1999), PhD: Information Science by the University of Brasilia (2003). She is currently Adjunct Professor IV of the Instituto de Ciência da Informação (ICI) of the Universidade Federal da Bahia. She coordinates the research group, Information Sciences: Cognition, Construction of Knowledge Representation and developing activities on the use of cognitive tools.

Guadalupe Vega-Díaz has been a tenured Associate Professor at the Graduate Program in Library Science at the Library of El Colegio de Mexico, a well known specialized research institution focused on Social Sciences in Mexico. She obtained her Ph. D. in Educational and Developmental Psychology at the National University of Mexico (UNAM). She is B.A. and Master in Library Science from the UNAM. Her main areas of research include: 1) The process of appropriation of information literacy in school students; 2) Information Literacy in Higher Education students, 3) Practice and situated learning communities, and 4) Information behavior in college students. She is currently Professor of the Information Literacy Course and Academic Coordinator of the Master Librarianship Program at El Colegio de México.

Index

J

K

L

M

N

O

P

CPSIA information can be obtained at www.ICGtesting.com
Printed in the USA
BVOW050748261111
276491BV00003B/7/P

9 781613 502013